CHINESE SONGS IN A FRENCH KEY

CHINESE SONGS IN A FRENCH KEY

How Judith Gautier's Book of Jade *Introduced Europe to Chinese Poetry*

PAULINE YU

Columbia University Press
New York

Columbia University Press
Publishers Since 1893
New York   Chichester, West Sussex

Copyright © 2025 Columbia University Press
All rights reserved

Library of Congress Cataloging-in-Publication Data
Names: Yu, Pauline, 1949- author
Title: Chinese songs in a French key : how Judith Gautier's book of jade introduced Europe to Chinese poetry / Pauline Yu.
Description: New York : Columbia University Press, 2025. | Includes bibliographical references and index.
Identifiers: LCCN 2025000770 (print) | LCCN 2025000771 (ebook) | ISBN 9780231209427 hardback | ISBN 9780231209434 trade paperback | ISBN 9780231557931 ebook
Subjects: LCSH: Livre de jade | Chinese poetry—Translations into French—History and criticism | Gautier, Judith, 1845-1917—Criticism and interpretation | LCGFT: Literary criticism
Classification: LCC PL3277.F3 G339 2025 (print) | LCC PL3277.F3 (ebook) | DDC 895.11009—dc23/eng/20250422

Cover design: Julia Kushnirsky
Cover image: John Singer Sargent, *Study of Judith Gautier by Lamplight*, ca. 1883. RCIN 917268, pencil and sepia wash. Used with the kind permission of the Royal Collection Trust.

GPSR Authorized Representative: Easy Access System Europe, Mustamäe tee 50, 10621 Tallinn, Estonia, gpsr.requests@easproject.com

For my children and grandchildren

Contents

1. "An elegant and original volume" by "the most singular of women":
   Invention or Translation?   1

2. "Going to China is like going to the moon":
   France Encounters China   17

3. "One of the most interesting characters of his time":
   Professor, Baron, Barnum, or Rake?   46

4. "For a woman the word 'impossible' no longer exists":
   The Challenges of Chinese Poetry   69

5. "The Celestial Empire unfurls completely throughout this book":
   The 1867 *Book of Jade*   100

6. "Brushing up against the famous":
   Judith Gautier's Artistic Connections   150

7. "Greatly enlarged and rigorously corrected":
   The Book of Jade, 1902   179

8. "Radiated beyond the scholarly world":
   An Extraordinary Afterlife   219

   Epilogue:
   "One of the most original talents in contemporary literature"   247

Acknowledgments 255

Notes 257

Works Cited 303

Index 319

CHAPTER 1

"An elegant and original volume" by "the most singular of women"

Invention or Translation?

On May 7, 1867, Alphonse Lemerre (1838–1912), Parisian publisher of the most avant-garde poets of the day, issued a volume of seventy-one poems that stunned and puzzled the French literary world. The collection—titled *The Book of Jade* (*Le Livre de jade*) and attributed to Judith Walter—announced its connection to Chinese culture by the calligraphy on its title and chapter pages and the names of the Chinese authors on whose work the individual pieces were declared to have been based. *The Book of Jade* had been scheduled for publication first in February, and then in April, which would have coincided nicely with the opening of the International Exposition on the Champ de Mars, at which the Chinese exhibition was awaited with special eagerness. But despite the predictable delay the timing was still propitious enough to capitalize on the interest in things Chinese that the exhibition was stirring among the population of Paris.

No one was fooled about the identity of the pseudonymous author, who was immediately recognized as Judith Gautier, the elder daughter of Théophile Gautier (1811–1872), one of the most prominent writers of the nineteenth century. It was likely, however, that Judith had no intention of fooling anyone. Her mother, Ernesta Grisi, a talented contralto, was the cousin of two even more acclaimed singers in the Grisi family, Giuditta and Giulia, and the sister of the renowned ballerina Carlotta. Born on August 24, 1845, Judith was therefore blessed with an impeccable artistic pedigree. Her education was equally remarkable. After two unhappy years at convent school, which "left many girls unable to carry on an intelligent conversation and deepened the intellectual gap between the sexes which the eighteenth century had begun to close,"[1] she was brought home and schooled primarily by her father, whose educational philosophy consisted primarily of letting her read. She enjoyed free run of his extensive library and the thrill of serving as his "research assistant" at age eleven on such projects as the writing of his novel based in Egypt, *The Romance of the Mummy*.[2] This may explain why even at the tender age of twenty-two she herself was already well published as Judith Walter, a pseudonym her father had suggested because it shared with Gautier a common root in the Old High German name Walthari, "lord of the forest."

One of Judith's most notable publications prior to *The Book of Jade* came about when her father asked her to review Charles Baudelaire's (1821-1867) translation of Edgar Allan Poe's (1809-1849) *Eureka: A Prose Poem*, subtitled "Essay on the Material and Spiritual Universe." Poe considered the 1848 essay his crowning achievement, but it was poorly received, and Baudelaire's 1859 French version—one of his many translations that made "Edgar Poe" not only more popular in France than America but also one of Judith Gautier's favorite authors—fared no better. Both Gautiers were interested in astronomy, so a treatise about the origins of the universe that discussed the movements of planets and stars, as well as the history of philosophy and sources of creativity, seemed an ideal assignment. When her father confessed that he found the piece a tough read and would like her to explicate it to him, she rose to the task. A week later she presented him with a detailed and incisive discussion of *Eureka*. Then, without her knowledge, Théophile submitted it to *Le Moniteur universel*, the official newspaper of the French government to which he had been a regular contributor on cultural topics. Shortly thereafter, in March 1864, Judith was shocked to see her review appear in the paper. Even more thrilling was the princely sum of 80 francs and 40 centimes she received for its publication. Perhaps most surprising was the letter she received from Baudelaire himself a few days later.

Théophile Gautier had sent the proofs of the article to the renowned poet, who initially thought Théophile wrote the essay himself. Understandably, Baudelaire was astonished to learn of its true authorship. His reaction to and appreciation of the young woman's insights into what he recognized as a deeply perplexing work provide an illuminating glimpse of his expectations: "I experienced a feeling that is hard to express, composed half of pleasure at having been so well understood, and half of delight in seeing that one of my oldest and dearest friends had a daughter truly worthy of him." He considered her astute analysis of Poe's work to be something that neither he himself at her age nor men more seasoned and erudite would have been capable of, thus proving what he would otherwise have deemed impossible, "that a young girl can find in books serious amusements altogether different from those so primitive and vulgar that occupy the lives of most women." And, he continued, "If I didn't fear offending you by defaming your gender, I would tell you that you've forced me to rethink the nasty opinions I've developed about women in general."[3]

Judith Gautier herself was unimpressed by her article. She considered it "poorly executed, clumsy, dry, and of a desolate conciseness,"[4] even though it did manage to raise the hackles of Catholic authorities outraged by the text's embrace of theories of creation that ran counter to religious doctrine.[5] Clearly undaunted, she continued to write at every opportunity, and she published several other pieces between 1864 and 1867, including numerous art exhibition reviews and some "variations on Chinese themes." But impressive as such publications on the part of a young woman might have been, they could not compare with the striking novelty of *The Book of Jade*. This began with its cover.

The title offered no hint of what was included, nor was any prefatory material helpful in identifying what sort of volume this was meant to be. The Chinese characters on the cover—should any of the book's first readers have been able to translate them—were only slightly more informative. (The four characters, *bai* 白 *yu* 玉 *shi* 詩 *shu* 書, can be translated literally as *White Jade Poetry Book*, but they correspond only partially to the French title, which does not contain the word "white" or "poetry.") Lacking any explanatory apparatus, and with words spaced out generously on fine paper, the elegant cover might reasonably have led prospective readers to wonder if the book should be taken as a precious gem—as treasured and enduring as jade, with a title that was as much "a poetic object as the collection itself."[6] Phrases in Chinese calligraphy, also untranslated, appeared as headings for each of the volume's seven sections. Judging by its contents and their layout on the printed page, the book would have resembled a collection of poems, even if no volume in the long tradition of anthologies in China had ever been called a "poetry book."[7] Inside appeared an enigmatic dedication to "Tin-Tun-Ling, Chinese poet," the author of three of the seventy-one poems claimed as sources for the works in the volume; the others who can be identified lived in China long ago. Any presumption that the pieces themselves were intended as translations would have been stymied by the notation that each was only "after" or "according to" (*selon*) the named source. Moreover, being extremely brief and lacking meter or rhyme or any other familiar characteristics of French verse, they did not look much like poems of the day.

白 玉 詩 書

LE

LIVRE DE JADE

PAR

JUDITH WALTER

PARIS
ALPHONSE LEMERRE, ÉDITEUR
47, *Passage Choiseul*, 47

M.DCCC.LXVII

1.1 Judith Walter, *Le Livre de jade* (Paris: Alphonse Lemerre, 1867). Public domain, Bibliothèque nationale de France Gallica, hereafter BnF Gallica

It was a rather perplexing package. *The Book of Jade* nonetheless captivated and intrigued the French reading public, and especially its literary luminaries. They disagreed in crucial ways in their estimation of its merits and, as well, of what it was trying to do, differences that would continue to frame its reception. But the book's first readers all clearly recognized its originality.

The first commentary on the volume came two days after its publication from Charles-Marie Leconte de Lisle (1818-1894), a leader of the literary group known as Parnassus (Le Parnasse), whose adherents met frequently at the offices of Alphonse Lemerre. As their name suggests, Parnassian poets turned their backs on what they considered the banality of contemporary life and looked for inspiration elsewhere—to places like Greece, India, and Asia—and preferably in the ancient past. Their guiding principles had been set out by Théophile Gautier himself in 1835, when he wrote in the preface to one of his novels that what is beautiful should serve no ethical or political purpose—the doctrine of "art for art's sake."[8] Rejecting the emotional effusions of romanticism, they sought in their writings a chiseled formal perfection that would be lofty, dispassionate, and adamantine in its description. Something, perhaps, like a Book of Jade. In a letter to his fellow Parnassian, José-Maria de Heredia (1842-1905), Leconte de Lisle writes:

> *The Book of Jade* was put on sale the day before yesterday. Lemerre has made it an elegant and original volume whose typographical appearance accords in a supple way with the pseudo-Chinese poems of Madame Judith Walter, the most singular of women and least comprehensible I know. This little book, furthermore, has this going for it, within the rare merit of a simple, graceful language, lightly colored and naturally feminine, in the best sense of the word, of having been written from beginning to end with a constant sense of *purity* and nobility. It goes without saying that one would find no analogue for it in China, which is definitely but a stupid, ridiculous, and cruel country.[9]

Leconte de Lisle's arch comment, like Baudelaire's letter, provides yet another backhanded compliment for Judith Gautier's accomplishment and manages to impugn her sources as well. While recognizing the beauty of the volume itself—the important consonance between how the poems looked on the page and what they said, as well as the elegance of her language—he slips in a dismissive note of bemusement about her own character. And to Baudelaire's blatant misogyny Leconte de Lisle adds his dose of racism. If Gautier's poems are only "pseudo-Chinese," it's not just because she is peculiar: Chinese civilization would simply be incapable of producing such beauty.

The poet Paul Verlaine (1844-1896) offers a more generous assessment of the book's achievements in a review published shortly thereafter, even if he also struggles to consider Judith Gautier as an author in her own right. Indeed, throughout his piece he can't resist noting her pedigree as the daughter of Théophile Gautier and, as of 1866, the wife of a fellow Parnassian, the prolific writer Catulle Mendès (1841-1909).

Verlaine's lengthy discussion of the book itself opens with an intriguing question: "How can one be Chinese?" For the French reader this would have recalled the incredulity of the eighteenth-century Parisians encountering an exotic foreigner for the first time, as depicted in Charles-Louis de Montesquieu's (1689-1755) *Persian Letters*: "Ah ha! The gentleman is a Persian? That's quite extraordinary! How can one be Persian?"[10] The original question was designed to cast a satirical light on the blinkered vision of the French society being chronicled by two visitors from afar. In Verlaine's hands, however, the comic rhetorical question is transformed into genuine praise, as he continues: "That's the secret of Judith Walter, the transparent pseudonym that conceals the brilliant personality of a young woman, recommended to the literate public by the double title as daughter of one illustrious poet and wife of another, and who is extremely likely soon to make even more renowned a name that already resounds among young Romantics." Verlaine attributes to the book an aspiration for *The Book of Jade* Gautier herself did not claim—"it presents itself as a translation of different Chinese poets, and I ask nothing more than to take it at its word"—but immediately observes that "here and there a very Parisian note, a delicately ironic accent, of which I suspect the literati with crystal buttons of the Celestial Empire are absolutely incapable, might warn you that the translation, since translation there is, is, at the least, very free." While admitting that he is not familiar with the language of the poets in the volume, he also believes that any "appearances of infidelity to the text" are more than compensated for by the undeniable charm and talent of the renditions.

Verlaine detects a "very Parisian note" to the pieces, an irony which he suspects is not rooted in Chinese culture. But he also astutely recognizes, unlike Leconte de Lisle, that they owe a debt to the borrowed tradition and cautions us not to infer from his previous remarks "that *The Book of Jade*, with its Chinese tint, is what one would conveniently call 'a Parisian book.' On the contrary, it would be impossible to be more Chinese, in the delicately eccentric and poetically precious sense of the word, than the author or translator of this delicious work."

Author or translator? Invention or translation? Chinese or French? What did they know about China or Chinese poetry that would allow this 1867 readership to judge? That, indeed, becomes the question. Verlaine moves on to provide a glimpse of the contents of the volume that both places it within a commonly shared literary tradition and points to aspects that are distinctively Chinese:

> Imagine a poet like Theocritus on the banks of the Yellow River, with exquisite oddities and enchanting surprises. At times the tone also becomes elevated, and the little idyll infused with tea, warm wine, and peach blossoms moves to a war tableau, a touching scene, sometimes to a deep thought, yet without ever breaking the rules which the author has imposed on herself, which are conciseness of expression, brevity of statement, and discretion in the methods employed.

Here the reference to the pastoral poet Theocritus establishes an important link between Greece and China, but Verlaine also discerns a crucial difference in style that inadvertently points to some of the most important characteristics of Chinese poetry. Succinctness of expression and economy of statement are in fact two hallmarks of classical Chinese poems, and it is much to Verlaine's credit that he recognized Gautier's own efforts to honor them. In these pieces she has demonstrated, perhaps, a conciseness that is not at all "desolate," as she thought her essay on *Eureka* had been. He notes the kinship of her methods to the widely admired prose poems of an earlier writer but declares that "if one gave me the choice, I would much prefer *The Book of Jade* for its greater originality, purer form, and more real and intense poetry." Verlaine's review concludes with a ringing prediction. The volume's "success is assured: Mademoiselle Théophile Gautier, Madame Catulle Mendès has just thereby affirmed a pseudonym, Judith Walter, that will certainly radiate, truly on its own, between the name of her father and that of husband."[11] Those two names would continue to flank, if not upstage, her own for the rest of her life.

The Book of Jade's reach was not limited to the Parisian literati. One indication of its remarkable popularity was an appreciative notice published in a French sports weekly, *Le Jockey*, a month after the book's publication. Most of the newspaper is dedicated to reporting results from horse races around the country, but it also includes a weekly summary of the "Talk of the Week." The columnist begins by lamenting the unusually dreary weather that May, for which he feels the best remedy is to sit by a warm fire with a good book. "In my lazy hours," he writes, "nothing pleases me more than a voyage, one of those voyages that happen without the traveler's leaving his armchair." *The Book of Jade* has offered him that opportunity, and he proudly announces that "I have come from China; I have seen China; I have penetrated the intimate life of the Chinese. It is Madame Judith Walter who has led me to the empire of flowers." Thanks to her he has dwelled among renowned poets on the banks of the Yellow River, "in lands where one scarcely knows, if indeed one knows at all, the names of Victor Hugo and Alfred de Musset. Oh, fame!"

Unsurprisingly, he identifies Gautier as her husband's wife and father's daughter. But he also recognizes her singular accomplishment: "Today she speaks and writes Chinese the way her father writes French. Elegant sentences, beautiful verses, and moral maxims escape from her brush and fall onto enchanted parchment. She knows the Chinese writers and poets, she has penetrated the intimate life of the Chinese; she has translated for us their most secret thoughts." After providing examples of poems that have particularly impressed him, the columnist concludes by offering what might be an explanation for having reviewed this book for a newspaper like *Le Jockey*. Perhaps because the volume's contents do not provide much evidence for a penchant for horse racing, he is appropriately silent on the topic. But he can assure his readers that "The Chinese are great lovers of nautical sports. Their poets celebrate the pleasure of navigating on rivers and spending entire days on a boat. They love, as we do, quiet nights and beautiful moonlight."[12] And, indeed, *The Book of Jade* abounds in such scenes.

As noted in the review, Victor Hugo (1802–1885), the senior statesman of French letters, may not have been someone who would have been known at the time in China, but he was surely the most distinguished of *The Book of Jade*'s early readers. Gautier sent a copy of the volume to a man she had never met but whose name "had radiated through her childhood" and who had left France because of his opposition to Napoleon III. She inscribed his copy with both his and her name transcribed phonetically in Chinese characters, and with a word-for-word translation of his name that sought to glorify his status as "the triumphant exile who strides with gravity and speaks of great and immortal things."[13] Several weeks later she received a letter from him thanking her for the gift, on whose first page, he writes, his name written in Chinese by her has "become a luminous hieroglyph, as if from the hand of a goddess." *The Book of Jade*, he continues "is an exquisite work, and let me tell you that I see France in this China and your alabaster in this porcelain."[14]

Like Verlaine, Hugo discerned in *The Book of Jade* qualities that made it difficult to consider it as deriving purely from the Chinese. His brief but telling comment recognizes that if these are Chinese songs, their key is decidedly French. What clearly, and typically, impressed him the most, however, was Gautier's rendition of his name, which she had attempted to translate in as "magnificent" a way as possible. (The size of the great writer's ego—he thought that the city of Paris should be named after him[15]—was well known.) The writer François Coppée (1842-1908) recalled that when he visited Hugo shortly thereafter in exile, the latter "spoke at great length about the dedication in *The Book of Jade*, which greatly surprised and charmed him."[16]

Later that year Coppée published his own review of the volume that, both generous and insightful, does not mention Gautier's family connections. He opens by lamenting the increasingly vulgarized taste for things Chinese of recent years that has made the culture's bronzes, ivories, porcelains, paintings, and silks mere commonplace in French furniture and decorative arts, rather than the domain of elite collectors. But this familiarity, he notes, does not extend to "their literature, which is, however, no less curious and no less original than the rest." Until now. "Madame Judith Walter has wished to make known and loved in France, in all their personality and their very essence, the Chinese poets she loves so much and knows so well, and she has just given us, in her *Book of Jade*, a translation of their most remarkable poems."

Like Verlaine, Coppée immediately goes on to question what he has just said: "Is it in fact translation of which one must speak, and is Madame Judith Walter very certain of the authenticity of all the poems she makes us read now?" But he then assures us that he wouldn't be surprised if, having absorbed their works, "she has become a Chinese poet as well and deserves to wear the jade button of officials of the first class on her ball gown." Whatever the case, he continues, "the poems of *The Book of Jade* are in their essence Chinese, and Madame Judith Walter has written them with all the grace and delicacy of the young Chinese women whom she shows us busy tracing characters with a brush as thin as an eyelash. The Celestial Empire unfurls in its entirety in this book," encompassing figures and landscapes in all their variety. "All of life's events and emotions—travel, war, dream, love—are expressed there in a form that is sometimes witty and clever, and sometimes poetic and tender, but always surprising and exotic, always Chinese." And he concludes by presenting three poems that illustrate "the refined subtlety and bizarre and penetrating charm of these poems, or of Madame Judith Walter's translation."[17]

We hear the same question: Is the "bizarre and penetrating charm" intrinsic to "these poems" or to her translation? Coppée's choice of conjunction brings to the fore both the appeal and the mystery of Gautier's book. While apparently convinced of the authenticity of the poems—he does not, as did Leconte de Lisle, call them "pseudo-Chinese"—he nonetheless cannot help suspecting that Gautier herself has added something very much her own to the mix. Most readers harbored such suspicions, although they framed them in different ways. An unidentified Parisian woman whose response to *The Book of Jade*—rather remarkably, just a month after its publication—crossed the Atlantic and is recorded in an American periodical, for example, makes a subtle distinction between translation and imitation. In a letter she reports that she has been reading "with infinite pleasure a volume of Chinese poetry by one of Théophile Gautier's charming daughters. Some of these prose poems are translated, and others imitated, from the Chinese; they are written with great delicacy and an exquisite charm of description, some sad as the rustling of the wind in the bamboos, others as bright and sunny as the brilliant colours of the birds and flowers they embalm." She observes that "great sentiment and beauty lie in the quaint, simple lines" of the poems, and "pervading them all is a breath of their native country." And she provides a rather unexpected reason (perhaps not so unnecessary, however, recalling Baudelaire's acid comments about young women) to acknowledge the "attentive study" that has produced such successful translations: Judith Walter "has long been battling against the difficulties of the Chinese language with a persistence that will aid me in proving that we *Parisiennes* are not all as worldly and shallow-minded as reputation scandalously whispers, and that more than one bright face, well known and sought after in Society, has, if not a private pair of blue stockings, at least well stocked bookshelves, and a student's desk in a quiet corner of her home."[18]

If this unnamed Parisienne recognizes the hard work that went into producing *The Book of Jade*, most of Gautier's known (and well-known) contemporaries were simply mystified, even as they were entranced. Her youth, her gender, and the sources, if undeniable beauty, of the work baffled the French literary establishment, which continued to discuss it long after its publication. In 1883 Robert de Bonnières (1850-1905) describes it as "a set of little prose poems that she says are borrowed from ancient Chinese poets, but which in reality belong to her alone."[19] The writer Anatole France (1844-1924) praises it in 1897 as "a perfectly beautiful book whose style gleams with a pure light," one that is inspired—"if one believes the author"—by Chinese lyrics, but he similarly doubts that Gautier has found in Chinese poetry "all the details of the delicate scenes contained in *The Book of Jade*; I doubt that the poets in the land of porcelain could have known before her such charm."[20]

"How can one be Chinese?" they asked of the "Chinese poet" to whom *The Book of Jade* had been dedicated and who tutored the young Judith Gautier. "How can this be Chinese?" they asked of a book that claimed roots in a culture they barely knew, and which both fascinated and repelled them. "How could she learn Chinese?" they asked of a young woman who had tackled the impossible language at an age when "young ladies usually only study piano, crocheting, and religion," or are "jumping rope," or "play at lifting up their first long dress."[21] Verlaine nonetheless suspected that "it would be impossible to be more Chinese" than the author of this book, and Gautier herself would come to agree with him.

In the most extensive biographical discussion of Judith Gautier written during her lifetime, Rémy de Gourmont sums up the collective reaction to her book:

> When in 1867, with *The Book of Jade* . . . the older daughter of Théophile Gautier made her debut in the world of letters, there was a stir of surprise and near revolt. One could not believe that this literature, so original and so coolly impersonal, was the work of a woman. It was like Gautier's but even more pure, more ironic, and more delicate, and the author, just married yesterday, was not even twenty years old! But Judith Gautier, who cared little about glory, cared even less about attending to these innuendos; she continued to write for her pleasure and for our delight.[22]

Gautier was not a teenager, as Gourmont thought, when the book appeared (she never bothered to correct this widespread error and was most likely responsible for it),[23] but he asked the essential questions. How could a young woman have accomplished this? Could the work's undeniable charm be attributed to a civilization about which France knew so little? Or to her own literary talents and originality? There was always her father to credit, and she herself would have been the first to acknowledge her family advantage. The question is what she made of her lineage.

―◆―

An extraordinarily prolific writer, Gautier would go on to publish more than fifty volumes of poetry, prose, and drama and well over a hundred essays and articles; she was known for her abilities as a painter, sculptor, musician, and marionettist as well. She studied and drew extensively on material from Egypt, Persia, India, and Japan for her creative work, but China remained her passion and, as Gourmont notes in his biography, "inspired her most beautiful books."[24] And of those many books, *The Book of Jade* gave her the most pleasure[25] and proved the most influential and widely read.

Most writing about Judith Gautier has focused on her biography, a task that she did not make easy despite producing three volumes of memoirs. She was inclined, as she put it, to "deny time. Dates and numbers escape from my memory as from a sieve."[26] Its outlines are unquestionably engrossing: daughter of one famous writer and wife, albeit only briefly and unhappily, of another, she was a woman whose success, prominence, and connections were almost unheard of for her time. She was, moreover, widely acknowledged to be beautiful, and contemporary commentators often talked of little else than her striking appearance, with its Grecian profile and penetrating gaze. As Anatole France writes in one of his "Feminine Sketches," she was blessed by family:

> She has the formal beauty of one of her father's strophes. Like a legend-
> ary princess, the
> fairies came to her baptism.
> Julia Grisi said to her:
> —"You will be beautiful."
> Carlotta:
> —"You will be charming."
> Théophile Gautier:
> —"You will be poetic."
> Better than poetic, she is poetry itself.[27]

But Gautier's talents were also very much her own. Her Sunday salons attracted a wide range of writers, musicians, and artists. Her introduction of Chinese poetry

1.2 Judith Gautier, photograph by Nadar (Gaspard-Félix Tournachon, [1820–1910]). BnF Gallica

in an innovative form placed her among the literary avant-garde of her day, even though the China she loved was long ago and largely of her dreams. Her critical appreciation of often controversial figures in other arts like music and painting proved equally visionary. She sat at the hub of a remarkable web of friendships. Muse, collaborator, friend, or rumored lover of such luminaries as Richard Wagner, Victor Hugo, and John Singer Sargent, Gautier was much more than the sum of her personal relationships, but they provided nonetheless much fodder for gossip and speculation.

As a journalist writing in 1904 observed, "the very life of Judith Gautier is a novel that would merit being recounted."[28] It is easy to agree with this, but it is also certainly true that the history behind her first book would be its most interesting chapter. My book, *Chinese Songs in a French Key*, will tell the story of that book. *The Book of Jade* not only enjoyed a lively reception upon its publication in 1867, but a second edition produced in 1902 both transformed its aspirations and revived its influence, which resounded throughout European letters and arts. It was reissued in its entirety or in part in five subsequent editions (in 1908, 1911, 1928, 1933, and 2004), was translated into numerous other languages—German, English, Italian, Portuguese, Spanish, Polish, Danish, and Russian—and provided the basis for at least one other popular anthology of Chinese poetry in French. This is a story of extraordinary networks and intersections—across languages and cultures, between scholars and artists, and across different media of expression. And its protagonist was a young woman of stunning audacity and vision. In setting her sights on the poets of China's distant past, Judith Gautier was undaunted by incredulity and skepticism regarding her youth and gender and generous and openminded in the face of the blatant stereotypes and prejudices of her era.

On this point a brief caveat may be in order. Sexism, racism, orientalism, and colonialism permeate every page of this story, which is hardly surprising for one set in nineteenth-century France. One could expend a great deal of energy critiquing these attitudes at every opportunity, and they certainly should be acknowledged. I have chosen, however, to focus on what Gautier and her Chinese tutor nonetheless were able to accomplish despite the benighted attitudes of their time, which they themselves sometimes shared.

What made this all possible? What was Gautier trying to do? How did she do it? What can an examination of her book tell us about nineteenth-century French conceptions of China, a country that many writers would see for the first time through *The Book of Jade*? I was given a chance to answer these questions years ago, after completing my doctorate in comparative literature. One of my advisors suggested that studying Gautier's *Book of Jade* might be well suited to my interests in classical Chinese and nineteenth-century French poetry and, because of important retranslations, could also benefit from my knowledge of German as well. What a perfect project for a comparatist! But like most students of comparative literature at the time, the last thing I wanted to do was compare, and theory—rather than literature—was all the rage. Translation was surely not abstract enough to interest hiring committees, and the topic was much too broad for an academic world that expected greater specialization and narrower focus. I was clearly not ready for Judith Gautier.

It is well past time to tell the story of *The Book of Jade*, a little work with an outsized influence and robust afterlife. Biographies of Gautier provide useful introductions to the overall arc of her life and works but have not delved deeply into the anthology itself, its reception, or its impact. Previous scholarship on the volume over the past century is limited at best. William Leonard Schwartz discusses Gautier in his still useful 1927 study of the representation of the Far East in French literature but criticizes her inattention to "linguistic accuracy" and the ease with which she wrote about countries she'd never visited as a "harmful" influence (he was the son of missionaries to Japan). Muriel Détrie's 1989 article on *The Book of Jade* as "a pioneering book" (*un livre pionnier*) was itself pioneering as the first even-handed examination by someone whose command of Chinese enables a judicious assessment of Gautier's translation efforts. Ferdinand Stocès, a Czech engineer and sometime translator of Chinese poetry, deploys his sinological background in several articles seeking to determine Gautier's sources. Min Ling resumes this search in her 2013 doctoral dissertation, the most extensive study thus far of *The Book of Jade* as a key element of the encounter between nineteenth-century French literature and classical Chinese poetry. Other valuable contributions in French include Yu Wang's discussion of the work in her book on anthologies of Chinese poetry in French; articles in two volumes published after the centenary of Gautier's death; and, especially, the ongoing work of Yvan Daniel, who edited the 2004 republication of *The Book of Jade* and is compiling the complete edition of her writings. In China the comparatist Meng Hua writes of Gautier as a translator who though "beautifully unfaithful" (*une belle infidèle* / *bu zhong de mei ren* 不忠的美人) nonetheless sparked a genuine interest in Chinese literature. Other brief discussions of the work in English include Richard Serrano's study of poetic borrowing across literary traditions, dissertations by Barbara Jessome-Nance and Laura Lauth, and my own previously published articles.[29]

This is, then, the most comprehensive study in any language of *The Book of Jade*, the first literary introduction of Chinese poetry to Europe. We will need to look in more than one direction to find answers to our questions about what Gautier accomplished and how she managed to do it. Historical figures and events helped to prepare the ground for the volume. Key individuals sparked and nurtured Gautier's interest. Scholars provided linguistic expertise and important guideposts. But in the end, it was she who recognized the commonalities that transcend cultural differences and the bold and imaginative strategies necessary to convey them to a broader public. As she so importantly realized, there are many paths that knowledge can take.

CHAPTER 2

"Going to China is like going to the moon"

France Encounters China

What did France know about China when *The Book of Jade* was published? Victor Hugo's praise of Judith Gautier for having bridged an almost unimaginable gulf in her works suggests how remote Chinese civilization may have seemed at the time. As he wrote to her in August 1869, "You possess within yourself the soul of Far Eastern poetry, and you infuse its breath into your books. Going to China is almost like going to the moon. You make this journey to the stars for us."[1] Yet the perplexed reception of the French reading public to her book does not reflect that in recent years much had happened to make China more familiar to contemporary Europe. Indeed, the 1860s have been called "the China decade"[2] in French letters thanks to a burgeoning interest inspired by developments in the domain of scholarship and by events in the real world. For Judith Gautier these two strands of influence were woven together by her father.

STUDYING CHINA: THE BIRTH OF SINOLOGY

China was the last of the great cultures to attract scholarly attention in Europe, long after philological skills had been honed on Latin, Greek, Arabic, Hebrew, and Sanskrit. Curiosity sparked only after Iberian sailors landed in China in 1513 and began publishing accounts of their expeditions. The Jesuit missionaries who proselytized in China from the sixteenth through the eighteenth centuries produced groundbreaking studies on Chinese and Manchu history, and especially on Chinese religion and ritual, thus establishing an important early foundation of scholarly knowledge.[3] Those sent from France first arrived in 1688 and were explicitly selected for their intellectual attainments, were named corresponding members of the Académie Française, and were instructed to send materials back that would "enrich the king's library" and "perfect the Arts."[4] This they did, even though they were understandably more interested in translating into Chinese those Western language texts—primarily on Christianity and science—that would advance their mission. Over the course of the eighteenth century, three series of multivolume compendia, of which the first was titled *Edifying and Curious Letters Written from Foreign Missions by Some Missionaries of the Society of Jesus*, communicated the Jesuits' findings about Chinese history, geography, culture, and industries. Often written in an elegant, vernacular French that conveyed the missionaries' genuine admiration for their subject, these volumes expanded the audience for information that had previously only been available to readers of Latin.[5] By 1760 Voltaire quipped that China was better known than certain European provinces.[6] Only three years later, however, French authorities closed down the Order of the Society of Jesus, with the Vatican following suit in 1773. The last Jesuit in China died in Beijing in 1795.

What the missionaries neglected to do was disseminate their knowledge of the language; they failed "to give their secret to the savants of Europe."[7] Ironically enough, sinology—the scholarly study of China's language and culture—was born only after all contact with China had been effectively cut off, with no surviving literate nonnative speakers in France, when on December 11, 1814, the faculty of the Collège Royal established a chair in Chinese and Tartar-Manchu languages. Founded by François I in 1530 as a humanistic alternative to the Sorbonne, which was dominated by medieval Latin-based scholasticism, the Collège Royal, which became the Collège de France in 1870, was conceived as an elite forum for the presentation of original research with only minimal encumbrance of registered students. From the start it had been committed to the purely textual study of languages other than Latin. Polymath chairholders in these languages had occasionally ventured on their own into Asian topics, but the chair in Chinese was the first of its kind in Europe.

Like their colleagues specializing in classical languages, the first three occupants of the chair—none of whom had ever set foot in the China—had neither an interest in treating their subject as a means of communication nor any direct contact with native speakers. They derived their pedagogical methods from the teaching of Latin, relying on the use of centuries-old literary texts for their examples. Even though these texts sometimes employed the vernacular, as opposed to classical, language, they were hardly suitable models for learning to speak effectively, not to mention the challenge of having to grasp how to pronounce nonalphabetic graphs. Unsurprisingly, another school focused on teaching the contemporary spoken languages came to be recognized as necessary for training students to navigate the real worlds of politics and commerce, leading to the establishment of L'École des langues orientales vivantes (School of Vernacular Oriental Languages) during the French Revolution in 1795. A chair in Chinese was created there in 1843, but no one who could speak the language, thanks to having lived in China, occupied it until after 1871.[8]

The first professor of Chinese at the Collège, Jean-Pierre Abel-Rémusat (1788-1832), assumed his post in January 1815. He commanded a host of modern and ancient languages, including Sanskrit, Persian, and hieroglyphics, but how had he learned Chinese? Although the Jesuit missionaries had prepared bilingual texts for pedagogical purposes, none were available to him. The Chinese dictionaries held by the national library were reserved for Chrétien-Louis Joseph de Guignes (1759-1845), a former diplomat whom Napoleon had commissioned in 1804 to produce a Chinese-Latin-French dictionary. He had an established scholarly pedigree: his father, Joseph de Guignes (1721-1800), had been a scholar of Syriac at the Collège who, among other findings, had claimed that Chinese was derived from Phoenician and that China had been an Egyptian colony. His son was happy to accept the emperor's assignment even though he knew Cantonese rather than Mandarin and was neither linguist nor lexicographer, on the condition that he be given exclusive access to the library's resources.[9]

In the lecture delivered upon his assumption of the chair, Abel-Rémusat vividly describes the daunting prospect of navigating such uncharted terrain in such inhospitable circumstances: "We are about to land on a deserted and still fallow land. The language which we will focus on in this course is only known by name in Europe.... We have no model to follow, no guidance to hope for; in a word, we will be on our own and will have to tap our own resources."[10] This is exactly what he had done—"without a teacher, dictionary, or grammar book"—when he began to study the language in 1806, at age eighteen, by reading a Chinese botanical treatise given to him by the collector Charles Philippe Campion, the Abbé de Tersan (1736-1819). Tersan seems to have had an uncanny eye for talent, for he also lent a print of the Rosetta Stone to a young Jean-François Champollion (1790-1832), who would eventually decipher its hieroglyphics. In some ways their laborious efforts to crack a linguistic code through triangulation among different languages were not dissimilar. Abel-Rémusat knew the plant world well, and thanks to the precision of the botanical drawings was able to identify each object, memorize the Chinese characters connected with them, and then extrapolate from there. Five years later he published the *Essay on Chinese Language and Literature,* which reflected substantial reading and translation of key classical texts.[11]

Abel-Rémusat's efforts were painstaking, and he was determined to make the way easier for others. De Guignes's selfishness rankled deeply: "It seemed as though the merit of knowing Chinese became greater if he possessed it alone. He guarded it jealously, like a treasure that might be lost if shared."[12] Through his more than three hundred publications, which ranged from the first grammar of Chinese for a European audience, published in 1822, to translations of literary works that provided a glimpse into daily life, Abel-Rémusat sought to make learning about China less mysterious and difficult than the Jesuits had made it seem.[13] He laid the groundwork for a more systematic study of the civilization, and his translations were read by the educated public. Still, huge challenges remained, as he confessed to a cousin: "I have learned the Chinese language rather well, but I still cannot read a Chinese book!"[14]

In 1832 Abel-Rémusat died in a cholera epidemic, and his most accomplished student, Stanislas Julien (1797-1873), was appointed to replace him. Julien had a phenomenal aptitude for languages. While a young seminarian he wanted to learn ancient Greek, which was not taught at his school and in fact was forbidden. So he obtained some Greek books and read them under his bedcovers at night. When caught in flagrante, he was forced to abandon the practice, but he'd already mastered the language, so the school created a new position and appointed him to teach his classmates. Julien then proceeded to learn English, Italian, Portuguese, Spanish, and German by memorizing dictionaries and absorbing grammatical rules inductively from books.

Julien continued his study of Greek at the Collège in his twenties, also picking up Arabic, Hebrew, Persian, and Sanskrit along the way, but nothing intrigued him as much as an explication of an early philosophical text one of his classmates was preparing for Abel-Rémusat's course in Chinese. Julien apparently decoded the passage in thirty minutes and then proceeded to translate it into Latin for the professor. Having "found his vocation," he abandoned Greek and switched to Chinese, acquiring a host of other Asian languages as well. After three months he had learned enough to complete his own translation of the complete text.[15]

For over four decades Julien dominated the world of European sinology with his research, and he established a monopoly on the field in France. Not content with his occupancy of the chair at the Collège and a second post as its chief administrator, he wangled a third appointment as adjunct curator of Chinese manuscripts at the national library. But he wished to expend as little effort as possible on these positions, despite his refusal to let anyone else lay claim to them. According to one obituary, "He hoped to have as few students as possible in his courses, and it always displeased him to see a crowd of readers of Chinese manuscripts arrive at the national library. He claimed—not without some reason—that most of his students ... were lazy indigents keeping themselves warm at the expense of the state."[16] Notwithstanding this disposition, he managed to make a cameo appearance, albeit unidentified, in Gustave Flaubert's (1821-1880) *Sentimental Education*. The novel's young protagonist, Frédéric Moreau, includes auditing "one-hour classes in Chinese or political economy" at the Collège in 1869—when Julien was teaching—as part of a daily routine to distract himself.[17]

Julien's personality "was as abominable as his scholarship was irreproachable. Jealous, irascible, peevish, he monopolized positions and dispatched all competition."[18] Much of his energy was devoted to vitriolic critiques of fellow sinologists, published in pamphlets with memorable titles like *A Simple Exposé of an Honorable Fact Odiously Distorted by a Recent Libel*, and *Obligatory Response to a So-Called Friend of Justice Who Hides Himself Under the Veil of Anonymity*.[19] Friedrich Neumann (1793-1870), for example, who had audited Abel-Rémusat's lectures with Julien and was appointed professor of Chinese and Armenian at the University of Munich, elicited this typically acerbic comment: "I'm sorry to say that Mr. Neumann, in whom I'm pleased to recognize a great enthusiasm for Chinese literature, has committed errors from the very beginning to the end of this piece. But my goal here is not at all to diminish the esteem that Mr. Neumann may enjoy as sinologist, nor to inspire in him any doubts about his knowledge of Chinese." Those who dared criticize him he simply accused of libel. But his most vicious diatribes were reserved for another former fellow student, Guillaume Pauthier (1801-1873), who had fancied himself an equally worthy contender for the chair vacated by their teacher. Julien never forgave Pauthier for such audacity. In one critique of the latter's translation of 21 pages of a 585-page text, Julien filled 136 pages of his own analyzing 13 lines that contained, by his count, 84 errors. "After this sample," he wrote, "it's rather easy to imagine what a translation of 300 pages, or 3,000 lines, would be like from the same author, if executed in the same manner by

M. Pauthier."²⁰ Pauthier didn't hesitate to return the favor in his reviews, and the two scholars feuded for four decades until they both expired, within a month of each other, in 1873.

Despite Julien's aversion to teaching he successfully obtained a fourth position, as chair of spoken Chinese in the School of Vernacular Oriental Languages, which he held from 1862 to 1871. Intent on preventing anyone else, and especially Pauthier, from securing the job, he offered to serve without salary, but the appointment was nonetheless a curious one, since his methods had not produced any students capable of speaking the language. This was pointed out in a pamphlet titled *Literary Charlatanism Unveiled: Or the Truth about Certain Professors of Foreign Languages in Paris*, published by Paul Perny (1818-1907), who as a former missionary *could* speak Chinese.[21]

Nor had Julien's methods managed to develop his own conversational abilities, as we learn from an account by Zhang Deyi 張德彝 (1847-1918), a young member of the first government-sponsored fact-finding mission from China, in 1866. A top graduate of the Tongwen guan 同文館 (Combined Language Institute), the official foreign language school that had been established in 1862, Zhang began as an interpreter on this trip, the first of eight expeditions charged with learning more about the "merits and weaknesses of Western countries"[22] and laying the groundwork for diplomatic relations. As China's first career diplomat, he then held several positions, including as English tutor to the emperor, and in 1901 was appointed Chinese ambassador to Great Britain.[23] He kept detailed diaries for each of his eight trips, and about a meeting with Julien he wrote that the French scholar "has studied Chinese for thirty years and understands the meaning of characters without having heard them pronounced. . . . He invited us to enter and sit down, but we didn't engage in any conversation out loud, because he could only communicate his thoughts in writing. He also brought out some works he had translated for us to read: they weren't entirely incoherent."[24]

The only one of Julien's students who managed to outlive him was Marie-Jean-Léon le Coq, Baron d'Hervey and Marquis de Saint-Denys (1822-1892), whom Julien had already asked to substitute for him, starting in 1868, in his spoken Chinese courses at the School of Vernacular Oriental Languages. Being as incapable of conversation as his teacher but considerably more modest, Hervey-Saint-Denys, as I refer to him hereafter in my narrative, only agreed to step in if he could hire native Chinese instructors—at his own expense—to assist him, a practice that had been introduced by the Japanese professor in the school, Léon de

Rosny (1837-1914). The Chinese position was filled in 1871 by a returning diplomat, Count Michel Alexandre Kleczkowski (1818-1886), who could speak the language, but Julien's death in 1873 opened up the bigger prize, the chair at the Collège de France. Paul Perny's screed about "Literary Charlatanism" was in fact primarily directed against Hervey-Saint-Denys, whom he accused of being "absolutely incapable of *speaking* or *composing* six lines of Chinese and of *translating from Chinese*."²⁵ This wasn't entirely true, and Hervey-Saint-Denys successfully sued for libel against Perny, who landed in prison for two months. Nineteenth-century French sinology, it seems, was "a combat sport."²⁶

Though he was appointed to the chair in the Collège de France in 1874, Hervey-Saint-Denys never garnered the same degree of respect as had Abel-Rémusat and Julien. As the bibliographer Henri Cordier commented: "I don't think I'm offending his memory in saying that the continuation of the work of these two scholars was a burden a bit too heavy for his shoulders.... We can consider the Marquis d'Hervey de Saint-Denys a shadow of his two predecessors, and, if this not be too vulgar an image, we could even say that he lived on the leftovers of a feast to which he'd been invited."²⁷ Since Cordier couldn't read Chinese himself, he might have had some difficulty gauging the value of what Hervey-Saint-Denys did in fact accomplish—and especially of the poetry translations he published in 1862. We will return to this volume to consider its possible connections to Judith Gautier's project, but its importance as the first scholarly translation of Chinese poetry is undeniable.

Unlike Julien, Hervey-Saint-Denys expended little effort to promote his sinological research, but his disinterested love for the culture impressed an elderly Manchu official named Binchun 斌椿 (1804-1871), who chaperoned the delegation that included the young Zhang Deyi, mentioned above. The French scholar visited Binchun in May 1866 at his hotel "on a rainy day with a gift in hand: a collection of Tang-dynasty poems, selected and translated into French by himself." Writing in his diary that Hervey-Saint-Denys was "an extremely artistic person, fond of wine and poetry, and had no interest in advancing his career whatever," Binchun invited the Frenchman back and presented as return gift a poem that praised him as a true amateur who could engage with him in the lofty conversations of Chinese sages, and thus a kind of soulmate.²⁸

Thanks to his wife Louise de Ward (1849-1930), an Austrian whom he married at the age of forty-six when she was only eighteen, the scholar was probably best known as a socialite, a fixture of mid-nineteenth-century high society in

2.1 The Marquis d'Hervey-Saint-Denys, 1884, photograph by Eugène Pirou (1841–1909).
Bibliothèque de l'Institut de France, public domain

2.2 Caricature of Hervey-Saint-Denys by Cham, from Félix Ribeyre, *Cham: Sa vie et son oeuvre* (Paris: Librairie Plon, 1884), between 154 and 155.
BnF Gallica

Paris, as an entry in the diary of the two most famous chroniclers of nineteenth-century Parisian society, Edmond (1822–1896) and Jules (1830–1870) de Goncourt, suggests: "The pretty Madame Hervey-Saint-Denis responded a few days ago to Alphonse de Rothschild, who was asking if her husband was jealous: 'No! he's too pretentious!'"[29] Charming, flirtatious, and serially unfaithful to him, she seems to have served as model for two princesses in Marcel Proust's grand opus, *In Search of Lost Time* (*À la recherche du temps perdu*). Hervey-Saint-Denys also appears as himself in the volume titled *Sodom and Gomorrah* (*Sodome et Gomorrhe*) of Proust's novel, as the donor of "a porcelain vase, Chinese of course, to M. de Charlus."[30] His dapper figure was captured in a caricature by his childhood friend and relative Charles Amédée de Noé, known as Cham (1818-1879).[31]

Strangely, however, Hervey-Saint-Denys vanished from the sights of both scholars and the larger literary readership. As an anonymous biographer commented in 1964, "One would believe that a man of d'Hervey's importance would not disappear without a trace," but despite having been professor at the Collège de France, president of the Académie Française, and a Chevalier of the Legion of Honor, he was, a hundred years later, curiously "unknown."[32] What others most remembered about him was his interest in the analysis of dreams, for which sinological colleagues ridiculed him. He wrote down his own dreams faithfully every morning upon awakening, published a book on how to "direct" them, and has been honored by oneirologists on both the centenary of his death and the sesquicentenary of his birth.[33]

PLUNDERING CHINA: THE YUANMINGYUAN

By the middle of the nineteenth century Paris was indisputably the center of Western scholarship about the "oriental" world, distinguished by vibrant connections between the scholars and the broader world of letters.[34] They practiced, however, what has been called "armchair sinology"[35]—as erudite men who had neither ventured out to the land they studied through ancient texts nor could speak a word of the modern language. Although their work was certainly better known than would be true today, real world events served to attract public attention in ways that no scholarship could hope for. And what could be more riveting than war?

Not every conflict manages to spark curiosity about the defeated nation among the victors, but the joint Franco-British expedition of 1860 succeeded in eliciting enough outrage—and brought back sufficient spoils—to keep China in the news for years. Britain and France had been engaged in separate military efforts for decades to achieve greater "freedoms" in China, which for the former focused on commerce and the latter, initially, on religion. Britain's victory in the First Opium War (1839-1842) produced the 1842 Treaty of Nanking, which forced the opening of five ports to British merchants and ceded the island of Hong Kong. In 1843 and 1844 the French diplomat Marie Melchior Joseph Théodose de Lagrené

(1800–1862) led an expedition to secure what France desired following this triumph, the legitimation and expansion of missionary activities; this they secured in the 1844 Treaty of Whampoa. These "unequal" treaties did nothing to reduce tensions, which escalated into a Second Opium War initiated by Britain in 1856; France joined forces the next year following the murder of a French missionary. Their victory in 1858 produced the even more humiliating Treaty of Tianjin, which among other concessions opened more ports, legalized the opium trade, and guaranteed the safety of missionary activity.

When it became clear that the Qing government had little intention of signing the treaty, Britain and France combined forces once again in 1860 to exact the emperor's compliance. After several military encounters, in September the Chinese ambushed and kidnapped a negotiating party that included the British consul, and the Europeans marched on the capital of Beijing in pursuit of the ruler and his forces. Led by General Charles Guillaume Montauban (1796–1878), the French forces arrived in early October at a vast palace compound on the outskirts of the city, the Yuanmingyuan (元明園, Garden of Perfect Brightness). They were surprised to find that the imperial family had fled. According to Captain Jean-Louis de Négroni (1820–?), a Corsican whose regiment was among the first to enter the grounds, the first thing the French soldiers did was to prepare a sumptuous repast from provisions in the imperial kitchens, which included "eels, trout, salmon, shrimp, capons, truffled turkeys; we saw that the imperial court of the son of heaven didn't always live on swallow's nests and shark's fin." They enjoyed excellent bottles from Champagne and Bordeaux and exquisite pastries as well. "We were at the height of bliss," he writes. "After a terrible day-long march, rest was already happiness. Being comfortable didn't spoil anything."[36] The British army under General James Hope Grant (1808–1875) and led by James Bruce, the Eighth Earl of Elgin (1811–1863), arrived the same evening, though the record does not indicate that their (British) priorities were culinary ones.

Constructed between 1709 and 1772 within a compound about the size of Central Park in New York, the Yuanmingyuan had been the residence of five Manchu emperors and official seat of government. Breathtaking in its majesty and beauty, it comprised over three thousand separate buildings situated within an elaborate complex of gardens and artificial waterways. In historical accounts it is often erroneously called the Summer Palace, which denotes a separate garden compound nearby that has been rebuilt and can be visited today. While most of the structures were Chinese in architectural style, more than forty were palaces that had been designed by Jesuit architects using European designs and materials. All of them were furnished with what represented the finest of the imperial collection of art and antiquities, mostly Chinese, but including as well several European pieces that had arrived as tribute.³⁷

The Yuanmingyuan was far too vast to represent in a single image, but thanks to woodcut copies of a set of forty paintings commissioned by the Qing emperor Qianlong 乾隆 (r. 1735-1796) that circulated in various compilations the compound was relatively well known to the French. This is the seventeenth view, which depicts the emperor's ancestral temple under the heading "Great Compassion and Eternal Blessings" (*hong ci yong hu* 鴻慈永祜), and which was included in a collection illustrating "Fashionable Anglo-Chinese gardens" (*Jardins anglo-chinois à la mode*).³⁸

Eyewitnesses found it difficult to put their impressions of the complex into words. Count Maurice d'Hérisson, who served as interpreter for the French, was

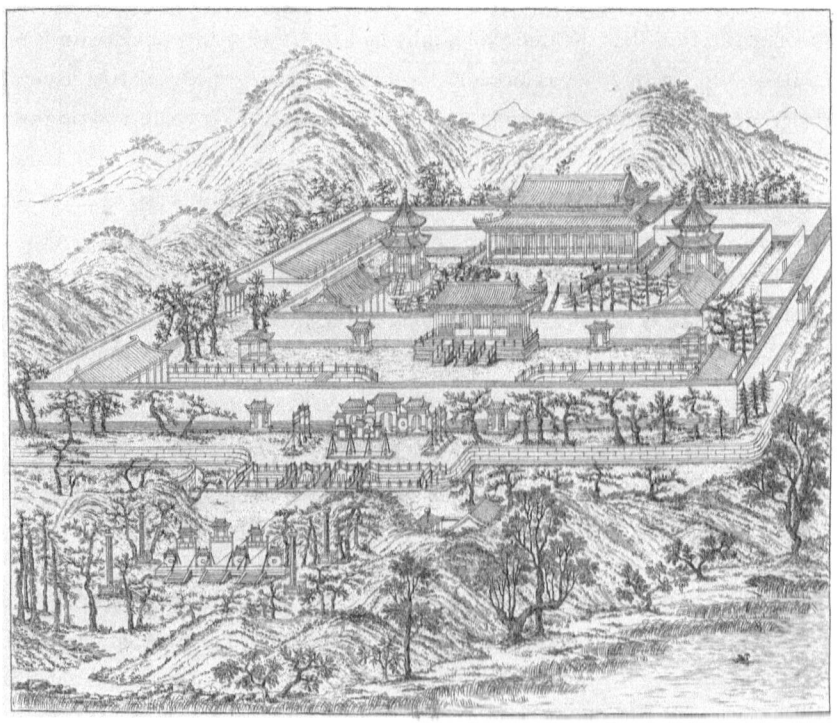

2.3 View 17 of the Yuanmingyuan, from [George-Louis Le Rouge, ed.,] *Jardins de l'empereur de la Chine* ([Paris: G.L. LeRouge, 1786]).
BnF Gallica

reminded of Versailles but declared language truly inadequate to the task: "I would now need, in order to describe all of the splendors offered to our eyes, to dissolve samples of every known precious stone into liquid gold and to soak in it a diamond feather whose bristles consist of the fantasies of an oriental poet raised on the knees of fairies and accustomed to frolicking from childhood in their chimerical treasuries."[39]

Having occupied the abandoned complex, the French and British military leaders set up commissions to select what they considered the finest objects to take back to their respective rulers, Emperor Napoleon III and Queen Victoria. (As the son of Thomas Bruce, the Seventh Earl of Elgin [1766-1841], who had "acquired" the famous Parthenon sculptures for Britain, James Bruce seems to have learned his father's lesson rather well.) Then they opened things up to their troops. The French and British argued over who started it all, and some blamed local Chinese brigands, but neither held back. Garnet Wolseley, who was quartermaster for the British troops, writes: "Indiscriminate plunder and wanton destruction of all articles too heavy for removal commenced at once.... Officers and men seemed to have been seized with a temporary insanity; in body and soul they were absorbed in one pursuit, which was plunder, plunder."[40] Négroni records in his memoirs that he wanted to save whatever he could of precious masterpieces that he feared were "at risk of total dispersion." Moreover, he considered it a patriotic act of noblesse oblige to bring back to France such artifacts, both for its greater glory but also to enable it to learn about China, for "the best way to come to know a country, to judge it, to appreciate it, is to see it in its artistic, industrial, and commercial products."[41] But it was looting, plain and simple, whose excesses were detailed in several other accounts.[42]

After two days of plundering the soldiers decamped to besiege Beijing. Having learned that the Chinese had tortured and executed some of its hostages, Lord Elgin ordered the total destruction of the Yuanmingyuan, what he considered "a solemn act of retribution"[43] that would also, he thought, compel the Qing government's acceptance of the as yet unsigned Treaty of Tianjin. His French counterpart, Baron Jean-Baptiste-Louis Gros (1793-1870), strongly objected to razing such a cultural treasure, as did General Montauban and most of his soldiers, although Négroni considered it to have been justly inflicted as "a necessity of war" and as appropriate retribution for the "atrocious cruelties" inflicted on "prisoners of the two most powerful nations of Europe."[44] So it was up to the British troops alone to set fire to the complex, whose largely cedar structures burned for two days. The conflagration, as well as a further threat to destroy the Forbidden

Palace in Beijing, finally succeeded in persuading the emperor to allow his brother to sign the treaty drafted in 1858, which now inflicted even more onerous terms on the Chinese government. It is estimated that approximately 1.5 million objects were either seized or destroyed by the British and French troops.[45]

The pillage of the Yuanmingyuan did not go unremarked in the French literary world. The Goncourt brothers decry the events in no uncertain terms: "There we are plundering China! We are raping and robbing Peking, the cradle, the most venerable cradle of art, of civilization! It's something the Huns would do: we have nothing more to reproach barbarians for. That is horrible, it's like watching someone rape his mother."[46] Victor Hugo revises the Goncourts' final metaphor in an oft-cited letter to a young Irish army officer whom he met while in exile on the isle of Guernsey and who asked his opinion about the Franco-British expedition. Hugo provides it in no uncertain terms, with language that also employs the same metaphor as his praise of Judith Gautier's writing. He begins by describing what he calls the Summer Palace as a veritable "marvel of the world," the highest embodiment of every French romantic fantasy of China as a land of dreamlike, fantastical, "chimerical art" engendered by "the imagination of an almost superhuman people"; it was, impossibly, "like a building on the moon." And now, he writes:

"This marvel has disappeared. ...

"One day, two bandits entered the Summer Palace. One plundered it, the other burned it."

And, he adds:

"I hope that the day will come when France, liberated and cleansed, will return this booty to plundered China."[47]

That, of course, did not happen. Meanwhile, a Pekingese dog taken from the Yuanmingyuan was sent to Queen Victoria. He was named Looty, and his picture still hangs in Windsor Castle.[48]

"A MOUNTAIN OF JADE"

The objects selected for Napoleon III and his wife Eugénie went on display in the Tuileries palace for three months and were then dispersed to various sites, including the "Chinese museum" (*Musée chinois*) the empress established at Fontainebleau.[49] The loot collected by British and French soldiers kept auction houses busy in both countries for the next two decades. Lord Elgin died in 1863, and his plunder began to be sold off the following year. But the most extensive collection in the hands of a single soldier had been assembled by Captain Négroni.[50] In his memoirs of the expedition, which include a complete listing of his booty, Négroni makes a point of noting that it had required a great deal of time and effort and the expenditure of his own funds to purchase objects from other soldiers to accumulate it all. Were he a person of greater means, he would have simply donated it to the state, which apparently was not interested in acquiring it at a reasonable price.[51] Instead, it was exhibited in several cities throughout Europe—first in Paris in 1864 and notably at London's Crystal Palace in 1865—in order to stimulate the interest of the art market.[52] Both Stanislas Julien and Hervey-Saint-Denys were able to acquire items billed as taken from the Summer Palace, no doubt from Négroni's collection. So, too, did Victor Hugo.[53]

Judith Gautier was among the many enthusiastic visitors when it went on display in Paris. Under the pseudonym Judith Walter she published a review of the exhibition in the journal *L'Artiste*, which her father had edited from 1856 to 1859. Mindful of the collection's provenance as almost entirely the spoils of invasion and plunder, the eighteen-year-old critic was nonetheless bedazzled by what she saw. As she puts it, the Yuanmingyuan "was like one of the palaces that the magicians in *A Thousand and One Nights* conjure up from the tip of their magic wand." Few people have had the opportunity to contemplate such "a profusion of marvels: it's a jumble of porcelain, a mountain of jade, a cascade of precious stones; you come out of it dazzled, and for quite some time everything seems ugly and dark as if one had looked into the sun."

There is no question about what impressed her the most: "The most interesting and most curious thing for us is without a doubt the series of jades. This stone, little known in our country, is unique to China, and the Chinese value it above all else; for them, it is the standard of the highest perfection: all beauty, all poetry, and all virtue are compared to jade." She is especially struck by the difficulty, delicacy, and intricate detail of the craftsmanship, which can be seen in the nephrite brushpot here, brought back from the "Summer Palace" to England. As Gautier writes: "Jade is extremely hard and can only be cut with diamond dust," yet the Chinese have managed to reduce it to a supple base for all sorts of shapes and ornament. Jade rings and bracelets that must have belonged to the empress spark visions of the slender Chinese arm that they had adorned. A little cup teems with carved flowers and foliage, of which "a whimsical branch extends carelessly over the rim like a clump of water-lilies on the edge of a lake," prompting her to imagine a nest nestled in a bouquet of marguerites and to wonder why some poet "hadn't traced, with the tip of her pen, one of those sweet poems of ineffable nuance?" And she asks which "mysterious port" will be the destination of the two children plying flowery oars in a graceful little jade boat. She notes that jade can also take on an imperceptibly green tint or, indeed, be unequivocally green, but—important in connection with the title of her book—it loses thereby some of the white stone's "beautiful transparency."

Gautier is initially less impressed by the porcelains but then discovers objects worthy of admiration, as well as paintings and drawings that strike her as surprisingly sophisticated (Westerners at the time were generally unappreciative of Chinese painting.) Then she moves to the textiles, from which emanates "a delicate perfume, a Chinese aroma that penetrates you; from these glittering crepes and light silks that unfurl escapes a distant dream that one would say was enclosed in their narrow folds." And her imagination takes flight, envisioning "fabrics carried by nonchalant Chinese women; one sees them behind their papered windows, balancing gently on their little feet that *resemble golden water lilies*. The flowery comparisons of poets come to mind; the cadence of verses hums in your ears like music; you are far away; Peking appears to you in a ray of sunlight and, in turning back you are completely stunned to find yourself on the rue de Rivoli."

After passing quickly over other features of the exhibition Gautier notes that Négroni had just published his account of the campaign in China, which she recommends as well written, keenly observed, and "full of interest for people who would be, like us, passionate about China."[54] And in addition to stoking her passion, the exhibit also provided her with countless ways of imagining its people, objects, and poetry that would shape her *Book of Jade*, on which she was already working, and, not the least, with the title image for that work.

THÉOPHILE GAUTIER AND CHINA

Judith Gautier's father had eagerly hoped to join the Anglo-French expedition, albeit before the sack of the Yuanmingyuan that yielded these treasures. He was rejected for military service by the French government, but his enthusiasm for the Orient had already sparked his daughter's imagination in many ways.[55] Théophile Gautier sat at the hub of mid-nineteenth-century French letters, and his

2.4 Brushpot of nephrite jade from the Summer Palace, Arthur Wells bequest (1882).
Courtesy of the Victoria and Albert Museum, London

Thursday salons and dinner parties featuring Ernesta's acclaimed risotto regularly convened the literary and artistic luminaries of the day. A poet, novelist, dramatist, essayist, artist, librettist, and critic, he was most active as a journalist, with a prodigious output of articles in the major periodicals of the day that would fill some three hundred volumes and provide an important source of income.[56]

Physically imposing, he was even more daunting intellectually. Gautier possessed, in the words of the Goncourt brothers, "the most astonishing good sense about literary things, the soundest judgment, a terrifying lucidity sparkling in very simple little sentences."[57] He was described as an "impeccable poet," the "perfect magician of French letters," and a "very dear and very revered master and friend" by Baudelaire, who dedicated his 1857 volume, *Flowers of Evil* (*Les Fleurs du mal*), with these words to him.[58]

Gautier's early and longstanding fascination with Chinese culture has been well documented, starting with a frequently anthologized poem titled "Chinoiserie" from 1838, which declares that he fancies neither the woman he's addressing nor any other Juliet, Ophelia, Beatrice, or Laura; rather, he writes, "The one I love just now is in China" (Celle que j'aime, à présent, est en Chine) in a porcelain tower where "she sings of the willow and the peaches' flower (chante le saule et la fleur du pêcher)."[59] The poem was as superficially indebted to Chinese literature as its title suggests, but two later works were more clearly inspired by texts that had recently been made accessible by scholars. In delving seriously into these sources for literary ideas Gautier distinguished himself from his many contemporaries whose fascination was less probing and enduring. Flaubert, for example, had long dreamed of traveling there and had also toyed with the idea of joining the Franco-British military venture, writing to a friend in 1859 that "I am at the moment a bit excited by the idea of a trip to China. It would be *easy* for me to leave with the French expedition. And I won't hide from you that I would happily leave all my work to head for the land of parasols and nankeen if I didn't have a mother who's starting to age and whom my departure would finish off."[60] Many of the Parnassian poets owed their relatively desultory interest in the Far East to Gautier's influence as well. But Théophile Gautier was certainly "the first imaginative French writer in the nineteenth century to discover the artistic possibilities" of Chinese texts recently translated by the first sinologists.[61]

As his daughter recalled in her memoirs, Gautier "was keenly interested in the ancient civilization of the Middle Kingdom. He had read the works of Abel-Rémusat and plays translated by Bazin; he had traveled intellectually to this land of dreams which remained nonetheless unreal for him."[62] Most notably, a Chinese tale that had been translated by a Jesuit missionary and published by Abel-Rémusat in his 1827 edition of *Chinese Tales* (*Contes chinois*) served as a fruitful source text for Gautier's 1846 novella *The Waterside Pavilion*, a story about two lovers who live in adjoining residences but whose relationship is temporarily foiled

2.5 Théophile Gautier, photograph by Nadar.
BnF Gallica

by disagreements and misunderstandings between their parents. In a letter to his editor, Gautier describes his plan to write "a Chinese tale" that will require research to "daub" with "local color" and explains: "You know that I'm no literary joker; you could do me a service that shouldn't bother you much and would help me greatly. If by chance you have the book in *L'Univers pittoresque* focused on China, you'd please me by lending it to me."[63] The book Gautier is referring to, from which he gleaned considerable information about Chinese gardens and architecture and which was titled "Modern China: Historical, Geographical, and Literary Description of this Vast Empire, based on Chinese Documents," was the work of none other than Stanislas Julien's nemesis Guillaume Pauthier.[64]

Another volume in his library was the *Selection of Stories and Novellas* (*Choix de contes et nouvelles*), drawn from a seventeenth-century collection of colloquial short stories selected from well-known anthologies titled *Wondrous Stories Old and New* (*Jin gu qi guan* 今古奇觀) and published in 1839 by Théodore Pavie (1811–1896). This included a tale about the noted Tang-dynasty poet Li Bo 李白 (701–762, also known as Li Bai, or Li Po), whom the French usually referred to by his alternate name "Li-Taï-Pé 李太白" (Li Taibo). He makes an appearance in one of Gautier's best known poems, an 1865 sonnet titled "La Marguerite," which begins:

Les poëtes chinois, épris des anciens rites,	The Chinese poets, in love with ancient rites,
Ainsi que Li-Taï-Pé, quand il faisait des vers,	Like Li Taibo when writing his verse,
Placent sur leur pupitre un pot de marguerites	Place on their desk a pot of marguerites
Dans leurs disques montrant l'or de leurs coeurs ouverts.	Whose disks show the gold of their open hearts.

Recalling the images from "Chinoiserie," Gautier then writes that the sight and fragrance of these flowers are more poetically inspiring than white peach blossoms or green willows, just as a real Marguerite had prompted the poem's composition by Gautier, who styles himself a "morose mandarin" and "aged rhymer" offering her yet another poetic bouquet.[65]

Théophile Gautier may have been thwarted in his effort to join the 1860 expedition to China, but he had already found what he jokingly considered a close substitute eleven years earlier, when an enormous Chinese junk was put on exhibit in London on the Thames. It had been acquired by English entrepreneurs in Canton who had managed to circumvent Chinese laws forbidding the sale of Chinese ships to foreigners and had spent several months on display in the United States. Billed as "the greatest novelty in Europe,"[66] it was included by the French railway office as a special feature of a deluxe weeklong package to London. Gautier made a trip to view the ship and reported on his experience in an article for *La Presse* published in June 1849.

"To go to China," he begins, "one embarks at Hereford Suspension Bridge, a couple of steps from Trafalgar Square, on one of those light paddle steamboats, aquatic omnibuses that constantly cruise up and down the Thames" to arrive at Saint Catherine's dock beneath the Tower of London "in less time than it would take for a short cab ride.... China was too far away, so they brought it to you. China found its way to you as did the mountain to the prophet."[67]

The ship itself, its furnishings, and other cargo spark his keen interest, offering a glimpse, through their craftsmanship and artistry, into the secrets of a previously "hermetically sealed" country. Even more absorbing are its occupants, who include sailors, a group of performing musicians, a painter, and a writer. Gautier wrestles with the contradictory impressions elicited by these encounters. Who is "barbaric" and who "civilized," he wonders, when one enters the domain and adopts the perspective of the other? He recognizes that various aesthetic features of Chinese objects might be considered ugly by classical Greek standards, but he can't help finding them attractive. And his curiosity about the people "from a human race that one encounters rarely in Europe" is profound. Under "this bronzed skin," angled facial apertures, and skull profiles so different from his own he wants to learn how "the soul of this unknown brother, worshipping other gods, expressing other ideas in another language, possessing peculiar beliefs and prejudices, can resemble our soul; we eagerly seek to divine, in the depths of eyes where the sun from the opposite hemisphere has left its light, a thought with which we might communicate and sympathize."[68]

From this point on, as news about the various conflicts in China reached Paris, Théophile Gautier's articles in leading periodicals were more and more "obsessed with China."[69] This is the curiosity he sparked in his daughter Judith. Both she and her sister Estelle were described by the Goncourts as seeming at times "the daughters of their father's nostalgia for the Orient," whose reading and activities were shaped by his interests. Even as teenagers they are said to possess a certain "air of oriental women" and "a sort of oriental languor" of their own.[70] But it was

Judith, who was widely recognized as "always the favorite child of her father,"[71] for whom his nostalgia became, at least artistically, a future. And it was he who provided her first encounters with it.

In May 1862 Théophile Gautier made another trip to London to report on the International Exhibition for *Le Moniteur universel,* and this time he invited his two daughters and their mother to join him. In her memoirs Judith Gautier vividly describes the many pleasures of her stay in England—once she'd recovered from the seasickness induced by the channel crossing—which included drinking beer, seeing chimney sweeps for the first time, and eating dinner with William Thackeray. Very little of the exposition itself struck her as memorable, although there were objects from the Yuanmingyuan on display.[72] One encounter, however, left "an indelible impression." While walking on the streets with her mother and sister one day she spies "two very strange persons, followed by a bunch of gawkers. It was two Japanese men, in their national costume." When the latter slip into a boutique to escape the crowd, Gautier and her family follow them inside. "I was fascinated," she writes. "It was my first encounter with the Far East, which from that very instant won me over." She had seen Asia's treasures, but never before its people.

Gautier describes the two Japanese men and their garments with impressive detail—their supple silk robes, the shield-shaped caps held on by white silk straps, and the delicately carved hilts of two swords that emerge, crisscrossed, from their belts of velvet and gold brocade. Sandals barely gripped by feet clad in white cloth socks articulated for the toes lend them "a soft and nonchalant gait." The taller of the two has a pale face, aristocratic nose, "a peculiar expression combining dignity, melancholy, gentleness, and indifference," and opens his fan with a single gesture. The other has a dark gold complexion, whose several pockmarks make him look like "a bronze old man somewhat ravaged by time."

The Japanese are as curious about the French family as they are of them, and as they chat briefly in a mix of English and French Gautier can almost sense "the perfume like the atmosphere of their legendary country" wafting about them. She does not mention this in her account, but the two men were in London as part of the first Japanese delegation to Europe,[73] sent by the government on the occasion of the International Exhibition to learn about the West and negotiate the opening of Japan to foreign trade. They had arrived the day before the fair opened and went on to tour other European countries over the course of a year. A public sensation, their appearance was even more transformative for Gautier, as she writes, "What a fateful encounter for me, what an unforgettable vision! An entire unheard-of world appeared before me, and a kind of intuition (which I always have when facing things that will captivate me) made me glimpse it in its entirety and revealed its special beauties to me."[74]

"AN AUTHENTIC CHINESE MAN"

If this brief meeting with two Japanese represented for Judith Gautier her first encounter with the Far East, she had yet to experience what she would call her true "discovery of China." Once again, she would have her father to thank for that. Her account of this episode in her memoirs begins with an undated visit from a close friend of the family, Charles Simon Clermont-Ganneau (1846–1923), who would later become a renowned archeologist known for sniffing out forgeries, most notably of the Dead Sea Scrolls. Still a teenager at this time, he was known to the family as Nono and had been treated like a son by Théophile Gautier after his father's death in 1851. In her memoir Judith Gautier recounts his retelling of an "adventure" that had occurred on some unspecified date several months earlier: "An extraordinary being had approached him on a street and asked him for information in an incomprehensible language. This being, rather small, had a strange yellow face with slanted eyes, which made the most amusing impression in the world under an old top hat that was too large and came down to his ears; he wore a tattered overcoat and worn-out shoes, bound together with strings." Despite this "sad disguise which made him look hideous," his origins were clearly recognizable: "he was a Chinese man, an authentic Chinese man, down on his luck, following a series of unfortunate incidents, on the pavements of Paris."

As Gautier tells it, Clermont-Ganneau spent a great deal of time to unravel the story of "this poor devil," whose name was Tin-Tun-Ling, often spelled with slight variations, and which in modern romanization would be Ding Dunling 丁敦齡 (1831–1886). In her telling Ding had been brought to France by a Monseigneur Callery, "bishop of Macao," who had engaged him to work on an edition of a Chinese-French dictionary, but his patron had soon passed away, leaving him without a means of livelihood and having acquired little French, since he had been able to lodge with his Chinese-speaking employer. When Nono met him, Ding was on his way to work for the sinologist Stanislas Julien, who evidently "was never in a hurry to pay him his meager salary." Taking an interest in his plight, Nono advised Ding to abandon his Western garb and don his "national costume" again, as well as to replait his queue, and immediately "the man was transformed into a very elegant vase." Newly attired to correspond with the French image of a Chinese, he met a woman who took pity on him and was on the verge of marrying him when she, too, passed away. Having heard this story and being moved by the plight of "this Chinese man, alone and without resources, so far from his chimerical homeland," Théophile Gautier could only imagine himself in Peking, "homeless, not knowing a word of Chinese." He and his daughters were much excited by the idea of meeting a living breathing human being from the "Celestial Empire": "this unbelievable creature thus actually existed, other than on screens and fans, with a head of ivory or a rice paper face."

In a 1910 interview with Raoul Aubry, Judith slightly condensed this account:

> One day, my father met Clermont-Ganneau, and this dialogue was exchanged between the two:
> "I have this Chinese man who is worrying me a bit. He came from his country with the bishop of Macao, and the bishop died. But one can't leave this poor devil without shelter, without aid. What can be done?"
> "He's all right, this yellow man?" asked Théophile Gautier.
> "But extremely so, and very cultivated."
> "Send me your Chinese man, we'll try to comfort him."[75]

It was decided to invite Ding to lunch the next day and to try to muster the resources to send him back to China.

Charles Clermont-Ganneau brought "the poor devil" to dine with the Gautiers, as requested. Judith Gautier describes how he greeted the family respectfully by raising and shaking his clenched fists before his forehead, and was clad in full "national costume," which consisted of "a blue gown of soft fabric under a black tunic of silk brocade, with little copper buttons. Following ritual protocol, he kept a little black satin cap on his head, decorated with a square mother-of-pearl button encased in gold filigree.... From his sleeves emerged halfway thin and aristocratic hands lengthened by nails that were longer than the fingers." In the photographs taken shortly after he is missing his cap, but the long nails and queue and two-piece Chinese garb he rarely changed are clearly visible.

Some version of this outfit appears in almost every account of Ding's activities in the newspapers of Paris until his death. It corresponds with the elements appearing in characteristic descriptions of Chinese in much of nineteenth-century European literature, typically reduced to sartorial details (long gowns for men, parasols or fans) and physical traits (the male queue, yellow skin, long nails, and slanted eyes).[76] And, indeed, in his much later recollection Georges Grison provides these several other customary elements of his appearance:

> He had a very tiny yellowish, wrinkled face adorned with a little moustache that one would have sworn was fake. His slanted eyes were protected by round, enormous glasses like those worn now by motorists and aviators. A long, thin queue flapped at his shoulders, falling down to his sky-blue silk skirt. On his head was a cap with a red button and on his feet white sandals. Under his arm was an enormous parasol of patterned paper brought from his home country.[77]

Judith Gautier continues by describing the gist of their first conversation, which presented real challenges. "We tried to exchange several sentences with him, but that wasn't easy because what little French he knew he pronounced in a rather unexpected way." When it became clear that Théophile Gautier intended to provide Ding with passage back to China, as he assumed would be desired, the latter responded in horror that he never wanted to return, for his head would be chopped off. What complicated intrigue or dangerous crime had he been involved with? Clermont-Ganneau, who had apparently learned enough Chinese to elicit a modicum of information from Ding, surmised from his interrogation that the latter had likely been involved in the Taiping civil war, which sought to replace the Manchu government by a Christian "Kingdom of Heavenly Peace" and ravaged much of China from 1850 to 1864. Indeed, one of his arms retained scars from an injury caused by an exploding weapon that had removed a large chunk of flesh. And it was during the famine caused by the warfare, while Ding was on the run, that he'd been rescued and converted by a missionary.

Ding clearly did not want to return to his home country, so Théophile Gautier came up with another idea. As his daughter recalls:

> "Do you want to learn Chinese," he says to me, "and learn about a country that is still virtually unknown, yet seems amazing? This melancholy marmoset

2.6 and 2.7 Ding Dunling (Tin-Tun-Ling), photographs by Jacques-Philippe Potteau (1807–1876).

©Musée du Quai Branly–Jacques Chirac, Dist. RMN-Grand Palais / Art Resource, NY

seems very smart. He must be educated, since bishop Callery chose him to work on his dictionary. Do you want to try to unwind this yellow man and see what lies hidden in his mysterious brain?"

Did I want that?!. . . .

I simply responded by turning a series of somersaults, which the Chinese man watched with his slanted eyes, his forehead totally creased, but out of courtesy without showing the slightest surprise.

And this was how Ting-Tun-Ling became Théophile Gautier's Chinese man.[78]

In a Paris with but a handful of native Chinese residents it appears to have been difficult to know how to categorize and process an "authentic Chinese man" in the flesh. In the passage above describing Ding's "national costume," Judith Gautier herself alludes to the difficulty of determining Ding's precise age from his appearance—still a familiar cliché about Asians—and writes that "he looked like a priest, a young female monkey, and an old woman, all at the same time." In a much later interview she remembered the thirty-year-old Ding as "a Chinese boy."[79] What was this "unbelievable creature," this "melancholy marmoset"? For Armand Silvestre, Théophile Gautier's kind reception of the "vagabond from the Far East" was easy to explain: "The great poet adored all animals, as those who knew him are well aware, as well as readers of his little known masterpiece which is called *The Intimate Menagerie*. He found room immediately for the outcast between his tomcat Enjolras and his female cat Éponine."[80] At times Ding seemed little more than an elegant decorative object. Théophile Gautier himself referred to Ding as an "amiable *magot*" or Chinese figurine (like the two large statues of officials that still overlook the patrons of the famous Café Les Deux Magots in Paris, which had been named after a shop that used to sell such pottery)[81] and was said to have commented that the Chinese man would look good on his mantel, between two vases.[82]

In later accounts Ding Dunling was sometimes promoted from house pet, household object, or houseboy to Théophile Gautier's "secretary." He never seemed to begrudge his reception in France and remained deeply grateful to the man who took him in. This is clear from the preface to a novel he published fourteen years after leaving China: "I've walked on the land of your ancestors, and I've found the people of the West kind and generous. One day, ten thousand times blessed, I met Théophile Gautier. His heart was vast and caring; he opened his home to me, and I entered it. He was for me like a celestial host and a benevolent light. He has bid farewell to the century: may his body rest in peace."[83]

Without Théophile Gautier's generosity we would have no story, and there are simple reasons Ding would always be called his "Chinese man." But the most influential position he would occupy was that of Judith Gautier's tutor, as her "professor of Chinese." He introduced her to the world of Chinese poetry, and she dedicated her *Book of Jade* to him. And his twenty-five-year sojourn has much to tell us about how, in fact, one could be Chinese in nineteenth-century Paris.

CHAPTER 3

"One of the most interesting characters of his time"

Professor, Baron, Barnum, or Rake?

He wasn't the first Chinese to arrive in Paris, nor would he be the last, but he was surely the most renowned of his countrymen in nineteenth-century France. No stranger to scandal, a rumored petty thief and cuckolder, he promoted himself shamelessly while negotiating Parisian society with remarkable adroitness. Tin-Tun-Ling / Ding Dunling and his activities were chronicled regularly in the countless newspapers, periodicals, and other publications that flourished in the French capital at the time. If always acknowledged as "Théophile Gautier's Chinese man" (le Chinois de Gautier), over the years he also became "the legendary Chinese man all Paris knows," "an elegant scholar and profound philosopher," and "one of the most interesting characters of his time."[1] His trial for bigamy, his death, and his funeral were all front-page news. Although described as "the most Parisian Chinese in Paris,"[2] he never came close to mastering the language of his adopted country, and he never tired of trying to introduce audiences to Chinese literature at Sunday matinees at local theaters. But though reviews suggest that his readings and performances were rarely truly understood or appreciated, his most important work had already been done, as Judith Gautier's Chinese tutor.

In addition to her memoirs, which recount Ding's first visit to the Gautier household, two other documents sketch the history of his arrival and residence in France: the court journal's report of his 1875 trial and Ding's own preface to the novel he wrote while in prison before it.[3] Just as Judith Gautier's life was thought worthy of being a novel, so, wrote her brother-in-law Emile Bergerat, "the novel of Tin-tun-ling himself was much more 'novelistic' than the one he wrote."[4] He played to Parisians' expectations of what an "authentic Chinese man" should be but also ended up surprising them.

FROM MACAO TO PARIS

In the preface to his novel Ding describes himself as "a scholar from the province of Chang-si," and trial reports confirm this. He was probably born on May 17, 1831, in Pingyang prefecture of Shanxi Province, in northeast China.[5] The son of a practitioner of Chinese medicine, he claimed to have earned the title of "flourishing talent" (*xiu cai* 秀才) at age eighteen. Though this was but the first rung on the ladder of civil service examinations leading to eligibility for government employment, it would have placed him in a distinct minority of the Chinese population and entitled him to be considered not just literate but someone qualified to teach others; it also provided him with the cap and gown that Paris would come to associate with him. That same year his father passed away and Ding may have decided to go to the capital of Peking, where, arriving destitute and hungry during a period of widespread famine, he was rescued by a Catholic priest who would only feed him if he was willing to be converted. Having not eaten for eight days, Ding agreed to be baptized, and he received the Christian name of Paul-Jean-Baptiste-Marie. This is his defense attorney's narrative; according to the prosecutor, he went straight to Macao and was baptized there.

Ding's possible involvement in the mid-century Taiping civil strife was brief at best.[6] We have no information about the course of his travels from the north to the south and how he might have engaged in the struggle. But he was certainly aware of it. In 1864 Judith Gautier published a sympathetic account of a legend associated with the leader of the revolution that she notes "has the merit of having been collected directly from the mouth of an inhabitant of the Celestial Empire," who was no doubt Ding Dunling.[7]

By 1852 Ding was in Macao, where he worked as a tutor and interpreter and married another convert to Christianity, Fan Alin 范阿林, who also appears in the records as Fan-Ha-Lin and Lusia-Tom-Alacer, in the chapel of Macao's Eglise Miséricorde. The couple had two children and remained in Macao until Ding left for Paris in 1861. As Ding writes in 1875, in the preface to his novel, "fourteen years have fallen into oblivion since I left the Middle Kingdom."

The man named Callery who brought Ding to Europe was not, as Judith Gautier asserts in her memoir, a bishop who was working on a Chinese-French dictionary. Joseph-Gaëtan-Pierre-Marie Callery (1810–1862), born Giuseppe Maria Calleri in the Piedmont region of Italy (then under Napoleon's control), was educated in France. He had indeed been ordained and went to China in 1833, where he learned both Chinese and Korean with the intention of proselytizing in Korea. Instead, he spent several years as a naturalist traveling throughout Asia, sending numerous specimens back to the Museum of Natural History in Paris, was dismissed while on a brief mission to the Philippines for allegedly inappropriate behavior, and then embarked on an active career as interpreter and sinological scholar. Callery returned to Paris in 1847 to take up a position as Secretary Interpreter for the Ministry of Foreign Affairs, where he translated an ancient classic and coauthored a history of the Taiping civil war. He also continued work on his *Dictionnaire encyclopédique de la langue chinoise* (Encyclopedic dictionary of the Chinese language [not Chinese-French]), of which the first of twenty projected volumes had been published in Paris in 1842.[8]

Callery was something of an anomaly in Paris: he was a scholar of China who could speak the language because he had spent time there. In 1854 Count Michel Alexandre Kleczkowski, who was then attaché at the French legation in Peking, communicated his concern about the lack of spoken facility being cultivated back home, where the School of Vernacular Oriental Languages had not yet hired anyone possessing it. Kleczkowski made the point that there may have only been one person in all of France qualified for any such appointment: Callery, who no doubt agreed.[9] He in turn sniped at the great "armchair sinologists" for their lack of firsthand knowledge of China and its culture and declared sinology to be "a thankless science in which very few people have been interested."[10] In addition he deemed it useless for diplomatic purposes: "One would not be a good ambassador to Rome today by virtue solely of understanding Horace or Tacitus well."[11] But neither was he immune to its constant battles. The arch-enemies Stanislas Julien and Guillaume Pauthier found common ground in their envy of Callery's spoken fluency and joined forces in an 1859 "vendetta" that accused the interpreter of having stolen six Chinese books from the national library. As scandal had dogged his career abroad, so it tinged his sinological activities, and though an investigation into the matter was inconclusive, he was unable to clear his name before his death in 1862.[12]

The previous year Callery had asked a friend in Macao to recruit someone who could copy his communications in Chinese, since the few Chinese he had encountered in Paris were illiterate stowaways from ships. Ding contracted for the job, which would pay a monthly salary of 150 francs. He left Macao in February 1861, arriving six months later after a harrowing trip that determined him never to set sail again. Disappointingly, the work as "secretary" turned out to consist mostly of doing Callery's laundry and waxing his boots,[13] but thanks to his employer's untimely demise it did not even last a year.

In her memoir Judith Gautier mentions Ding's employment by Stanislas Julien after Callery's death, but there is considerable confusion as to when and how this happened and what it involved. One story has it that Napoleon III himself brought Ding over from Macao to serve as pronunciation drill instructor for Julien at the Collège de France.[14] This is certainly untrue, if only because Julien never employed drill instructors. It is quite likely, however, that Ding did work for Julien to provide the Chinese characters for the bilingual editions of some of the scholar's works, for his presumptive calligraphy is contained in Julien's translations of texts like the *Three Character Classic* and the *Thousand Character Essay*.[15] This may be the assignment that Gautier recalls, for which Julien so begrudged paying him his salary. We know that Ding performed similar work for Léon de Rosny, the Japanese specialist at the School of Vernacular Oriental Languages. Between 1863 and 1864 he provided the calligraphy for Japanese and Chinese language manuals de Rosny was preparing, and he most certainly penned the characters for the professor's *Dictionary of Ideographic Signs in China (Dictionnaire des signes idéographiques de la Chine)*, published in 1864.[16] Ding enrolled in de Rosny's Japanese class during the 1863-64 school term and was even initiated into Freemasonry by his instructor.[17] He also served as drill instructor for the Marquis d'Hervey-Saint-Denys for approximately six weeks during May and June 1870 when the latter filled in for Stanislas Julien at the school and decided to emulate de Rosny's innovative practice of using native speakers for pronunciation drills.[18]

The stories about Ding's relationships with the two scholars of Chinese do agree on one fact—that he managed to antagonize both for the same reason. In a 1910 interview Judith Gautier recalls:

> Stanislas Julien, who saw [Ding] at our house, had developed a true antipathy to him. For this knowledgeable orientalist that was Stanislas Julien did not speak a single word of oriental languages; he deciphered most marvelously the most obscure manuscripts and figured out the most unbelievable dialects, but the contemporary language remained beyond his reach. He was discomfited by the thought that this Chinese nobody could say "Good day, Mr. Scholar" to him and that he could not reply. He was very humiliated. So he attributed to our Chinese a most bizarre origin and thought him qualified to be only a chauffeur or a cook."[19]

50 *Professor, Baron, Barnum, or Rake?*

As for Hervey-Saint-Denys, one report of the trial that limns the arc of Ding's career notes that after his introduction to the Gautier family,

> Tin-Tun-Ling found ways to give Chinese lessons. His fortunes rose. In 1870 he was named drill instructor for Chinese pronunciation for the Marquis d'Hervey-Saint-Denis, professor of Chinese language at the Collège de France. Unfortunately for Tin-Tun-Ling, he knew Chinese and had an irascible personality. One fine day in the middle of a class he is said to have interrupted the professor, saying to him: "You not know Chinese, not at all." This exceeded his modest responsibility as pronunciation drill instructor.[20]

Though this account gets the name of the institution wrong (this would have occurred at the School of Vernacular Oriental Languages, not the Collège de France, where no spoken language was taught), it probably explains why Ding's employment for Hervey-Saint-Denys lasted less than two months. He sought, nonetheless, to be elected as a member of the first International Congress of Orientalists meeting in Paris in 1873, and when this effort proved unsuccessful, "Théophile Gautier's famous Chinese man" threatened "to rip apart any sessions claiming to deal with the Chinese language."[21]

TUTOR TO THE GAUTIERS

Ding had secured his first and most important engagement with the Gautiers in summer 1863, and he soon became a well-known fixture of the household. Théophile Gautier found lodging for him not far from his own house, and his work as Chinese tutor to daughters Judith and Estelle began immediately, as is documented by an entry in the Goncourt brothers' diary. While at dinner with the Gautiers, the brothers are entertained by the daughters' story of having dined with a Chinese man the day before; they run "to look for the Chinese slipper he gave them, stammering the Chinese words he had spoken." "This suits them like a perfume from the Orient, these pretty and mischievous Parisian Orientals." After dinner in the living room Judith even recites from a Chinese grammar book, no doubt the one Abel-Rémusat had compiled.[22]

Four other diary entries record Ding's appearances at the Gautiers' house, and his influence. After a dinner in April 1864 the Goncourts note that "the daughters chat about absolutely nothing other than the Chinese they are learning."[23] An entry in May 1865 begins:

> It's an amusing table we're sitting at chez Gautier. It looks like the *table d'hôte* at a tower of Babel, the last caravansary of romanticism, a mix of people from all nations, which Gautier is accustomed to and proud of.
>
> The other day at his table there were twenty individuals, speaking forty different languages, with whom one could have made a trip around the world without an interpreter. Tonight next to Flaubert, Bouilhet, and us there is a real Chinese, with his slanted eyes and his red-currant velvet jacket, the Chinese professor of the Gautier daughters.

Although Ding seems to have shed his traditional costume this evening, his authenticity and novelty are not in doubt. Flaubert also wrote about this dinner the next day: "Yesterday we dined at Theo's, where there were twenty people at table, including a Chinese man with whom My Lord chatted in Chinese."[24] "My Lord" (Monseigneur) was the novelist's honorific for his close friend and mentor Louis Bouilhet (1821-1869), to whom *Madame Bovary* had been dedicated. Bouilhet was deeply interested in Chinese language, literature, and philosophy and, according to an earlier entry in the Goncourt diaries, "is studying Chinese in order to write a Chinese poem." Four years later the writer and editor Charles Yriarte (1832-1898), mourning the death of Bouilhet, whose first work had been a long narrative poem titled *Miloenis*, recalls what appears to be the same evening: "That Bouilhet was an indefatigable worker. He'd taken it upon himself to learn Chinese all on his own, and one day when we were dining at Théophile Gautier's with Tin-Tun-Ling, known as 'Théo's Chinese man,' the author of *Miloenis* only had ears and eyes for the scholar, in order to master through practice those solitary studies."[25]

In June 1866 Ding is noted again as a dinner guest and identified as "the real Chinese man."[26] And years later, in December 1873, Edmond de Goncourt and Flaubert spot Judith Gautier at the entrance to Père Lachaise cemetery after the funeral of François Hugo, Victor's fourth child. After an extensive description of the "strange and almost terrifying beauty" of this "lethargic creature" who possesses "the undefinable quality and mystery of a female sphinx, of flesh made of a substance that lacks modern nerves," Edmond takes note of her companions: "And the young woman has, as foils to her dazzling youth, on one side the

Chinese Tsing with the flat face and turned up eyes and on the other her mother, the aged Grisi, who in her wrinkled and shrunken state looks like an old consumptive monkey."[27] Goncourt may have erred in remembering Ding's name, but he has clearly not lost his bite.

Meanwhile Ding Dunling found a way to record himself visually for posterity. He participated in an ethnographic project to document human racial types, a collection of well over one thousand photographs taken by several photographers, with the majority attributed to Jacques-Philippe Potteau (1807–1876), for the "Anthropological Collection of the Museum of Paris" between 1855 and 1869. Many of these consist of studio portraits, in both frontal view and profile, of individuals identified generally by their country of origin. Ding Dunling's portraits as a "Chinese from Peking" (figures 2.6 and 2.7 in chapter 2) were taken around 1865. Another pair of later photographs labels Ding as a "Chinese literatus from Shanxi" and served as the basis for engravings illustrating an anthropological study of the human race.[28]

Ding Dunling's activities deeply fascinated the Parisian public and were widely recorded. Part of that interest derived from the sheer novelty of his presence. The paltry number of Chinese in France at the time appears to have shrunk before it began to grow. An article from 1878, the year the first embassy from China was established in France, notes that there are only eleven Chinese nationals in Paris, compared to eight hundred Japanese. Of those eleven, three are waiters, six merchants, and two are men of letters—with one being Ding himself.[29] By 1882, there were only nine members of the "Chinese colony" of Paris that could be profiled, in an article that leads off with Ding Dunling: "Everyone has met Tin-Tun-Ling, with his black gown, short coat, queue that flops against his back, and umbrella under his arm. Those who have never met him only have to head to Place Louvois at 4 p.m., the exit of the national library, where you'll be sure to find him. Tin is, in point of fact, a scholar."[30]

Two years later an article written during the brief Sino-French Tonkin War and titled "Desinification" states that there are only four.[31] However undocumented these numbers may be, they make the point. Ding was newsworthy by simply being there. And he seemed to be everywhere, a solitary habitué of the street as distinctively dressed—complete with the Chinese version of top hat and monocle—as the figure of the dandy or flaneur that so fascinated Baudelaire. When a sportswriter listed the names of glitterati watching the Grand Prix de Paris horse race at Longchamps in 1878, Ding finds his place among the noblemen, politicians, generals, actors, and other notables in attendance.[32]

3.1 and 3.2 Ding Dunling, engravings from Armand de Quatrefages (1810-1892), *Histoire générale des races humaines: Introduction à l'étude des races humaines* (Paris: Hennuyer, 1889), 430-31. Based on photographs by Jacques-Philippe Potteau.
BnF Gallica

Ding's association with the Gautier family guaranteed his newsworthiness. Théophile and Judith both wrote about him in letters and memoirs, and other family members and friends were similarly inspired to record what one referred to as "those remarkable incidents sprinkled through the life of Tin-Tun-Ling."[33] Catulle Mendès even grants him equal billing with the likes of Théophile Gautier, Hugo, Mallarmé, and Verlaine by including him in *Figurines of Poets* (*Figurines des poètes*), a small collection of "literary portraits," a genre popular in the late 1860s. "A Chinese man?" he begins, and quickly responds: "Yes, really. Are there so many French poets that we don't have the time to pay attention to a Chinese poet? Besides which, Ting-Tun-Ling is a Parisian. Have you met on the boulevard or at the theater a small man whose face is the color of brass lamps, with a droll mouth and sparkling eyes, who wears a two-layered gown of light silk on top of scarlet wool pants and a cap on which gleams the button of a Kin-Jen? That's him. He walks, he speaks, he laughs. Nothing frightens him and nothing surprises him. He knows our civilization as well as that of the Celestial Empire, Paris like Peking." Mendès then provides several examples of witty ripostes from Ding to insinuations that he knows nothing of French or French literature and goes on to say: "But remaining Chinese at the bottom of his soul, he doesn't forget that he was a poet in his home country, and he pours it out in nostalgic quatrains," providing an example that was included in Gautier's *Book of Jade*. "Isn't it charming?" concludes Mendès, with the faintest of praise: "I don't know if Li Taibo is the equal of Victor Hugo, but Ting-Tun-Ling is certainly worthy of Belmontet."[34]

For Émile Bergerat, the husband of Judith's younger sister Estelle, Ding's only saving grace was the gratitude to Théophile Gautier he expressed in the preface to his Chinese novel. Bergerat describes it as "a moving cry from someone uprooted," "charming," and "delicious," but then the mean-spiritedness that infuses his article takes over. Ding's homage to Gautier, he writes, is "like the yelping of a good puppy to its master, and the brief sentences by which he expresses the great tenderness of his life sound like those moaning complaints of dogs confronting what is an incomprehensible phenomenon to them, absence." Not surprisingly, Bergerat echoes Armand Silvestre's characterization of Ding as belonging to the great writer's "'intimate menagerie,' among the cats, the dogs, the birds, and the white mice of his Noah's ark."

This passage is among the more anodyne of the racist slurs of this piece. Bergerat was also responsible for one of the most enduring rumors about Ding— that he was a petty thief. Judith Gautier's memoirs make no reference to his possibly light fingers, but the details of Bergerat's account proved memorable. When one of the daughters saw from a window that Ding was coming, he begins, the "other sister would rush to the dresser and, with a turn of the key, would secure their contents. The arrival of the Chinese man was always greeted by the sound of drawers closing. I've never known a man who borrowed more silently than this Celestial." One day, Bergerat continues, Ding managed to take some silver cutlery, which the girls spot sticking out of his pocket. When they chide him for stealing—if he was short of money he only needed to ask—he insists that in the Orient it would be considered not thievery but commerce. At this point Théophile Gautier emerges from his room with his cat Éponine on his shoulder, and intervenes, "philosophical and serious," to defend the "mutualist" moral tradition of his guest over the prosaic, self-centered interests of his daughters' "turkey brains." And he asks them how they could begrudge a set of silver cutlery, which is only silverplate anyway, to "a mandarin of the first class from the province of Shanxi who commands the eighty thousand words of his language when you barely know three hundred of your own?"[35]

A LITERARY ENTREPRENEUR

Ding Dunling embarked on an ambitious career of both publication and performance, often with the help of his patrons. The first was an essay titled "Chinese New Year" ("Le Jour de l'an en Chine"), which outlines traditional customs around the holiday; signed by him, though no doubt penned by Judith Gautier, it was published several times between 1866 and 1872.[36] Théophile Gautier also requested of his friend, the editor Charles Yriarte, that he look kindly on a submission from "my poor Chinese man": "if you could accept the article by Tin Ton Lin, you would please me and be of service to him."[37] And, indeed, in fall 1867 Yriarte reported: "Our rather overworked life has some curious compensations. Yesterday . . . a mandarin scholar Tin-Tun-Ling, clad in a gown with the button of his class and trailing his long queue, came to offer us a manuscript for *Le Monde illustré*." The following summer a piece of short fiction by Ding (and surely edited by his student)—titled "The Justice of the Son of Heaven" ("La Justice du fils du ciel") and recounting "the tribulations of a husband in the Middle Kingdom"—was published in four parts by the journal.[38] It was probably also around this time that Judith Gautier introduced Ding to Alexandre Dumas (1802–1870), at a lunch hosted by their friend Robelin on some unspecified date. As she writes in her memoir, "That day I presented Ting-Tun-Ling to him, and we requested very solemnly the authorization to translate *The Three Musketeers* into Chinese." She does not record Dumas's reply.[39] Ding and Gautier never translated the novel, but a decade later he may have served as model for a character in a work by another friend of the Gautiers, Jules Verne (1828-1905), *Tribulations of a Chinese Man in China*, published in 1879 and his only novel set entirely in China. One of its main characters, the philosopher Wang, is revealed to be a former Taiping rebel who is a scholar with exactly the credentials Théophile Gautier had attributed to Ding: mastery of the eighty thousand Chinese characters and a civil service examination degree.[40]

In addition to dedicating her *Book of Jade* to Ding and including three of his poems in the volume, Judith Gautier published a "Chinese Poem" ("Poëme chinois") by him titled "The sad night" ("Ié-man") in romanized form, with a French translation, "La Nuit triste," in the *Revue des lettres et des arts*. The recently established journal was published by Armand Gouzien (1839-1892), who had much admired her work and came to respect Ding's talents as well.[41] Her system of transcription is unorthodox, which makes it difficult to extract the original Chinese text, but the French version suggests that Ding was quite familiar with well-worn evocations of melancholy in the Chinese poetic tradition. The most widespread introduction of his literary talents to the Parisian public, however, occurred in dramatic performances and poetry readings in the 1870s and 1880s. He was clearly the first Chinese to appear on a French stage, speaking Chinese, and announcements and reviews of his appearances, usually at the large music hall, Élysée Montmartre, or the Théâtre Rossini, often received front-page billing in the daily newspapers.

Some of Ding's performances received especially extensive press coverage. In May 1874 *Le Petit Journal* announced "at the Élysée Montmartre a concert that should signal something utterly new and bizarre. The Chinese man Ting-Tun-Lin, well known in Paris, will recite there a piece of poetry of his own composition!" An article in *Le XIXe Siècle* the same day bills him as "the celebrated Chinese artist and author" and a veteran of "the Imperial Theater of Peking" to boot (which he certainly was not). It notes that the orchestra and choir will be at least three hundred strong and predicts that this "irresistible attraction quite different from the luminaries of our top theaters will undoubtedly attract all of Paris," concluding, however, that "dilettantes should be advised."[42]

The same event had received a rather more sardonic billing in the theater column of *Le Figaro*:

> We rarely speak about concerts—and for good reason—and certainly wouldn't have about the one Alexis Collongues, first violinist at the Opera, will give Monday at the Elysée Montmartre, if something bizarre had not brought it to our attention.
>
> Tin-Tun-Ling, whom you know well, the Chinese man of Théophile Gauthier and of Catulle Mendès, will appear on the platform to recite *Tchu-Tien* (*Spring*), poetry of which he is the author. But Mr. Collongues hasn't wished to force the French to hear Chinese without translating it immediately afterward. Thus as soon as Tin-Tun-Ling has finished his little chinoiserie, an artist from the Théâtre-Français, Mr. Charpentier, will recite it in French.
>
> If you understand it, it won't be as amusing anymore.[43]

Announcements of forthcoming performances like these tended to be intrigued by the promise of an "interesting" experience. Actual reviews, however, proved to be somewhat more mixed. One matinee at the Théâtre Rossini in July 1874 received front page coverage in *L'Événement*, with a perplexed and not entirely appreciative description of the program of poetry, short fiction, and drama presented by Ding, performed by both him and two fellow Chinese. For Bixiou, the front-page reviewer of *Le Gaulois* on the same day, the matinee provided "a marvelous and paradoxical spectacle" orchestrated by Ding himself, whom "everyone knows: everyone has met this little man with the intelligent and smiling face on the boulevards, with his gown of black silk, his skullcap, and his long braided queue." Tongue firmly in cheek, he continues: "I don't need to tell you that Tin-Tun-Ling speaks French very well—and even that rumors have quickly spread that Tin-Tun-Ling was but an apocryphal Chinese, a pseudo-Chinese, having never eaten the least bit of swallow's nest, incapable of appreciating the taste of dog meat cooked in its fat, and not knowing the first word of the first work by the great scholar Confucius." But this decisively Chinese performance has succeeded in reaffirming Ding's native identity, although the reviewer confesses that he might have preferred otherwise. Reviewing for *Le Figaro*, Gaston Vassy minces no words in his devastating pan of the afternoon, which he also sees as "the bizarre Tin-Tun-Ling's" attempt to convince fellow Parisians that he is "a true Chinese." He notes that Judith Gautier herself, despite her affection for Ding, was seen retreating into her loge and then making an early exit.[44]

Ding remained undaunted by this reception, and notices of subsequent performances are sprinkled throughout the city's periodicals, with increasingly more positive reviews. It cannot have hurt that he donated his talents to at least two well-received benefit performances. *La Petite Presse* reports in August 1874 that he participated in an evening program held at a local high school to benefit the poor by chanting Chinese poems, provided also in French translation. The review reprints the two poems and concludes by congratulating the school for an excellent evening.[45] The next year, after massive flooding of the Garonne River in June devastated the city of Toulouse, Ding again took it upon himself to respond with a humanitarian gesture, much to the astonishment of *Le Figaro*, which announces that "Tin-Tun-Ling, the now famous Tin-Tun-Ling, is a philanthropic Chinese" who is "organizing, to benefit the flood victims, a Chinese performance at the Passy Theater. You read correctly, a Chinese performance. Tin will recite an epic poem of his own composition about the floods; then he will perform himself, with three of his compatriots, still in Chinese, of course, an occasional piece entitled *The Overflowing of the Yangzi River*."[46]

The French public learned to appreciate Ding's efforts. *La Petite Presse*, for example, describes his performance at a "Chinese matinee" in 1878 as simply "brilliant." Other French performers reciting poetry and playing the piano and violin had been roundly applauded, "but the session's honors went to our friend Tin-Tun-Ling, who recited several pieces of Chinese verse of his own composition," with a French translation following as well. Two of Ding's poems, indeed, "earned a real ovation for the poet and 'son of heaven.'"[47] Similarly, a front-page article in *L'Événement* reports two years later that "the matinee given yesterday at the Atheneum by the celebrated Chinese poet Tin-Tun-Ling, whom all Paris knows" was "very brilliant." Two of his compatriots, "star singers" who "lent their assistance to the amiable Tin," were the first to grace the stage. "Their original singing, strange and infinitely variable, surprised the audience, which called for a group encore." Ding then recites his own poetry in Chinese, followed by Judith Gautier's translations. The poems are "charming, filled with lofty poetic ideas and very sweet feelings. Mademoiselle Felcourt recited them in French with talent and earned for the poet Tin a real ovation." The article reports that, much encouraged by his great success, Ding is planning more performances, which leads to the concluding happy thought that "the capital is in the process of being equipped with a Chinese theater!"[48]

SCANDAL!

Ding's other comings and goings continued to merit occasional press coverage. When the 1878 International Exposition brought two Chinese "giants" back to Paris, Ding served as guide and go-between to an interested journalist, who reported that the excellent English of the Chinese made it easier to communicate in that language than to rely on "Tin's peculiar French, for which a second translator would not be entirely useless."[49] But nothing attracted the attention of the French reading public like his arrest on charges of bigamy in 1873 and his trial two years later. He had already acquired a reputation as something of a ladies' man. Rumors circulated about his seduction of young women and cuckolding of more than one husband, most of which can probably be traced to a rather confused account provided by Zhang Deyi, the young interpreter on delegations sent from China who wrote about his meeting with Stanislas Julien in 1866. A second mission was sent in 1868 to establish formal diplomatic contacts with the United States, Great Britain, and France and was led by the Manchu Zhi Gang 志剛, the Chinese Sun Jiagu 孫家穀, and the American Anson Burlingame (1820–1870), who had served as minister to China. They arrived in Paris at the beginning of 1869.

The delegation stayed for eight months in France, mostly in the capital, and one of their many social events appears to have included Ding Dunling. Zhang's diary records that Zhi Gang and Sun Jiagu invited several French guests to dinner in February 1869 at their lodging, among whom were the mother and sister of someone whose name is rendered in Chinese as Ou Jian 歐建 and a "Ding Dunling from Shanxi." Zhang notes that the group "chatted and dined most convivially until one in the morning" but then continues:

> I've heard that Ding Dunling is a vulgar character who had an affair with the consul's young daughter four years ago. Furious, the consul banished him to the lonely isle of London, whence he was able to return to the French capital only upon the consul's death two years later.
>
> And then he made off with the wife of a tailor, who reported him to authorities; they jailed him for two years. Now he is Ou Jian's secretary, and people say he's been a guest behind the bed curtains. I've also heard that newspaper articles report that Ding calls himself a "recommended man."[50]

This passage is intriguing for several reasons. Who was Ou Jian, who curiously is not specified as being present at the dinner?[51] Given Ding's connection to them, one might reasonably take this to be a reference to one of the Gautiers. In his 1948 volume of criticism Qian Zhongshu excerpts this passage and declares that Ou Jian is Théophile Gautier, whom Qian assumes Ding had cuckolded.[52] But though Gautier did have two younger sisters, his mother died in 1848 and thus could not have been a dinner guest in 1869. Nor, since Gautier never officially married any of the several women with whom he had relationships, would it have been easy to portray him as a victim of adultery.

Two contemporary Chinese scholars believe that Ou Jian refers to Judith Gautier, whose mother was still very much alive and who did have a younger sister Estelle.[53] As a virtual member of the household Ding had access to her quarters, but mainly to deliver correspondence from her fiancé. Given their difference in status he would never have been considered a suitor, and no rumors ever circulated to that effect. It is difficult, furthermore, to give credence to any of the other tales Zhang Deyi recounts in this diary entry. From 1865 to 1867 Ding could not have been in exile in London: Judith Gautier writes in her memoirs that he was an almost daily presence at her house while they worked on their poetry translations. Nor, judging from scattered newspaper reports of his various activities in Paris already cited, could he have been imprisoned from 1867 to 1869. And finally, he never claimed to have been a successful examination candidate at the second, provincial level (*ju ren* 舉人, "recommended man") but merely of the first, prefectural degree (*xiu cai*, "flourishing talent").

This would not be the first example of the appeal of unfounded rumors nor should one assume that Ding was incapable of such peccadilloes. As Maurice Dreyfous writes in recounting his memories of life in Paris during the mid-nineteenth century, "the unlucky Tin was destined for judicial adventures born of entanglements with women," but Parisian chroniclers had a hard time keeping these stories straight. Differing versions of his cuckolding of both a tailor and a fruit merchant, along with the ingeniously successful defense arguments by often renowned lawyers, provided rich fodder for memoirs and scandal sheets.[54]

While such tales deserve a generous sprinkling of salt, there was no denying the charge of bigamy that led to Ding's arrest and imprisonment for two months in 1873. On January 6, 1872, he had married a French teacher named Caroline-Julie Liégeois.[55] Five months later she learned that he had a wife and children and denounced him as a bigamist; after a lengthy investigation, which included research into his background in Macao, he was incarcerated in Mazas prison. The trial, which took place in June 1875, was nothing less than a sensation: the daily court journal (*Gazette des tribunaux*) provided a blow-by-blow account of the witnesses' testimony, which was repeated verbatim or paraphrased in countless other newspapers as well. The opening paragraphs of the report suggest some of the reasons:

> Today the court hall is particularly animated. The space reserved for witnesses has been invaded by a curious public. A great number of lawyers in robes have crowded into the hearing. It's not every day that one sees a Chinese man passing through the criminal court.
>
> For this is all about a true and authentic subject of the Celestial Empire. It's the Chinese man whom Paris has known for fifteen years, the protégé of Théophile Gautier, the assistant of M. Catulle Mendès, the assiduous reader at the National Library, Ding Dunling, who is about to appear before the jury under the serious accusation of bigamy.
>
> The guards bring him in. He's wearing the traditional costume in which we've come to know him. His braid of black hair still bobs on his back.... Atop his head perches lightly the same black cap adorned with gold lace and ornamented, in front, with a precious button of mother-of-pearl; for Ding Dunling, as we know, is a scholar. He has the equivalent of a bachelor's degree. His mother-of-pearl button is the insignia of a *xiucai*. Translated literally: his talent is flourishing.

The transcript opens with the plaintiff's lawyer, Monsieur Chévrier, citing evidence gathered in Macao—from Ding's wife, his brother-in-law, and the priest who presided over his nuptials—regarding Ding's first marriage and children. All of this is affirmed by a court clerk in Macao who claims to have known Ding well. No written records can confirm the marriage, however, because sacraments administered by missionaries to new Christians were not documented. The widow of Joseph-Marie Callery testifies that upon receiving a contract for employment from her husband Ding had specified that a certain sum should be paid in advance to his wife. That he had been married in Macao and intended to support his spouse seems incontrovertible.

The presiding judge, Monsieur Bondurand, then interrogates both Ding himself and several witnesses. Availing himself of the linguistic help of Gabriel Devéria (1844-1899), son of the well-known painter Achille Devéria (1800-1857) and on leave from his work as interpreter for the French government at various posts in China,⁵⁶ Ding testifies that his union with the woman he knew as Fan-Ha-Lin was not an officially documented marriage with a primary wife, which would have required "a contract and signatures," and that she was but a secondary wife or concubine. There had been "confusion" about the role of a missionary priest in the ceremony, which was simply to provide a "Christian benediction." Even though he had initially shared his salary with Fan, once three years of separation without contact had passed the relationship was considered terminated according to Chinese law. He had thus been a free man in 1872.

Charles-Edouard Comte, who had known Ding for five years and served as a notarized character witness to the process authorizing the marriage to Liégeois, then takes the stand and confirms that he had been told that Ding was the son of a "baron Tin-Tun-Ling," which he concedes was a garbled translation of a title. Judith Gautier—whose name had notably not been mentioned in the opening paragraphs of the story—then testifies in support of Ding's claims, identifying herself as the twenty-three-year-old wife of Catulle Mendès. (She was twenty-eight at the time.) In response to the judge's statement that Ding's French wife had left him because he beat her, Gautier shares Ding's account of their wedding night, which suggests a rather different tenor to their young relationship. After insisting, over his objections, that he acquire theater tickets for the evening, his bride decided to stay in the hotel, but she also declined to join him in bed and refused to budge from her chair all night. As for the question regarding his prior marriage, Gautier also refers to the Qing legal code, collapsing two separate statutes to affirm that because Ding and his wife had not seen each other for more than three years he could be considered released from that relationship, which he had in any event never mentioned to her. Finally, Gustave Lafargue, a writer and composer who was to remain a close friend of Ding's for the rest of his life, declares that Ding had only agreed to marry the teacher after her vigorous pursuit of him—"she was determined to use all her forces to marry him"—and her unkept promise to translate and gain a greater audience for his writings.

In his closing argument the prosecutor Chévrier acknowledges the defendant's appeal: "He is known to all of Paris. Chinese and intelligent, he quickly acquired that notoriety which often waxes and vanishes within the space of twenty-four hours, but which—more fortunate than others—he retained for twelve years." He notes that while Mademoiselle Liégeois had wanted to marry a Chinese man, having "satisfied her whim she quickly repented." She has, moreover, disappeared from the scene and may have decamped to New York.⁵⁷ While acknowledging that he has little to offer in face of the informed, compelling testimony of Judith Gautier based on the Qing legal code—"I should have studied Chinese!"—he implores the jury to render a wise judgment on a curious case.

The concluding argument of Ding's defense attorney Pierre-Elzéar Bonnier-Ortolan (1846–1916) is a tour de force. Described by Maurice Dreyfous as "a lyric poet in his spare time and a sometime lawyer,"[58] as Pierre Elzéar he was well known to the Parisian public. His gift with words provided Ding with an impressive advantage over his accuser. He provides a vivid overview of his client's many travails in both China and France and supplies yet another unexpected element of local color when describing his first wedding night in Macao. In accordance with custom, "he'd been given one of the young woman's little shoes, perfumed with musk and sandalwood, which he was supposed to wear close to his heart for three days." Then the day of the union arrives, and "Tin-Tun-Ling finally lifts the red veil that covers his wife's features. A terrible deception! She is ugly, pockmarked, and bloated, and to compound the horror, her feet are enormous. Twenty-five years have passed since that day, and the unfortunate man still can't speak about it without chills." Despite this disillusionment, Bonnier-Ortolan declares, Ding provided for his wife and produced two children. (She now had four.)

Among Ding's many virtues, Bonnier-Ortolan adds, was his loyalty to France during the Franco-Prussian War. He had even tried to enlist in the battalion consisting of foreign "friends of France" but had been refused because of his frail constitution. But he managed to provide support of a different sort, as one of his colleagues had recently told him: "Your Chinese man contributed to the defense of Paris. He maintained our spirit and courage. After having eaten the bread of the siege, after having listened all night to the din of gunfire, we loved finding him trotting here and there with his cheerful costume, with his queue, his umbrella—sole concession that he had felt it necessary to make to European civilization. He comforted and amused us, and we went home consoled."[59]

Bonnier-Ortolan concludes his summation with a moving account of his first visit to Ding in prison, during which he asks if his client has any message to convey to Judith Gautier. "The poor Chinese man looked at me sadly and said: "Listen, make me happy. I entrusted Madame Mendès with a little bird in its cage. Prison is truly sad; now I see what it's like. Tell Madame Mendès to set my warbler free." To which the lawyer only needs to add: "Gentlemen of the jury, you will do right by Tin-Tun-Ling to set him free." Which they proceeded to do, unanimously.

The victory is a subdued one. "Monsieur Lafargue and a great number of friends of the poor Chinese man come to shake his hand. Tin-Tun-Ling appears deeply moved. He embraces Madame Mendès effusively."[60] When he leaves the hall of justice Ding is surrounded by a host of curious people hailing his release from prison. It turns out that among the most dedicated followers of the trial were readers of the *China Mail*, published in Shanghai. The paper had covered his arrest for bigamy and, in order to satisfy its curious readers it paid a not inconsequential sum of 1,425 francs for a telegram relaying the jury's verdict.[61] The London *Times* also ran a two-column story on the trial of "Tin-Tun-Ling, a Chinaman" on June 12, 1875.[62] Ding himself did not appear to mind the news coverage. A cover cartoon in the satirical journal *Le Sifflet* bears his signature and statement, in Chinese and his typical broken French, authorizing the publication of a cartoon memorializing his predicament.[63]

The story of Ding's trial proved endlessly fascinating to the French press, which devoured and reprinted the transcript, jokingly wondered if Ding might be a Mormon, and engaged in discussions about the merits of bigamy. The story traveled abroad as well, as exemplified by an uncharitable and error-ridden piece called "A Chinaman's Marriage" by the Scottish author Andrew Lang (1844–1912).[64] But Ding then found yet another way to make the news, by publishing a short Chinese novel barely one month after his acquittal. Titled *The Little Slipper* (*La Petite Pantoufle*), and in Chinese *The Stolen Little Slipper* (*Tou xiao xie* 偷小鞋), it was bound in yellow fabric Chinese-style, unpaginated, and meant to be read from back to front. Translated by Charles Aubert (1840–1927), who was secretary to Catulle Mendès, and produced by Richard Lesclide, "the most adventurous of all Paris editors,"[65] the elegant volume was printed on China white paper with six watercolor illustrations by Frédéric Chevalier.

Its preface, dated June 25, 1875, is addressed "to the French public" and explains the circumstances of its composition:

> In 1872—I had lost my mind—I got married, and for this reason I've been deprived of my liberty for more than two months. But I wasn't angry or resentful, and in prison I've written a book that will introduce you to some of the customs of my country, as far away as the stars.
>
> The same sun illuminates us; the same heaven shelters us; may you be for me like brothers who live under the same roof, in the same light.[66]

Professor, Baron, Barnum, or Rake? 65

3.3 "Monsieur et Mesdames Tin-Tun-Ling," cover cartoon by Henri Meyer, *Le Sifflet*, June 20, 1875.
BnF Arsenal Gallica

Did Ding actually produce a Chinese text for *The Little Slipper*? There is no record of it, and Aubert's name does not figure among the ranks of French writers capable of translating from the Chinese. But Ding could certainly have provided the raw material for Aubert's "translation." The novel comprises nine short chapters and employs motifs familiar to readers of early modern Chinese stories and plays, especially those categorized as examples of the consequences of folly or criminal court cases. Set in the Tang dynasty, it is the story of a lascivious monk who craves the beautiful wife, named Lan-Yin, of a young man and discredits her integrity by duping her maid to obtain one of her slippers, the discovery of which outside her quarters indicates that she has been unfaithful with someone. After the husband promptly divorces her, another wealthy man appears, claims to realize her blamelessness, and proposes to marry her. The maid recognizes him as the monk in disguise and arrives at the wedding chamber just in time to spirit Lan-Yin away, seduce and inebriate the monk, compose her confession, and hang herself. Body and statement discovered, the monk confesses under appropriate torture and is sentenced to decapitation. And the young couple is happily reunited.

In his final paragraph Ding declares that he wrote the story "for the glory of Lan-Yin, who was a faithful spouse, for the enjoyment of benevolent readers who might be interested in her troubles, and to serve as an example to husbands whose souls are agitated by the dragons of jealousy." His recent celebrity ensured a robust reception for the book. One review opens, for example: "To those who still maintain that preventive imprisonment is a useless cruelty, we will proceed to say that the Chinese scholar from the province of Shanxi, the secretary of Théophile Gautier, the illustrious Tin-Tun-Ling, in a word, has used the leisure afforded by an accusation of bigamy to compose *The Little Slipper*." And it affirms that "everyone will want to obtain this bizarre specimen of a book."[67] Another reader is especially moved by Ding's prefatory letter to the French public, declares that the novel itself "lacks neither emotion nor narrative charm," and appreciates "the exemplary morality" of its conclusion.[68] Writing for the newspaper of the Worker's Party, yet another reviewer praises the rich, original detail of the novel and declares that it "leaves nothing to be desired."[69] Perhaps most interestingly, copies of the book were sold for 25 francs at the benefit performance Ding mounted for victims of the 1875 Toulouse floods, to whom the proceeds of the sales would be donated. But there was more. As one attendee from the publishing house writes, "the oddities of the famous Barnum pale next to the ideas of our friend Tin-Tun-Ling," for he brought to the concert hall, "while drying the tears that filled his eyelids, the cord with which his heroine [the maid] had hanged herself." He hints that purchasers of the book's new edition might even be able to obtain a strand of the rope.[70]

Ding Dunling died of complications from pneumonia on November 13, 1886, at the age of fifty-seven, having received the last rites and in the bosom of friends. The announcement about his funeral was sent to newspapers all over Paris, and several of them, like *Le Figaro*, made it front-page news:

> Everybody knew, and many quite closely, Tin-Tun-Ling, that Chinese scholar so French in his heart, whom Théophile Gautier had adopted and who had collaborated on several novels with the master.
>
> Tin-Tun-Ling died rather suddenly two days ago, at the home of his friend, Monsieur P. Dumas, who had cared for him for several years with a devotion beyond all praise.
>
> The invitations had been sent in the name of Monsieur P. Dumas and of Monsieur Paul de Cassagnac, in whose family Tin had found the deepest affection, an affection which he deserved, moreover, in every respect.
>
> It was amid a considerable crowd that the cortege left yesterday from 65 Rue Dulong for the church of Sainte-Marie des Batignolles, where the funeral ceremony was celebrated.
>
> The Chinese embassy in its entirety, several students at the École orientale where Tin-Tun-Ling had taught, a great number of journalists and writers made a point of offering a last tribute to this fine man, and many accompanied him to the cemetery of Saint-Ouen.[71]

Judith Gautier had paid for his funeral.[72]

Not every obituary was as kind as this one. One front-page article in *Le Voltaire* opens by regretting the demise of someone truly original, whom all Paris had come to know and who was "for a long time an indispensable ornament at every premiere, the necessary relation for whoever claimed to be a friend of scholars. Behind them he seemed their caricature, a role that pleased him—and the dinners encouraged him." The writer mentions Ding's reputation as a petty thief and includes an interview with Judith Gautier's sister Estelle, who makes a point of correcting the *Figaro* article—Ding's limited French would never have allowed him to collaborate with her father on any novel—and stresses that he "was never taken seriously" by her family, which treated him like a toy. But the author nevertheless concludes: "Let us take Tin for the gentle innocent that he was, and one might say that he was both the least and the most Chinese of all Chinese."[73] Another front-page piece provides a droll, error-ridden account of "the strange destiny of this eccentric Chinese," an "adventurer who seemed to have descended on a parasol" to engage in one "ingeniously Chinese" scheme after the next, but the writer also believes that Ding must have merited the kindness meted out by his many friends. Moreover, "he died a good Christian, which redeems many faults" and was, undeniably, "the only one of his kind in Paris."[74] Yet another obituary, after recounting episodes from Ding's checkered past, reflects on how much has changed during the twenty years since his arrival in Paris. As Verlaine did when reviewing Judith Gautier's *Book of Jade*, the writer recalls Montesquieu in observing that Ding arrived "at a time when we could easily say 'How can one be Chinese?' China seemed unreal." Warfare, diplomacy, travel, and knowledge have changed all that, and while Paris "has not yet been invaded by the Chinese like the American West, their country will soon seem no stranger to us than [the suburb] Asnières." Ding Dunling "arrived exactly at a time when he was still an object of curiosity; perhaps he's also departing on time. The globe is shrinking before our eyes."[75]

If, indeed, China seemed less distant from Paris in 1886 than it had twenty years earlier, it is in no small part owing to Ding Dunling's arrival, presence, and tutelage of Judith Gautier. As many of these comments and anecdotes have suggested, he embraced his adopted city and its folkways and strolled as naturally on its boulevards as residents born there. Émile Bergerat describes him as "a representative of "*la Chine boulevardière*" who kept "his homeland in his boots."[76] Parisians certainly persisted in regarding him as an eccentric curiosity, a grifter, and a lady's man, and he never hesitated to capitalize on his exoticism, speaking pidgin French and wearing his scholar's cap atop a plaited queue. But they grew as accustomed to him as he to them. As they ended up considering him a Parisian to the core, perhaps familiarity was able to breed something more than contempt. And an important element of that familiarity was his collaboration with Gautier, his most devoted student, on *The Book of Jade*, which proved to be the most influential introduction to Chinese poetry in nineteenth-century Europe.

CHAPTER 4

"For a woman the word 'impossible' no longer exists"

The Challenges of Chinese Poetry

Ding Dunling first appeared at the Gautier household in 1863, and as Judith Gautier recalls in her memoirs, the months leading up to that summer had been filled with a series of desultory "independent studies" for the young teenager. Her father believed that "reading is the key to everything, and that the most marvelous thing is that a child can learn to speak and read, so he left the library at our disposition and urged us to rummage often through it." Largely left to her own devices, she flitted from astronomy, her first and longstanding passion, to math, and then geology. Her friend Charles Clermont-Ganneau ("Nono") was learning Persian and shared some of the poetry he was reading with her. There were also the many piano pieces for four hands that she practiced with her sister Estelle, and lessons in drawing and painting. But she was getting bored when "the arrival of the Chinese man Ting-Tun-Ling and the discovery of China brought new work for me to do."[1]

Ding quickly made himself at home, she writes, and "his slight silhouette in his blue gown and black vest, his impish face with half-closed eyes under his satin cap, which in accordance with protocol he never removed, became familiar to us and no longer seemed unusual; the exile blended in with us, and we missed him when he wasn't there." But he was rarely absent, for despite having been settled in separate lodging close by, he showed up for lunch without fail every day.[2]

The first task was to learn Chinese. Gautier doesn't mention the grammar book that she showed the Goncourt brothers, but she and her tutor did have a copy of the 1813 Chinese-Latin-French dictionary that Joseph de Guignes had cribbed from a version compiled by the Dominican cleric Basilio Brollo de Gemona. Beautifully printed with each character two centimeters square, the volume, which they jokingly referred to as their "pocket dictionary," was of impressive size but

4.1 "Melles Théophile Gautier" (Estelle and Judith), photograph by Nadar.
BnF Gallica

limited utility and reliability.³ It was, as the sinologist Paul Demiéville puts it, "a true piece of furniture, with enormous Chinese characters," and at best "a typographical curiosity."⁴

Judith Gautier soon found a reason to put her language learning to work, something that did not prove to interest her sister Estelle for long: "Right away I wanted to read the poets and try to translate them."⁵ Indeed, she had no sooner begun to "babble" Chinese than she determined

> to undertake the most difficult and impossible task, which disheartened the most knowledgeable sinologists—that of translating the untranslatable Chinese poets.
>
> Tin-Tun-Ling, the Chinese scholar in distress in Paris whom my father had taken in, had become my professor. When this lofty resolution took root in my mind, the poor Chinese man was deprived of all peace and quiet. No more of the lazy naps he was so fond of, deeply ensconced in an armchair, no more idle daydreams while strolling along the paths of the garden; he had to grapple with the 214 keys of the Chinese dictionary, an enormous, splendid, but imperfectly referenced tome, whose secrets were not easily extracted.⁶

THE CHALLENGES OF TRANSLATION

Why Chinese poetry, and was it truly untranslatable? From Ding Dunling, who as an educated scholar was familiar with the classical tradition, Gautier had learned that poetry was in fact the most esteemed literary genre in China, with a history that extended back for well over two millennia. Compiled by the sixth century BCE, the anthology known as the *Shi jing* 詩經, the *Classic of Poetry* or, more commonly, *The Book of Songs*, had attained the stature of scripture, largely thanks to legends of Confucius's involvement in its compilation and to his many invocations of its importance and utility. In the hands of later scholars its 305 poems—which range from simple folk songs to ritual hymns—were seen as important vehicles of both emotional and political expression, an important function that came to be conferred on the genre as a whole.⁷ Confucius was also associated with the belief that the responsibility of the educated class was to serve the government (which he himself sought to do, unsuccessfully, throughout his lifetime), and poetry not only addressed this ideal thematically but also became a means of measuring one's ability to fulfill it. Even for poets who for religious or other reasons chose to reject this mandate, the question of service would constitute an important theme of their work.

In China poetry was thus not just a form of personal expression; it was also an extremely important means of establishing and communicating social and political identity. Over the centuries writing poetry became an activity integral to the daily life of the educated class, an accepted currency of personal, social, and political exchange and thus a skill any bureaucrat would be expected to master and display. This was especially true during what is commonly agreed as the period of its greatest flourishing, the Tang dynasty (618-907). It was during the Tang that the cultural importance of poetry became especially evident, and poetic composition even began to be tested at times on the most difficult and prestigious level of the civil service examination, as a means of demonstrating one's ability to master tradition and manipulate language in creative and meaningful ways, both quickly and on demand.

Celebrations at court might be memorialized poetically by officials in attendance, often at the command of the ruler and as competitive displays of one's competence.[8] Other rhythms of elite social life were also expected to be marked in poetic form. Officials were constantly moved from one post to another, lest they develop dangerously powerful connections in any one location. This generated many reasons to compose poetry. As Arthur Waley (1899-1966) once observed, "It would not be an exaggeration to say that half the poems in the Chinese language are poems of parting or separation."[9] A bureaucrat accepts a new post: his colleagues bid him farewell, and he leaves them a keepsake poem in exchange. He returns from a mission, and they welcome him back. Someone visits a friend, and both host and guest honor the occasion with a poem, and when the guest departs, the host may accompany him to the first post station, where they both write another. If the friend is not at home, the disappointed visitor might leave a piece—perhaps brushed quickly on a garden wall, to convey his regret at having missed him—and requiring any later editor to go to great lengths to recover these scattered poetic graffiti. Not all Tang poetry is occasional, by any means, but it's easy to see why the many circumstances inspiring—or compelling—the composition of a poem generated an impressive number of works. *The Complete Tang Poems*, compiled by imperial edict in the eighteenth century, contains some 49,000 poems by over 2,200 poets, but a fraction of the myriads that must have been composed over the course of the dynasty. And it's also easy to understand, given the necessary premium on swiftness of production, the motivations behind the development and refinement of shorter and more highly regulated forms.[10]

From *The Book of Songs* on, most Chinese poetic forms originated from literati appropriation of popular songs, and though the ties to musical performance attenuated greatly over time, the importance of sound in structure and composition remained strong. A line was the basic prosodic and grammatical unit. End rhyme was a consistent feature throughout the tradition, usually on even-numbered lines, thus establishing the couplet as a key building block, along with a relatively short line. In *The Book of Songs* lines of four characters—all monosyllabic and in ancient times normally equivalent to discrete words—predominate, especially in the anonymous folk songs that comprise more than half of the anthology, which also frequently employ the stanzas, incremental repetition, and refrains familiar in popular songs throughout the world. Sometime in the second century a preference for five- and then seven-character lines emerged, with their slightly greater expressive potential, and the four-character line already seemed archaic.

Beginning in the fifth century the four tones of medieval Chinese (which are not the same as in the modern spoken language) also became an important element of poetic composition. This attention to the auditory features of the language led to the development of what became known as "recent-style poetry" (*jinti shi* 近體詩), which demanded manipulation of variables like tones within set patterns and greater concentration of expression within increasingly shorter pieces. Older forms, which came to be known as "ancient-style poetry" (*guti shi* 古體詩), permitted greater metrical freedom and maintained their popularity as well. The dominant examples of the "recent-style" were "cut-off" quatrains (*jue ju* 絕句) and "regulated verse" (*lü shi* 律詩), poems of four or eight lines with five or seven characters per line. In addition to these restrictions on length, they required poets to conform to parallel structures of tone, syntax, and meaning within couplets, to avoid repeating any word within those couplets, and to adhere to one rhyme throughout. However constraining they may seem, such prescriptions could facilitate the swift composition demanded by the numerous courtly and social occasions in which Tang poets would find themselves because they established limits to an otherwise daunting range of choices. The emphasis on tones also provides an important reminder that the sounds of Chinese poetry were even more important than the visual impact of the characters themselves.

We can see these rules at work in one of the most famous examples of regulated verse, a poem by Du Fu 杜甫 (712–770), who was commonly paired with Li Bo but was eventually singled out as the tradition's greatest, for his unwavering, if unfulfilled, commitment to the Confucian ethic of public service, his expressive depth and scope, and the technical innovations of his language. Not only does he chronicle the troubles of his times, never shying from critique when appropriate, but he also interweaves them constantly with his own personal history, on which public events impinged in intimate and painful ways.

When an upstart general launched a rebellion against the Tang and took over the capital of Chang'an, Du Fu was held there for several months. This poem was written while he was in captivity in spring 757 and is given below in four versions: Chinese characters and romanization on the left, and literal and word-for-word translations (the latter italicized) on the right.

春望	SPRING GAZE
Chun- wang+	spring gaze
國破山河在	The country shattered, mountains and rivers remain.
guo+ po+ shan- he- zai+	*country break mountain river remain*
城春草木深	The city in spring: grasses and trees are thick.
cheng- chun- cao+ mu+ shen- (R)	*city-wall spring grass tree thick*
感時花濺淚	Feeling the times, flowers drip tears.
gan+ shi- hua- jian+ lei+	*feel season flower splash tear*
恨別鳥驚心	Regretting separation, birds startle the heart.
hen+ bie+ niao+ jing- xin- (R)	*regret parting bird alarm heart*
烽火連三月	Beacon fires nonstop for three months;
feng- huo+ lian- san- yue+	*beacon fire consecutive three month*
家書抵萬金	A family letter worth ten thousand gold pieces.
jia- shu- di+ wan+ jin- (R)	*family letter equal ten-thousand gold-tael*
白頭搔更短	White hairs scratched grow even shorter:
bai+ tou- sao- geng+ duan+	*white head scratch more short*
渾欲不勝簪	Soon unable to hold a hatpin on.
hun- yu+ bu+ sheng- zan-(R)	*hardly will not bear hat-pin*

For purposes of poetic composition, tones were divided into two categories, "level" (*ping* 平) and "deflected" (*ze* 仄), indicated above by the minus and plus signs, respectively. Du Fu follows one of the limited set of established tonal patterns, which create variety within a line (no more than three words of one category in a row); antithetical mirroring within each couplet (a level tone in the first line of a couplet is matched by a deflected tone in the corresponding word of the second, with deviations allowed in the first word), with the middle couplets observing parallelism of meaning and syntax as well; and one rhyme (R) throughout the poem, always in the level tone (in the Tang dynasty, all of the final words of each couplet here would have rhymed; pronunciations have changed). But these mechanics of tonal alternation were relatively easily deployed. More striking is how Du Fu takes advantage of other conventions of regulated verse and grammatical features of classical Chinese in general to deepen and complicate the meaning of the poem.

Irony begins with the title, for spring is conventionally the season of renewal and joy, and there is no hint of the wartime scene that will follow. The opening couplet, as it should, sets the theme with stark but dramatically juxtaposed images that develop this irony. What might normally have provided consoling testaments to the permanence of nature, the "mountains and rivers" that "remain," also serve as painful contrasts to what is being destroyed by strife, "the country shattered." And the grasses and trees within the city's walls are only lush because untended and overgrown during war. Nature endures, apparently oblivious of the enormity of human loss.

Or is it? The compressed syntax of the second couplet, which must not only be tonally but syntactically and semantically parallel, yields more than one possible reading. All Chinese poets could take advantage of the classical language's lack of inflection for tense, number, gender, case, voice, mode, and person. Few constraints limited how words could modify one another. Especially in recent-style pieces, poets could enhance this density of expression by eliminating most of the grammatical "glue" that clarifies relationships between elements of a line and relying principally on concrete images and their juxtaposition to convey meaning. But Du Fu exploits the resulting potential for multivalence and ambiguity more than most, and especially in this second couplet. The subjects of both lines are unspecified. Who is feeling the sadness of this season? Does the almost perverse beauty of the flowers elicit the speaker's tears? Or, in an example of pathetic fallacy, does the dew on the blooms suggest that they are weeping metaphorically in sympathy? Similar questions arise in the next line about who resents parting and whose heart is alarmed: Are the birds themselves "startled" by the human pain of separation or as indifferent as the flowers might, in one reading be, even as they move the speaker? Both, after all, like the natural world, will persist.

As Du Fu's gaze narrows in focus from the grandly cosmic and distant to the highly specific and proximate images of spring in the first half of the poem, it shifts in the second half to the larger human context and finally to his own individual plight. Like the second couplet, the third demands parallelism and here moves from an oblique reference to the continuing warfare—readers would have known that beacon fires were used to send messages between garrisons during times of emergency—to his own separation from his family, which makes a letter so precious. How long has this been going on? Not only for "three months" (*san yue*) running, but also, since the same characters denote the third month, or March, perhaps consecutively from March to March, or an entire year. The final couplet typically avoids an obviously declarative conclusion, choosing an image whose significance must be inferred. The almost comical reference to his balding pate in the last couplet continues the trust Du Fu has placed throughout the poem in evocative imagery, refuses overt lament, and invokes only indirectly the ultimate core of his grief. It is not just the agonized concern for the devastation of war that is ravaging his hairline, thus making it difficult to keep the clasp holding a cap of office attached to his increasingly scanty hairs: the problem is that he has no cap to wear, he has no position from which to act.[11]

Nowhere in the poem does Du Fu use even one word to denote his anguish explicitly, yet it comes through all the more powerfully for that very reason. Without the long history and rich intertextual references of the tradition, thanks to which many objects, places, and motifs came to trigger increasingly well-recognized ideas, this lexical economy would have been impossible. The exploitation of allusions—whether to historical people or events or other texts—enriched poetry's evocative power while retaining a succinctness of expression. But not every reference was widely identifiable, which created sometimes challenging impediments to interpretation. This is especially true of poetry from the later years of the Tang dynasty.

All this may help to explain why, despite the centrality of poetry—and especially that of the Tang dynasty—to the Chinese cultural tradition, so few translations were attempted by Europeans once they first began to encounter these materials. Translators would need to unpack and explain historical and textual references, not to speak of supplying the grammatical infrastructure elided in the original but required in their own inflected languages. There were other reasons as well. The Jesuit missionaries in the eighteenth century had translated selected poems from *The Book of Songs* into French and the complete anthology into Latin, but they considered them valuable primarily as documents of cultural, historical, or religious interest, rather than as literary artifacts. Although they were clearly familiar with the major figures and recorded many anecdotes surrounding them, lyric compositions by individual poets were of minimal utility to their proselytizing goals. But they also recognized how difficult it would be to translate works from a language whose origins and grammar were so different from their own, and whose poetry was so concise yet so steeped in allusion. As a consequence, concluded two Jesuit priests who wrote extensively about Chinese culture, it was in fact simply untranslatable: "one really couldn't dream of translating the verse without abandoning the poetry." Because the brilliance of China's poetic language was drawn from "their traditions and their scriptures, from their literature and their customs, from the totality of their ideas and convictions, from their way of conceptualizing and expressing things, no doubt much farther away from us than even their country, to want to bring them into our language would be to make the Chinese ridiculous and the translations untenable."[12] One of the missionaries, who had produced a few translations from *The Book of Songs*, confessed that he felt "as if I were copying a miniature with a piece of charcoal."[13]

Like the clerics before them, the first sinologists were most interested in literature as a window into the customs of Chinese culture, and prose and drama provided the richest veins to mine such information. But they were also no less daunted by the challenge of translating poetry. Abel-Rémusat, the first chairholder at the Collège de France, declared that "Chinese poetic language is truly untranslatable. One could add that it's often unintelligible. Because in Europe we're deprived of the aids that would be indispensable to decipher these enigmatic compositions, we find ourselves reduced to a kind of conjectural operation whose success is never perfectly demonstrated."[14] For his part, although he did translate several individual poems, Stanislas Julien agreed with many scholars that they needed more reference works before tackling the more challenging genre, perhaps a complete dictionary of Chinese poetry, which he thought he would be able to compile in a few years if "I had the advantage of living in China, of being able to obtain examples of all poetic genres along with commentaries and paraphrases, and—what is even more precious—with the immediate consultation of Chinese scholars themselves."[15]

Although they transmitted significant biographical and historical information about Chinese poets, early efforts at translation by missionaries and scholars were limited, scattered, and largely focused on *The Book of Songs*, with almost no examples drawn from the corpus of Tang lyrics.[16] The situation was no different elsewhere, with the only substantive discussion of Chinese poetry in any European language consisting of a lecture titled "Poeseos Sinensis Commentarii, or the Poetry of the Chinese," delivered in May 1829 to the Royal Asiatic Society by Sir John Francis Davis (1795-1890), who would become head of the East India Company and then the governor of Hong Kong. Davis understood well such formal features of the poetry as rhyme and parallelism, and he demonstrated good judgment in the verses he translated from *The Book of Songs* and some unnamed poets. But they were very few.[17]

A "MOST CURIOUS COLLECTION": HERVEY-SAINT-DENYS'S ANTHOLOGY

Were Chinese poems in fact truly "untranslatable"? The Marquis d'Hervey-Saint-Denys provided his answer to the contrary when he published a volume titled *Poetry of the Tang Dynasty* (*Poésies de l'époque des Thang*) in 1862.[18] Despite a scholarly reputation that did not radiate as brightly as that of his predecessors Abel-Rémusat and Julien (he certainly lacked the latter's flair for self-promotion), Hervey-Saint-Denys's command of both Chinese and French equipped him well enough to craft translations that struck readers as faithful, informative, and even elegant. He was clearly aware of the challenges, as he writes in the preface to the volume:

> Literal translation is more often than not impossible from Chinese. Certain characters sometimes express, as we've seen, an entire scene that can only be conveyed by a paraphrase.
>
> Certain characters absolutely demand an entire sentence to be interpreted usefully.
>
> One must read a Chinese verse, penetrate the image or thought that it contains, and force oneself to grasp its main point and to preserve its force and color. The task is perilous; and painful as well, when one perceives real beauties that no European language could ever retain.[19]

POÉSIES

DE L'ÉPOQUE DES THANG

(VIIe, VIIIe et IXe siècles de notre ère)

TRADUITES DU CHINOIS

POUR LA PREMIÈRE FOIS

AVEC

UNE ÉTUDE SUR L'ART POÉTIQUE EN CHINE

ET DES NOTES EXPLICATIVES

PAR

LE MARQUIS D'HERVEY-SAINT-DENYS

PARIS

AMYOT, ÉDITEUR, 8, RUE DE LA PAIX

MDCCCLXII

4.2 The Marquis Hervey-Saint-Denys, *Poésies de l'époque des Thang* (Paris: Amyot, 1862). BnF Gallica

Hervey-Saint-Denys's nearly hundred-page-long preface to his collection is titled "The Poetic Art and Prosody of the Chinese" ("L'Art poétique et la prosodie chez les Chinois") and provides a useful historical survey of the tradition from the sixth-century BCE *Book of Songs* to the Tang dynasty, as well as an introduction to the key prosodic features of Chinese poetry. He was clearly familiar with Davis's essay, while occasionally taking issue with some of the Englishman's critical preferences, and he also drew on discussions of Chinese poetry and poets provided by the Jesuit missionaries. He discusses the typical syntax of individual lines, the important grammatical elasticity of words, and the structural relationships and movements from line to line. He explains the use of rhyme, rhetorical devices like metaphor, parallelism, and reduplication, and the importance of allusion. And he recognizes that the characteristic succinctness of Chinese poetry enhances the evocative power of the genre: "A poem cannot be considered perfect unless all of its characters hold together to the point that not a single one can be eliminated without obscuring the meaning and destroying the thought."[20]

Hervey-Saint-Denys lavishes attention on the two greatest Tang poets, Li Bo and Du Fu, leading off his anthology with substantial introductions to and selections from their works in deference to the places they occupy within the Chinese tradition.[21] Their poems make up forty-six of his ninety-eight titles. Subsequent poets follow in chronological order. In arranging the poems according to authorship and chronology he observes conventions established by the Chinese poetic anthologies he drew upon. A biographical notice prefaces each set of poems, which are accompanied as well by explanatory annotations. The translations reveal his predilection for longer works in older, more narrative styles that offered the kind of documentary information about the culture in which he was most interested—his first book had been on Chinese botany—and most of his selections are thus ancient-style poems. They often present fewer impediments to translation, even while also requiring more footnotes.

Hervey-Saint-Denys's volume was intended to be a work of scholarship: it presented itself proudly as the first translation of poetry from the most important period in the history of Chinese poetry with all the explicatory accoutrements, but it did not lack for literary merit. He was applauded for having filled a lacuna in knowledge of China "with the talent and taste that distinguish him."[22] Julien himself, not known for complimenting his own students, chimes in, although he also typically manages to claim his own due credit: "M. d'Hervey de Saint-Denys continues with equal zeal and success the Chinese studies which he began under my direction more than twenty years ago. He has given us some truly remarkable compositions of the most famous poets of the Tang dynasty, which he has translated with as much elegance as fidelity."[23] To some eyes, however, the volume was distinguished, like the translations of the Jesuits, "by a complete lack of poetic qualities,"[24] yet its readership was surprisingly broad. One later sinologist observed that though Hervey-Saint-Denys's translations "sparkle neither with philological rigor nor with French formal elegance, they were noticed in the literary salons of the Second Empire."[25] Another offers even more mincing praise. Translating Chinese poetry is "an arduous enterprise" because it is "almost impossible, once one has grasped the author's intentions, to make them comprehensible to a foreign reader without ample commentary." Given that difficulty, "putting aside the blunders and the ponderousness of the translation, the *Poetry of the Tang Dynasty* of Hervey de Saint-Denys offered a rather good example of the dose of erudition that can be acceptable to a public of nonspecialist readers."[26]

A significant audience of nonspecialists did indeed take interest in his anthology. Critics initially expressed some perplexity about the nature of the work, calling it "the most curious collection of oriental literature," if not "one of the most curious books of its time." But they also recognized the insights it granted into similarities shared by vastly different cultures, even one "whose bizarre names will frighten the ears a bit." Hervey-Saint-Denys had thus provided a "true service" in teaching French readers that "henceforth the history of literature would be incomplete if it neglected the Chinese poets."[27]

The volume's continued appeal to contemporary writers is documented by entries in the *Journal* of the Goncourt brothers. A few years after its publication, they note that the poems' frequent injunctions to drink remind them of the epicurean themes of Western poets like Horace: "How extraordinary! Chinese poetry—at least what we know of it—is Classical."[28] Ten years later Edmond de Goncourt directly quotes the first line of a poem translated by Hervey-Saint-Denys in lamenting a spell of unusually dry weather:

"A storm without rain, with a wind that emerges as if from the warm mouth of a poet. It seems to me that my intellectual faculties are evaporating. . . .

Oh! the lovely little rain that knows so well when we need it, so says the Chinese poet, well, then, will this lovely little rain ever fall again?[29]

Another entry in their *Journal* suggests that Chinese poetry was a topic of conversation at Parisian dinners, no doubt because of the publication of the volume, but also that not everyone shared in the enthusiasm. "Never before, in the Goncourts' memory, had one known such furor for or against Far Eastern poetry, such spats between Jules and Edmond on one side, Renan and Berthelot on the other." The influential historian Ernest Renan (1823–1894) vented his opinion at a gathering the brothers recorded in June 1864: "Renan is very up in arms, very talkative, and very violent this evening. He unleashes himself against poetry of words, poetry that is useful for nothing, that contains nothing, poetry of the Chinese, of orientals."[30] But he seems to have been an exception. Flaubert's close friend Louis Bouilhet was among those to find extensive inspiration in Hervey-Saint-Denys's volume, which "occupied a place of honor in his library." His study of Chinese poetic forms enabled the French writer to devise new structures for his own poems and "to write truly charming exotic pieces by simply adding rhythm and rhymes to d'Hervey Saint-Denys's translation."[31] The poet Stéphane Mallarmé (1842–1898) also possessed a copy of the collection.[32] But despite a readership that sinologists today can only dream of, the impact of the scholar's book would pale in comparison with that of Judith Gautier's *Book of Jade*, published five years later. As one of Hervey-Saint-Denys's own biographers admits, her Chinese poems were even "better suited to the literary milieu of the day" and thus upstaged her predecessor's, which "languished for a long time in the obscurity of orientalist studies, covered with the dust of contempt."[33]

AT WORK IN THE LIBRARY

Were Judith or Théophile Gautier among the readers of Hervey-Saint-Denys's *Poetry of the Tang Dynasty*? Neither one of them refers to it at the time it was published, and scholars have disagreed on how much overlap exists between his selections and the poems in *The Book of Jade*. Although it is almost as difficult to recognize these affiliations as it is to identify Gautier's sources, there are many more than some have thought, and some of her variations were likely prompted by material in the scholar's preface as well. Given their interest in the general topic and the fact that writers in their world had it on their shelves, they most certainly were familiar with it. But even though she must have had access to a copy of the scholar's work when undertaking her first labors, she usually chose not to follow its scholarly lead and simply used it as an occasional starting point for her own compositions.

Instead, Gautier tells us that she and Ding embarked on their task by visiting the national library on the Rue de Richelieu, the only repository for Chinese books in Paris, to peruse the original sources for the poems themselves. Now known as the Bibliothèque Nationale de France, the library changed its name over the course of its history to reflect the many changes in French government, but the Chinese collection is still held in the same complex they visited. Gautier instantly fell in love with her work there, which began sometime in the late summer or fall of 1863, when she was but a teenager: "Almost every day, accompanied by Ting, who took the place of chaperone, I settled myself in the manuscript room and we leafed through the collections of poetry to find within them poems to our taste and copy them, so we could take them home and study them at our leisure. I really loved this solemn and austere environment, so calm and so studious; it imposed itself on me a bit and I only dared speak in a very low voice." She also recalls, however, an incident from that first day that almost prevented her from ever returning. When a staff member announces at 4 p.m. that the library is closing, Gautier glances up, notices that no one else is budging, and decides to finish copying the poem she has found. Three more shouts from the impatient employee elicit an angry response from another patron, who chastises him especially for having been so "insolent" to Gautier, a young woman—most likely the only one there. More harsh words are exchanged, the room erupts in turmoil (which she describes as "brouhaha"), and as Gautier quickly flees, with the very perplexed Ding trailing behind her, someone is seen to brandish an armchair overhead.[34]

Such incidents in the august reading room were no doubt as rare then as they are now, and Gautier and Ding persevered at their task, poring over the anthologies of Tang-dynasty poetry held by the library as well as editions of the works of both Li Bo and Du Fu, and copying out the works that most pleased them. Ding was certainly familiar enough with the canon to point Gautier toward several "chestnuts" that are still recited by schoolchildren today as well as his own personal favorites, and professor and student collaborated at home to put them into French. Gautier struggled to keep her tutor on task, "because whenever Ting sniffs some work ahead he runs away from me on all limbs."[35]

Given the imperfect nature of their respective foreign language abilities and the weakness of the one dictionary they had at their disposal, their labors must have been curious, indeed. But they certainly impressed all visitors to the household. In July 1865, when Marguerite Dardenne de la Grangerie, the woman who had prompted Théophile Gautier to write the sonnet titled "La Marguerite," visited the family for the first time she absorbed the scene "with the curious eye of a bird," as Judith Gautier recounts in her memoir:

> Tin-Tun-Ling was standing, next to the huge dictionary, in our usual corner of the drawing room; he leaned toward the guest, who, having perhaps taken him for a vase, was completely startled.
> —"Monsieur is Chinese?" ...
> I explained to her, without thinking that it would be at all astonishing, it seemed so natural to me, that I had been working since his arrival with my professor Tin-Tun-Ling.
> —"This is a household that is far from banal," she said, smiling.[36]

Gautier and Ding eventually realized that it would be much more convenient if they could borrow the books they were consulting and work at home. She writes that this occurred "later," but it was in fact considerably later, in February 1866. This significant exception to the rules required permission from the head of the library, which Théophile Gautier successfully secured.

The archives of the Bibliothèque contain three communications regarding the request, the first from the beginning of February 1866 sent from Gautier to Jules Taschereau (1801-1874), the administrative head, which requests permission for "Mademoiselle Judith Gautier, who is studying Chinese language, to take out manuscripts in order to be able to continue at home the work that she does not have the time to complete during the brief sessions of the library because they demand extensive attention." Taschereau consults Stanislas Julien, at the time adjunct curator of the Chinese collection in addition to chair at the Collège de France, who proposes a grudging and qualified assent to this request. Acknowledging the awkwardness of turning down someone of Théophile Gautier's stature he suggests that the loan be limited to novels because the library holds so many. Taschereau, however, appears to have decided to err on the side of generosity, and the memo of his response to Gautier recognizes that Julien's limitation would not allow Judith to undertake her project to translate poetry. He will therefore allow her to borrow any volumes of poetry other than the works of Li Bo and Du Fu, which he considers irreplaceable, although she could, and certainly did, consult them onsite.[37]

There were not that many volumes to lend. At the time Gautier and Ding began their labors the Bibliothèque only held four anthologies of Tang poetry, two of which Hervey-Saint-Denys also notes that he consulted. Unlike the scholar, Judith Gautier also includes poems by the Song-dynasty poet Su Shi 蘇軾 (1036-1101) in her *Book of Jade*, presumably at Ding's suggestion and found in the edition of his complete poetry held by the library.[38] Once allowed to take books home, Gautier and Ding settled themselves down "to work in a corner of the living room next to the window overlooking the street," although, to repeat a theme, she constantly had "to struggle against the very oriental laziness of Ting-Tun-Ling, who monopolized the big armchair and happily fell asleep there."[39] Since she began to produce translations more than two years before the Bibliothèque granted permission for her to borrow books, much of her early work was based on texts she and her tutor had copied out in the library, which may explain some deviations from her sources.

"VARIATIONS ON CHINESE THEMES"

Gautier wasted little time before publishing the first fruits of her collaboration with Ding Dunling. In January 1864 what she called "Variations on Chinese Themes" appeared under the pseudonym Judith Walter in the periodical *L'Artiste*. An unsigned footnote from the journal's editor Arsène Houssaye (1815-1896) explains: "This transparent pseudonym conceals the daughter of a great poet, a woman twice over by virtue of both beauty and poetry. In her article on the new book by Figuier she has proved that her thoughts have traveled worlds both visible and invisible. Today, in translating the Chinese poets better than Stanislas Julien, she proves that *for a woman the word 'impossible' no longer exists.*"[40]

Could one have expected a more stunning endorsement of a young woman's aspirations in 1864? This extraordinary compliment may overstate the comparison between Julien and Gautier—Houssaye was, after all, a good friend of Théophile, a previous editor—but it provides a surprisingly warm welcome for her audacious venture. Hervey-Saint-Denys had toiled for twenty years before publishing his translations at age forty; she had been studying Chinese for but a few months and was only eighteen years old. Significantly, of course, hers were not presented as translations. She referred to the poems inspired by her first readings of

Chinese poets as "variations," displaying sometimes tenuous connections to their sources.

What *were* her sources? Although Gautier's rendering of their names is at times uncertain and often deviates from the romanization system used to represent Chinese in French, it is possible to recognize the names of most of the poets whose work inspired her. In the January 1864 issue, under the title of her first set, she states that her variations were based on the poetry of Li-taï-pé (Li Bo), Thou-fou (Du Fu), Than-jo-su (Zhang Ruoxu 張若虛 ca. 660–ca. 720), Houan-tchan-lin (Wang Changling 王昌齡 ca. 690–ca.756), and Haon-Ti—this last not identifiable as the name of a Chinese poet. It is very difficult, however, to determine specific attributions for poems, which are all unnamed. This is also true of a second set of eight "Variations on Chinese Themes" published eighteen months later in the June 1865 edition of *L'Artiste*, where, in addition to listing Du Fu and Li Bo, she adds Su-Tchou (perhaps Wei Yingwu 韋應物 [737–ca. 792], who was also known as Wei Suzhou 韋蘇州), Sou-ton-po (Su Dongpo 蘇東坡 or Su Shi), and Kouan-tchau-lin, presumably Wang Changling. She also includes a poem by "M. Ting-Tera-Lin," which must be a typo for Ting-Tun-Lin / Ding Dunling, who is described as a "young Chinese in Paris" (*jeune Chinois emparisé*).[41]

The following year Gautier published a third set, "Moonlit Evenings: Little Chinese Poems,"[42] in the *Revue du XIXe siècle*, another of Houssaye's periodicals. As the title suggests, she has organized these selections around a single theme and has also become more confident about her efforts. These six selections (one of which consists of five separate pieces) are now called "poems," each of which is now linked with a specific name, though still only "according to" or "after" the poets Li Bo, Du Fu, Zhang Ruoxu, and Li-hu-tchou, this last writer again unidentifiable. The aspiration to present her versions as actual translations might have been tempting, but she managed to resist it.

Given the circumstances, haste, and less than systematic preparation for her labors it is remarkable that connections between her compositions and their possible sources of inspiration are discernable at all. These are, after all, "variations." The titles have changed, the poems have been truncated or expanded, internal elements have been modified, added, or subtracted, and little to no vestige of an original's formal properties remains. Specific cultural references and allusions have been replaced by imagery that would be more familiar to a French reader. Gautier has retained the fondness for short forms and their conciseness evident in Chinese poetry, but whereas both traditional Chinese and contemporary

French poems were governed by rules of meter and rhyme, using forms with an even number of lines and an equal number of syllables per line, Gautier has chosen to opt instead for longer, unrhymed, rhythmically cadenced lines in short stanzas of unequal length and uneven number.

Although there was little critical response to the poems Judith Gautier published in these periodicals between 1864 and 1866, they foretold what would appear in her acclaimed 1867 *Book of Jade*. She carried over all but one of the twenty-three titles, occasionally revised but most only minimally so, and they make up more than a third of its contents. One poem from January 1864 set may serve as a preview of what lay in store:

LA FLÛTE MYSTÉRIEUSE	THE MYSTERIOUS FLUTE
Un jour, par-dessus le feuillage et les fleurs embaumées, le vent m'apporta le son d'une flûte lointaine.	One day, above the foliage and fragrant flowers, the wind brought me the sound of a distant flute.
Alors j'ai coupé une branche de saule, et j'ai répondu une chanson.	So I cut a willow branch and responded with a song.
Depuis, la nuit, lorsque tout dort, les oiseaux entament une conversation dans leur langage.⁴³	Since then at night, when all is asleep, the birds begin a conversation in their language.

This represents one of the rare cases where a Chinese source can be readily identified, a well-known heptasyllabic quatrain by Li Bo. But in Gautier's hands its title and content have been transformed.

春夜洛城聞笛	LISTENING TO A FLUTE ON A SPRING NIGHT IN LUOYANG
誰家玉笛暗飛聲	From whose house does the jade flute's sound come wafting in the dark?

散入春風滿洛城	Scattered by the spring wind, it fills all of Luoyang city.
此夜曲中聞折柳	Tonight among the tunes I hear the song of "Snapping Willows":
何人不起 故園情 [44]	In whom would this not arouse thoughts of one's home?

Chinese poets were constantly on the move thanks to the demands of their bureaucratic posts, but as a fundamentally agricultural people rooted to family, they were not typically possessed by wanderlust. This is one of thousands of poems evoking the feelings of a traveler nostalgic for his home (literally, the "old garden") and was written when Li Bo was in the city of Luoyang, the historic eastern capital of China and a common destination. For centuries willow branches were broken off as parting gifts because the word for "willow" (*liu* 柳) is homophonous with the word for "stay" (*liu* 留), and "Snapping Willows" was a traditional song for farewells. This information, as well as the recognition that sadness is the primary emotion evoked, would have all been explained to her by Ding Dunling and readily recalled by a reader familiar with Chinese poetic conventions but would require annotation in a translation for the European reader.

Gautier, typically, obviates that need by changing the title to delete the specific place reference and eliminating it altogether within the poem itself. She also ignores the allusion to parting made by the song title. Instead, the willow branch she breaks off becomes an instrument, now plied by the speaker, whose song echoes that of the flute. In addition to the wind, flute, willow, sound, and song, another key element of Li Bo's poem remains, the nighttime setting, when the senses of hearing and smell are keenest. The birds, however, are new; their singing presence marks the season as spring, as in the Chinese source, and suggest an echoing resonance between human and natural worlds. Their nocturnal song also evokes a trope familiar to French readers from well-known stories of courtly love about a woman waiting by her window because the nightingale's song has kept her awake. Gautier thereby transforms the poem from a lament about homesickness to an oblique evocation of secret romance. It has become domesticated, and thereby accessible to a French reader.[45]

At the same time, however, Gautier's poem, which lacks both rhyme and meter, resembles formally neither its inspiration nor any French lyric of its day. With only three lines, it is even shorter than Li Bo's quatrain, though each line is typographically twice as long. In a poem about sounds her attentiveness to auditory effects is clear from the generous use of alliteration ("f" in the first line, "l" in the third), assonance ("eu," "an," "ui," "or,"), and repetition ("j'ai"). The three short lines also create a miniature narrative in a world of connected sonic events: hearing the distant flute prompts ("Alors") the speaker to sing her song, and since then ("Depuis") the birds converse in their own language. (It is only surprising that Gautier omits the delectable fact that the flute is jade, but she had not yet seen Négroni's collection of treasures.) These adverbs establish a causal relationship among the various sounds, an explanation that the original poem does not provide. At the same time, she withholds any overt comment about the significance of the scene, leaving it to the reader to complete what Chinese critics would call "the meaning beyond words."[46]

As the titles of the three published selections suggest, Gautier is most interested in the themes of what she has read, and she has astutely recognized ones that resonate throughout the collections of classical Chinese poetry. The corpus is rife with evocations of the passage of time, signaled typically by references to sunset, autumn, and winter, and a concomitant anxiety about aging, no matter how young the poet: Gautier has clearly recognized their significance. Some of her variations lament the "white frost" or "white silk" that may blanket the dark tresses of the female speakers as they age and others the sorrows of separation from a loved one. A fretful insomnia whose causes remain unspecified and a general sense of equally unexplained ennui suffuse much of the Chinese poetic corpus with a deeply melancholic tone and pervade Gautier's variations as well. But her dramatis personae also reflect interests that were very much her own. Unlike Chinese, French requires an indication of person, so if not expressing a situation or emotions in the first person, she typically chooses a young woman as her protagonist, who if in the original was often an allegorical stand-in for the male author. And while Tang poets often refer to the act of writing, none would describe themselves as having "traced characters similar to the black hair a woman smooths with her hand," as she does in her 1864 "While I was singing of nature" ("Pendant que je chantais la nature").

Gautier's reliance on scenic description and concrete visual imagery in her "variations" takes a cue from the Chinese tradition, and natural elements like flowers, trees, the moon, the wind, and stars abound. But what she notices are the resemblances to human actions and constructs, and her poems therefore teem with comparisons between the two domains. She sees resemblances everywhere.

In some cases she will employ a metaphor, like the white frost or silk on black tresses. Far more frequently, however, she employs explicit similes: peach blossoms that flit like pink butterflies ("Indifference to summer's sweetness" / Indifférence aux douceurs de l'été), a cool wine as transparent as jasper ("Thoughts of the seventh month" / Pensées du septième mois), and frost-covered trees that resemble women's powdered faces ("A thought written on the white frost" / Pensée écrite sur la gelée blanche). One entire poem in her January 1865 set of variations consists of a series of similes and concludes by celebrating the way nature imitates humans ("A poet laughs in his boat" / Un poète rit dans son bateau).

Such explicit comparisons were much less common in the Chinese originals and, along with Gautier's attention to the varieties and vagaries of feeling and perception (as in frequent phrases like "it seemed" or "one would think"), suggest that an active observer is very much at the center of these variations. Nonetheless, her emotional reticence and willingness to rely on simple description of a tableau, rather than an extended comment or an explanation, resonate with characteristics of the Chinese poems that inspired her. Like them, she usually allows her images to speak, however obliquely, for themselves, to embody feelings and thoughts rather than articulate them explicitly. When Verlaine described Judith Gautier as having imposed certain "rules" on her poems, "which are conciseness of expression, brevity of statement, and discretion in the methods employed," he surely did not know that these same features were shared by her Chinese sources. She managed to intuit and convey them successfully, even in her very first efforts, versions that ventured far from the realm of literal translations.

"MARITAL EPISODE"

As Judith Gautier worked with Ding Dunling between 1863 and 1867 on "the most difficult and impossible task" of translating Chinese poetry, her personal life developed in ways that came to frame that task. One of them provided an anticipatory mirror image of her tutor's later brush with bigamy. In July 1865, while picnicking on the Seine, she and her family were introduced to a Persian general named Mohsin-Khan by the journalist Dardenne de la Grangerie and his wife Marguerite. Mohsin-Khan was a descendant of the Prophet Muhammed on his maternal side and had been sent by the shah to France on a special mission. He is accompanied on the summer outing by a colleague at the Persian legation in

Paris. These are not Montesquieu's two young ingenuous visitors from his *Persian Letters*, however, but rather tall, elegant gentlemen who write and speak French perfectly and are accomplished poets and musicians. Judith impresses them by reciting a line from the Koran she had learned from her friend Clermont-Ganneau, and her father, "so smitten with the Orient, was completely seduced by these two Persians."[47]

Mohsin-Khan appears to have been equally taken with Judith Gautier, whose hand in marriage he soon requests from Théophile. To his surprise, he is rebuffed. She learns only indirectly of the main reason, from Marguerite Dardenne de la Grangerie: the general had first to extricate himself from a "temporary marriage" in Persia. If Ding Dunling's first marriage had ended thanks to the spouses' separation of more than three years, so could this entanglement—which was just as "secondary" as Ding's—be formally dissolved within a specified time frame. Théophile insists on awaiting this resolution and urges Mohsin-Khan to reduce his visits to the family in the meantime. Instead, the resourceful general manages to find ways to cross paths with them at parties and to book adjoining loges at the theater. He asks that Judith not marry anyone else during his year's absence: he will certainly return and, moreover, will be entrusted with important diplomatic functions that could ensure her happiness and prove decisive.

As Judith becomes more and more uncomfortable with the idea of another woman languishing in Persia, it also turns out that Théophile Gautier is not as "smitten with the Orient" as she had thought. Despite Mohsin-Khan's "charm, intelligence, and obvious goodness," her father harbors certain fears about the "ferocious tempers" of "Orientals," which her suitor denies, declaring to his daughter: "'You are like a plant born by chance in foreign soil,' he said to me; 'you should be a Persian princess: don't reject this opportunity to fulfill your destiny.'" But Judith refuses to commit herself, and when Mohsin-Khan returned one year later, as ambassador to London, she had "left the paternal nest" for someone else.[48]

Indeed, already sometime in 1863, the same year Ding Dunling entered Gautier's life and she began her study of Chinese, she had met and fallen in love with the writer Catulle Mendès. About the circumstances of their relationship she is curiously silent in the second volume of her memoir, which ends on the eve of her marriage. She did, however, recount—much later—part of the story to her companion Suzanne Meyer-Zundel (1882–1971), which provides an important emotional context for her readings of Chinese poetry: the desperation of a longing that marriage never slaked.

Gautier and Mendès had met at the famous popular classical music concerts organized from 1861 by the conductor Jules Pasdeloup (1819-1887) in the Cirque Napoléon, now called the Winter Circus, a large circular arena with a seating capacity of five thousand. Starting in 1862 Pasdeloup began to include works by Richard Wagner and other modern composers in his programs, which lured the writers and artists who were early fans of the German musician to the Sunday performances. Théophile Gautier had been one of the first, as was his daughter, who attended regularly with her sister and mother.[49]

Contemporary descriptions of Gautier and Mendès suggest that from certain perspectives they could not have been better suited for each other. She was consistently described as "one of the most perfectly beautiful creatures one could ever see," with an allure both classical and exotic that combined "the moon face and lotus eyes" of Hindu goddesses with the Grecian profiles on the medallions of Agrigento.[50] Mendès was equally striking, resembling "a young, sculpted Apollo slimmed down by a Renaissance artist," "Prince Charming," or a "pretty blond Christ."[51]

In addition to their enthusiasm for Wagner, Mendès shared with Gautier an early engagement with the world of letters. His literary reputation had been established as precociously as hers. Poet, novelist, dramatist, critic, indefatigable journalist and chronicler of contemporary affairs, by 1861—when not yet twenty—he had already founded one influential periodical, *The Fantastic Review* (*La Revue fantaisiste*), which was the first such publication in France to declare itself for the controversial German composer.[52] He soon sat at the center of the circle of young poets who would gather at his apartment on weekday evenings and whose work he published in a journal called *The Contemporary Parnassus* (*Le Parnasse contemporain*).[53] Alphonse Lemerre's subsequent decision to publish three selections of their works under the same title made both the name and the fame of the group.[54] The first volume, in 1866, declared its homage to Théophile Gautier by leading off with five poems by him (including his sonnet to "La Marguerite"); it also included works by central Parnassian figures like Leconte de Lisle, Heredia, Banville, and Coppée, as well as venerable and future luminaries like Baudelaire and Mallarmé.

Judith Gautier was not among the women included in the three volumes of *The Contemporary Parnassus*, but she was sometimes called "the only female Parnassian" (l'unique Parnassienne). Like Mendès she regularly attended the Saturday salons of the group's leader Leconte de Lisle, where "she sparkled with her beauty and intelligence" and attracted the poetic homage of several in the group.[55]

4.3 Catulle Mendès, photograph by Nadar.
BnF Gallica

While she shared certain literary predilections—for an imagined purity of distant times and cultures, the glorification of the figure of the poet, and the crafting of dispassionate, descriptive tableaux—unlike them she generally sought to de-exoticize her material, and she also rejected the adherence to metrical norms demanded by traditional French verse.[56] She later confessed that she found their struggles for such perfection "a bit contemptible and rather ridiculous" and likened their writerly efforts to the "torture" of the endless prowling of "beasts in a cage."[57] But they were nonetheless among the most enthusiastic first readers of *The Book of Jade*, having been as influenced as she by Théophile Gautier's fascination with China.

In a poem published in the 1866 volume of *The Contemporary Parnassus* titled "Épilogue," but better known as "Weary of bitter repose" ("Las de l'amer repos"), Mallarmé suggests the nature of this inspiration when describing an art that aspires to

Imiter le Chinois au coeur limpide et fin	Imitate the Chinese of limpid and subtle heart
De qui l'extase pure est de peindre la fin—	Whose purest ecstasy is painting the end—
Sur les tasses de neige à la lune ravie—	On his cups of snow stolen from the moon—
D'une bizarre fleur qui parfume sa vie	Of a strange flower that scents his transparent
Transparente....[58]	Life....

The Chinese aesthetic offers a salutary alternative to what he describes earlier as "the voracious Art" (l'Art vorace) of his contemporary world, as Mallarmé here "prefigures the methods of condensation, suggestion and juxtaposition...that would generate the ambiguities and demandingly blank spaces of his later poetry."[59] Citing this excerpt, M. Marc Chadourne highlights the role of Ding Dunling as "Judith's tutor, Gautier's mandarin, and the Yellow Eminence of Parnassus," "a living Buddha" from whom poets in Théophile's orbit came to drink "the celestial manna"[60] of Chinese culture. While this is clearly an overstatement, that the Parnassians were associated with an interest in Chinese poetry became clear when a group of writers led by Paul Arène (1843-1896) published an anonymous parody of their first collection of poems, which he titled *The Contemporary*

Parnassicle (*Le Parnassiculet contemporain*). The preface features the visit of one Si-Tien-Li, "a Chinese poet and mandarin of the first class" clad in an embroidered orange tunic and a cap with a crystal button, to a meeting of the group, whom he had understood to be "a seminary of young writers infatuated with Chinese verse." Although he does not find them, as he'd imagined, passing their lives "in porcelain palaces full of flowers, women, and rare birds amid vast summer gardens where water sings forever deep within marble basins," a setting that could have been taken from Judith Gautier's variations, he recites one of his poems to the opium- and hashish-smoking group, and their own compositions follow.[61]

Si-Tien-Li's host and the leader of the "Parnassicle" is "a young man with golden locks," no doubt referring to Catulle Mendès, who was as closely linked with Ding Dunling as were Judith and Théophile Gautier. Indeed, a hostile profile of Mendès written about this time wonders: "Look, do you write only for the dozen little comrades who at your evenings lean back in their chairs and swoon when your verses are read, and for the young Chinese man who follows you at six paces when you deign to show yourself to people?"[62] But Mendès was never as exclusively identified as she with the "Orient" and ranged broadly over the field of contemporary French letters; he was even more prolific than Gautier, and a much friendlier profile later called him "the most accomplished man of letters living—master of all the artifices and secrets of literature."[63]

What Judith Gautier certainly did not share with Catulle Mendès was a reputation tainted by scandal. His *Fantastic Review* survived for only nine months, thanks to Mendès's decision to publish in it his off-color verse drama, *The Novel of One Night* (*Le Roman d'une nuit*), which was deemed an outrage to public morals. He was sentenced to a month in prison and paid a fine of 500 francs, and his father's subsequent decision to stop providing him with support doomed the journal and created financial issues for the rest of his life.[64]

Mendès dedicated a volume of poetry titled *Philomela* to Théophile Gautier in 1863, but that tribute does not seem to have been sufficient to sustain the older writer's initially positive opinion of his daughter's suitor, whom he had taken care to warn, on his first visit, about a cigarette that was burning dangerously close to his fingers: "Look out, Catulle, you're about to burn your claws." Théophile was at first primarily worried about Mendès's impecuniousness but had to admit that he was both talented and charming.[65] But already by the latter's second visit Gautier's welcome had cooled, and when Mendès inquired whether consent might be granted to marry Judith (who at eighteen was underage), he was told to come back in a year. Judith Gautier alludes vaguely to "disturbing information that had reached my father's ear,"⁶⁶ but others did not hesitate to speculate. In addition to the pornographic writings and subsequent prison term, there were rumors about his alcoholism, philandering, drug use, and generally dissolute life. In the antisemitic atmosphere of nineteenth-century France it did not help that he was half Jewish. He was rumored to be gay and was even later named as one of Oscar Wilde's three French "intimates" during the English writer's trial.⁶⁷ At the same time it also seems to have been an open secret that while courting Judith Gautier, Mendès became involved with another woman, Augusta Holmès (1847–1903), a composer of English and Irish parentage who had added the French accent to her name and who was another avid fan of the Pasdeloup concerts.⁶⁸ Her relatively deep pockets were appealing to him, and he would go on to have five children with her, two of whom were born before his marriage to Gautier and one of whom died in infancy.⁶⁹ Three of their girls (Huguette, Claudine, and Helyonne, born in 1871, 1876, and 1879) were memorialized in a painting from 1888 by Auguste Renoir, *The Daughters of Catulle Mendès*, which hangs in New York's Metropolitan Museum of Art.

Small wonder, then, that some descriptions of Mendès veer from the angelic to the diabolical. He was called "a poet of mysterious intentions" and "brother of Edgar Poe," perhaps even "a Mephistopheles who's assumed Christ's visage." One observer added:

> It's not to Baudelaire's collection that one should have given the title *Flowers of Evil*.
>
> Didn't this same Baudelaire, the professor of corruption, say of Catulle Mendès:
>
> "I love this young man; he has every vice."
>
> This comment is entirely correct. M. Catulle Mendès possesses a rare talent, precious, exquisite, and corrupt.⁷⁰

Mendès took it upon himself to announce his engagement to Judith Gautier prematurely (in 1863) and publicly, something her father forced him to recant, equally publicly. Théophile Gautier was adamantly opposed to a union that he believed was "fraught with the worst of dangers."⁷¹ This he could do until she turned twenty-one in August 1866, and the resulting standoff etched a painful rupture between father and daughter that scarred both their lives. Her mother Ernesta's decision to side with the young couple led Théophile to leave the household, relegating him, as he grumbled to the Goncourts, "at the age of fifty-four to a student's studio."[72]

The enforced (if occasionally violated) separation generated a passionate cache of letters from Judith Gautier to Catulle Mendès during the year before their eventual marriage that Suzanne Meyer-Zundel includes in a chapter titled "Marital Episode" in her eclectic collection of reminiscences from the almost fifteen years she spent as Gautier's companion. The desperate and plaintive declarations of Judith's love for Mendès in the letters, which are undated though clearly not in chronological order, belie the attitude of impassivity and indifference for which she would become known. Meyer-Zundel may have correctly intuited, however, that although "for those who didn't know her she seemed like someone whose heart could be touched by nothing and no one," nonetheless, "a volcano smoldered beneath the snow."[73] Equally interesting, however, is the fact that the billets-doux were delivered by none other than Ding Dunling.

As Meyer-Zundel tells us, "It was generally 'the Chinese man' of Théophile Gautier, Ting-Ton-Ling, completely devoted to his benefactress Judith, who took it upon himself to deliver to the lovers the letters or short notes that they secretly exchanged." Meyer-Zundel's explanation for Ding's gratitude has been confused by the haze of memory—she attributes it to Gautier's crucial role in exculpating him from the charge of bigamy which occurred ten years later—but five letters themselves make clear how important was his role as messenger.[74] "Ting is going to you and I will stay where you are not. He seems to have no idea how lucky he is," Gautier complains in one, going on to describe her nocturnal bouts of insomnia. Another night she is tormented by terrible dreams until "Ting came into my room with a large volume of Chinese poetry; your letters were inside and the nightmares flew away." A third letter frets that "that monster Ting didn't come and you'll think that I haven't written to you today because of that ridiculous dance," a costume ball that she attended as the male pantomime Pierrot, in "absurd" contrast to "the wave of chiffon that submerged" her family. Yet another complains that "I've waited for your letter all day. Ting comes back, and he has no letter. I have a crazy desire to climb to the second floor and jump out the window. I swear to you that if I had your bottle of laudanum I would have drunk it today." And a fifth note bewails the fact that "Ting has left, it's fate. For some time everything has gone against me—my letter won't arrive and you will curse me again."[75]

The correspondence appears to extend from approximately August 1865 (a year before she declares she will be "free," on her twenty-first birthday) to March 1866.[76] Although she and Mendès could not have secreted notes within volumes of Chinese poetry until after she had secured permission to borrow them from the library in February 1866, the anguish and longing expressed in her letters also suffused Gautier's readings of and selections from the poems from the very start, whose beginnings coincided with her relationship. Mendès, for his part, chose to publish some of his own desperate correspondence with Gautier, thinly disguised as "Love Letters" from "Olivio" to "Mademoiselle Olivia," whom he describes as having departed two years prior for China and now residing in "Tin-Ling on the Yellow River in Manchuria."[77]

Théophile Gautier eventually relented, granting permission for the wedding to take place four months early, on April 17, 1866. He did not attend, but his editor at *Le Moniteur universel*, Julien Turgan (1824-1887), and Gustave Flaubert served as witnesses for Judith, although they didn't attend the wedding breakfast out of respect for her father. The writers Auguste Villiers de l'Isle-Adam (1838-1889) and Charles Leconte de Lisle stood for Mendès and attended the breakfast, along with her mother Ernesta, her sister Estelle, and Ding Dunling.[78] But her father's worries may have been all too well founded, as the marriage barely survived his death six years later in 1872, one which a friend believed had been indirectly hastened by his agony over the struggle with his daughter.[79] The couple's separation in 1874 was ratified judicially four years later. In 1896 they were granted a divorce; such proceedings in France had been reestablished in 1884 after a hiatus of almost seven decades.

News of the foundered marriage spread quickly throughout the Parisian literary world, with Mendès evidently primarily worried about controlling the damage to his relationships with eminent figures within those circles.[80] This effort was largely unsuccessful, and a figure who had been at the center of the artistic avant-garde vanished from prominence almost as mysteriously as Hervey-Saint-Denys did from his field; small wonder that a recent collection of essays about him is titled *Catulle Mendès: The Enigma of a Disappearance*. "It wasn't just a simple man of letters who disappeared, but a half-century of literary Paris, of which he was the sonorous tribune,"[81] observed one contemporary. And a second agreed that "all of Mendès's defects disappear before the greatness of soul with which he devoted himself to everything he found beautiful, no matter the author."[82] Mendès died horribly in 1909 from an ether- and sleep-fogged tumble from a train outside of Paris, but he had already revealed that "greatness of soul" in praise for his ex-wife's *Book of Jade*.

Judith Gautier herself tells us little about the six short years with Mendès, during which they maintained their busy literary and social life and took several important trips together. Suzanne Meyer-Zundel was convinced that her friend would surely have forgiven Mendès for whatever humiliation and pain he had inflicted on her had he been inclined to return. Because "first loves," she writes, are "always the most powerful and enduring, their memory lasts for long years and leaves indelible regrets in one's heart."[83] Other infatuations, as we will see, may have mitigated the distress caused by their relationship. But its many frustrations nonetheless left their own imprint on what mattered most to her, the selection of poems for her *Book of Jade*.

CHAPTER 5

"The Celestial Empire unfurls completely throughout this book"

The 1867 *Book of Jade*

THE 1867 INTERNATIONAL EXPOSITION

While Judith Gautier was rousing her tutor Ding Dunling from his beloved naps to help her prepare *The Book of Jade* for publication, Paris was eagerly awaiting the opening of the International Exposition in April 1867. The world's fair would offer the host country the opportunity to showcase its own imperial power and industrial achievements, and "France and its Colonies" occupied nearly half of the main exhibition building on the Champ de Mars. But Parisians were also curious to learn what they might about countries from Asia, which were participating for the first time in a world's fair. Japan and Siam had responded enthusiastically to the invitation the organizers extended in 1865, eager to acquire a new European market for their goods. China, however, had refused.[1] Still dealing with the internal strife caused by the Taiping conflict, the country was less interested than its neighbors in cultivating international commerce and was also still smarting from the damage inflicted by the Anglo-French expedition that had sacked and burned the Yuanmingyuan.

But how could China not be represented, in a decade that had brought it to the forefront of the French public's attention? None other than the Marquis d'Hervey-Saint-Denys stepped up and offered to take responsibility for mounting an exhibition that would allow the display of goods from China, and at his own expense. After heavy lobbying by several colleagues the French government agreed, appointing him "special commissioner for China" to work with Jules de Lesseps (1809–1887), who served as general commissioner for most of the Oriental section.[2]

Assisted by the Baron Eugène de Méritens, who had served for fifteen years as head of the maritime customs service in China, Hervey-Saint-Denys worked for the next eighteen months to assemble items for the exhibit. Most came from private collections in Paris, including his own, and many had been looted from the Yuanmingyuan as trophies of the Anglo-French military triumph. The local merchant on the rue Tronchet supplied Chinese provisions for sale in its bazaar. The main structure, which in addition to this market housed a tea house and space for theatrical performances, was designed—like the other buildings in the Oriental section—by the architect Alfred Chapon (1834-1893), who had never set foot in China. For inspiration Chapon turned to what had been the emperor's own copy of an album of paintings that had been completed for him in 1744. Titled "Forty Views of Yuanmingyuan," the album had been pillaged from the main drawing room of the palace by Colonel Charles Dupin and thus "saved" from destruction in the subsequent fire; it was given to the national library in 1863. Chapon selected the emperor's favorite tea kiosk, to which he had retreated daily, as model for the Chinese pavilion, around which were planted trees and flowers imported from China. As Raoul Ferrère observes in his essay about the garden complex for the French Imperial Commission, "To create at the Exposition a true Chinese dwelling in all of its gripping reality, to introduce Europeans to a civilization and interior life of a still little known even though much talked about people, to reestablish in Paris what no longer exists in Peking, such was the goal which had been proposed and which has been achieved in a most felicitous way on the Champ de Mars."[3]

The fair featured fifty-two thousand exhibitors and attracted some eleven million visitors, including several heads of state. *Le Figaro* ran a daily column reporting from the fair for nearly four months.[4] Not everyone was thrilled. Even before it opened, the Goncourt brothers decried it as "the last blow of what is the Americanization of France, of Industry taking precedence over Art, of the steam thresher usurping the place of the painting."[5] And there was no denying the even more vulgar atmosphere of the cheap entertainments in the park outside the main pavilion displaying these technological achievements, which led *Le Figaro* to suspend its coverage.[6] Spectacles of another sort included Chinese individuals of unusual size. Hervey-Saint-Denys can be seen at the far left of an illustration of the two attractions.

As for the Chinese pavilion, Ferrère's review vividly describes the story of the construction of "an edifice whose loss China will always weep over." Its effect is

5.1 The Chinese tea pavilion at the Exposition of 1867 as rendered by Alfred Chapon, in *L'Exposition universelle de 1867 illustrée*, publication internationale autorisée par la Commission impériale, ed. François Ducuing, 2 vols. (Paris: Imprimerie Générale Ch. Lahure, 1867), 1:136.
BnF Gallica

5.2 "Giant and dwarf" from China at the Exposition of 1867 with Hervey-Saint-Denys at the far left, from *L'Exposition universelle de 1867 illustrée*, 1: 35.
BnF Gallica

simply "thrilling. One feels gripped, if I may use that expression. Each detail possesses such a powerful stamp of originality that it's impossible not to cry to oneself: that must be real." He is especially impressed that Hervey-Saint-Denys and Méritens have managed to import teen-aged Chinese girls to serve tea, a major triumph over the obstacles of Chinese law. Male Chinese gardeners had been brought over to tend the native plantings as well. And he concludes that "everything in this garden had been studied with an infinitely detailed care and love," creating "a living reproduction of a civilization unknown to us yet nonetheless an important part of the human race."[7]

Others did not share Ferrère's appreciation of the Chinese exhibit. There was some grumbling over the extra admission Hervey-Saint-Denys had been allowed to charge to help defray some of his costs. Another report for the Imperial Commission complained about the limited representation of the full range of Chinese art—there were no paintings and sculptures, for example—and the fact that most items on display were luxury objects for the export market that did not provide a glimpse into the daily life of commoners.[8] Hervey-Saint-Denys's good deeds did not go unpunished; his subcontractors sued him for nonpayment of expenses, generating a substantial legal file revealing, among other details, that the sinologist had personally housed the seven "imported" Chinese personnel for nine months, and that he had spent a total of 85,580 francs, of which only 14,000 had been offset by revenues.[9]

For his efforts, however, Hervey-Saint-Denys was named a Chevalier of the Legion of Honor.[10] He was also memorialized as host of one of the more famous social events of the time, noted by the Chinese general Chen Jitong 陳季同 (1851–1907) in his discussion of the pleasures of Chinese cuisine: "During the Exposition of 1867 the Marquis d'Hervey de Saint-Denys gave a Chinese dinner whose menu was drawn by the celebrated caricaturist Cham: there were the most terrifying things on it." After recounting how a German woman had much enjoyed a dish of sea slugs, a Chinese delicacy, until informed of their name—at which point she thought she could feel them moving in her throat—Chen goes on to assure his readers that though "there are doubtless people in China, as everywhere else, who eat rather eccentric things, that's not true in general. I'll repeat here that never in my life have I known or seen anyone eat cat or dog."[11]

Judith Gautier visited the Asian exhibits frequently and offered her assessment in a series of four reports for *Le Moniteur universel*. One offers tactfully qualified praise of the Chinese pavilion, whose objects provided by collectors and merchants "suffice to introduce us to the Middle Kingdom;" "they didn't get things wrong." She especially admires the porcelains and describes the Marquis d'Hervey-Saint-Denys, in the face of "the abstention of the Son of Heaven," as a "worthy" substitute for him.[12] In an earlier report, also for *Le Moniteur*, Théophile Gautier appears equally underwhelmed by the exhibition, commenting that a real Chinese acting troupe should have been brought over to perform in the theater. He reserves his fascination for the "most authentic" Chinese girls in the teahouse, who recall for him a poem in *The Book of Jade* that begins: "I plucked a peach blossom and brought it to the young woman whose lips are more pink than the little flowers." "Chinese beauty," he writes, deserves a "Chinese madrigal."[13] His article appeared just twelve days after the publication of his daughter's book in May 1867.

A COLLECTION OF "CHINESE MADRIGALS"

The Book of Jade includes seventy-one short "Chinese madrigals," each of which spans at least two printed pages thanks to an unusual typographical generosity. They are arranged into seven categories—Lovers / Les Amoureux (17 titles), The Moon / La Lune (9), Autumn / L'Automne (12), Travelers / Les Voyageurs (6), Wine / Le Vin (8), War / La Guerre (7), and Poets / Les Poëtes (12)—a thematic focus that had already been signaled in Gautier's earlier articles. The volume includes twenty-two of the twenty-three poems Gautier had previously published from 1864 to 1866, with one of the earlier titles that had initially consisted of five sections now broken down into five separate poems, for a total of twenty-seven imported works. She made minor editorial changes but altered their typographical presentation.

In choosing to compile a collection, Judith Gautier was probably inspired by the anthologies she had been allowed to borrow and was thus drawing from the most venerable of literary practices in China. The sixth-century BCE classic *The Book of Songs*, after all, was itself an anthology. Over the centuries compilations of poetry—sometimes commissioned by rulers but more often a labor of individual scholarly love—proved among the most important sources enabling an understanding of literary history, theory, and value in China. The process of selecting poems to be published together not only ensured their preservation but also signaled their special value from the point of view of the compiler. Ding Dunling may have explained that their arrangement also indicated what characteristics were felt to matter most in their understanding and appreciation.

From the volumes she borrowed Gautier would have learned that most Chinese anthologies arranged their contents by form, author, chronology, or some combination of the three. The 305 poems in *The Book of Songs* were almost all anonymous and were arranged by subtype, and within the largest category further by geography. The next two major literary anthologies date from the sixth century CE. The *Selections of Refined Literature* (Wen *xuan* 文選), compiled between 520 and 530 under the leadership of crown prince Xiao Tong 蕭統 (501–531) of the Liang dynasty, sorts its contents first by genre, and then further by topic and chronology. Spanning the millennium since *The Book of Songs* but explicitly excluding canonical and philosophical works, it aimed to be broadly comprehensive, representative, and rigorously selective in its choices of what it considered to be the best literary writing. A roughly contemporaneous anthology, *New Songs from the Jade Terrace* (*Yutai xinyong* 玉臺新詠), compiled under the patronage of Xiao Tong's younger brother Xiao Gang 蕭綱 (503–551) by the court poet Xu Ling 徐陵 (503–583), also sorts its contents by genre and then by author in chronological order, but its scope is vastly less sweeping: the majority of its works are poems in pentasyllabic meter written within the previous century and are examples of the mildly erotic "alluring songs" that suited its patron's taste. The handful of Tang-dynasty anthologies of Tang poetry that have survived continue this focus on authorship and are generally arranged accordingly, also in chronological order. Those compiled during later dynasties usually sort first by metrical form (regulated verse or ancient-style, pentasyllabic or heptasyllabic lines), and then by author as well.

In deciding to arrange her selections by theme, therefore, Judith Gautier forged a path of her own. The Bibliothèque did hold five editions of the *Selections of Refined Literature*, whose poetic works are arranged in categories like hunting, palaces and halls, travel, rivers and seas, natural phenomena, and warfare, but there is little evidence from her compositions, which were mostly derived from Tang poetry, that she consulted it. Only one poem that she drew from is included in that imperial anthology, and it was also readily available to her in another collection that she relied on heavily. It is tempting to think that the romantic, boudoir-centered poems in *New Songs from a Jade Terrace* might have inspired her foregrounded theme of Lovers, not to speak of its title, but the library did not hold a copy of it at the time she and Ding Dunling were working. The two popular and comprehensive

Qing-dynasty anthologies of Tang poetry (*Compiled Explications of Ancient and Tang Poetry* and *Compiled Selections of Tang Poetry*) she borrowed, as well as the collections of the poetry of Li Bo and Du Fu she read onsite, relied on formal characteristics, authorship, and chronology to arrange their contents. The lone exception to this practice in the library was the *Linked Pearls of Tang Poetry*, an eighteenth-century compilation of poems categorized by themes, such as history, retreat, landscape, animals, flowers and trees, the seasons, farewells, amorousness, banquets, the court, and laments. *Linked Pearls* includes poems drawn from all periods of the Tang dynasty but favors heptasyllabic regulated verse exchanged among officials, especially from the late Tang, of which there appear to be few examples in *The Book of Jade*, but Gautier may have taken inspiration from a simple perusal of its table of contents for her organizing principle, and perhaps even her title.[14]

Gautier may also have looked at contemporary French collections for ideas on how to structure *The Book of Jade*. Like most Chinese anthologists, Hervey-Saint-Denys's *Poetry of the Tang Dynasty* arranged its contents by author in chronological order, except for Li Bo and Du Fu, whose works he placed first because of their stature. Because he was most interested in providing information about Chinese daily life from the content of his materials, the formal characteristics of the poetry were not his primary concern; in any case, it would not have made sense to sort his materials according to prosody in translations. Among collections of French poetry, the readiest example to hand was the 1866 *Contemporary Parnassus*, which arranged its poems by author as well. Charles Baudelaire's 1857 *Flowers of Evil* may also have offered a different example to Gautier.[15] This collection, the poet's first and most influential, was pathbreaking in its engagement with the dark side of life in a rapidly modernizing Paris; it was deemed a masterpiece by some and a scandal by others. Baudelaire was charged with offending public morals, and six of the volume's poems were suppressed, but *Flowers of Evil* established his preeminence on the contemporary literary scene. Although obviously not a compilation of works by more than one author, as an anthology it was renowned for its purposeful architecture and its deliberately thematic structure. Baudelaire organized the poems in the volume under distinctive headings—Spleen and Ideal, Parisian Tableaux, Wine, Flowers, Revolt, and Death—and while most differ in emotional tonality from those of Gautier, not to speak of their focus on modern life, there is an interesting overlap of one category (Wine), and the poems in general share a melancholic tone and fascination with sensory imagery.

Whether or not any of these previous collections served to influence Gautier as she compiled her own, her decision to arrange her pieces by topic demonstrates that she did not regard them primarily as historical, or even biographical, documents but rather as literary artifacts. She had already made this impulse clear in her first efforts published in *L'Artiste* in 1864 and 1865, which she describes as "Variations on Themes" gleaned from her reading of Chinese poetry. Her poems are presented only as "after" those of a Chinese poet, so any arrangement by author or chronology would have made little sense, although she might have chosen to group pieces linked to the same poet together. (Significantly, the table of contents for the volume lists poems by theme and title, without attribution to authors.) A thematic structure may have been the best strategy for dealing with variations of sometimes shaky attribution, but it also suggests that for her the historical identification was of secondary importance anyway; she was thinking literarily, unlike her sinological predecessors. Having grouped one set of poems under the rubric "Moonlit Evenings" in 1866, she easily found some more. The themes she identifies do in fact course through the body of predominantly Tang-dynasty poetry that Ding Dunling introduced her to, but she has extracted and embellished them with her own set of predilections and experiences. In addition to jade flutes, porcelain cups, and other precious objects that she may have seen in the Negroni exhibit, images of flowers, boats, flowered boats, mirrors, water, and the moon fill the pages of *The Book of Jade*, which is also obsessed with the process of writing itself. We see politics solely from the perspective of an imagined imperial boudoir and warfare through the eyes of women left behind. Notably scarce are the historical and religious topics, social critique, and glimpses of official life that we also readily find in the poetry of the Tang. But she has not invented the ones she chooses to foreground.

LOVERS

Many have wondered about her decision to place a section on Lovers (Les Amoureux) at the very beginning of the collection: Was this just evidence of the romantic obsessions of a young woman impatiently awaiting her marriage? The section is the largest (with 17 out of 71 titles), and her second edition published in 1902 would expand the number (to 42 of 110). Arthur Waley, one of the most gifted translators of Chinese poetry into English, is most famously associated with the idea that Chinese poets didn't write about love. Writing in "The Limitations of Chinese Literature," he asserts that whereas the European poet is conspicuously preoccupied with it and "tends to exhibit himself in a *romantic* light, in fact, to recommend himself as a lover," the Chinese poet "recommends himself not as a lover, but as a friend." Relationships between men and women, he argues, are less important than male friendship, into which poets invested the emotional energy that in Europe would go to love. The rare woman poet generally presents herself as a rejected wife "cast adrift by her lord or sent back to her home," with male poets often assuming the same voice to speak allegorically of their fall into political disfavor. While it's true that Tang poets often imitated folk songs written in the voice of women and found the abandoned palace lady a convenient figure for their own fears of political disfavor, Waley's blanket statement has been contested. James J. Y. Liu politely replied that while "some Western translators" may have overemphasized the importance of friendship over love, "there *is* a great deal of love poetry in Chinese,"¹ going back to *The Book of Songs*, spanning centuries of largely anonymous folk songs, and rippling through the works of poets from the Tang dynasty onward.[16] But there is certainly not as much as the lovelorn young woman led her readers to believe, in leading with Lovers.

Every section in *The Book of Jade* is headed by a six-character Chinese phrase that highlights images or actions that might be associated with the theme. Few readers of the volume have paid attention to the phrases; they are not translated and thus serve primarily as decoration—both exotic and authentic—and their awkward mix of registers in Chinese suggests that they were of Gautier's own devising. For the Lovers section the phrase reads "Yellow gold willow leaves float on water" (Huang jin liu ye fu shui 黃金柳 葉浮水).¹ As noted earlier, willow branches were associated with parting in Chinese poetry, but Gautier's willow leaves, bobbing on the waves, here serve as signs or messages for lovers. Boats also float on water in many of the poems, both separating and connecting the individuals in question.

Not all of the poems contain these title images, including some of the most interesting pieces in the section, but all of them are about encounters or relationships between men and women. Several of them also demonstrate how well Ding has helped Gautier to understand her sources, even as she chooses to deviate from them. A good example is her poem "Birdsong in the evening" ("Chant des oiseaux, le soir"), which Hervey-Saint-Denys also translated. Though hers is only "after Li

Bo," it is based on one of the poet's best known poems, which had been composed to a traditional folk song title, "Crows calling at night" ("Wu ye ti" 烏夜啼); it was included in the two major anthologies she consulted as well as in Li's collected works. The two French versions follow a literal translation into English and the Chinese original provided below, whose stock figures of the crows and the weaving girl would have appeared in any poem written to this song title:

黃雲城邊烏欲棲	Amid yellow clouds by the city wall, crows are about to roost.
歸飛啞啞枝上啼	Flying back, they cry "caw-caw" atop the boughs.
機中織錦秦川女	At her loom weaving brocade is the young woman of Qin,
碧紗如煙隔窗語	The blue-green gauze like mist, and voices outside the window.
停梭悵然憶遠人	She stops her shuttle and sadly thinks of the person far away.
獨宿空防淚如雨[17]	Alone at night in the empty room, her tears are like rain.

LE CRI DES CORBEAUX À L'APPROCHE DE LA NUIT

Près de la ville, qu'enveloppent des nuages de poussière jaune, les corbeaux se rassemblent pour passer la nuit.

Ils volent en croassant, au-dessus des arbres; ils percent dans les branches, en s'appelant entre eux.

La femme du guerrier, assise à son métier, tissait de la soie brochée;

Les cris des corbeaux lui arrivent, à travers les stores empourprées par les derniers rayons du soleil.

CROW CALLS AT NIGHTFALL (HERVEY-SAINT-DENYS)

Near the city enveloped in clouds of yellow dust, crows gather to spend the night.

They fly cawing above the trees; they pierce the branches, calling to one another.

The soldier's wife, seated at her loom, was weaving embroidered silk;

The crows' cries reach her through blinds purpled by the last rays of the sun.

Elle arrête sa navette. Elle songe avec découragement à celui qu'elle attend toujours.
Elle gagne silencieusement sa couche solitaire, et ses larmes tombent comme une pluie d'été.[18]

CHANT DES OISEAUX, LE SOIR

Au milieu du vent frais les oiseaux chantent gaiement sur les branches transversales.
Derrière les treillages de sa fenêtre, une jeune femme qui brode des fleurs brillantes sur une étoffe de soie écoute les oiseaux s'appeler joyeusement dans les arbres.
Elle relève sa tête et laisse tomber ses bras; sa pensée est partie vers celui qui est loin depuis longtemps.
"Les oiseaux savent se retrouver dans le feuillage; mais les larmes qui tombent des yeux des jeunes femmes comme la pluie d'orage ne rappellent pas les absents."
Elle relève ses bras et laisse tomber sa tête sur son ouvrage.
"Je vais broder une pièce de vers parmi les fleurs de la robe que je lui destine, et peut-être les caractères lui diront-ils de revenir."[19]

She stops her shuttle. She thinks disheartened of the one she still awaits.
Silently she reaches her solitary bed, and her tears fall like summer rain.

BIRDSONG IN THE EVENING (JUDITH GAUTIER)

Amid the cool wind the birds sing gaily on the crosswise branches.
Behind the window screen a young woman who embroiders brilliant flowers on silken cloth hears the birds calling joyously in the trees.
She raises her head and lowers her arms; her thoughts have sped to the one far away for so long.
"Birds know how to find one another again in the foliage, but tears falling from young women's eyes like torrential rain don't call back the absent."
She raises her arms and drops her head over her needlework.
"I'll embroider a poem among the flowers of the gown meant for him, and perhaps the characters will tell him to come back."

Gautier and Hervey-Saint-Denys make very different choices, even as they both address, like the traditional folk song, the theme of a couple separated. The differences also suggest that while Gautier must have had recourse to Hervey-Saint-Denys's versions, she relied on her own independent readings of the sources. As she would have learned from Ding and the annotations to Li Bo's poem, it is dense with allusions, but, unlike in "The mysterious flute," here she chooses to incorporate them into her poem rather than delete or transform them. She also retains more of the material from the original poem than does her scholarly predecessor.

Why do her crows caw "gaily" and "joyously" to each other? As Hervey-Saint-Denys explains in a footnote to his translation, the associations of their evening cries are quite different in Europe and China. In the former they would likely evoke the presence of a nearby battlefield littered with carcasses, whereas in the latter they signal a joyous reunion, since crows were thought to rejoin their mates, whom they locate with their cries, on treetops at nightfall. Li Bo's poem situates his protagonist in Qin, the far northwest of China, where desert dust mixed with clouds would be yellow. Hervey-Saint-Denys jumps from the identification of this location to the inference that the absent husband is a soldier at war on the frontier, despite having just pointed out that the crows' cawing is not necessarily associated with battle. Gautier, by contrast, highlights the significance of the crows' ability to communicate with and find each other, as Ding and the commentators' notes would have explained, with the reference to their cries as happy, almost human, "voices" that contrast with the woman's inability to summon "the one far away," even with her tears. And unlike Hervey-Saint-Denys she brings to the fore the allusion, also annotated, to the most famous weaver from Qin, a fourth-century woman named Su Hui 蘇蕙, who with her husband, Dou Tao 竇滔, had been exiled there. When he was assigned to a position in a more salubrious location he took his favorite concubine with him, but Su Hui refused to go along. She composed a palindromic poem that was woven in five colors into an eight-inch-square piece of silk brocade and sent it to Dou Tao. Laid out in sections, its 841 characters arranged in a square of 29 characters on each side could be read vertically, horizontally, diagonally, backward, and forward as more than two hundred different poems. (Such is the virtue of classical Chinese, where words are uninflected, grammatically mobile, and almost all monosyllabic.) When he received her gift, which only he could read in its entirety, he sent his concubine away and invited Su Hui to join him; "their love and affection had doubled."[20]

Gautier recognizes this as a remarkable story and dramatizes it in her poem, slightly embellished in its details and featuring a more empowered central figure whose actions will be more effective than her tears. It is nonetheless true to Li Bo's poem and the contrast it draws between birds and humans. Her concise tableau deftly balances the action within it: just as the woman raises her head and lowers her arms when listening to the crows, she lowers her head and raises her arms as she prepares to weave. Patterned repetitions like these throughout *The Book of Jade* demonstrate her attention to the rhythmic and musical aspect of her pieces.

Another celebrated legend about a neglected woman is attached to the poem "The fan" ("L'Éventail") which Gautier labels as "after" a poet named Tan-Jo-Su.[21] It is in fact based on a well-known "Song of complaint" ("Yuan ge xing" 怨歌行) attributed to a first century BCE court lady with a similar name, Ban Jieyu 班婕妤, or Lady Ban, whose position as favorite of the Han emperor Cheng 成 was jeopardized by the machinations of another concubine. The poem describes a white silk circular fan that knows its value during the hot summer months but dreads the cool winds of autumn that will relegate it to storage—just as the speaker tacitly fears that her lord's affection for her will end. Ban Jieyu's poem is presented entirely from the point of view of the fan; the comparison to the woman did not need to be spelled out. Gautier, however, cannot rely on this cultural knowledge, so her poem is spoken in the voice of a "new wife" who has just been visited for the first time the night before, in the "perfumed chamber," by her husband. And in her version the fan's situation is inscribed on the object itself, which after reading aloud the woman speaker then sees as alarmingly analogous to her own. Her choice may have been more apt than she could have realized, for though readers wanted the poem to be voiced by Ban Jieyu, or some court lady enjoying the emperor's favor, another interpretation is plausible. "Rather than a poem comparing a court lady to a fan, we might well have a poem actually on a fan, implicitly compared to a court lady," since professional poets were often called upon to compose on an object: "if a third-century poet had been asked to write on a circular fan, the piece [attributed to Lady Ban] would have been appropriate."[22]

This was not a Tang-dynasty work, and some scholars have assumed that Gautier only learned about it from Hervey-Saint-Denys's preface to his collection, in which he mentions, as part of a longer discussion of women in Chinese poetry, a wife who compares herself to a fan that may be cast aside when the weather cools. He does not refer to Ban Jieyu by name, nor does he provide the text itself, but it's clear that he is alluding to her story. Gautier could have been intrigued by this reference, but given the fact that she explicitly names "Tan-Jo-Su," a quite plausible misreading or mishearing of Ban Jieyu, as her source, she seems to have actually encountered the poem, and Ding Dunling could have pointed Gautier to available sources for the original text, one of which was the anthology that includes pre-Tang as well as Tang-dynasty pieces and was one of the two major texts she used.[23]

In a third poem included in the Lovers section commentators generally read the relationship depicted allegorically, but Gautier clearly found its appeal stronger if taken literally. "The virtuous wife" ("L'épouse vertueuse") is based on a poem by the mid-Tang poet Zhang Ji 張籍 (776–ca. 829), "Song of the faithful wife" ("Jie fu yin" 節婦吟), which is included in both of Gautier's main anthological sources and was also translated by Hervey-Saint-Denys as "A woman loyal to her duties" ("Une femme fidèle à ses devoirs").[24] In Zhang Ji's poem a woman receives a gift of two pearls, which she temporarily affixes to her red silk gown, but because she is already married and determined to be faithful she returns them to her suitor. Her rejection, however, is a tearful one, for she wishes she had met him before her marriage, leading one commentator to wonder whether "faithful" was the right word.[25] As Hervey-Saint-Denys tells us, the poem was traditionally read as Zhang Ji's allegorical profession of loyalty to his ruler during a time of civil warfare; poems written in the voice of women were often interpreted in this way. Gautier distills the eight lines of the source to four, deleting background information and the traditional political reading, and her final image ingeniously transforms the tears into metaphor: "At the tips of my lashes, see these two trembling tears: these are the pearls I give back to you." (Au bord de mes cils, voici deux larmes tremblantes; ce sont tes perles que je te rends). We can see here her recognition of an unrealized aesthetic potential presented by her materials.

These three examples illustrate the extent to which Gautier kept her Chinese sources in mind even as she produced variations that would be more readily understood or appreciated by her French audience. Two of the most admired poems in her collection, however, cannot in fact be linked to any classical Chinese text. The first is a poem "after" her tutor Ding Dunling, titled "The shadow of the orange leaves" ("L'ombre des feuilles d'oranger"):[26]

La jeune fille qui travaille tout le jour dans sa chambre solitaire est doucement émue si elle entend tout à coup le son d'une flûte de jade;	The young girl who works daylong in her lonely room is gently stirred if she suddenly hears the sound of a jade flute;
Et elle s'imagine qu'elle entend la voix d'un jeune garçon.	And she imagines that she hears the voice of a young man.
A travers le papier des fenêtres, l'ombre des feuilles d'oranger vient s'asseoir sur ses genoux;	Through the paper windows, the shadow of the orange leaves comes to settle on her knees;
Et elle s'imagine que quelqu'un a déchiré sa robe.	And she imagines that someone has ripped her gown.

Did Ding Dunling compose a Chinese original for this poem? Some readers have had their doubts, but he was likely familiar with the tradition of mildly erotic folk songs popular during the dynasties preceding the Tang, in which one might well encounter a desiring woman imagining her own disrobing. Given his louche reputation, such a projection would not be surprising, although the other works attributed to him in the volume address more somber themes. The elements of the poem—the solitary young woman and the jade flute, its repetition of phrase, rich assonance, and withholding of emotion and comment—recur throughout the collection and were hallmarks of Gautier's style. A likely collaboration between tutor and student, "The shadow of the orange leaves" would become one of the most frequently retranslated works from *The Book of Jade*.

Even more popular was another poem in this section, which takes us unequivocally into the territory of invention. "The house in the heart" ("La maison dans le coeur") is attributed to Du Fu:

Les flammes cruelles ont dévoré entièrement la maison où je suis né.	Cruel flames completely devoured the house of my birth.
Alors je me suis embarqué sur un vaisseau tout doré, pour distraire mon chagrin.	So I embarked on a gilded vessel as distraction from my grief.

J'ai pris ma flûte sculptée, et j'ai dit une chanson à la lune; mais j'ai attristé la lune qui s'est voilée d'un nuage.	I took my sculpted flute and chanted a song to the moon; but I saddened the moon, which hid behind a cloud.
Je me suis retourné vers la montagne, mais elle ne m'a rien inspiré.	I returned toward the mountain, but it failed to inspire me.
Il me semblait que toutes les joies de mon enfance étaient brûlées dans ma maison.	It seemed as if all the joys of my youth had been burned in my house.
J'ai eu envie de mourir, et je me suis penché sur la mer. À ce moment, une femme passait dans une barque; j'ai cru voir la lune se reflétant dans l'eau.	I wanted to die, and I leaned over the sea. At that moment, a woman passed by in a boat; I thought I saw the moon reflected in the water.
Si Elle voulait, je me rebâtirais une maison dans son coeur.²⁷	If She wished, I would rebuild myself a house in her heart.

There is no poem in Du Fu's corpus with the title "The house in the heart" and no work that corresponds even remotely to Gautier's piece. It may have been inspired by a famous and quite different poem in which the Tang poet describes how an autumn gale blows off the roof of his thatched hut.[28] Each piece does end with a visionary hope for the future: for Du Fu that he could build a shelter for all similarly bereft souls, and for Gautier's speaker that a new dwelling might be rebuilt in the heart of the unidentified woman.

"The house in the heart" proved to be one of "Du Fu's" most famous poems. It would be retranslated more frequently than any other poem in *The Book of Jade*, at least six times into English alone, and it was selected as one of the "hundred most beautiful poems in the world" in 1979, although erroneously attributed to another French poet, Louis Laloy (1874-1944).[29] One of Gautier's first "Variations," published in January 1864 when she was eighteen, it bears the least resemblance of all the works "after" Du Fu to any of his works, and, for that matter, to any Chinese poem. There are elements more closely associated with the more whimsical Li Bo, whose jade flute (here "sculpted") we have encountered already in "The mysterious flute." A set of four poems titled "Drinking alone beneath the moon," for example, involves a fanciful exchange with the moon, which he invites to drink with him, and another quatrain features him communing calmly with a mountain. And according to one popular legend, Li drowned when leaning down to embrace the reflection of the moon in the water.[30] This poem may be a pastiche of such allusions, misattributed to Du Fu, but even Li cannot account for the concluding line's romantic fantasy.

THE MOON

Whatever liberties she chose to take with "The house in the heart," Gautier was also capable of respecting both the letter and the spirit of her sources, as is evident in another poem "after" Du Fu that appears in The Moon (La Lune), the next section of *The Book of Jade*. It is a well-known twilight scene titled "Gazing over the wilds" ("Ye wang" 野望):

清秋望不極	In clear autumn gazing has no bounds,
迢遞起層陰	Far in the distance arise layered shadows.
遠水兼天淨	Distant waters meet the sky untainted;
孤城隱霧深	The lone city wall is hidden deep in fog.
葉稀風更落	Leaves sparse, and more blown down by the wind,
山迴日初沈	Mountains remote, where the sun begins to sink.
獨鶴歸何晚	The solitary crane returns so late—
昏鴉已滿林 [31]	Dusk crows already fill the forest.

Gautier calls her poem "Evening walk on the plain" ("Promenade le soir dans la prairie"):

Le soleil d'automne a traversé la prairie en venant de l'est; maintenant il glisse derrière la grande montagne de l'ouest.	The autumn sun has crossed the plain coming from the east; now it slips behind the large mountain to the west.
Il reste une lueur dans le ciel; sans doute le jour se lève de l'autre côté de la montagne.	A glow remains in the sky; no doubt day is dawning on the other side of the mountain.

Les arbres sont couverts de rouille, et le vent froid du soir décroche les dernières feuilles.	The trees are covered with rust, and the cold evening wind detaches the last leaves.
Une cigogne veuve regagne son nid solitaire, tristement et lentement, comme si elle espérait encore voir revenir celui qui ne reviendra plus.	A widowed stork reclaims her solitary nest, sadly and slowly, as if she yet hoped to see return the one who will never return.
Et les corbeaux font un grand bruit autour des arbres, pendant que la Lune commence à s'allumer pour la nuit.[32]	And the crows caw noisily around the trees, while the Moon begins to light up for the night.

Du Fu's poem balances the many contrasts perceptible at a moment of transition on a frontier landscape, and commentators have admired the multiple layers of vision between which his gaze shifts: the boundless clarity offered by the autumn sky as opposed to the increasing obscurity of evening clouds and fog blanketing the city wall, and the details of windblown leaves nearby contrasted with the distant sunset glow behind the mountains. He suggests a temporal contrast as well in noting how long the lone crane has been absent from her nest and how soon the crows have returned to theirs. As we know from Li Bo's "Crows calling at night," the latter have also come back to their mates. The desolation of the scene evokes Du Fu's melancholy as he contemplates the landscape far from his home.

In her version Gautier retains both his somber tone and his attention to transitional moments, both past and present, tracing the sun's path from east to west, juxtaposing the sunset with a presumed sunrise on the other side of the mountain and adding—perhaps to justify inclusion in this section—the rising moon. Dusting the falling leaves with metaphorical "rust" to describe their autumnal tinge, she also explains for her audience the poignancy of the contrast between the situations of the two birds, whose function as analogues is highlighted by the description of the stork as "widowed." She rearranges and reinterprets from the perspective of an abandoned woman, but the fundamental elements of Du Fu's starkly evocative poem remain.

The Chinese heading for this second section of *The Book of Jade*, The Moon, reads "Poems on enjoying the moonlight and talking of feelings" (Wan yue tan qing shi ci 玩月談情詩詞), thus thematically closely related to the first group but linked by a focus on "*la Lune*," which is capitalized in each one. Its nine poems had all been published in Gautier's "Moonlit Evenings" in April 1866, and Chinese sources can be easily identified for almost all of them. Five pieces attributed to "Tan-Jo-Su" are based on a much longer poem, not by Ban Jieyu, however, but rather one of the two surviving compositions of an early Tang poet with a more similar name, Zhang Ruoxu 張若虛 (660?–720?) and certainly the one for which he is best known. Titled "Spring, river, flower, moon, night" ("Chun jiang hua yue ye" 春江花月夜), the name of a traditional song, it consists of nine quatrains that develop themes suggested by those five paratactically assembled words. The poem engages in philosophical ruminations on transience—suggested by the endlessly flowing water and the cycles of the moon and the seasons, which both mirror and contrast with the human condition—and focuses as well on the same particularly human problem addressed in the first section, the separation between a man and woman.

"Spring, river, flower, moon, night" was included in both of Gautier's main anthological sources and had also been translated by Hervey-Saint-Denys. Whereas in 1866 she had published the pieces as sections of a single poem titled "By the river edged with flowers" ("Près de la rivière bordée de fleurs"), thus retaining the ties to her source, in 1867 she breaks them down into five shorter poems of three to five lines, with separate titles. Each focuses on one aspect of the larger poem, although the connections are at times attenuated. "The peaceful river" ("Le fleuve paisible") muses on the passage of time evoked by the movements of both moon and river. "A poet looks at the moon" ("Un poète regarde la lune") describes the moon as more engrossing than the sound of a woman's singing and provides in its final line a good example of Gautier's exuberant overreading of a line. In describing the moonlight on the river, Zhang Ruoxu writes that "fish and dragons dive and leap, the water forms a pattern" (yu long qian yue shui cheng wen 魚龍潛躍水成文), where the word for "pattern" (*wen* 文) used to describe ripples also means "writing." In Gautier's variation, this becomes "The moon reflects itself in the eyes of poets as in the scales of dragons, those poets of the sea" (La Lune se mire dans les yeux des poètes comme dans les écailles brillantes des dragons, ces poètes de la mer). "On the river edged with flowers" ("Sur la rivière bordée de fleurs") focuses in three short lines on the speaker in a solitary boat who spies his match in a lone cloud above. As the moon rises in the sky, mirrored in the river, both cloud and speaker find solace. "On the edge of the small lake" ("Au bord du petit lac") seizes on stray images to describe the effect of moonlight on various elements of the landscape. And "A woman facing her mirror" ("Une femme devant son miroir") draws on the section of Zhang's poem that describes the abandoned woman at her toilette.[33]

The most celebrated quatrain depicting a lonely woman included in the section titled The Moon is based on one by Li Bo, which Gautier titles "The jade staircase" ("L'escalier de jade"). Li's poem, "Complaint on the jade steps" ("Yu jie yuan" 玉階怨), deploys a song title that was typically used to express the resentment of a courtesan who has not been "favored" by her lord, a tradition going back to the complaint of Lady Ban discussed above.

玉階生白露	On the jade steps arises white dew.
夜久侵羅襪	In the long night it penetrates silk gauze stockings.
卻下水晶簾	Then she lowers the crystalline blind,
玲瓏望秋月[34]	Tinkling bright, to gaze at the autumn moon.

Critics over the centuries greatly admired Li's poem for its remarkable restraint, especially when compared with previous examples of poems written to the same title, which usually contain the same elements—a solitary woman on an autumn evening by a richly screened window. Li's version is markedly less explicit than its predecessors in its presentation of her actions and emotions. We are provided little information about the woman or her experience, that she has been waiting in vain for her lord. The dew could have served as an image of imperial favor, but here the soaked silk stockings tell us rather of a long night spent on the steps alone. Nor does Li employ a single word to express the resentment that is signaled by the title. As if still hopeful for a visit, the woman returns to her quarters to gaze mutely at the autumn moon, whose gleam through the clinking crystal-beaded curtain completes the tableau of chilly, somber whiteness drawn by each line of the quatrain. The poem's evocative power depends on what it refuses to say.

Such restraint is possible with a readership familiar with the elements of the tradition, which both Ding and the annotations would have explained to her, but Gautier recognizes that her audience might require a different approach. Her first version of "The jade staircase" appeared in "Moonlit Evenings" in 1866:

120 *The 1867* Book of Jade

Malgré la douce clarté de la pleine lune, l'Impératrice remonte son escalier de jade.	Despite the gentle light of the full moon, the empress ascends her jade staircase again.
Il est déjà tout brillant de roses.	It is already glistening with roses.
Le bas de sa robe baise doucement le bord des marches.	The gown's hem gently kisses the steps' edge.
Le satin blanc et le jade se ressemblent.	The white satin and jade look alike.
Le clair de lune a envahi la chambre de l'Impératrice; en passant la porte, elle est toute éblouie.	Moonlight has invaded the empress's chamber; passing the door, she is completely dazzled.
Devant la fenêtre, sur le rideau brodé de perles de cristal, on croirait voir une société de diamants qui se disputent la lumière;	Before the window, on the curtain embroidered with crystal pearls, a host of diamonds seems to vie with the light.
Et par terre on dirait une ronde d'étoiles.[35]	And on earth one would call it a circle of stars.

This is one of the few previously published poems that Gautier significantly revised over the years. For the 1867 *Book of Jade* she tinkered primarily with the spacing; she consolidates the seven units of the earlier version to five here and adds an explanatory conjunction in the fourth:

Sous la douce clarté de la pleine Lune, l'Impératrice remonte son escalier de jade, tout brillant de rosée.	Under the gentle light of the full moon the empress ascends again her jade staircase, glistening with dew.
Le bas de la robe baise doucement le bord des marches; le satin blanc et le jade se ressemblent.	The gown's hem gently kisses the edge of the steps; the white satin and jade look alike.
Le clair de Lune a envahi l'appartement de l'Impératrice; en passant la porte, elle est toute éblouie;	Moonlight has invaded the empress's chamber; passing the door she is completely dazzled;

Car, devant la fenêtre, sur le rideau brodé de perles de cristal, on croirait voir une société de diamants qui se disputent la lumière;	For before the window, on the curtain embroidered with crystal pearls, a host of diamonds seems to vie with the light;
Et, sur le parquet de bois pâle, on dirait une ronde d'étoiles.	And, on the pale wood floor, one would call it a circle of stars.

Gautier retains the emotional economy of Li Bo's poem, if not its verbal abstemiousness. Though her title refrains from any explicit reference to feelings or situation, she feels obliged to explain the opulence of context suggested by a "jade staircase," so her protagonist becomes not just a courtesan but the empress herself. The rest of her poem, however, expands on the imagery of whiteness and light contained in the source and suggested by the qualities of jade and crystal, to the exclusion of even Li's oblique reference to the courtesan's plight. He speaks of the dew as penetrating, literally "invading" (*qin* 侵), her silk stockings, whereas Gautier describes the woman's gown as gently kissing the staircase, and the dew ("*rosée*," corrected from "*roses*" in the first version, which must have been based on a transcription error) simply glistens brilliantly. The "invasion" is transferred instead to the light of the full moon filling her quarters, which dazzles and confuses her perception: as she rolls down the crystalline blind, the prismatic effect of the light broken up by the honeycombed jewels creates a host of diamonds competing with the moonlight above and a circle of stars twinkling on the floor, reversing what might be their expected locations. Each image is as shattered as her hopes.

Gautier transforms elements of the original scene, so admired for the way in which it conveyed profound emotion without referring explicitly to it, into one that requires no explanation. Its unified miniature tableau reminded readers of the relatively new genre of prose poem, of which Aloysius (a pseudonym for Louis Jacques Napoléon) Bertrand (1807–1841) is generally considered the first practitioner. His volume *Gaspard of the Night* (*Gaspard de la Nuit*), published posthumously in 1842, contains a series of vignettes set in early modern Leiden and Dijon inspired by the etchings of Rembrandt van Rijn and Jacques Callot, each of which consists of a prose prologue and epilogue enveloping four verse couplets. Intrigued by this example, Charles Baudelaire began experimenting with the form in 1855, although he sought to depict scenes from contemporary life and eschewed Bertrand's uniform structure and commitment to versification. Baudelaire's prose poems appeared over the next decade in various journals and were published posthumously in 1869 in a volume that included a dedicatory preface addressed to his editor, Arsène Houssaye, with a description of what had motivated him: "Who among us has never, on those days full of ambition, dreamed of the miracle of a poetic prose, musical but without rhythm and rhyme, supple and abrupt enough to adapt itself to the lyrical movements of the soul, the ripples of daydreaming, the herky-jerky of consciousness?"[36]

Judith Gautier seems to have been susceptible to this dream as well. As she tells us in her memoir, her first literary effort consisted of something she wrote to distract her father from dealing with a childhood escapade that might have had dire consequences for her and her siblings. She describes the piece, which was titled "The return of the swallows" ("Le retour des hirondelles"), as "a sort of poem in prose, arranged in stanzas," and it succeeded in impressing Théophile Gautier—who thought her composition worthy of Heinrich Heine—sufficiently to exculpate the guilty crew.[37] Years later, after the publication of her *Book of Jade*, she recalls that her father was very interested in the Chinese translations she was working on with Ding Dunling and even tried to put some into verse. Although the drafts of his efforts had been lost, she retrieves from memory the concluding couplet from his version of "The virtuous wife," discussed above, whose heptameter replicated that of the Chinese original: "Before having been thus joined / If only I had known you!" (Avant d'être ainsi liée, / Que ne vous ai-je connu!) As she goes on to note:

> He liked my first book a great deal and did me the exquisite and surprising honor of writing a few lines about it à propos of Baudelaire's prose poem, "Blessings of the moon" ("Les bienfaits de la lune"): "We know nothing analogous to this delicious morsel other than the poetry of Li Taibo, translated so well by Judith Walter, where the empress of China drags through the beams of glistening moonlight, on her jade staircase, the folds of her white satin dress."[38]

Baudelaire's "Blessings of the moon" bears little resemblance to Gautier's "The jade staircase." Its five long paragraphs depict a moon obsessed with a young woman to the point that its "blessings" seem more like a curse. But her poem reveals the influence of the earlier example. Notable, for instance, is the fact that he also capitalizes "la Lune," and Baudelaire's moon descends "its cloud staircase" just as Gautier's empress ascends hers of jade. Her moonlight "invades" the bedroom, while his fills the room with "a luminous poison," a thinking and speaking light. First published in *Le Boulevard* on June 14, 1863, "Blessings of the moon," along with other examples of Baudelaire's prose poems, provided an important model for Gautier of unrhymed compositions that display both the grammatical shape of prose and the auditory features of poetry.[39] The appeal of the stanzaic structure to Gautier can be seen in the consolidation from seven to five strophes during the years 1866 to 1867. And, indeed, throughout the volume Gautier revises the spacing of her previously published versions and insists on a typography that creates short narrative blocks separated by generous amounts of white space.

"The jade staircase" would remain one of Gautier's most admired poems. Verlaine is said to have composed his "Clair de lune" after falling under its spell, and his poem was then adapted musically by Claude Debussy.[40] As late as 1900 the writer Henry Céard (1851-1924) would recall, echoing Gautier's account of her father's praise: "With *The Book of Jade* of Madame Judith Gautier, we come to know more profoundly the Chinese poets. It appears that the delicious morsel where the empress of China drags, among the rays, on her jade staircase sparkling diamond-like in the moon, the folds of her white satin gown, is a skillful orchestration of a poem of Li Bo, and a felicitous translation of a perfectly authentic piece."[41]

AUTUMN

The next section of *The Book of Jade* includes twelve poems whose theme, Autumn (L'Automne), is central to the Chinese poetic tradition. Their emotional register is generally appropriate to the melancholy associated with the season, although Gautier's Chinese heading, "Autumn poems on the joys of roaming the scene" ("Qiu shi you jing kuai le" 秋詩遊景快樂), does not provide the tonal cue we might expect. The section contains the other two poems attributed to Ding Dunling, both of which address the inevitability of aging and mortality, themes typically associated with the season. Some of the poems in this group are easily identifiable, such as "The pavilion of the young king" ("Le pavillon du jeune roi"[42]), after a well-known work by the early Tang poet Wang Bo 王勃 (649-676) titled "Prince Teng's tower" ("Teng wang ge" 滕王閣) and also translated by Hervey-Saint-Denys, in which a standard evocation of the transience of worldly glory is made more poignant by the poet's own short life. Gautier retains and even embellishes upon descriptions of the costly objects associated with pleasures of the past—the tower had been the scene of a famous banquet that Wang Bo described in another work—as well as the contrast between that fleeting human joy in the structure above and the enduring flow of the river below.

Several other poems in the Autumn section are less easily linked to a Chinese source, mostly because of uncertain transcriptions of poets' names or the greater liberties taken with text and title. Seven of the poems in the section were imported with minimal revision from Gautier's first variations published in 1864 and 1865, where she made no attempt to connect author with work. Some names like "Haon-Ti" may never be identified, but "Han-Ou," who becomes "Han Yu" and then "Heu-Yu" in later editions, is probably the late Tang poet Han Wo 韓偓 (844-923). Gautier's "A young girl's cares" ("Le souci d'une jeune fille") appears to be a blend of lines from the first and third poems in his set of three quatrains "Written in imitation of Cui Guofu's style" (Xiao Cui Guofu ti 效崔國輔體),[43] which gently limn the concerns of a solitary young woman. It also includes direct quotations from Hervey-Saint-Denys's translation of the same two poems in his anthology, as the italicized portions of her version demonstrate:

澹月照中庭	A pale moon shines on the inner courtyard.
海棠花自落	Crabapple blossoms tumble down on their own.
獨立俯閒階	I stand alone, head bowed, on empty steps.
風動鞦韆索	The wind stirs the rope and leather swing.
羅幕生春寒	Through gossamer bed curtains arises spring's coolness.
繡窗愁未眠	By the patterned window from sadness I haven't yet slept.
南湖夜來雨	On South Lake rain arrives at night,
應濕采蓮船	Certain to dampen the lotus-picking boat.

HERVEY-SAINT-DENYS

IMITATION DE TSOUI-KOUE-FOU	IN IMITATION OF CUI GUOFU
La lune éclaire silencieusement la cour intérieure;	The moon silently lights up the inner courtyard;

Les fleurs du *haï-tang* s'effeuillent d'elles-mêmes;
J'incline la tête, je fixe un regard distrait sur les marches du perron,
Où passent et se meuvent les ombres de la balançoire, que le vent tourmente.
La fraîche humidité du printemps m'a saisie, au fond de mes rideaux de soie;
Ma chambre solitaire est froide; je m'attriste et ne puis dormir.
J'entends, durant la nuit, venir la pluie, qui tombe avec bruit dans l'étang;
Hélas! mon petit bateau sera mouillé. Comment ferai-je, demain, pour cueillir des fleurs de nenuphar?

The flowers of the *hai tang* drop by themselves;
I bow my head and look distractedly at the steps of the staircase,
On which pass and move the shadows of the swing, buffeted by the wind.
The fresh dampness of spring has gripped me through my silk curtains;
My lonely room is cold; I'm saddened and cannot sleep.
I hear through the night the arriving rain, which falls loudly into the pond;
Alas! My poor boat will get wet. How will I manage tomorrow to pluck the lotus blossoms?

LE SOUCI D'UNE JEUNE FILLE

JUDITH GAUTIER

La lune éclaire la cour intérieure, je passe *la tête* par ma fenêtre et je regarde *les marches* de l'escalier.
Je vois le reflet du feuillage et aussi *l'ombre* agitée de *la balançoire que le vent* secoue.

Je rentre et je me couche dans mon lit treillagé; la *fraîcheur* de la nuit *m'a saisie*; je tremble dans *ma chambre solitaire*.

The moon lights up the inner court, I stick my head out the window and look at the steps of the staircase.
I see the reflection of foliage and also the swaying shadow of the swing stirred by the wind.

I go back and lie down in my latticed bed; the night's coolness has gripped me; I tremble in my lonely room.

| Et voici que *j'entends tomber la pluie* dans le lac! *Demain mon petit bateau sera mouillé*; *comment ferai-je pour aller cueillir les fleurs de nénuphar?* | And now I hear rain falling in the lake! Tomorrow my small boat will be all wet; how will I manage to go pluck the lotus blossoms? |

This significant overlap of words should dispel any doubts that Gautier consulted Hervey-Saint-Denys's translations, even as she chose not to use them consistently to produce her own "faithful" versions. In this case hers is both more concentrated and, thanks to the block-like stanzas, more fluid.[44] Her attribution to "Han-Ou" is a simple misreading of his "Han Ouo." The springtime setting of the poem is curious for placement in "Autumn," but the middle song of the original trio does in fact refer to the fall. The situation of a lonely, worried, sleepless woman clearly resonated with Gautier, a plight she presents with greater restraint than her scholarly predecessor. The poem's annotations observe how effectively the poems convey the speaker's loneliness through natural imagery rather than outright lament, without even mentioning the season that prompts sadness, and Gautier succeeds in doing the same.

Another poem in this section, "Autumn evening" ("Le soir d'automne"), which clearly belongs here and also focuses on the plight of a young woman, is attributed to a poet with an even more perplexing name, "Tché-Tsi."

La vapeur bleue de l'automne s'étend sur le fleuve; les petites herbes sont couvertes de gelée blanche,	The blue mist of autumn spreads across the river; white frost blankets the tiny grasses,
Comme si un sculpteur avait laissé tomber sur elles de la poussière de jade.	As if a sculptor had sprinkled jade dust on them.
Les fleurs n'ont déjà plus de parfums; le vent du nord va les faire tomber, et bientôt les nénuphars navigueront sur le fleuve.	The flowers have already lost their scent; the north wind will topple them, and soon the lotuses will float on the river.

Ma lampe s'est éteinte d'elle-mème, la soirée est finie, je vais aller me coucher.	My lamp has flickered out by itself, evening has ended, I will retire.
L'automne est bien long dans mon coeur, et les larmes que j'essuie sur mon visage se renouvellent toujours.	Autumn is so long in my heart, and the tears I wipe from my face keep coming back.
Quand donc le soleil du marriage viendra- t'il sécher mes larmes?⁴⁵	Oh, when will the sun of marriage dry my tears?

"Tché-Tsi" turns out to be the Tang poet Qian Qi 錢起 (722-ca.780), whose poem titled "In imitation of the old song 'Autumn nights are long'" ("Xiao gu qiu ye chang" 效古秋夜長) had also been translated by Hervey-Saint-Denys as "A memory of ancient times evoked by a long autumn night" ("Souvenir de l'Antiquité évoqué par une longue nuit d'automne").⁴⁶ His translation follows the original Chinese and literal version:

秋漢飛玉霜	Under autumn's Milky Way the jade frost flies;
北風掃荷香	The north wind sweeps away lotus fragrance.
含情紡織孤燈盡	Stifling her feelings, she spins and weaves as the single lamp flickers out.
拭淚相思寒漏長	She wipes her tears, longing for him; the cold water-clock drips endlessly.
檐前碧雲靜如水	Before the eaves the blue-green clouds are as still as water;
月弔棲烏啼雁起	Under the moon crows roost and crying wild geese rise up.
誰家少女事鴛機	In whose house does a young girl weave a mandarin duck at her loom,
錦幕雲屏深掩扉	The brocade bedcurtain and mica screen deep behind closed doors?
白玉窗中聞落葉	From within her white jade windows she hears the falling leaves:
應憐寒女獨無依	One should pity the poor young girl alone without support.

La Voie lactée brille dans un ciel d'automne, et le grésil voltige en parcelles de jade;	The Milky Way gleams in the autumn sky, and frost flies in bits of jade;
Le vent du nord emporte les parfums du nénuphar.	The north wind carries lotus perfumes.
Une jeune femme concentre ses pensées. Elle dévide de la soie, aux lueurs affaiblies de la lampe solitaire;	A young woman focuses her thoughts. She winds silk by the weak light of a solitary lamp;
Elle essuie des larmes; elle trouve bien longues et bien froides les heures de veillées que marque sa clepsydre.	She dries her tears; she finds the evening hours marked by the waterclock truly long and cold.
Les nuages purs, qui courent sur l'azur celeste, passent seuls devant sa demeure.	The pure clouds that race across the celestial azure pass alone in front of her dwelling.
La lune est le seul hôte de pavillon, où l'on n'entend que le croassement des corbeaux et le cri des oies sauvages.	The moon occupies the canopy alone, where one only hears cawing of crows and the cry of wild geese.
Quelle est-elle donc cette jeune femme qui brode sur son métier l'oiseau *youèn*?	So who is this young woman who embroiders on her loom the *youèn* bird?
Qui s'abrite à grand'peine dans ses rideaux de soie, derrière son paravent incrusté de nacre,	Who takes shelter with difficulty in silk curtains, behind her mica-encrusted screen,
Et qui, de sa chaste fenêtre, regarde tristement tomber les feuilles?	And who, sitting chastely at her window, looks sadly at the falling leaves?
Quelle est-elle cette jeune femme qu'il faut plaindre, qui souffre, et que personne ne soutient dans son isolement?	Who is this young woman whom one must pity, who suffers, supported by no one in her solitude?

Composed to a traditional song form, Qian Qi's poem is steeped in imagery and allusions that evoke the loneliness of a young woman thinking of someone far away. Its repeated images of "jade" must surely have confirmed for Gautier the aptness of her volume's title. The cold autumn sky (the character *han* 漢, which she takes to be the Han River—whose proper name she characteristically deletes—denotes here the Milky Way), white jade frost, and flowers' fading fragrance all set the scene by which a young woman, silently weeping and waiting, embroiders late into the night until the light of her single lamp flickers out. By contrast, the crows have roosted—presumably having found their mates—and the wild geese are stirring under a companionable moonlit sky. Qian Qi draws yet a second contrast with another young woman who has woven the image of the mandarin duck (*youèn*), a traditional symbol of conjugal bliss, probably for her bedspread, and who has retreated—presumably not alone—behind a brocade bedcurtain and mica screen. If she were to hear leaves falling outside her white jade window, he writes, would she not pity her less fortunate counterpart? Hervey-Saint-Denys notes that Qian Qi was employing a highly allusive poetic form that would be traditionally separated into two parts joined by a central couplet, which he indicates through his spacing. But he neither explicates the references nor distinguishes between the two women, and Gautier chooses to forgo them altogether. She reduces the ten lines of the original to six and distills its many images to two simple tableaux: the autumnal scene outside and the woman weeping in her room. As if tacitly evoking the original Chinese song title, "Autumn nights are long," Gautier uses that very image to describe with great poignancy the woman's sadness ("Autumn is so long in my heart"), and the cause of her grief could not be clearer. Whereas the original poem is narrated from the perspective of a third person observer, Gautier has also clearly shifted the point of view to the woman herself. Both the imagery and the situation retained from Qian Qi's poem must have resonated irresistibly for the young writer anxiously awaiting her own marriage.

TRAVELERS

The fourth section of *The Book of Jade*, Travelers (Les Voyageurs) is headed by the Chinese phrase "Floating on a flowery boat and reading lovely lyrics" (You hua chuan guan e ci 遊花船觀娥詞). At six poems it is the smallest group, and perhaps the most disparate, and none of the pieces evokes the promise of this heading. Two simply describe the difficulties of travel, and a third, "The big rat" ("Le gros rat"), attributed to "Sao-Nan" in 1867 and then Tao Han 陶翰 in 1902, but clearly based on a poem from *The Book of Songs* with that title ("Shuo shu" 碩鼠), decries a metaphorical rodent despoiling the grain of the speaker, who vows to escape to another country.[47] The remaining three focus on nostalgia for one's home, and of them "The inn" ("L'auberge") is based on what is probably the single most famous classical Chinese poem, a quatrain by Li Bo that has been translated countless times and is still memorized by schoolchildren today:

靜夜思	QUIET NIGHT THOUGHTS
牀前明月光	Before my bed the bright moon shines;
疑是地上霜	I took it for frost on the ground.
舉頭望明月	Raising my head I gaze at the bright moon;
低頭思故鄉[48]	Bowing my head I think of home.

Readers over the centuries have admired how a disarming simplicity of diction and imagery in this poem can suggest deep feeling with extraordinary effectiveness. A fixture of the classical poetic canon, it has traveled widely through popular culture, from textbooks to T-shirts, men's ties, and women's lingerie. The poem is easily memorized, thanks to its brevity (at only twenty characters, the shortest possible poem), the repeated rhyme (on all but the third line), the repetition of words ("bright moon" and "head"–unorthodox in a poem of such brief length), and the parallel structure of the last two lines ("raise head" / "lower head"). But it is also accessible because it rings so many familiar cultural bells. Because government bureaucrats were frequently transferred, farewell poems populate most Tang poets' collections and typically invoke the sorrow of parting. Here, however, there is no overt indication of emotion, nor even that the speaker is traveling. It is easy to imagine awakening in (as it turns out) a strange bed and being so initially disoriented that the moon's light on the ground is mistaken for frost, a misperception that explains psychologically what would otherwise simply function as a metaphor. Having realized the source of the light, the speaker then looks up at the moon, which countless travelers before and after would do, and which reminds him that those left behind are seeing the very same orb in the sky; it's a longstanding trope of separation and connection at the same time. And that leads him, looking down, to explain the context of the poem, as he thinks of home—in the poem, his "native province"—which he has journeyed from. Everyone in China had one—it is the phrase still used to ask where one is from—and attachment to it was deeply embedded. Li Bo thus successfully evokes a situation (a traveler away from home) and feelings (sadness and homesickness) without a single word of explicit emotion or contextual background, making it all the more powerful in its impact. As Hervey-Saint-Denys observes writing about this poem in his introduction, and echoing comments made by countless Chinese scholars, it would be difficult "to say less and at the same time to mean more."[49]

If in Li Bo's poem, as well as in Hervey-Saint-Denys's translation, there is no explicit reference to the fact that the speaker is traveling, Gautier leaves no doubt for her reader, from the very title and the first line:

Je me suis couché dans ce lit d'auberge; la lune, sur le parquet, jetait une lueur blanche.	I lay down on the bed at the inn; the moon cast a white gleam on the floor.
Et j'ai d'abord cru qu'il avait neigé sur le parquet.	And at first I thought it had snowed on the floor.
J'ai levé la tête vers la lune claire, et j'ai songé aux pays que je vais parcourir et aux étrangers qu'il me faudra voir.	I raised my head toward the bright moon, and I thought of the lands I would traverse and of the strangers I would have to see.
Puis j'ai baissé la tête vers le parquet, et j'ai songé à mon pays et aux amis que je ne verrai plus.	Then I lowered my head to the floor, and I thought of my own land and of the friends I'll never see again.

However unrecognizable her source might be by the title of her rendition, it is immediately apparent from its content, which retains the elements of the original, albeit significantly expanded. And while, unlike Li Bo, Gautier provides the context, like him she refrains from overt expression of emotion. Her preference for the shape of prose, rather than a lineated poem, is also clear.

WINE

For her fifth section, Wine (Le Vin), Gautier devised the heading "Discussing wine, making music, and presenting poems" ("Tan jiu zuo yue ti shi" 談酒作樂提詩). The eight pieces in the section unsurprisingly develop the traditional association of drinking with carpe diem sentiments. (Contemporary scholars have established the fact that the word *jiu* 酒 is more appropriately translated as "ale" rather than "wine," but the effects and associations remain the same.) A typical example is a quatrain "after" the poet Wang Wei 王維 (699–761), "To forget one's thoughts" ("Pour oublier ses pensées"):

Réjouissons-nous ensemble et remplissons de vin tiède nos tasses de porcelaine.	Let's rejoice together and refill our porcelain cups with warm wine.
Le frais printemps s'éloigne, mais il reviendra; buvons tant que nos lèvres auront soif,	The cool spring is gone, but it will return; let's drink while our lips are thirsty,
Et peut-être oublierons-nous que nous sommes à l'hiver de notre âge,	And perhaps we'll forget that we are in the winter of our years,
Et que les fleurs se fanent.[50]	And that the flowers are fading.

This is based on a "Song of farewell to spring" ("Song chun ci" 送春詞) included in one of Gautier's main sources, although it is only uncertainly by Wang Wei:

日日人空老	Day after day men age in vain,
年年春更歸	Year after year spring returns again.
相歡在尊酒	Let's delight together with a goblet of wine:
不用惜花飛[51]	No need to pity the flowers in flight.

Gautier retains the familiar imagery in the poem, which contrasts the inexorability of human aging with the cyclical recurrence of the seasons, but she rearranges the order of the original four lines to 3 2 1 4. Moving the third line about drinking to the beginning conveniently allows her to foreground her reason for assigning the poem to the section on wine, and she also expands the description of each image to create a fuller tableau.

This section includes a well-known early poem by Du Fu that celebrates a group of hearty drinkers, "Song of the eight immortals of drinking" ("Yin zhong ba xian ge" 飲中八仙歌), which Hervey-Saint-Denys had also translated.[52] Here the connection to a source is readily apparent, however remote; even her renditions of the names of the eight individuals are approximate at best. She titles her poem "To eight great poets who drank together" ("À huit grands poètes qui buvaient ensemble")[53] and recognizes that the twenty-two lines of Du Fu's heptasyllabic ancient-style poem would be more easily digested in smaller bits. So she breaks it down into eight separate sections, each addressed to one figure and containing the same number of lines Du Fu had devoted to each.

Of the eight drinkers in the poem, all friends of the poet, the most renowned was Li Bo, of whom Du Fu writes "Li Bo with one jug has a hundred poems" 李白一斗詩百篇, or in Gautier's version, "Li Taibo, you raise your cup, and before putting it back on the table you've made a hundred poems" ("Li-Taï-Pé, tu soulèves la tasse, et avant de la reposer sur la table tu as fait cent poëmes"). Four of the twenty-two lines in Du Fu's piece honor the poet with whom he is most often paired, more than any of the remaining seven, and it may be thus appropriate that of the eight poems in this section on "Wine" three are attributed to this most famous drinker in the Chinese poetic pantheon. They do not include some of Li's best known works on the topic, such as his "Drinking alone beneath the moon" mentioned above, but among them is a poem intriguingly titled "The porcelain pavilion" ("Le pavillon de porcelaine"):

Au milieu du petit lac artificiel s'élève un pavillon de porcelaine verte et blanche; on y arrive par un pont de jade qui se voûte comme le dos d'un tigre.	Amid a small artificial lake rises a green and white porcelain pavilion, reached by a jade bridge that arches like a tiger's back.
Dans ce pavillon quelques amis vêtus de robes claires boivent ensemble des tasses de vin tiède.	In this pavilion some friends clad in light gowns drink cups of warm wine together.

Ils causent gaiement ou tracent des vers en repoussant leurs chapeaux en arrière, en relevant un peu leurs manches,	They chat gaily or sketch verses while pushing their caps back and lifting their sleeves a bit,
Et, dans le lac où le petit pont renversé semble un croissant de jade, quelques amis vêtus de robes claires boivent, la tête en bas, dans un pavillon de porcelaine.[54]	And in the lake where the small inverted bridge looks like a jade crescent, some friends clad in light robes drink, their heads below in the porcelain pavilion.

Gautier's poem "after Li Bo" depicts a genial gathering of friends drinking wine and writing poetry in a setting that captures the height of stunning artifice: a pavilion of porcelain on a man-made lake over which arches a jade bridge. She describes the scene as if it were itself carved from a block of jade, with its frozen beauty doubled in the last stanza by a reflection of the group in the smooth surface of the lake below. This highly crafted representation of a craft at the height of exquisiteness and cultural value was to make the poem enormously popular with retranslators working after Gautier in a fin-de-siècle era that glorified artifice. But it is a curious work for a poet associated more commonly with spontaneity and artlessness.

There is, in fact, nothing called "The porcelain pavilion" in Li Bo's collected works, and its source is a poem by him titled "Banqueting at the Tao family pavilion" ("Yan Tao jia tingzi" 宴陶家亭子):

曲巷幽人宅	On a winding path to the hermit's dwelling,
高門大士家	Through lofty gates to the gentleman's house:
池開照膽鏡	The pond opens out, a mirror reflecting one's gall;
林吐破顏花	From the forest sprout flowers that make one smile.
綠水藏春日	Verdant waters harbor the springtime sun;
青軒祕晚霞	Azure porticoes store dusk's rosy clouds.
若聞絃管妙	If one's heard these marvelous pipes and strings
金谷不能誇[55]	Even Golden Valley cannot be praised.

Li Bo's piece typifies the sort of composition poets might toss off at a social occasion to praise the generosity of their host, who in this case remains unidentified. But his surname Tao 陶 is important because it is also the word for "pottery," and Gautier has chosen to read it as referring to the pavilion itself, though upgrading it to porcelain.[56] It is clear, moreover, that she has rewritten virtually the entire poem, while contracting it from eight lines to four. She has retained few of the original scenic details of a natural environment—winding path, tall gates, forest, flowers—and the green waters and azure balconies have become a jade bridge over what is now no longer a natural body of water but an "artificial lake." She has also transformed the many allusions of the original poem, which Ding would have explained to her, to similes more comprehensible to a French reader. The image of the arching tiger's back may be how she incorporates the original description of the pond from a legend as a "gall-reflecting mirror," clear enough to afford a view of one's bodily organs. The gall bladder was thought to be the seat of courage, which a tiger would plausibly embody, and one might imagine a green and white jade bridge replicating the stripes on its body.

The clarity of the pond sets up the final image of what is her main focus, the scene of poets drinking and composing verses to which Li Bo himself only obliquely alludes. For this Gautier and Ding draw on an annotation from the poet's collected works that explains the reference to Golden Valley, a place rich in natural beauties where an extravagantly wealthy man, Shi Chong 石崇 (249-300) gave a famously lavish party in 296 at which music was played, wine drunk, and poetry written under competitive circumstances, which increased the consumption of wine and produced a small collection of poems. Unlike Li Bo she brings their activities into the poem. But their poetic product becomes in Gautier's last line a visual artifact capturing both the actual scene above and the reflection of the inverted bridge (now a "jade crescent") and the friends themselves, upside down in the water's clear surface. And her repetition of phrases from the first two lines provides a formal analogue to the mirroring she describes.

In 1873 Gottfried Böhm (1845-1926) published the first (and only complete) retranslation of Gautier's volume, which offered versions in various German rhymed forms of the 1867 edition. It contains a typographically intriguing version of this poem.[57]

Gautier's "Porcelain pavilion" would become one of the favorites of later translators working from her text, and small wonder why. Replicating the shapes of a "Chinese style" structure rising above the lake and the arched bridge leading to it, as well as their reflection in the water below, and crafting his rhyme scheme

Das porzellanene Pavillon.

Nach Li-Tai-Pe.

Lieblich
Hell erhebt sich
Aus des Sees Mitte
Ein Haus, nach Chinesen Sitte.
Aus Porz'lan in grün und weißen Stücken.
Dorthin führen kühngeschwung'ne leichte Brücken,
Gleichend ganz des Tigers braun und gelb geflecktem Rücken, —
Lustig zechende Genossen, welche bunte Kleider tragen, —
Trinken klaren, lauen Wein aus Tassen in des Herzens Wohlbehagen,
Plaudern fröhlich, schreiben süße Verse, die erblühten tief in dem Gemüthe,
Stülpen rückwärts ihrer seidnen Kleider Aermel und vom Haupte fallen ihre Hüte.
Aber in des Wassers leicht bewegten, weiten, wonn'gen, schwanken Spiegelwogen
Gleichet einem Halbmond nur der Brücke umgekehrter, leichter Bogen
Und man sieht die lustig zechenden Genossen all, die bunten,
Fröhlich plaudernd sitzen dort, gestreckt das Haupt nach unten.
Und das Lusthaus selber auf des Felsens Rücken,
Aus Porz'lan in grün und weißen Stücken,
Aufgeführt nach Väter Sitte,
In des Sees Mitte
Abwärts senkt sich
Lieblich!

The Porcelain Pavilion

Lovely,
Rising bright
From lake's midst,
A house, in Chinese style,
Of porcelain tiles green and white.
Boldly arching, delicate bridges lead there
Like a tiger's brown-and-yellow striped back.
Joyously carousing fellows, clad in colorful clothing,
Drink clear warm wine from cups, their hearts at ease—
Chat gaily, write sweet verses blooming deep within their souls,
Sleeves of silken clothes tossed back, caps falling from their heads.
But in the water's gently rippled, broad, and dappled mirror-waves
Just the light, inverted bridge's arc, similar to a crescent moon,
And one sees all the joyously carousing fellows, colorful,
Seated, chatting gaily there, heads stretched downward.
The house of mirth itself, on the back of the rock,
Of porcelain tiles green and white,
Built in ancestral style,
Into lake's midst
Sinking down,
Lovely!

5.3 Gottfried Böhm, "Das porzellanene Pavilion," in *Chinesische Lieder aus dem* Livre de jade *von Judith Mendès* (Munich: Adermann, 1873), 82.
Courtesy of the British Library

to accord with the shape, Böhm's image renders graphically clear the formal artistry of her piece and the importance of the mirroring repetitions within it. The genial young poets and the natural world surrounding them have been captured as timeless art.

WAR

In choosing War (La Guerre) as her sixth theme, Gautier tapped into a topic with deep roots in the Chinese poetic tradition, one which extended back to *The Book of Song*'s complaints about the hardships of a soldier's life or celebrations of military victories.[58] Nor was warfare a stranger to poets during the Tang, whose government waged constant battles, both defensive and imperialistic, against neighbors across northern borders. Anyone sent to a bureaucratic post on the frontier may have witnessed battle scenes at first hand, and some poets Gautier drew on for her poems were known for their compositions inspired by that experience. But her distinctive perspective on the theme is signaled by the Chinese phrase with which she heads the section: "Weaving brocade with a palindrome to give as a poem" (Zhi jin hui wen gei shi 織錦回文給詩). This alludes to the story of Su Hui's palindromic poetic message woven in silk and sent to her absent husband, which Gautier had found so appealing as background for Li Bo's "Birdsong in the evening." In keeping with that inspiration, the seven poems she includes in this section focus primarily on departures of men for war or on the perspective of the women left behind, and three of them include references to women weaving or embroidering for their husbands.

The Su Hui legend clearly left its imprint on Gautier's poetic imagination, which roams especially freely in this section. It is impossible to identify the poet named Roa-Li, the putative source of Gautier's poem "Farewell" ("Les adieux"[59]), but the poem centers on a wife's parting gift to her soldier husband of a piece of silk on which, like her third-century counterpart, she has embroidered characters with a message to him to return as soon as possible. "The red flower" ("La fleur rouge"), attributed to Li Bo, rewrites in a more imagistically dramatic fashion the situation of the young wife working alone by her window depicted in his "Birdsong in the evening," alluding to the same story but concluding by recalling a second one as well:

En travaillant tristement près de ma fenêtre, je me suis piquée au doigt; et la fleur blanche que je brodais est devenue une fleur rouge.	While working sadly next to my window I pricked my finger; and the white flower I was embroidering became a red flower.
Alors j'ai songé brusquement à celui qui est parti pour combattre les révoltés; j'ai pensé que son sang coulait aussi, et des larmes sont tombées de mes yeux.	Then I thought suddenly of the one who'd left to fight the rebels; I imagined that his blood was also flowing, and tears fell from my eyes.
Mais j'ai cru entendre le bruit des pas de son cheval, et je me suis levée toute joyeuse; c'était mon coeur qui, en battant trop vite, imitait le bruit des pas de son cheval.	But I thought I heard the sound of his horse's hooves, and I stood up in joy; it was my heart that, beating too fast, sounded like his horse's hooves.
Je me suis remise à mon ouvrage près de la fenêtre, et mes larmes ont brodé de perles l'étoffe tendue sur le métier.[60]	I went back to my work next to the window, and my tears stitched pearls on the fabric stretched on the loom.

Gautier's inventiveness—the transformation of the white rose to red, the parallel streams of blood and tears, the painful mistaking of heartbeats for horse hooves—as well as her impulse to construct her poem on repetition with variations emerge clearly here. Her final innovation, however, rather than employing the Su Hui story of embroidered words, imports instead the concluding image from her translation of Zhang Ji's "The virtuous wife," in which she transforms two pearls from the original poem to the woman's tears.

Of the three poems in this section attributed to Du Fu, "Departure of a great leader" ("Le départ du grand chef") may have been inspired by the poet's well-known piece titled "The newlyweds part" ("Xin hun bie" 新婚別), in which a young wife laments her husband's departure for war the morning after their wedding. It had also been translated by Hervey-Saint-Denys.[61] For Du Fu the point could not be clearer than he puts it in his poem, "Marrying a woman to a man on campaign / is no better than leaving her by the side of a road" (Jia nü yu zheng fu / Bu ru qi lu pang 嫁女與征夫 / 不如棄路旁), but Gautier's message is the converse of his. Whereas Du Fu's wife urges her husband to focus on his military duties without her, her variation leaps into the realm of fantasy, for the woman joins him at the front after a swallow takes pity on her weeping by her western window; the bird's flight was so swift that in comparison his horse's gallop was as slow as a tortoise's. "The newlyweds part" may also have inspired another piece attributed to Du Fu titled "The spouse of a young woman arms herself for combat" ("L'époux d'une jeune femme s'arme pour le combat"[62]), in which a husband instructs his wife to leave her needle in the red silk on the loom and bring him his weapons for war.

The "western window" from "Departure of a great leader" reappears in the title of a quatrain attributed to Wang Changling, which is based on the poet's "Complaint from the women's quarter" ("Gui yuan" 閨怨):

閨中少婦不知愁	Within her chamber the young wife knows nothing of sorrow.
春日凝妝上翠樓	On a spring day fully made up she climbs the blue-green tower.
忽見陌頭楊柳色	She suddenly sees at the head of the path the color of the willows
悔教夫婿覓封侯[63]	And regrets having urged her husband to seek fame and glory.

Wang Changling was renowned for his mastery of heptasyllabic quatrains like this which rely on restraint and objective imagery to convey the pathos of a situation, and he composed several pieces based on traditional folk song titles that were classified as laments—by implication in the voice of women. Indeed, the two anthologies which Gautier most relied on include two songs, titled "Spring complaint from the Western Palace" ("Xi gong chun yuan" 西宮春怨) and "Autumn complaint from the Western Palace" ("Xi gong qiu yuan" 西宮秋怨), that harken back to the "Song of complaint" about the fan of the courtesan Lady Ban, who retired to the Western Palace when she lost favor with the emperor. These two poems appear closely before Wang Changling's "Complaint from the women's quarter" in the volumes and may account for the "western window" in Gautier's title. But her poem is not about Lady Ban, and, indeed, the *Explications of Ancient and Tang Poetry* explicitly notes that these are the words of the wife of a soldier on military campaign.

Gautier's "By the western window" ("De la fenêtre occidentale") follows this annotation but focuses on developing the implications she discerns in the last two lines of the poem:

À la tête de mille guerriers furieux, à la bruit forcené des gongs, mon mari est parti, courant après la gloire.	At the head of 1,000 raging warriors, to the wild clash of gongs, my husband departed, chasing after glory.
J'ai d'abord été joyeuse de reprendre ma liberté de jeune fille.	I was at first pleased to regain my liberty as a young girl.
Maintenant, je regarde de ma fenêtre les feuilles jaunissantes du saule; à son depart elles étaient d'un vert tendre.	Now I see from my window the yellowing willow leaves; when he left they were a delicate green.
Serait-il joyeux, lui aussi, d'être si loin de moi?[64]	Would he also be pleased to be so far from me?

For Wang Changling the poem charts a moment of painful discovery on the part of the young woman, whose realization of the significance of her husband's departure is prompted by the sight of the willows by the road outside the tower she has ascended on a lovely spring day. Willows symbolized the sorrow of parting in traditional poetry because the two words were homophones, and her encouragement of his ambitions, she now sees, has imperiled their happiness together. For Gautier there is a different sequence of discoveries that would be more plausible for a young Frenchwoman than one in Tang China: after initially delighting in her newfound "liberty" upon her husband's departure she suddenly wonders if he is also enjoying their separation. As was the case in "The mysterious flute," Gautier ignores the connection between willows and farewells, and for her the sight of the leaves would evoke sadness only if their yellowing signaled the passage of time; the spring setting of the original poem thus shifts to autumn. Her variation nonetheless retains the concluding open-ended quality of Wang's quatrain and reminds us of her own personal distress.

POETS

The seventh and last section of *The Book of Jade* is dedicated to the theme of Poets (Les Poëtes); its twelve poems equal those of "Autumn" in number and are exceeded only by the seventeen in "Lovers." As a writer herself whose Parnassian colleagues could not have been more obsessed with the mission and craft of poetry, Gautier must have found this topic appealing, and the Chinese heading for the section, "Poets prevail over a hundred rulers" (Shi jia sheng bai jun wang 詩家勝百君王) makes her point about the relative longevity and impact of literature versus politics. Two of the poems address the occasional challenges of writing. "Indifference to the mildness of summer" ("Indifférence aux douceurs d'été") laments a boredom that renders the speaker incapable both of appreciating the beauties of nature and of crafting poems, and "The white page" ("La feuille blanche") describes the agonies of the paper that remains blank while the inked brush dries, a desolation of inspiration that even a walk amid nature cannot revive.[65] It is, as Denise Brahimi observed, an "anguish" worthy of Mallarmé.[66] But most of the poems in the section evoke instead the miraculous potential of the written word, stimulated most often by wine, and the special character of poets themselves.

Gautier does not hesitate to make this point with whatever material she can find, as with one of the two poems in this section attributed to the Song-dynasty writer Su Shi, "The poet walks up a mountain enveloped by fog" ("Le poëte se promène sur la montagne enveloppée de brouillard"):

> Le poëte se promène lentement sur la montagne; au loin les pierres couvertes de brouillard lui semblent des moutons endormis.
> Il est arrivé en haut très-fatigué, car il a bu beaucoup de vin; et il se couche sur une pierre.
> Les nuages se balancent au-dessus de sa tête; il les regarde se rejoindre et voiler le ciel.

> The poet walks slowly up the mountain; from a distance the rocks covered in fog look like sheep asleep.
> He has arrived at the top very weary because he's drunk a lot of wine; and he falls asleep on a rock.
> The clouds dance above his head; he watches them merge and veil the sky.

Alors il chante tristement que l'automne approche, que le vent devient frais, que le printemps prochain est éloigné encore.	Then he sings sadly that autumn is nigh, that the wind is cooling, that next spring is still far away.
Et les promeneurs qui viennent admirer la beauté de la nature l'entourent en battant des mains, et ils s'écrient: "Voici assurément un homme qui est fou!"67	And the strollers who come to admire nature's beauty surround him, clapping their hands, and exclaim: "Here's a man who is certainly crazy!"

Su Shi is the only Song-dynasty poet represented in the 1867 edition of *The Book of Jade*. His inclusion testifies to the original research Gautier conducted with Ding's guidance in the library, since there were no previous translations into French available for her to consult. Su must have been a special favorite of her tutor because there are seven poems "after" his works in the volume, one-tenth of all the pieces, and an eighth was added in 1902. While it is difficult to identify source texts for some of them, which would have been composed almost two centuries later than the examples from the Tang that inspired most of Gautier's volume, in this case we have something that approaches an actual translation, even with her typical variations, more closely than anything else in the book:

登雲龍山	CLIMBING CLOUD DRAGON MOUNTAIN
醉中走上黃茅岡	Drunkenly I run up Yellow Thatch Hill.
滿岡亂石如群羊	On the whole hill jumbled rocks resemble flocks of sheep.
岡頭醉倒石作牀	Atop the ridge I tumble down drunk, with a rock as my bed,
仰看白雲天茫茫	And look up at the white clouds in the vast sky above.
歌聲落谷秋風長	My song's sound dips into the valley on long autumn winds.
路人舉首東南望	People on the path raise their heads to gaze southeast:
拍手大笑使君狂	They clap their hands and chortle aloud, "The prefect is daft!"68

Although Gautier collapses the seven lines of the original into five, each of which presents a self-contained vignette, she retains almost all the elements of Su Shi's poem, which is distinctive for its humorous self-deprecation, unusual imagery, and unorthodox formal properties, such as rampant repetition and an uneven number of lines—all of which befit the poem's context of composition. (As prefect of nearby Xuzhou 徐州 at the time, Su Shi was tapping into a tradition of officials who sought to assure the populace of their harmlessness.[69]) The simile of rocks to sheep is there in her version; so are the use of a stone for a bed and the concluding judgment, to clapped hands, of the passers-by. She does make changes: she identifies her speaker explicitly as a poet, who ascends the hill slowly rather than running; her sheep are sleeping; her clouds dance overhead; her poet's song is no longer carried by the autumn wind but rather about autumn, the wind, and the too-distant spring; and her observers have ventured out to seek the beauties of nature. As in other instances she deletes the specific place names in the title and the poem itself, which helps to de-exoticize her version, along with Su Shi's reference to himself by his official title, and she feels it necessary to explain something that would have been evident to a Chinese reader, that the poet's stupor is owing to an excess of wine. She wants her renditions to be accessible without annotation.

If Su Shi offers Gautier an image of a poet who is willing to poke fun at himself, an even more appealing image in this section is of someone whose drunken songs can move the gods. Her principal exemplar of this power is Li Bo, and a poem she attributes to him, "The sages dance" ("Les sages dansent"), opens the section and provides tropes that run through many of its other pieces. There is no work with this title in Li's corpus: Gautier appears to be improvising from elements from his "River song" ("Jiang shang yin" 江上吟), a heptasyllabic twelve-line poem that celebrates extravagantly an outing on a river boat at which music is performed, wine generously poured, and poetry composed:

木蘭之枻沙棠舟	With gunwales of magnolia, a pear-wood boat:
玉簫金管坐兩頭	Jade flutes and golden pipes seated at both ends.
美酒尊中置千斛	Fine wine in goblets is poured by thousands of barrels,
載妓隨波任去留	The singing girls sway to and fro with the waves.
仙人有待乘黃鶴	Celestial immortals can ride mounted on yellow cranes;
海客無心隨白鷗	The seaside traveler aimlessly follows white gulls.

屈平詞賦懸日月	Qu Ping's poetry hangs suspended with sun and moon;
楚王臺榭空山邱	The Chu kings' terrace and palace are but mountain ruins.
興酣落筆搖五嶽	Fully inspired I lower my brush and five March-mounts quake;
詩成笑傲凌滄洲	A poem complete I laugh with pride, reaching paradise.
功名富貴若長在	Deeds, fame, wealth, and honor: if they last forever,
漢水亦應西北流[70]	The Han River will also have to flow northwest.

Li Bo's poem actually inspired two different pieces by Gautier; her "River song" ("Chanson sur le fleuve") retains his title but is much shorter, and it appears earlier in the section on Wine:

Mon bateau est d'ébène; ma flûte de jade est percée de trous d'or.	My boat is made of ebony; my jade flute is pierced with golden tone holes.
Comme la plante qui enlève une tache sur une étoffe de soie, le vin efface la dispute dans le coeur.	Like the plant that removes a stain on silk fabric, wine erases discord in one's heart.
Quand on possède de bon vin, un bateau gracieux et l'amour d'une jeune femme, on est semblable aux Génies immortels.[71]	When one has good wine, a delicate boat and the love of a young woman, one resembles the immortal spirits.

Li Bo's original is rich with allusion, and Gautier ignores the many specific references that would have required annotation and discouraged a French reader, who would not need to know, for example, that the boat was constructed of two different woods: laurel magnolia for sturdiness and wild pear for buoyancy; her boat is simply made of ebony. The two kinds of wind instruments Li mentions as synecdoches for the musicians on board—one with holes (*xiao* 簫) and the other without (*guan* 管)—were not made of jade or gold but rather bamboo, but that conventional hyperbolic description was too appealing for her not to take literally. Gautier also happily retains the reference to Daoist spiritually advanced beings popularly known as "immortals" whose special status is signaled when yellow cranes fly them away.

In addition to its title, Gautier's "River song" retains some key elements of Li Bo's poem, however revised: the ebony boat, the wine, the women, and the immortals. But it is only in "The sages dance" that Gautier recoups Li's celebration of music and poetry and its celestial audience. In his poem Li alludes to a well-known anecdote from a Daoist classic to suggest that the legendary immortals (who had made their way into Gautier's "River song") are even less compelling as a model—because they depend on cranes to fly—than the freedom to follow without purpose gulls by the shore.[72] The story, which Ding must have recounted to her, features a man whose guilelessness enabled him to roam freely with the birds; he loses their trust when his father asks him to bring some home with him, and the gulls stay dancing in the sky. "The sages dance" transforms them into her receptive audience—cloud-borne sages who understand her better than humans on earth:

Dans ma flûte aux bouts de jade, j'ai chanté une chanson aux humains; mais les humains ne m'ont pas compris.	With my jade-tipped flute I sang a song to humans; but the humans did not understand me.
Alors j'ai levé ma flûte vers le ciel, et j'ai dit ma chanson aux Sages.	So I raised my flute to heaven, and I spoke my song to the Sages.
Les Sages se sont réjouis; ils ont dansé sur les nuages resplendissants;	The Sages were delighted; they danced on resplendent clouds;
Et maintenant les humains me comprennent, lorsque je chante en m'accompagnant de ma flûte aux bouts de jade.[73]	And now humans understand me, when I sing accompanying myself with my jade-tipped flute.

Typically, she fashions her extracted material into a miniature drama that concludes by returning to its beginning with a key variation—a key revision to her earlier version of the poem—for the power of her song has been transformed by its celestial audience. In both content and narrative arc it recalls the fascination with the transformative power of art that was implicit in "The mysterious flute." There the sound of a flute inspires the speaker to use a willow branch to play her own song, to which the birds then respond with theirs. Here she plays a song on her jade flute that is at first only understood by the sages, but their dancing then enlightens the initially uncomprehending human audience.

The second half of Li Bo's "River song" focuses on what poetry can do, opening with a comparison between the third-century BCE writer Qu Yuan 屈原, or Qu Ping 屈平, a loyal minister who was calumnied, forced into exile by his ruler, the king of the southern kingdom of Chu, and ended up committing suicide. The poetic rhapsody he is said to have penned before his death, Li Bo points out, has survived as long as the heavens, while his ruler's lofty buildings lie in ruins. Significantly, the annotation to this line in one of the anthologies Gautier consulted even provides the overarching theme for this section: it notes that one can easily see "how greatly [Qu Yuan's] poetic composition prevailed over the king of Chu."[74] Exhilarated by drink, Li Bo continues, he can set brush to paper and move even the most massive and stable of mountains, the five sacred peaks that symbolically marked the five directions of the empire (the four cardinal points plus center); with this poetry one can approach the immortality of the denizens of the Eastern Isles, Daoist transcendent beings. And his final couplet disdains the appeal of worldly fame and fortune: if they had any staying power, the Han River would be able to reverse its course and flow northwest rather than southeast.

None of these allusions would travel well into French translation, but Gautier picks up on the elements that are central to Li Bo's poem—music, wine, Daoist immortals, and poetry—as ingredients for an experience that transcends consciousness and time, and she intersperses them freely throughout this section. It is Li Bo himself who most frequently embodies their confluence, and it is therefore fitting that two of the poems in the section are drawn from the most renowned set of compositions linking two Tang poets: Du Fu's poems to or about his then much more famous colleague (in the 1902 edition she added a third). Although literary history in later centuries conferred on Du Fu the mantle of China's greatest poet, it was the better-known Li Bo whom the younger poet especially revered, and whose scrapes with the government worried him. More than a dozen of Du's poems address the older poet, praise him, and even dream of him. Gautier's "In praise of Li Taibo" ("Louange à Li-Taï-Pé") may be based loosely on Du Fu's "Thinking of Li Bo on a spring day" ("Chun ri huai Li Bo" 春日懷李白), which compares Li to other respected poets, stresses the unrivaled uniqueness of his poetry, and longs for the day when they might drink a goblet together.⁷⁵ Gautier dispenses with the various allusions to other poets and simply describes Li as "the first among men" (le premier des hommes) whose language is poetry itself, as song is that of the birds. Du Fu in her version conveys his "adoration" for Li "from the shadows" of someone unknown (De celui qui t'admire dans l'ombre, reçois cette adoration inconnue). And picking up on Li Bo's own description of the inspirational effects of drinking in "River song," she also writes of him that "when you drink golden wine, poetic ideas come to you on the cloud of intoxication" (Lorsque tu bois le vin doré, sur le nuage de l'ivresse te viennent des idées de vers).

"Dedicated to Li Taibo the twentieth day of the twelfth month" ("Envoi à Li-Taï-Pé: Le vingtième jour du douzième mois") is loosely based on the opening of Du Fu's "Twenty couplets sent to Li Bo the twelfth" ("Ji Li shi er Bo er shi yun" 寄李十二白二十韻). Although Gautier has mistaken the references to Li Bo's place in family birth order and the number of rhymed couplets in the poem for a nonexistent date, she gets the opening allusion right. Du Fu's poem begins:

昔年有狂客	In years past there was a crazy guy
號爾謫仙人	Who named you "the banished immortal."
筆落驚風雨	Your brush once lowered roused wind and rain;
詩成泣鬼神⁷⁶	A poem complete made gods and spirits weep.

As the Qing-dynasty editor tells us, Du Fu's first couplet alludes to the story that when He Zhizhang 賀知章 (ca. 659-744) met Li Bo, he named him "heaven's banished immortal." Both He and Li were among the "eight immortals of drinking" Du Fu had celebrated in the poem discussed earlier. And the succeeding couplets go on, in increasingly allusive language, to celebrate Li Bo's fame and their friendship, to lament the hardships he suffered while in exile (he had been implicated in a rebellion), and to hope for a resolution. Gautier's version is content understandably to focus on the opening images, into which she sprinkles some from other poems as well:

Ton nom est Ti-Sié-Jen, la goutte d'eau intarissable, et tu es au rang des Sages immortels.	Your name is Ti-Sié-Jen, the inexhaustible drop of water, and you are the equal of the immortal Sages.

La sceptre du Fils du Ciel est moins puissant que ton pinceau; moins fort est le sabre du guerrier.	The emperor's scepter is less powerful than your brush; less strong is the warrior's saber.
Dans le ciel pur de l'été rien ne fait présager l'orage; mais tout à coup le vent amasse des nuages, et la pluie se précipite.	In the pure summer sky nothing predicts the storm; but suddenly the wind gathers clouds, and the rain rushes down.
De même sur le papier sans tache le souffle de ton génie fait pleuvoir de noirs caractères; ce sont les larmes de ton esprit qui coulent silencieusement de ton pinceau.	Similarly on the blank paper the breath of your genius rains black characters; these are the tears of your spirit that flow silently from your brush.
Et, lorsque la pièce de vers est finie, on entend autour de toi les murmures d'admiration des Génies invisibles.[77]	And when the poem is finished, we hear around you murmurs of admiration from the invisible Spirits.

This is one of the few instances where she retains a term in its (somewhat garbled) romanized form: Ti-Sié-Jen" corresponds to Du Fu's *zhe xian ren*, or "banished immortal," which Gautier provides with a new meaning, an "inexhaustible drop of water" equal to the immortals themselves. Her second line introduces the notion that literature prevails over worldly might, as already seen in Li Bo's "River song," a power suggested by the ability to stir up wind and rain that Gautier retains from Du Fu. She then provides a parallel to this image with the metaphor of inked words falling on white paper as the silent tears of the poet's brush, which—as had also been the case in "River song"—have the power to move the spirits of nature.

In referring to Li Bo's ability to evoke another realm, Du Fu was deploying images associated with the "banished immortal" by others as well as himself. For Gautier there could not be a more apt embodiment of a notion that was as hoary in classical China as in the West, that writing endures and can transcend the limits of time. And so her final poem, attributed to Li Bo,[78] celebrates "The eternal characters" (Les caractères éternels[79]) that tumble onto paper like plum blossoms on snow. Unlike the blossoms, and the other objects of nature to which they can be compared—mandarin oranges carried in a woman's sleeve or white frost under the sun—she concludes, "the characters I let fall on the paper will never be erased" (les caractères que je laisse tomber sur le papier ne s'effaceront jamais). Surely, she hoped, her own *Book of Jade* might enjoy the same fate.

CHAPTER 6

"Brushing up against the famous"

Judith Gautier's Artistic Connections

In her 1867 *Book of Jade* Judith Gautier found a way to introduce Chinese poetry to a French public poised to receive it, even if ambivalent about what it found. For her the word "impossible" truly did not exist. Over the next several decades she displayed a similarly remarkable openness to and embrace of new developments in other literary and artistic domains. As Anatole France observed, she had "a sense of all the arts."[1] Her visionary enthusiasms expressed themselves in prolific publications and a web of personal relationships that ensured the public's familiarity with both her byline and her biography. In addition to revealing her talents across a multitude of genres, Gautier knew, impressed, or influenced an extraordinary range of European, American, and Asian cultural luminaries. Despite her own modest disclaimer about the intrinsic interest of her life, that it "would scarcely be worth recounting had it not often brushed up against those of very famous artists," there are good reasons others deemed it "a novel worth recounting."[2]

Gautier wrote more than twenty-five books between 1867 and 1902, which included historical novels set in places like Japan, India, Palestine, and Persia; short stories, plays, poetry, and ethnographies; and scores of articles and reviews. If *The Book of Jade* was the work that on later reflection she realized had given her the most pleasure, it may have been because it was the only one that was not driven primarily by financial need. Within a year she had expanded her repertoire from Chinese poetry to fiction, whose episodic publication provided welcome income. In March 1868 *La Liberté* announced the forthcoming serialization of a novel titled *The Imperial Dragon* (*Le Dragon impérial*), which it predicted was "destined to be a great success. It has the double advantage of being as entertaining as a novel of adventures and as detailed as a historical novel." The periodical further tantalized its readers by calling attention to the "eminently remarkable work by a young woman of twenty years who knows Chinese like a mandarin and already possesses the style of her father the great colorist." (Gautier was almost twenty-three at the time.) The novel appeared in thirty-three installments, and with its last chapter *La Liberté* proclaimed it a great success, owing to "the dramatic violence of the action, the bold strangeness of the characters, the splendor of the descriptions, and the beauty of its style. This novel establishes the place of Madame Judith Gautier among our foremost novelists."[3] Alphonse Lemerre published it in book form the following year.

The Imperial Dragon paints a very different China from that of *The Book of Jade*. Set in the seventeenth century during the reign of the Qing emperor Kangxi— Gautier specifies the year 1676 using the Chinese calendar—it features a peasant who is recognized, thanks to the dragon-shaped shadow he casts, by the two other main characters, his fiancée and a scholar, as destined for rule. Told from the scholar's point of view, the novel tracks the trio's adventure-packed journey to the capital of Beijing and attempted rebellion, which is ultimately thwarted and leads to their collective, bloody demise. While not based on actual events, the novel may be drawing from accounts of the recent Taiping civil war—about which Gautier had written, with Ding as informant—and perhaps also from his account of *The Peach Blossom Fan*, a well-known traditional drama set during the fall of the Ming dynasty.[4]

The imagined China of *The Imperial Dragon* seemed as real as, and was no doubt preferable to, the actual country for the famous readers who enjoyed it. Judith Gautier's vivid, violent, and intrigue-packed narrative and her colorfully detailed depictions of the Chinese capital and the Forbidden City were especially admired. They were, regardless of some skeptics, surprisingly accurate and precise.[5] Mallarmé was given a copy as a gift from his friend Henri Cazalis and deemed it "a great marvel." Villiers de l'Isle-Adam compared it to "a world's fair and a real voyage to Asia," a "literary discovery of China" whose "prodigious sense of local color was more effective and profound than any other experience."[6] Anatole France praised the power of her imagination and a "style limpid in its brilliance."[7] For Rémy de Gourmont it was "surely a work of genius, and surely one of the three or four most beautiful literary works ever produced by women." For him the derivation of her talent was eminently clear: its lack of sentimentality in depicting deep passions and the horrors of war proved that there was "the heart of a man, indeed a superior man, in this woman that prolongs for us the marvelous gifts of her father."[8]

One of the novel's proudest and most enthusiastic fans was in fact Théophile Gautier, despite the estrangement caused by her marriage to Catulle Mendès. In a conversation with Edmond de Goncourt her father compared it favorably to Flaubert's 1862 historical novel; it is "*Salammbô* without the heaviness." He goes on to describe his daughter as "the most amazing creature in the world, a marvelous brain," but a brain that existed as if "on a plate" unconnected to her person and behavior, leaving her "as childish and silly as possible: 'She is but an instrument, a tool before a sheet of paper.'" Four years later Goncourt records that Gautier "took me aside to speak extensively and tenderly about *Le Dragon impérial* and his daughter. One senses that he is proud of having created this brain," which has been able to understand in such depth and scope the great historical epochs of the world. But if responsible for her existence Gautier also disavows responsibility for his daughter's gifts, even as he barely credits her. "She created herself, she alone made who she is, we raised her like a little dog that is allowed to run about under the table; no one, in other words, taught her to write."[9]

Théophile Gautier found it difficult to recognize in his daughter the intensity of effort on which he and his Parnassian colleagues liked to pride themselves. But though Judith may have been able to write with apparent ease, she had not shirked the research necessary to produce her work. Ding Dunling (her father's other pet) had taught her about China and was Gautier's most important personal source for the historical background, characterization, and form of *The Imperial Dragon*, where she tapped into the poetic imagination already on display in her first book. Having learned from Ding that traditional Chinese novels could include a great deal of poetry, she begins each chapter with a poetic epigraph and embeds individual poems throughout the text. Of the fifty poems in the novel, six were taken from *The Book of Jade*.

Gautier returned the favor by promoting Ding's literary career. In addition to including three of his poems in *The Book of Jade*, she published another in both romanized Chinese and French translation, his article on the "Chinese New Year," and a serialized tale titled "The Justice of the Son of Heaven." Although the latter two bore his byline, both were probably penned by her. Gautier and Ding also went together to meet the first Chinese emissaries to Paris. A short piece in the *Revue des lettres et des arts* in January 1869 describes a visit by Gautier, fluently speaking Chinese and accompanied by Ding, to meet two members of the young

Chinese delegation making their tour of Europe. Gautier herself describes this encounter with Zhi Gang and Sun Jiagu in some detail in an article published the following week. She writes that, having been instructed by Ding, she greeted her hosts on bended knee with fists raised together overhead, a gesture of courtesy reciprocated by the Chinese, who then urged their guests to be seated on couches under a canopy of silk "in a parlor lavishly decorated in contemporary style with which the exotic garb of the two mandarins contrasted most strangely." After desultory conversation about current affairs in China they soon turned to the topic of literature and poetry. The two mandarins, she observes, were true literati: "they love serious works above all, and when the poet Tin-tun-ling remarked to them that in France one neglects the serious side of literature for the frivolous, the special envoys politely refused to believe him." Intrigued by aspects of European music (Why is the violin played on the shoulder rather than the knee?), they are especially astounded by trains that "depart as soon as they arrive," velocipedes (an early form of bicycle which had just appeared in Paris in 1863), and the French language itself, with its peculiar distinctions of gender.[10]

Ding Dunling's brief appointment in 1870 as drill instructor for Hervey-Saint-Denys at the School of Vernacular Languages probably provided an opportunity for Gautier to meet the distinguished sinologist. Although she had not chosen to rely on his translations in producing most of her variations, she did turn to his *Poetry of the Tang Dynasty* as an important source for her discussion of Chinese poetry during the 1870s. This can be seen in a section called Poetry and Poets (Poésie et Poëtes), part of a much longer chapter titled "The Chinese" (Les Chinois) that takes up almost two-thirds of a book appearing in 1879, called *Foreign Peoples* (*Les Peuples étranges*). Gautier had published most of the sections as *Notes on China* (*Notes sur la Chine*) on topics ranging from music to medicine to funerary practices, under the pseudonym F. (for Ferdinand) Chaulnes in the *Journal officiel* from 1875 to 1876.[11]

The opening paragraph of the Poetry and Poets section makes clear how captivated Gautier was by legends of the genre's power: "In China, poetry is the magic key that opens all doors, the sign of nobility before which even the most elevated will bow down, the celestial privilege that makes one to whom it is entrusted untouchable." Poetry can earn the trust and friendship of a ruler, the most enviable positions, a peasant's worship, and an executioner's release. No wonder, then, that "the Middle Kingdom is the paradise of poets."[12] What follows is a history of the Chinese poetic tradition going back before *The Book of Songs* which is largely based (without attribution) on the extensive historical essay provided by Hervey-Saint-Denys as an introduction to his volume of translations. She credits the scholar for having put the names of Chinese poets "on everyone's lips" and even identifies a few of the poems she includes as having been translated by him, but most of the examples in the essay are either unacknowledged, lightly revised versions of his pieces or her own variations from *The Book of Jade*. Gautier repeats some of Hervey-Saint-Denys's errors—such as the dates for Li Bo and Du Fu—and adds some transcription mistakes of her own; she also embellishes her account with invented dialogues and an imagined poetry contest between the two great poets. Of the two, like Hervey-Saint-Denys she believes that Du Fu's "talent will certainly be preferred by all European readers,"[13] and she therefore devotes the lion's share of her attention to his biography. However unmindful she may have been of scholarly niceties, by this time Gautier had acquired a more systematic understanding of Chinese poetic history to supplement the introduction Ding had provided.

VICTOR HUGO AND RICHARD WAGNER: MUSE, DISCIPLE, "HYPHEN," OR MORE

Meanwhile Gautier's engagement in the larger cultural sphere led to intimate friendships with two towering figures, Victor Hugo and Richard Wagner. That both men were significantly closer in age to her father than to her has been duly noted by biographers, some of whom have explored the psychological implications of the possible attraction. That they were also well-known womanizers is evident in the many books that discuss their multiple paramours. Whether or not she was entangled in their amatory nets—she referred to herself rather as a "disciple" of each—she may, at the least, following the subtitle of one biography, have been their muse.[14]

Victor Hugo had greatly appreciated her flattering rendering of his name inscribed in Chinese on the copy of *The Book of Jade* that she sent to him, "an exquisite work" which he praised in language characteristic of his time:

> You are the daughter of a poet and the wife of a poet, daughter of a king and wife of a king, and yourself a queen. More than queen, Muse.
> Your dawn smiles on my shadows.
> Thank you, madame, and I kiss your feet.[15]

6.1 Victor Hugo, photograph by Nadar.
BnF Gallica

He also admired *The Imperial Dragon*'s "powerful and graceful art" and its evocation of a distant China as far away as "a journey to the stars." She paid him the homage he expected in their correspondence and meetings. With her husband Catulle Mendès she went to Brussels to visit him after he had left his exile in Guernsey in October 1869, and she was at the Gare du Nord with thousands of others for his triumphant return to Paris in September 1870. There were dinners together with Catulle, with her increasingly ill father, with her mother, and occasional encounters *à deux*.

Gautier's adulation of Hugo was public, one she shared with a population that honored his literary accomplishments as well as his political principles, but his fondness for her was expressed in rather more intimate terms. In July 1872 Hugo published a sonnet dedicated to her and titled "Hail, goddess, the dying man salutes you " (Ave, Dea, Moriturus te Salutat), which—as befits the title—focuses on the contrast between his age and her beauty while claiming that "our two destinies are closer to each other / than one would think" (nos deux destins sont plus près l'un de l'autre / Qu'on ne croirait). Hugo was seventy at the time, Gautier not quite twenty-seven. The poem was named one of the hundred most beautiful sonnets in French.[16] Two more intimate poems from Hugo's pen in April 1874 suggest a deeper entwinement. The first, "To Madame J." (À Madame J.) opens by calling her "Venus, / the beauty of beauties" (Vénus / Belles des belles) and closes: "You are marble inhabited / by a star" (Vous êtes un marbre, habité / Par une étoile) And the second, "The snow that is not cold" ("Nivea non frigida"), suggests that such feminine pallor can be deceiving, "and one can be on fire / even though made of snow" (et que l'on peut être de feu, / Étant de neige).[17]

These three poems, plus scattered letters and entries in Hugo's personal notebooks suggesting in code that they kissed, have led many to assume that there must have been more. One biographer concludes from the tone of their correspondence and his poems to her that it would "be surprising if there had been no love affair between Victor Hugo and Gautier's elder daughter."[18] Hugo's long-time mistress Juliette Drouet was certainly displeased when she learned about the poems and considered infidelity "already confirmed by the sole fact of desire."[19] The liaison, if it ever occurred, was in any event not of long duration, nor did it leave a lasting imprint on either life.[20] Hugo soon moved on to an affair with Drouet's maid, and Gautier's writings are silent on the topic. But Hugo did look after her. Well aware of her persistent financial difficulties, in 1881 he made the same request of the French government that he had submitted on behalf of her father years before—that she be granted a pension—and succeeded again.[21] When he died in 1885, she appeared shortly after to make a much-admired wax death mask of her revered "Master."

Richard Wagner was the other "Master" in her life. Neither man thought much of the other—unsurprising in light of their outsized egos. The admiration she and Catulle Mendès shared for Wagner "remained as intolerable . . . to Hugo as their admiration for Hugo was to Wagner."[22] It is difficult to imagine which of them would have been more chagrined to learn that Gautier trained her dog Grimace to jump up on her hind legs when she heard each of the great masters' names.[23] Her esteem for the German composer was the only sentiment that came close to competing with her passion for Asia: "two cults, in fact, absorbed her life, enriched every moment, and sustained her spirit above trivial contingencies and petty worries: enthusiasm for Wagner and love of the Far East."[24] Gautier famously stated in a 1910 interview, "I am a Chinese woman." But she also once firmly declared, "I was born a Wagnerite."[25]

If her interest in China and Japan was both visionary and antiquarian, in promoting Wagner's work she was a modernist, unequivocally embracing what he proclaimed as the "Music of the Future" (la musique de l'avenir).[26] Even before attending her first concert she displayed a premonition of his talent, as recounted in her memoirs. In 1861, when she was but sixteen, she and her father were awaiting her mother outside one of Wagner's first performances of *Tannhäuser*, where they could hear the crowd loudly blowing hunting whistles, the equivalent of hissing. When the composer Hector Berlioz passing nearby noted this negative reception gleefully to Théophile Gautier, Judith didn't hesitate to chide him, without knowing who he was: "One can see that you are talking about a colleague. . . . And that without a doubt it's a question of a masterpiece." Though her father had to scold her for her rudeness, he was secretly amused by her discernment and also proud that he had been one of the first to appreciate the German composer's work.[27] She wrote that her first encounter with Wagner's music was both fascinating and terrifying: "I felt as if on the edge of an abyss, the bottom of which I would surely have to touch: it was a vertigo of the mind."[28] She was soon a regular fan herself, with her sister Estelle, at the Sunday Pasdeloup concerts, as was Catulle Mendès. In September 1868 the couple went to Baden for a performance of *Lohengrin*, after which she published the first of three articles explaining and defending the German composer's innovations to a hostile French public and praising him as "the greatest musical genius of our era."[29] As a cartoon by Félix

6.2 Richard Wagner, photograph by Franz Hanfstaengl (1804-1877).
BnF Gallica

Régamey that appeared on December 12, 1868, in *Paris-Artiste* makes clear, though the craze for Wagner was widely shared by the avant-garde writers of the day, she was identified as among his most ardent supporters. The cartoon is labeled "The apotheosis of M. Pasdeloup," and the muse depicted "in Japanese garb placing a crown on the head of Pasdeloup is Madame Judith Gautier, who had just published *The Book of Jade* [a copy of which she holds in her left hand]. The hands of

6.3 "The Apotheosis of M. Pasdeloup," cartoon by Félix Régamey, *Paris-Caprice*, December 12, 1868, in John Grand-Carteret, *Richard Wagner en caricatures* (Paris: Larousse, [1892]), 211.
BnF Gallica

those applauding Wagner's music are chasing away firemen and their whistles. All young artists, like all young writers, supported the composer of *Tannhäuser*."[30]

Gautier sent her articles to Wagner himself for corrections of her "errors," and she was stunned to receive an appreciative response from him, in early November 1867, expressing a hope that he might visit Paris and meet her. When that didn't happen, she used a commission she and Catulle Mendès received to report on an international art exposition in Munich as a pretext to suggest that they might stop on the way at his home in Tribschen, in Lucerne, Switzerland. To her surprise, in early July 1869 Wagner graciously took her up on this proposal: countless other fans had sought to visit him without success, and he was rumored to be surrounded by a vast harem of women "of all countries and all colors" and to be extremely averse to guests.[31] Gautier and Mendès traveled to Lucerne with their friend and equally ardent Wagnerian Villiers de l'Isle-Adam and stayed for over a week in July 1869, making a second stop on the way back to Paris in September. Her account of the trip, published in 1909, proved wildly popular; it went to five editions and was translated into English.[32] As many have noted, she rather comically fails throughout to mention the presence of her husband, with whom relations were already strained, referring explicitly and quite frequently only to Villiers. Mendès, for his part, returned the favor by omitting her from his correspondence about the journey as well. Among other distractions, Augusta Holmès had shown up in Munich, too.

Gautier's recollections of her encounter with Wagner are nothing if not hagiographical, as she struggles to explain "this prodigious genius to those of another era." He is "the Master" and "the Great one," a "Jupiter on Olympus," whom she and her companions revere as "apostles and disciples." He is "the greatest god of art," indeed, "evidently superhuman." His talents comprise "Apollo and Orpheus blended into a single lyre" and transcend those of Homer, Aeschylus, Goethe, Beethoven, and even Shakespeare. His home is "sacred soil," a "temple of genius," and his workspace a "sanctuary" and "the holy of holies." But her reminiscences also suggest the genuine warmth of Wagner's hospitality toward his guests, whom he would later refer to as a "dear Trinity" worthy of being named "chevaliers" of "the Holy Guard of the Grail." The composer invites them for a light supper almost every evening, sometimes opening for them one of the many bottles of champagne sent him by his "good friend" Chandon. He plays excerpts on the piano for them from his works, and Gautier even tries her hand at a duet for four hands with the great man himself.[33]

She also became a confidante of Wagner's mistress Cosima von Bülow, who had already borne a daughter and son by him to add to the three daughters she brought from her marriage to the pianist and conductor Hans von Bülow. Cosima had refrained from seeking a divorce, thinking that her father, the composer Franz Liszt, who had been von Bülow's teacher, was opposed. While in Munich, Gautier decided to meet directly with Liszt and discovered that he in fact did not object to the idea, a finding she quickly reported back to Tribschen. She and Mendès helped celebrate the subsequent divorce in July 1870 on their return from another trip to Munich for a performance of *The Valkyries*, and the celebration of Beethoven's centenary; after the August 1870 marriage Gautier was named godmother of the couple's son Siegfried.

The Franco-Prussian War erupted almost immediately, and the German composer's insensitive anti-French comments led to a brief hiatus in their relations, which Mendès, though remaining devoted to the music, never resumed in person. But Gautier made three more trips to the Wagners after the peace, each time in the company of the Dutch pianist and composer Louis Benedictus (1850–1921), a descendant of the philosopher Spinoza, who like von Bülow had been a student of Liszt. He would remain inseparable from Judith Gautier for the rest of her life though she rejected his repeated entreaties to marry him, having found one marriage to be enough.[34] The next visit, in August 1876, included attending the first Bayreuth festival, for which Wagner conducted three complete cycles of *The Ring of the Nibelungen*. Gautier and Benedictus returned in September 1881 and then again in July 1882 for a performance of *Parsifal*, for which she would eventually produce a French translation published in 1893, working from Cosima's rough draft.[35]

A cache of thirty-five letters from Wagner, sixty-eight letters from Cosima, and scattered reminiscences recorded by her companion Suzanne Meyer-Zundel provided, once again, rich fuel for speculation about the nature of her relationship with a famous man. Almost all of her own letters to him were destroyed. Many of Wagner's early letters to her, through 1873, were also addressed to Mendès, but the tone of his correspondence to her alone for the two years after her visit in 1876, when he was composing *Parsifal*, shifts markedly in level of intimacy and is rife with passionate declarations of her physical attractiveness and his amorous desires. As the editor of Wagner's letters to Gautier comments, "for some there is no doubt that Judith was Wagner's mistress."[36] But others are convinced that she was more than a little embarrassed by the excesses of Wagner's effusions and certainly disappointed by his repeatedly negative opinion of the quality of her friend Benedictus's musical compositions. She could also quite reasonably have become annoyed by Wagner's incessant requests, which he jokingly always refers to as the "serious" matter of their correspondence, to send him precious goods from Paris: creams and perfumes for himself and his bath (he was particularly fond of essence of rose, and each scented letters to the other with rose water[37]), sachets for his dresser drawers, fine leather gloves, silks and satins (with color and yardage specified) for his furniture, and numerous gifts for his wife and daughter, no expense to be spared. However passionate and studded with exclamation points Wagner's declarations of love for Gautier may have been, there is little evidence that they were more than rhetorical expressions of a "cerebral passion" or that she ever reciprocated.[38] He acknowledged her advice on "Eastern thought and culture, contributing to the ambience" of *Parsifal* by sending her a copy of the text, thus making her the first person to whom he ever entrusted his work,[39] but she never succeeded in persuading him to write an opera based on Asian themes. A gilded Buddha sat in his office, after all, but although she shipped him several classical Vedic and Buddhist texts, he never turned toward Eastern religion for sources.

Gautier remained what she called Wagner's "best disciple," and she was indeed considered "the Wagnerian high priestess in France," who "did more than anyone else to promote his music in France."[40] Back in Paris she organized a celebrated series of six Wagnerian "evenings" in 1880, and later in life she fashioned elaborately costumed marionettes of wax or clay to perform Wagner's operas in her apartment and elsewhere.[41] Both of her residences paid tribute to the composer as well. Gautier fell in love with the coast of Brittany thanks to Albert Lacroix, Victor Hugo's editor to whom she'd given a novella to publish. He lost the manuscript and offered her by way of apology a vacation on one of the properties he had developed in St. Énogat, next to Dinard and west of St-Malô on the mouth of the Rance River. Gautier was so charmed by the location that she borrowed money to buy land and build a house for herself, which she named Birds' Meadow (Le Pré des Oiseaux), after the German poet Walther von der Vogelweide (1170–1230), "Walther of Birds' Meadow." He figures in two of Wagner's operas,[42] and Walther was also the German equivalent of Gautier and her first pseudonym. Completed in 1877, Gautier's house rose just steps above the beach of St. Énogat and stands there today. Gautier received notable visitors regularly there; the Wagners never made it

6.4 Judith Gautier's house at St. Énogat, Le Pré des Oiseaux.
Author's photograph

despite repeated invitations, but Claude Debussy composed *La Mer* while her guest.[43]

Gautier also became a renowned hostess at the Paris apartment she bought at 30, rue Washington, two blocks from the Champs-Élysées, in 1885. Her eyrie on the barely visible fifth floor of the building became renowned for the Sunday salons, followed by dinner for the especially lucky, that she hosted for her many friends—writers, painters, musicians, Chinese diplomats, and other luminaries of the Parisian fin-de-siècle who enjoyed hearing her anecdotes about her father, her own life, and the many memorable figures who had already passed through it. Numerous regulars described in detail the peculiarities of her apartment—the ceiling so low one could touch it, the vermilion-lacquered walls on which she painted Asian fans, the long sofa draped with Persian carpets that took the place of the usual chairs, the profusion of exotic decoration, and the hanging plants on her terrace that turned it into a "modern Babylon"—all of which made it difficult to believe one was still in the heart of Paris. Her niece described it as "a pagoda, or rather a minuscule palace of the 1,001 Nights where, as soon as one crossed the threshold one felt separated from the real world." And visitors would be entranced as "the entire nineteenth century, as with Aladdin's magic lamp," emerged "from her charming mouth."[44]

Like her Pré des Oiseaux, the apartment made clear who her "Master" was, even as it displayed the homage of others. One 1887 visitor describes it as an extremely interesting "storage house inhabited by memories," or perhaps "it would be better to say it's a temple rather than a storage house, a temple in which Wagner is the god." The "relics" were everywhere. A gilded bronze bust of the composer, who had died in 1883, was "enthroned" on the fireplace mantel, one of the last photographs taken of him, signed, decked the piano, and a "strangely glowing" painting depicting a scene from legends of the Rhine hung in a corner. A drawing by Paul-Jacques-Aimé Baudry (1828–1886) that had served as frontispiece for the published *Parsifal* was also on the wall. And among Gautier's most treasured possessions shared with visitors was a copy of *Tristan and Isolde*, which bore the inscription: "A pitiful story set to music to please Mme Judith Gautier. Richard Wagner."

But there was much more in the cramped attic, which Gautier referred to as her "gutter." Its low ceilings reminded visitors of a cabin on a boat, "but a boat returning from the China seas carrying rich collections from over there; in a chaos as ingenious as artistic this Parisian woman who composes verse in Chinese has

6.5 Judith Gautier's apartment building in Paris at 30, rue Washington. The plaque above the door reads: "Judith Gautier of the Académie Goncourt, poet, writer, dramatic author, lived in this house from 1872-1917."
Author's photograph

brought together fabrics, embroideries, fukusas [Japanese square cloths used for wrapping gifts or for the tea ceremony], all pell-mell with a capricious fantasy." Like "a miniature museum" the apartment also contained numerous mementos of other important figures in her life, including the poem Victor Hugo composed after the death of Gautier's father in 1872, the sonnet he'd written to her earlier the same year, and his letters. There was an inscribed portrait of Franz Liszt, an enamel medallion from the hand of Claudius Popelin (1825-1892), and a painting by the prominent contemporary artist Pierre Puvis de Chavannes (1823-1898). Most notable among the works of art, however, were the several portraits of Gautier produced and given to her by "John Sargent" (1856-1925).[45]

JOHN SINGER SARGENT

John Singer Sargent shared with Gautier her enthusiasm for Wagner, and her early defense of the artist's work, which had provoked mixed reactions among the French public, provides another index of her critical acumen. The young American had arrived in Paris in 1874 to study with the portraitist Charles Auguste Émile Duran, known as Carolus-Duran (1837-1917), who appreciated his student's talent enough to have him do a portrait of himself. But Sargent's famous painting first known as *Madame **** and now *Madame X* required an unusually discerning eye, which Gautier was one of the few to display in her review of the Salon of 1884 in which it was exhibited. This striking portrait of the Louisiana native Virginie Amélie Avegno Gautreau (1859-1915), who had married a wealthy French banker and captivated Parisian society with her beauty, both baffled and scandalized contemporary viewers with its sculptural profile of Gautreau and her long, distinctively pointed nose, her spectrally pale skin contrasting sharply with a low-cut black gown whose thin jeweled strap originally fell provocatively off her shoulder. The public hated the painting, which Sargent had hoped would open doors to more commissions from Parisian society; he later repainted the strap back on Gautreau's shoulder and left the next year for London, keeping the painting for himself. Gautier, however, while acknowledging it as "a singular figure before whom visitors stop with mouths agape, not knowing what they're seeing," describes it as a "delicious arabesque," "the exacting image of a modern woman religiously traced by a painter who is a master of his brush." All of its elements, she notes, from skin tones that range from blue to heliotrope to pink, to half-closed eyes shadowed by velvet, "have a somewhat chimerical effect, which is solely owing to the chimerical beauty that the canvas evokes." Not everyone will understand its "charming strangeness," she concludes, but "like all rare and surprising things, it will turn every head."[46]

Four years later in a review of the 1888 Salon she coyly asks, "Whom will we ask to make our portrait?" and, after running through the names of some of the accomplished figure painters on display, she answers: "Well, John Sargent attracts us even more; there is in his style a nervous grace, a *singular* poetry that makes us prefer him above all. Thus it is he who shall have the honor of painting us."[47] That honor she seems already to have conferred on Sargent, who completed several informal, noncommissioned portraits of Gautier—three oils, a water color, two sepia ink wash drawings, and two pencil sketches—around the time of his *Madame X*.[48] The two had likely met through the writer and translator Emma-Marie Allouard-Jouan (1836–1918), who was also friends with Madame Gautreau, had been painted by Sargent, and had a country home in Brittany; the three women socialized there and in Paris.[49]

Sargent's best-known portraits of Gautier were done in oil. One, *Judith Gautier*, which hangs in the Detroit Institute of Arts, depicts her standing with her hand resting on her piano, wearing a long, cream-colored gown with a bow at the neck whose luster contrasts with the dark, lamplit interior of her living room. It presents Gautier in an intimate setting that nonetheless insists on her imposing presence and signals what elements of her life, like the piano, were important to her. The loose gown of the sort she favored—contemporaries called them "kimonos"—and the flowers in her hair lend an appropriately exotic air. The painting demonstrates well what the first review of Sargent's work in English pointed out, his "wonderful power of suggesting a mysterious sentiment by light.... No one could compete with him in treating the mystery of real light and shadow, wrapping figures in a half gloom."[50] Another, known as *A Gust of Wind*, is more indebted to Impressionist influences in its outdoor setting, evocative, quickly brushed style, and flat surfaces, and catches her on the sand near her beach house trying to hold onto her hat in the stiff breeze.

The precise dates of the portraits have not been documented, but there are many reasons to think that the 1883 to 1885 time frame makes sense. Virginie Gautreau's country house in Brittany was not far from Gautier's, across the mouth of the Rance, and Sargent frequented both; they had friends in common in addition to Allouard-Jouan, like the well-known socialite-gynecologist Samuel Jean

Pozzi (1846-1918), who was also famously painted by Sargent wearing a bright red dressing gown.[51]

A "veritable gallery of Sargent's works shows Gautier in a variety of informal poses and settings" and serves as testimony of their friendship and "evidence of the spell she cast on him."[52] (One especially charming drawing in pencil and sepia wash, *Study of Judith Gautier by Lamplight*, is in the collection of the British royal family and has been reproduced on the cover of this book.) Eleven years his senior, Gautier shared with Sargent not just a passion for Wagner's operas—he made the pilgrimage to Bayreuth, too—but a more far-ranging love of music and all the arts, not to speak, of course, of his own work, in which she had recognized "a *singular poetry.*" While it's unlikely, as was suggested decades ago, that the relationship went further than that, there is no doubt that Gautier was extremely "important for Sargent on both personal and professional levels in the 1880s."[53]

The only proximately datable portrait by Sargent of Gautier is one he gave to the Japanese painter Yamamoto Hōsui (1850-1906), who had arrived in Paris as secretary to the Japanese delegation to the International Exposition in 1878 and stayed for nine years. Yamamoto studied Western painting technique with Jean-Léon Gérôme (1824-1904) at the École des Beaux-Arts and established his own atelier in Paris in 1880. Inscribed "to Monsieur Yamamoto / Souvenir of St Enogat / John S. Sargent," the small pencil sketch places both artists at Le Pré des Oiseaux in Brittany in the early 1880s.[54]

Yamamoto had met Gautier through her brother-in-law, Émile Bergerat, and painted a portrait of a woman in 1882 that is the first oil by a Japanese painter of a European subject; after his return home he established a school that taught French-style painting.[55] While a visitor at St. Énogat he also decorated the wooden panels of the small guest house she had built in the garden and jokingly called her "cigar box." The typical Japanese motifs that adorn the four walls—bamboo, plum blossoms, pine, birds and cranes—can still be seen today.[56] Most famously, however, he provided the illustrations for her translation of Japanese poetry, *Poems of the Dragonfly* (*Poèmes de la libellule*), which was completed in 1884 and published in 1885.

Japan had been Gautier's first "discovery" of Asia, when she visited London with her family in 1862 and encountered the visiting members of the Japanese delegation to the world's fair, but she did not return to it until the 1870s. Paris had in the meantime been swept up in the wave of *japonisme* stimulated by the arrival of Japanese prints around 1860, their influence on Impressionist

6.6 "Judith Gautier." Pencil sketch, ca. 1883. Tokyo University of the Arts.
Photograph courtesy of the Tokyo University of the Arts / DNPPart.com

painters, and the country's exhibits at the international expositions of 1867 and 1878. For Gautier once again a personal relationship was key: she became good friends with two young Japanese students who arrived in Paris in 1871. One, the Marquis Saionji Kinmochi (1849–1940), studied law, and for nine years frequented the city's literary and artistic circles, where he met Gautier. After returning to Japan he was posted as ambassador to other European countries and then became an important political leader back home, serving as prime minister twice. He represented Japan at the Paris Peace Conference in 1919.[57] The second was Komyoji Saburo (1847–1893), whom Gautier knew as Mitsouda Komiosi; he also studied law and served as a diplomat after his return to Japan until his early death.[58]

Gautier dedicated *Poems of the Dragonfly* to Komiosi, but Saionji was her collaborator and remained a lifelong friend; she made sure to send him a copy of the book in Japan, to which he had returned, and dedicated a later play to him. She knew no Japanese, but Saionji was considerably more comfortable in French than Ding Dunling. Working with him Gautier selected eighty-seven poems composed over the course of several centuries in traditional *tanka* form, thirty-one syllables in five unrhymed lines arranged in a set pattern of 5-7-5-7-7; she inadvertently repeated one poem, so the volume contains eighty-eight pieces. Saionji first prepared a French prose translation, which Gautier put into rhymed verse that largely replicated the syllable count in French feet of the original and observed prosodic rules about the alternation of rhyme categories. Direct and spare, these poems have been described as "a remarkable feat of versification" that achieves "an astonishing concretion and concision."[59] Unlike *The Book of Jade*, where she rendered the rhymed Chinese verse into unrhymed "stanzas" that rarely corresponded in number to the originals, in *Poems of the Dragonfly* Gautier produced a more standard literary translation, perhaps because she had reliable cribs to work from. She captures well themes like evanescence that permeate the poetry, and the volume includes in an appendix all of Saionji's prose versions, inviting readers to compare; in a few instances the original poem in romanized Japanese also appears on the same page as the translation. Her success at capturing the spirit of the originals was acknowledged by contemporary readers like the well-known collector of Japanese art, Philippe Burty (1830–1890), who commented that she "had collected Japanese poems just as the Japanese themselves collected fireflies in miniature cages."[60] In addition, to orient her readers, she included as introduction a translation of the preface to the first Japanese imperial anthology of poetry. Here, as well as in works of fiction and drama based on Japanese themes, one Japanese scholar believes that Gautier revealed a surprisingly impressive familiarity with the culture: "At the age of 30, she already knew rather well the history, language, customs and traditions of Japan, which was exceptional at the time."[61] The comment about her linguistic facility is a generous one, but she was remarkably well-attuned to the sensibilities of the texts she read.[62]

Poems of the Dragonfly was intended to be as much a work of art as it was of literature. It was published by Charles Gillot, both an expert printer and a seasoned collector of Japanese fine arts, and it featured eight monochrome illustrations by Yamamoto of typical motifs from nature—bamboo, waterfalls, birds, and the like—printed in different colors and repeated throughout the volume as backdrop for the translations. Enthusiasts familiar with the recently discovered Japanese aesthetic "all praised the absence of symmetry in Japanese art," so the asymmetrical layout of every page was surely intentional, as on the main title page, where a large dragonfly whose wings are inscribed with Japanese characters holds aloft the background of the translations and their date of completion, spring 1884.[63] Twenty of the eight hundred copies were produced in a deluxe edition containing seven full-page water-colors by Yamamoto.

THE BOOK OF JADE IN A "BIBLE OF DECADENCE"

At Gautier's recommendation Yamamoto also illustrated an edition of a collection of poems titled *The Bats* (*Les Chauves-souris*) by Gautier's good friend, Robert de Montesquiou-Fézensac (1855-1921). Poet, painter, fellow *japoniste*, and aristocratic dandy, Montesquiou was one of the regulars at her Sunday salons in Paris and a frequent visitor to St. Énogat as well. It was he who had christened the small garden house in which he stayed the "hat box" or "cigar box." His fondness for Japanese decorative arts is something for which his biographer credits Gautier: thanks to her he learned "how to talk about fukusas, netsukes and kakemonos."[64] Well known throughout the city for his hyperaestheticized and unconventional lifestyle, he was described by Proust in a 1905 essay as "a professor of beauty"[65] and likely inspired the figure of Baron de Charlus in the novelist's *In Search of Lost Time*. But even before that he served as a model for Jean Floressas des Esseintes, the main character in the writer and art critic Joris-Karl Huysman's (1848-1907) *Against Nature* (*À Rebours*), "a magnificent and scandalous novel" published in 1884 that ensured that "well before Montesquiou wrote a single verse" he became "one of the most viewed characters of his time."[66]

Described by Julian Barnes as a "dreamily meditative bible of decadence,"[67] the novel tells the story of a young nobleman—the last in his line and plagued by dyspepsia, insomnia, ennui, and various nervous disorders—who seeks shelter from what he perceives as the disgusting assaults and displeasures of modernity. Montesquiou's decoration of his own apartment in Paris had become renowned for its exotic extravagance, thanks to rumors spread by the dealers who furnished it. Huysmans first learned about the apartment from their mutual friend Mallarmé,[68] and the description of des Esseintes's construction of his refuge structures the novel. Proust may have been known for his cork-lined bedroom, but Huysmans's protagonist's country house cloisters him within leather-lined walls and ceilings, and heavily curtained windows impervious to sunlight and the outside world. He prefers artificial sounds, smells, and tastes to anything natural—a special "sustainer" extracts the quintessence of nourishment from food that his delicate stomach can't digest—and he ultimately finds that nutrition administered by enema may be the best cure for his gastrointestinal ailments. Seeking artificially synesthetic pleasures, he develops a special "mouth organ" that dispenses liquors that taste like musical instruments. His favorite works of art turn their backs on contemporary subjects. Huysmans shared with Gautier an admiration for the young painter Gustave Moreau (1826–1898), whose fondness for exotic subjects and dreamlike suggestiveness made him "a prefiguration" of the aristocratic protagonist.[69] In a bit of poetic license he places two of Moreau's well-known paintings of Salomé on the walls of des Esseintes' house.

One notable episode centers on a tortoise des Esseintes purchases, thinking that it might accentuate the colors of his Persian rug. Finding its shell insufficiently luminous he glazes it with gold and then encrusts it with precious stones in Japanese patterns of flowers. Not only does the bejeweled animal fail to move brightly across the carpet but it soon expires. According to Montesquiou's biographer, the idea of acquiring a turtle, "truth be told," was Judith Gautier's, who was said to have owned a rhinestone-bedecked tortoise that wended its way among her flowerpots.[70] But the sad fate of des Esseintes's pet could surely not have been envisioned or wished for by a renowned animal lover who was always described as flanked by her extensive menagerie, which ranged from cats and dogs to snake, monkey, lizard, mice, warbler, a crow named Wotan, and a blackbird that could sing Wagner's music, and which traveled to and from Paris to St. Énogat with her every season.[71]

Gautier's *Book of Jade* makes a surprise appearance toward the end of *Against Nature*. Des Esseintes spends a great deal of time examining and rearranging the books in his library, which was based on Montesquiou's own. Works in Latin and the poetry of Baudelaire, Poe, and Mallarmé are special favorites. He is especially fond of the prose poem and its distillation of the power of narrative from otherwise tedious analysis and description; it represented "the concrete juice, the osmazone of literature, and the essential oil of art, ... a succulence developed and reduced to a drop." As the acknowledged master of the form, Baudelaire occupies pride of place, and an exquisitely illuminated and finely lettered copy on the best vellum of his work titled "Anywhere Out of the World" hangs prominently above the fireplace mantel. Des Esseintes treasures in particular a special anthology of prose poems he had printed for his private use, "a little chapel" which contains more pieces from Baudelaire, from Aloysius Bertrand and Villiers de l'Isle-Adam, and "some extracts of that delicate *Book of Jade*, whose exotic perfume of ginseng and tea mingles with the aromatic freshness of water that babbles under the moonlight throughout the entire book." After an extensive perusal of his entire library that culminates with this volume, he concludes that "there would probably be no further addition."[72]

STATESMEN AND DIPLOMATS

The Book of Jade also attracted considerable attention outside France and inspired many additions to the library of literary retranslations in other European languages, all by writers with no knowledge of Chinese. The Bavarian statesman Gottfried Böhm had already published his *Chinese Songs from the Book of Jade by Judith Mendès* in 1873, with German versions of sixty-nine of her seventy-one poems.[73] Most of his compositions are quatrains with rhyme on the even numbered lines, and they all significantly expand on Gautier's originals, distancing them even further from the Chinese originals. They capture the content of the French renditions but certainly not their economy. Still, his diamond-shaped depiction of the reflected image in the water of the young, wine-drinking poets in his translation of Gautier's "Porcelain pavilion" displays a rare graphic imagination and caught the attention of important early readers.

In 1882 the Italian statesman Tullo Massarani (1826-1905) published a complete translation of Gautier's collection into Italian: *The Book of Jade: Echoes of the Far East brought into Italian verse following the readings of Madame J. Walter.* His volume includes a 125-page introduction based on research into the most important available French missionary and sinological sources, for which Massarani provides a bibliography. He reproduces the Chinese characters for the title and thematic sections from Gautier's volume, follows her practice of identifying each piece as "after" or "adapted from" a poet, and employs a variety of prosodic forms, all rhymed, for his translations.[74]

Another notable translation of forty-eight selections from *The Book of Jade,* titled *Chinese Songbook,* was published by the Portuguese poet and diplomat António Feijó (1859-1917) in 1890. Feijó himself does not mention his source, but a second edition dedicated to "Madame Judith Gauthier" appeared in 1903 that includes reviews of the first volume and a new poem celebrating a character from her *Imperial Dragon.* This edition served as the basis for the American diplomat and businessman Jordan Herbert Stabler's (1885-1938) English translations of Chinese poetry, now thrice removed from the originals, published in 1922 and titled *Songs of Li-Tai-Pe.* Despite the title, Stabler's volume is not in fact limited to the poetry of Li Bo but includes English versions of half of the forty-eight poems in Feijó's *Chinese Songbook.* Stabler's introduction provides personal background and context for his work on the volume: that he had spent two years with the Portuguese diplomat when both men were posted to Stockholm; that Feijó had labored for six years on his translations, with substantial consultation of French and Portuguese sources on Chinese literature; and that he had invited his young American colleague to try his hand at English versions based on his Portuguese renditions, knowing that Stabler had translated some poems of François Villon (1431-1463). He writes that though the *Chinese Songbook* "may be termed a reconstruction—yet Feijó has so identified himself with the very nature of the Oriental poetry he interprets, that his verses appear as fresh as the originals." And he describes Judith Gautier herself as "one of the greatest living authorities on Chinese literature in Europe."[75]

Feijó departs from Gautier's seven themes and arranges his translations instead into four sections of twelve poems each based on the seasons, starting with spring. Stabler does the same for his twenty-four poems, and both men generally employ quatrains with various rhyme schemes. The dramatic transformation wrought by this linguistic peregrination can be seen in one example, the first two quatrains of Stabler's "The Stairway of Jade," which is based on Li Bo's single quatrain of that title and her "Jade staircase":

> The youthful Empress slowly mounts,
> While the Lanterns dim and fade,
> In the Full Moon's dazzling Light,
> The great Stairway of Jade.
> Its Steps lightly kiss as she passes,
> The Fringe of her Robe, which is made,
> Of green Brocade, half celestial,
> The hue of Imperial Jade.[76]

Like Feijó, Stabler reprints the passage from Huysmans's *Against Nature* alluding to *The Book of Jade*'s "exotic perfume of ginseng and tea" as epigraph for his volume, and he also refers to it in his introduction. In addition, he translates the French preface that had been provided for Feijó's *Chinese Songbook* by the Chinese general Tcheng-Ki-Tong, or Chen Jitong.

CHINESE ADMIRERS

Gautier might have found in Chen Jitong an intriguing mirror image of her own interest in bridging cultures. Having begun learning French in 1869 while studying naval engineering and navigation at the Fuzhou Navy Yard, Chen arrived in Paris in 1875 as secretary to a delegation of Chinese students sent to study Western science and technology; he was the only one to volunteer for the mission. He lived there for fifteen years, married a French woman, and became secretary and military attaché to the legations in Berlin and Paris, where he parlayed his linguistic facility, cosmopolitan self-confidence, and military title into a literary profile that likely made him "at the time in the West the most famous living Chinese author."[77] This assessment stemmed from the seven books, some of them wildly popular, that he published in French to introduce aspects of Chinese culture to the Western public, and, in particular, to correct common and irritating misperceptions about China that his ten years abroad had made all too familiar. Most widely read was his *The Chinese Painted by Themselves* (*Les Chinois peints par eux-mêmes*), which sought to "present China as she really is, to describe Chinese customs with all the knowledge I have of it, but with a European spirit and taste." The book appeared in 1884, was translated into English the following year, with other languages to follow, and focused on topics like marriage, the family, religious practices, education, language, and literature.[78] It was followed by *Les Plaisirs en Chine* in 1890, translated immediately as *Bits of China* and five years later as *Chin-Chin, or the Chinaman at Home*, which aimed to provide "a tableau of our private amusements and our small public celebrations" by describing various festivals, competitions, games, and other activities.[79] The reference to Hervey-Saint-Denys's famous dinner party appears in this book in a discussion of Chinese cuisine that Chen hoped would dispel widespread rumors that Chinese ate dogs and cats. Chen also wrote on the theater of China, translated a selection of Chinese short stories, and wrote a novel based on a well-known Tang-dynasty classical tale.

Chen Jitong does not mention Judith Gautier by name, but his preface to Feijó's collection delivers high praise for the work on which it was based. Its promise, he believes, begins with the image of jade, which Chen reminds his reader refers to something "rare and precious." "The title alone of *Book of Jade* is thus for an educated Chinese a promise and would prevent even the most audacious of critics from doubting the value of such a work: it is perfect from its very cover, or at least it should be." And, indeed, he quickly goes on to affirm that it is indeed "a masterpiece" comprising works of the best Chinese poets and "worthy of the admiration of all the literati in the world." Chen recognizes and particularly recommends poems by the great Tang poets Li Bo and Du Fu, who succeed in expressing profound emotions with the utmost simplicity. "Poetry is humanity's first language," he declares, but "an arduous task" to translate. He therefore "can only commend those poets who've had the generous idea of translating the most esteemed works of their colleagues in the Far East" because bringing the poetry of two civilizations together is an important first step in achieving international understanding and thereby peace and harmony.[80]

There is no record of encounters between Gautier and Chen, but it's likely that their paths crossed at some point. They were both acquainted with and admired by Anatole France, who wrote about them in *The Literary Life* (*La vie littéraire*), his four-volume collection of essays about notable writers of his time. Chen had been only one step removed from Ding Dunling when he provided a preface—in both Chinese and French—to a novel by the writer René de Pont-Jest (1830–1904) for which Ding had provided the plot outline, thus leading to some confusion about its authorship. And Gautier's volume, along with Hervey-Saint-Denys's, served as important references for Chen's discussions of Chinese poetry in his books on China.[81] But Chen was not the only Chinese diplomat to admire the fruits of Gautier's labors, for she and Ding were invited to meet more than once with the young scholars who were included in the first delegations sent by the Chinese to visit the United States and Europe in the 1860s. From the establishment of the first Chinese mission to France in 1878 she enjoyed regular contact with many of the official envoys, as their host at dinners, theater, and salons and as their guest at events hosted by them. The first ambassador, Guo Songtao 郭崧焘 (1818-1891), stayed for less than a year in Paris, and there is no record of their meeting (though Guo did meet Hervey-Saint-Denys), but his successor Zeng Jize 曾紀澤 (1839-1890), who served from 1878-1884, records in his diary a visit from Gautier, whom he had met through Prosper Marie Giquel (1835-1886), a French naval officer who had spent over two decades in China in various military and diplomatic capacities. An entry in Zeng's journal notes that "On the sixth day of the third month of the seventh year of the reign of Emperor Guangxu (April 4, 1881) Giquel (Ri Yige 日意格) came, accompanied by Madame Judith Gautier (Xudide Goujiye 徐狄德 勾吉野). We talked for a long time. This French woman has done research in Chinese culture."[82]

Gautier took special pleasure in the opportunity to introduce Chinese envoys to her other great passion, Wagner. A profile published in February 1890 records in vivid detail how she, a "fanatical admirer," led a group from the embassy to a performance of *Rienzi*, interested in finding out what kind of impression Wagner's music would have on these Asian dignitaries, who occupied two loges of the Théâtre-Lyrique. "From the first chords of the orchestra their exhilaration surged into delirious paroxysms. They jumped up, urged one another to applaud, gesticulated, and cried out loud, while the entire hall pointed their opera glasses at them and ignored the performance to focus instead on this multicolored riot, this stupefying torrent of admiration."[83]

As Rémy de Gourmont tells us, Gautier regularly opened her home to Chinese diplomats and other visitors: "The little salon of Judith Gautier is a corner of China: no Chinese of the upper class has ever spent time in Paris without coming to drink green tea, to peruse the precious manuscripts stored there or the lacquer chests, and to admire this modern Li Yi-an who has revived, on European soil, the poetic delights that enchanted the refined spirits of the Song dynasty." Agnès de Noblet writes that Gautier "knew, more or less, the entire colony of cultivated Chinese in Paris; they found recourse in her as the interpreter of choice," and she would frequently take Chinese visitors, "in caravans," out to visit the Louvre and the National Library, chatting easily in their language.[84] But she became especially close to the two envoys who arrived at the turn of the century, Yu Geng 裕庚 (?-1905), who was ambassador from 1899-1902, and Sun Baoqi 孫寶琦 (1867-1931), who served from 1902 to 1905. Gautier would end up writing poems in French to both of them, but it was Yu Geng himself whose own poem provides an opening benediction for the second edition of Gautier's *Book of Jade*, which appeared in 1902.

Another *Book of Jade*? What led Gautier to prepare a new version, and how different was it from the first?

CHAPTER 7

"Greatly enlarged and rigorously corrected"

The Book of Jade, 1902

The French public's interest in China and things Chinese had not abated in the years since the 1867 *Book of Jade*. The timing of a second edition early in the new century was equally propitious. Interest in the first edition had been piqued by both the plunder-rich aftermath of the Anglo-French expeditions at the beginning of the 1860s and the first Chinese exhibit at the Paris International Exposition—even though Hervey-Saint-Denys had had to stand in for an official government presence. In 1902 similar roles were played by the Boxer Rebellion of 1899–1901 and the 1900 Exposition, once again in Paris. The former, an anti-imperialist insurrection directed primarily against the missionary privileges that had been secured after the Opium Wars, was ultimately suppressed by an eight-nation coalition that included France. Significant looting occurred, as it had leading up to the destruction of Yuanmingyuan, but Chinese sieges of the European legations generated great hostility in the press, and the victorious foreign powers demanded significant reparations for the losses incurred by their citizens. The story of the 1900 International Exposition in Paris was a happier one, for the Chinese government chose for the first time to mount its own exhibit and sent official representatives. China was still in the news and on display for a France more fascinated than angry, and the moment for a new volume on its poetry was surely ripe.[1]

Gautier greatly welcomed the opportunity to produce a second edition of her debut collection. As she later recalled, after describing her labors with Ding Dunling and the manuscripts at the library:

> *The Book of Jade* was the result of that fine effort, which, though relentless and earnest, never assured me completely about the accuracy of the poems that

comprised that little volume; moreover, I didn't dare affirm that they had been precisely translated so I only said "after such and such a poet," leaving it to be understood that they had been inspired by him, interpreted. Later I picked up *The Book of Jade* again. I greatly enlarged and rigorously corrected it, and this time I was able to affirm it as translated from the Chinese.

I believe, to my great displeasure, that certain readers prefer, no doubt owing to its rarity, the first edition, which is fortunately out of print.[2]

Although Gautier's "corrections" were minimal, the evidence for her greater command of the language in 1902 is compelling. And the new edition was indeed significantly expanded, from 71 to 110 pieces, with most of the new poems (25) going into the first section, Lovers.[3] Gautier made several other changes, in addition to adding new front matter. She dropped the Chinese headings for the seven sections and added an eighth, The Court (La Cour), containing six new poems. Because the poems are now presented as real translations, she associates each with a poet. The table of contents reflects this change by listing poems by theme, title, and author. Some previously uncertain attributions have become works of "unknown" or more conveniently identified poets; Ding Dunling, for example, receives credit for a fourth poem, which in 1867 was "after Tse-Tié," a name that would still be difficult to identify. On the other hand, some that had been correct in 1867 were revised wrongly in 1902. She tinkered with the sequence of poems within each section, sometimes grouping them by author—perhaps a nod to Chinese anthological practice, or to Hervey-Saint-Denys's example—and sometimes chronologically, but in neither case consistently. There are Chinese characters for each poet's name, occasionally in Gautier's own calligraphy, but these were deleted in the 1908 reprinting of the edition, perhaps because she had realized that many of the attributions were shaky or their representation flawed. The characters for Du Fu, for example, were printed upside down on one page, and in other instances names and graphs were mismatched.

Judith Gautier expected the second edition of *The Book of Jade* to be published in fall 1901, but like her first book it was slightly delayed. At the beginning of 1902 it was issued from the house of Félix Juven. He was a relatively young publisher whose list included humor, well-known foreign authors like Arthur Conan Doyle, and a number of popular contemporary French writers. Although the titles were less highbrow than those of Alphonse Lemerre, who had been responsible for the first volume, Juven's print runs were typically on the large size.[4] Perhaps more important, he would be publishing the first volume of Gautier's memoirs,

The Necklace of Days (*Le Collier des jours*), later that year, with the second volume, *The Second Strand of the Necklace* (*Le Second Rang du collier*), in 1903, following its serialization. The appearance of her distinctive anthology could only enhance interest in her memoirs, and vice versa.

This book presented itself quite differently from its predecessor, and the unusually extensive front matter provides important background on her intentions.

The title on the first page is the same in French as before, but its Chinese name has been simplified to *Yu shu* 玉書 (*Jade book*), characters that now appear boldly in what looks like Gautier's own calligraphy (in 1867 the characters for *Bai yu shi shu* 白玉詩書 had been printed). This second version is as unlikely a title for a Chinese poetic anthology as was the first but is a literal rendering of its French counterpart. A new subtitle proclaims definitively that these are "poems translated from the Chinese"; they will thus no longer be simply described as "after" Chinese poets. The author's surname is now Gautier, to which she had returned in 1876 after the death of her father and her separation from Catulle Mendès. And this new edition has been "considerably enlarged" and "decorated with borders and engravings around the text after Chinese artists." The improvisation, then, will be visual rather than textual.

A special message appearing as an insert after the title page by Félix Juven (and thus lost in many currently available digitized versions) makes all of these points and adds a new one. "For more than forty-five centuries," he begins, China has been chanting "melodious poems of love and battle, marvels of pure grace and genial irony" that are as "innocent and tender as ours but with a more refined elegance." With a "brilliant style put at the service of her oriental erudition," Judith Gautier in her *Book of Jade*, her "literary debut," ensured that French readers would no longer be unfamiliar with "these Asiatic discoveries." Now, however, "at a moment when China imposes itself on our concerns and our studies," *The Book of Jade* deserves to be looked at again. It will be enlarged and re-edited, "in a mauve and delicate setting like the strophes it frames." Juven underscores both the context and the fact that this is a *new* edition, thanks to the addition of numerous previously unpublished pieces and illustrations by Chinese artists, all of which will be presented to French readers by "a sort of ballad-madrigal with an utterly 'Celestial' charm" composed by the Chinese ambassador to Paris himself.[5]

What does Juven mean by "mauve?" The term identifies the volume as very much of its time. Available in aniline form, and thus artificially, only since the middle of the nineteenth century, "mauve *was* the modern colour par excellence,

LE
LIVRE DE JADE

POÉSIES TRADUITES DU CHINOIS

PAR

JUDITH GAUTIER

NOUVELLE ÉDITION CONSIDÉRABLEMENT AUGMENTÉE
ET ORNÉE DE VIGNETTES ET DE GRAVURES HORS TEXTE
D'APRÈS LES ARTISTES CHINOIS

PARIS
FÉLIX JUVEN, ÉDITEUR
122, RUE RÉAUMUR, 122

Tous droits réservés.

7.1 Judith Gautier, *Le Livre de jade*, Paris: Félix Juven, 1902, BnF Gallica

not only because it had been invented thanks to new scientific means, but also because it entailed new ways of seeing." As a synthetic pigment it highlighted the artificiality of art itself, appreciated by writers and artists alike. Mauve was a fugitive, "transitional, liminal hue" that "the French literary avant-garde of the *fin de siècle* embraced in all its infinite synaesthetic variations."[6] And its chromatic suggestiveness was equally favored by the Impressionist painters who began using blotches of shades of purple, rather than black, to create shadows. Used to describe both visual and written texts, mauve pointed to the intersections among the arts so appealing to turn-of-the-century artists. Gautier herself had called attention to John Singer Sargent's participation in this "culture of mauve" when she described the striking hints of blue and heliotrope in his depiction of Madame Gautreau's complexion. Here Juven attributes to both the book and its poems the same evocative and distinctively modern qualities of the paintings she admired, without even knowing that traditional Chinese critics had long pointed to the pictorial possibilities of their verse.

The front matter continues. A separate page informs us that five special numbered copies on "China [paper]," known for its quality and durability, have been printed. We then discover that this new edition of *The Book of Jade* is no longer dedicated to Gautier's tutor Ding Dunling, who had died in 1886. Instead, she writes: "To / Emperor Ham Nghi / Exile from Annam / I offer the fragrance of these immortal / flowers." This is preceded by a short, untranslated dedication in classical Chinese signed by Gautier in her own calligraphy. Then follows an essay by Gautier herself titled "Prélude," which serves as her preface to the collection. And finally, in both Chinese and French—translated by Gautier—the promised "ballad-madrigal" contributed by the Chinese ambassador, an eight-line heptasyllabic poem. Compared with the first edition of *The Book of Jade*, which arrived without any preparatory information, the drumroll introducing this volume is a long and leisurely one.

INTRODUCING THE COLLECTION

Ham Nghi (1871–1944) was a recent addition to Gautier's circle of friends but one with whom she quickly became infatuated. He had been the eighth emperor of the Nguyen dynasty of Annam,[7] whose nominal reign as a teenager, under two regents, lasted only one year, from 1884 to 1885. When the French gained control over all of Vietnam in 1885 after a successful two-year military struggle with

China, Ham Nghi's regents launched an insurrection against their new "protectors." Ham Nghi fled from the palace and spent three years engaged in guerrilla warfare against French forces. He was betrayed, captured, and forced into exile in Algeria in 1888, where he was known as the Prince of Annam, received a pension and residence from the French government (who wanted to keep him viable as a potential ruler), and was welcomed into the high society of Algiers. Allowed regular visits to Paris as early as 1897, he took sculpting lessons from Rodin.[8] He became a painter and sculptor of not inconsiderable talent and married a French woman, with whom he had three children.

"Ham Nghi" (咸宜, "Entirely proper") was the name of his reign, which alludes to a phrase in a dynastic hymn from *The Book of Songs* that affirms the legitimacy of the first ruler of the Shang dynasty and, by inference, his own. As a ruler he would not have been referred to by his taboo given name (Nguyen Phuc Ung Lich), so he used his familiar name, Xuan Tu (春子 "Spring's son"), which he usually reversed when in France to correspond to French word order; Gautier therefore also called him "Teu Soune" (Tu Xuan).[9] Having heard about his tragic fate, she wrote a long now-lost play celebrating him in 1896 called *Les Portes rouges* (The red gates) and set her mind on meeting him during one of the annual two-month visits to France that the government allowed him to make. According to Suzanne Meyer-Zundel it was her friend the poet Pierre Louÿs (1870–1925) who succeeded in introducing her to Ham Nghi, in June 1900. Over the course of the next fourteen years she frequently met him and, often, his family in either Paris or St. Énogat. A correspondence of some ninety-three letters and poems documents her fascination with the young man twenty-six years her junior, which bordered on adoration and "desperate love." She wrote three acrostic poems, of which each line begins with the letters of his title or name (Ham Nghi, Prince D'Annam, Teu Soune); a fourth refers to him as "Buddha," a title befitting her custom of burning incense before his portrait.[10] The only time she left the European continent was to visit him and his family in Algeria in 1914.

Gautier repeatedly urged Ham Nghi to send her poems or essays in Chinese that she could translate and hoped that he would collaborate with her as she was preparing this second edition of *The Book of Jade*. He declined consistently, pleading that he had forgotten whatever classical Chinese he'd known for French. In February 1901 she wrote asking permission to dedicate the volume to him, an offer he accepted with pleasure even as he made clear that he could not write anything for her in Chinese. And in a letter a year later she informs him that he will be receiving one of the five special copies of the volume she had requested. It is "his" book: "Your book has finally appeared, and I am sending you a copy on China paper printed especially for you. I will be happy if the work has your approval." In March 1902 he writes back, thanking her for "the charming dedication" and complimenting her on "the profound erudition with which your *Book of Jade* is imprinted. A Chinese who reads this book will be completely surprised to see it signed... by a French name."[11]

The import of Gautier's short dedication in Chinese to Ham Nghi is clear and simple. "The great emperor Ham Nghi," it begins, has tragically been unable to realize his talent and ambition far and wide, unlike other contemporary rulers, who cannot in fact compare with him. "There is no one who doesn't lament what he has encountered and the many restraints on his aspiration." The early history of distant Vietnam has been transmitted thanks to the written record, which will not perish; Gautier wishes to present these compositions, in place of flowers, in humble tribute to this unfortunate ruler. As her even shorter dedication in French declares, these flowers are also immortal.

The flowers reappear at the beginning of the "Prelude" that follows, an introduction that marks this second edition as an undertaking with distinctively new scholarly ambitions. In her essay on poetry and poets, published in her book *Foreign Peoples*, Gautier had described China as the "paradise of poets" because of the doors poetic composition could open and the fame it could earn. Here she begins by describing a different—also "more just and infinitely more durable"—process by which "glory" was attained by Chinese poets, taking off from anecdotes of how collections were created when writers were not "presumptuous" enough to compile their own. At social gatherings one might recite a composition that others would copy down, causing "the name of a poet to waft like a sweet perfume." Or a poet might himself write a poem on a door or wall that some discerning reader would appreciate and copy down. The works of certain poets would emerge from this process of communal recognition, in "a kind of plebiscite." And sometimes, perhaps by imperial decree, thus "consecrated by renown," they might be gathered like a "bouquet of rare flowers" in a compilation that would enable "their verses to be enhanced and contrast in a charming diversity." Although she does not make the point, what is an "anthology," after all, if not literally a "garland" or "gathering of flowers," going back to its first exemplar, Meleager's first-century BCE collection of epigrams with that title? Her simple metaphor places her volume in a long and distinguished tradition.[12]

Continuing the image, Gautier then moves on to discuss two poets from among those whom "posterity has gathered, from across the ages, for the bouquet of immortality," writers whose precious works merited preservation despite not having been published during their lifetime. Li Bo and Du Fu are the greatest of these, whose mutual precedence has been subject to debate, but how can one rank them? "When two eagles have grabbed their prey, they say, and rise out of sight, who could then recognize which of them has flown closer to heaven?" This is an almost verbatim quote from Hervey-Saint-Denys's discussion of the difficulty of comparing the two in the introductory essay to his selection of poems from Li Bo in *Poetry of the Tang Dynasty*. Gautier goes on to describe the distinctive qualities of his work—"an original and concise form that plays with difficulties, a colorful style with rare and choice images, full of allusions, innuendos, and frequent irony"—and borrows from the many anecdotes in the scholar's volume to illustrate the reasons behind Li's appeal: his drunkenness, his violations of protocol, his reported disappearance at the end of his life accompanied by two celestial immortals on the back of a dolphin. Although some might want to insist that Li Bo had simply drowned, "who would want to believe that?" As does Hervey-Saint-Denys, she points out that a temple had been built in his honor, demonstrating why China is such a "noble country"; it is, after all, the paradise of poets.[13]

Du Fu receives less attention in this essay, but Gautier begins her discussion by stating that many have preferred him to Li Bo. Hervey-Saint-Denys had been one of them and thought that most European readers would agree, though he does not explain why. Gautier provides her reasons: "With less strangeness, less that is unexpected, his poems are as vivid as those of his great friend, whom he honored as his teacher; they are more easily translated, possessing more naturalness, clarity, compassionate tenderness, and emotion confronting the sorrows of humanity. Less Chinese, perhaps, they are more universal, closer to us."[14] Those who have wrestled with the compressed syntax and dense allusiveness of Du Fu's late work might disagree that it is more easily translated, but the poignant humanity of his poetry is what matters to Gautier. What can bring these Chinese poets closer to their French audience? In both cases she seeks likenesses that might make them approachable to her reader. For Li Bo it was Omar Khayyam, another passionate drinker who sought consolation in wine, throwing "the veils of inebriation, like a gold-spangled shroud, over the bitterness of this life and fear of the next." As for Du Fu, Hervey-Saint-Denys had compared him to the similarly exiled Ovid, but Gautier finds a closer and more exalted French counterpart for him.

Following his separation from the affairs of the capital, she writes, his poetry "exhaled most vividly his chagrin and his regrets. One can observe a curious coincidence there. Poets have similar souls in different times and places. Ten centuries before Victor Hugo, the Chinese exile counts the years by the visual evidence nature brings him. 'It's now twice that I've seen the chrysanthemums bloom,' says Du Fu. 'For the third time I see the apples ripen,' says Victor Hugo during the third October of his exile."[15] Gautier is looking for comparisons; she wants to make her readers see something they can recognize in Chinese poetry.

There is a third poet discussed in this "Prelude" for whom Gautier did not need to look far to find a likeness, for the two women were compared almost immediately. Li Qingzhao (1084–1155?) 李清照, whom Gautier refers to by her alternate name, Li Yi'an 李易安, is probably the best-known woman poet in premodern China, and Gautier's translations of six lyrics attributed to her were new to the second edition of *The Book of Jade* and the first to appear in any Western language. We will return to her remarks here when discussing the poems below, all of which, incidentally, reflect work that could not have been indebted to Hervey-Saint-Denys. Gautier concludes her essay by pointing to further areas of similarity and difference between Chinese and European poetry, such as attention to syllable count, rhyme, the cesura, and a penchant for four-line strophes, and she presents a word-for-word breakdown of a quatrain translated later to illustrate distinctive prosodic features. The ideographic nature of the Chinese language also has "a very original charm" of its own. Finally, she notes that both traditions are rooted in music and song, although she imagines that Chinese poets always sang their works accompanied by the stringed instrument known as the *qin* 琴 or zither. Once again, she is seeking to bring two cultures together in calling it a "lyre," but the superiority of one remains clear: Chinese poets were singing their songs to the lyre "twelve centuries before Orpheus," and they are "certainly the only ones on the face of the earth still singing in the same language and to the same melodies."[16]

This "lyre" reappears in the poetic epigraph contributed by Yu Geng, the Manchu ambassador from China to Paris. Gautier's relationship with Yu Geng seems to have been especially cordial. They exchanged poems, and Gautier even included translations of pieces by Yu Geng's two sons, Charles Xingling Yu 裕 馨齡 and John Xunling Yu 裕 勛齡 in this second edition of *The Book of Jade*.[17] Yu Geng's benediction was brushed dramatically on letterhead from the imperial Chinese legation, an improvisational gesture that pays high tribute to Gautier and her effort; the Chinese original would not be reproduced in subsequent editions of the volume.

7.2 Yu Geng, Chinese ambassador to France 1899–1902.
Public domain

Her translation into French of the "Strophes improvised by His Excellency Yu Geng, Ambassador of China to Paris" ("Strophes improvisées / par Son Excellence Yu-Keng / Ministre de Chine à Paris"), dated Paris, April 1901, captures well, with some explanatory embellishment, the gist of his message:

7.3 Epigraph from Ambassador Yu Geng to the 1902 *Livre de jade*.
BnF Gallica

Sur un ordre souverain, me chargeant d'une ambassade, j'ai dû quitter mon pays, pour me diriger, à travers les océans, vers l'Occident lointain, vers Paris, l'illustre ville.

Le navire avance, peu à peu; je franchis la mer Rouge, le canal de Suez; tout ce chemin qu'une fois déjà j'ai parcouru.

Car c'est mon second voyage, et je retourne là-bas, cette fois, comme si j'allais à un rendezvous.

Under sovereign orders charging me as ambassador, I had to leave my country to travel across the oceans, toward the distant West, toward Paris, the illustrious city.

The ship advances bit by bit; I cross the Red Sea, the Suez Canal; this entire route that I traveled once before.

For this is my second voyage, and I'm returning there this time as if for an appointment.

190   The Book of Jade, 1902

Trente années, déjà!...Que d'événements! que de transformations! sujets de réflexions sans fin!...	Thirty years already! How many events! How many transformations! Endless food for thought!...
Et cependant, voici que mon esprit retourne vers les temps disparus: je me souviens des voyageurs intrépides, qui, dans une embarcation faite d'un tronc d'arbre creusé, s'en allaient à la découverte.	And yet, see how my mind returns toward times past: I recall those intrepid voyagers who, embarking in a boat made of a hollow tree trunk, set off for discovery.
Entre les vagues bondissantes, je regarde, espérant voir apparaître la belle déesse Siang-Ling, tenant dans ses bras blancs la lyre d'or; j'écoute, croyant entendre les chants suaves de la divine musicienne qui donne l'inspiration...	Amidst the surging waves I look out, hoping to see the beautiful goddess Xiangling, holding in her white arms the golden lyre; I listen, thinking I hear the sweet songs of the divine musician who provides inspiration...
Mais ce n'est pas Siang-Ling qui m'apparait; celle que je rencontre, c'est une poétesse d'Occident, qui, à ma joyeuse surprise, serre sur son coeur les poëmes de mon pays!...	But it's not Xiangling who appears to me; the woman I meet is a poetess from the West who, to my happy surprise, clasps to her heart the poems of my country!
J'écris alors, pour elle, ces quelques vers, et je suis heureux, en lui tendant le feuillet, à l'idée que nous pourrons longuement causer ensemble des poètes et de la poésie.[18]	And so I write these few verses for her, and I'm delighted, in offering her the page, by the thought that we'll be able to chat at length together about poets and poetry

As Yu Geng reflects on the thirty years that have passed since his first trip to Europe, he recalls the first mariners setting off for parts unknown but also clearly knows his destination. And he likens the woman who greets him to the legendary goddess of the Xiang River playing the zither.[19] Gautier adds the "white arms" and lyre to make clear whom he's referring to: she is the Western woman who has learned to embrace the ancient poems of China to her heart. During his three-year posting to Paris they met frequently, and Yu Geng was an admiring reader of her writings on Chinese culture.[20] She could not have asked for a more enthusiastic benediction to her collection.

In addition to the extensive front matter, this would be the first edition to include the visual art promised by Félix Juven to highlight the "mauve" resonances between visual and verbal beauty. A limited set of images of vases, flowers, dragons, rocks, and the character for "jade" in Gautier's writing repeats at regular intervals throughout the volume at the end of each poem. There are also occasional full- or, more commonly, two-page illustrations drawn from Chinese manuscripts—a scholar playing his zither, various mythological characters, travelers on horseback, social gatherings, an inebriated Li Bo, and so on—that are related to the theme of the section in which they appear; some of these are repeated as well.[21]

EXPANSIONS AND CORRECTIONS

As had been the case with the first edition of *The Book of Jade*, Gautier offered a preview in 1901 of most of her prospective additions in two journal publications: "Chinese Poems from All Ages" and "Some Great Chinese Poets and the Poetess Li Yi'an."[22] The first set opens with the "Improvised strophes" from Ambassador Yu Geng and is followed by twenty-three new poems without commentary. The second consists of interspersed sections of most of her upcoming "Prelude," providing background for nine new translations. All of them would be included, virtually unchanged, in the 1902 volume.

The first five pieces in "Chinese Poems," she tells us, were "borrowed" from *The Book of Songs* (*Le Livre des vers*),[23] but her sources are all easily recognizable as folk songs from various regions included in the classical anthology. In 1902 she identifies four of them unambiguously as direct translations and even points us to the source texts. They focus on courtship and marriage and thus appropriately open the amplified section on Lovers, with titles of her own devising—"A young girl" ("Une jeune fille"), "Forbidden love" ("Criminel amour"), and "Return to the kingdom of Qi" ("Retour dans le royaume de Tsi")—that clarify their theme. Gautier's relative fidelity to the original songs suggests that translation is indeed her goal here, although she makes one interesting final swerve in a poem she titles "Vengeance" ("Vengeance"):

—Ah! Voilà que le coq chante! dit-elle...	Ah, the cock is crowing! she says...
—Non, dit-il, la nuit est profonde, il ne chante pas encore...	No, he says, the night's still deep, it's not crowing yet...
—Lève-toi, lève-toi! soulève le store de la fenêtre, interroge le ciel.	Get up! get up! raise the window shade, look at the sky.
—Hélas! l'étoile du matin déjà monte à l'horizon!	Alas! the morning star has already risen to the horizon!
—Ah! c'est l'aurore! il est temps! il est temps! Mais avant de t'éloigner, venge-nous de celui qui nous sépare.	Ah, it's dawn! it's time! it's time! But before leaving me, avenge us on the one who's separating us.
Prends ton arc, et tue le coq.[24]	Take your bow and kill the cock.

Hervey-Saint-Denys had translated this passage in discussing *The Book of Songs* in the introduction to his anthology, and Gautier's version corresponds closely to his (which is based only on the first half of the original song) until her final lines.[25] In these last two lines, as well as the next stanza of the original song, the woman reminds her lover of his responsibility to go out and shoot wild fowl that she will prepare for them to enjoy together with wine and music. As traditional commentators explain, she wants to remind him of his proper duties. This fails to interest Gautier, who chooses to keep her poem rooted in the aubade tradition that scolds the rising sun, or, in this case, punishes its herald. She adds a footnote in the 1902 volume to make clear that this is an "interpretation" of a piece from *The Book of Songs*, not an inadvertent misunderstanding, labeling it as well an "anonymous" composition.

The selections first published in "Chinese Poems" and "Some Great Chinese Poets" enabled the expanded 1902 *Book of Jade* to offer "a relatively vast and well chosen panorama"[26] of the tradition, compared not only to the limited number of translations available at the time but also to the first edition. The 1867 volume had focused on the Tang dynasty, with only twelve of seventy-one titles linked to sources from other epochs (one from *The Book of Songs,* one to Ban Jieyu of the Han, seven from the Song dynasty Su Shi, and three from Ding Dunling). In 1901 and 1902 Gautier ranges from the sixth-century BCE *Book of Songs* to the Han dynasty, translating two well-known pieces composed by second-century BCE emperors; through the heart of the book, poems from the eighth-century Tang and eleventh-century Song dynasties; and up to the Qing dynasty in the nineteenth century, with the three works written by Yu Geng's sons and another attributed to the statesman Li Hongzhang, whom Gautier probably met when he visited France in 1896.[27] Her renditions now observe scholarly conventions more closely. They do not stray drastically from original sources—which are almost all recognizable, unlike those in the 1867 edition—although she still occasionally truncates works with impunity, changes titles, and introduces puzzling deviations. Perhaps more confident than before, in herself and in her readers, she translates longer works and retains names and place references in romanized Chinese, rather than resorting to generic terms. While some critics have assumed that the generally greater "accuracy" of these poems can be credited to her consultation of Hervey-Saint-Denys's versions, in fact only seven of the thirty-two titles included in the two 1901 preview publications had been translated or discussed by the sinologist, and only one of the seven previously unpublished new titles in the 1902 edition.[28] Readers of the 1867 edition may have had reason to doubt that Chinese sources could be found for all of its poems, but fidelity had not in any case been her primary goal then, even though—as we've seen—she understood more than many have thought. In 1902 she has resolved to translate faithfully, an effort evident despite her literary polish and inventiveness. Indeed, the modern editor of *The Book of Jade* was able to examine drafts of her poems preserved by the family of Suzanne Meyer-Zundel and discovered how systematically Gautier proceeded: "This work presents itself vertically in three columns reading from left to right, the first containing the Chinese characters for the poem, the second a phonetically romanized transcription of the character, and the third presents different possibilities for translation into French—whether in word for word form and/or more developed formulations. These documents prove, if it were still necessary, that *The Book of Jade* is indeed a translation."[29]

This claim can only realistically pertain to the new additions to her anthology, nor is it the case that this ambition prevented her from choosing to deviate from the text, as in the last line of "Vengeance." But Gautier now had the linguistic skills to present a reasonably close approximation of original Chinese texts when she chose to, and at least twenty-nine of the thirty-nine additions in 1902 can in fact be linked to those sources.[30]

The 1901 articles include five new poems by Li Bo and one significant revision of a sixth from 1867; the 1902 volume would add one more, and all but one of the new additions were placed in the section on Lovers. Gautier's additions provide insight into the range of Li's interests, including his fondness for composing to traditional song titles. Two works that stay close to the original are both heptasyllabic quatrains in the voice of a young bravo, a subgenre of traditional folk songs, both of which involve amorous encounters set, appropriately, in spring, the season for love. In one, "Some good luck on the path" ("Une bonne fortune sur le chemin," first published in "Chinese Poems"), the speaker, while riding on horseback, meets a woman in an elegant carriage who coyly shows him where she lives. The second, "Youth" ("Jeunesse," which was included in "Some Great Chinese Poets"), contains the same evocative image of flowers being trampled by the young man's horse on his springtime travels; his indecision about where to stop is resolved when, smiling, he spots a barmaid in a wine shop. Gautier captures another of Li's many voices in her "Forbidden flower" ("Fleur défendue"), which depicts a young fern-picker in a boat who is saddened by the sight of the beautiful lotuses on the water.[31]

Li Bo also invokes contemporary history in two songs that point obliquely to the fateful infatuation of the Tang emperor Xuanzong, who reigned from 712 to 756, with his beloved Yang Yuhuan 楊玉環, on whom he bestowed the highest title of imperial consort, Yang Guifei 楊貴妃, in 745. Hervey-Saint-Denys had already translated both of them, so Gautier had his notes to guide her. She chooses to ignore them in a much abbreviated version of one piece, "Drunkenness of love" ("Ivresse d'amour," first published in "Chinese Poems"), which alludes indirectly to Yang by featuring another femme fatale, the fifth-century BCE beauty Xi Shi 西施, who was sent as a gift by one ruler to another, his mortal enemy, in hopes of distracting him; the plan succeeded, and the besotted king was defeated in battle. But her rendition of a set of three poems that Li Bo was said to have composed while drunk and on imperial command, "Strophes improvised before Emperor Minghuang [Xuanzong] and his beautiful favorite Taizhen" ("Strophes improvisées devant l'empereur Ming-hoang et sa belle favorite Taï-tsun") accurately and succinctly conveys the poet's artful manipulation of both allusion and flattery; the entire sequence evokes Yang's legendary allure without once mentioning her name.³²

Gautier also translated one of Li Bo's best-known farewell poems, "Farewell to a friend" ("Song youren" 送友人), in a manner that illustrates both her observance of and occasional deviation from the norms of translation. Her "Departure of a friend" ("Le Départ d'un ami") was included in the 1901 "Chinese Poems" and opens the 1902 volume's section on Travelers. It is followed below by the original in Chinese and a literal English translation:

Par la verte montagne, aux rudes chemins, je vous reconduis jusqu'à l'enceinte du Nord.	By the verdant mountain, on rough paths, I lead you back to the Northern rampart.
L'eau écumante roule autour des murs, et se perd vers l'orient.	The foaming waters flow around the walls and vanish toward the east.
C'est à cet endroit que nous nous séparons....	It is here that we leave each other....
Je m'en retourne, solitaire, et je marche péniblement. Il me semble, maintenant, que j'ai plus de dix mille *lis* à parcourir.	I return alone, walking wearily. It now seems that I have more than ten thousand *li* to traverse.
Les nuages légers flânent, paresseusement, comme mes pensées.	The light clouds drift lazily, like my thoughts.
Bientôt le soleil se couche, et je sens plus vivement encore, la tristesse de la séparation.	Soon the sun sets, and I feel more intensely again the sadness of separation.
Par-dessus les broussailles, une dernière fois, j'agite la main, au moment où vous allez disparaître.	Above the brush I wave my hand one last time, just as you're about to disappear.
D'un long hennissement, mon cheval cherche à rappeler le vôtre.... Mais c'est un chant d'oiseau qui lui répond!³³	With a long whinny, my horse tries to call out to yours.... But it's a bird's song that replies!

青山橫北郭	Green peaks extend along the north rampart,
白水遶東城	White waters wind around the east city wall.
此地一為別	From this place once taking leave
孤蓬萬里征	A lone tumbleweed journeys ten thousand miles.
浮雲遊子意	Floating clouds: a wanderer's thoughts;
落日故人情	Setting sun: an old friend's feelings.
揮手自茲去	Waving hands we go from here:
蕭蕭班馬鳴 [34]	*Xiao xiao* the parting horses neigh.

Li Bo relies on simple imagery to set the scene, the departure of an unnamed friend into a landscape extending across unknown distances and far-reaching rivers and mountains. He also relies on images—rolling tumbleweed, floating clouds, setting sun—to suggest the panoply of emotions associated with parting, travel, and friendship without having to name them explicitly, such as the sorrow of separation, uncertainty about what lies ahead, worry about aging, and comfort in an enduring relationship. There are no tears, just the wave of a hand between friends and the whinnying of horses that can sense they are heading off in different directions.

Gautier retains the poem's title, and the bones of the original are readily apparent in her translation despite her impulse to explain and embellish the traditional associations of these images that readers unfamiliar with Chinese poetry might not recognize. As in many other poems added in 1902, she challenges her readers with a Chinese term that would have been excised in 1867, *li*, a measure word for distance (about one-third of a mile), which she could have easily approximated to *lieue* or "league." Even more surprising is her conclusion to the poem. The binome *xiao xiao* is an onomatopoetic rendering of a horse's neigh, to which the line's final word "cry" refers; this is made clear in the annotations in the anthology Gautier consulted. But in her version, a bird's song responds to the horses instead. Was she perhaps inspired by the fact that *xiao xiao* can also be used onomatopoetically to suggest a bird's wings in flight? More likely she has been persuaded by the ideographical appeal and, in fact, actual etymology of the word to dissect the final graph of the line, *ming* 鳴; it consists of elements meaning mouth *kou* 口 and bird *niao* 鳥, once referring to the sound of birds and then extended to denote the cry of any number of animals, including horses. This original contribution to Li Bo's poem evokes the same atmosphere of resonance in nature as does his. It also anticipates a controversial method later employed by Florence

Ayscough and Amy Lowell in their 1921 collaborative translation efforts that sought to "split-up" a character to foreground its visual effect.[35] As has been noted, Ayscough was probably "the most advanced sufferer from the character-splitting fallacy"[36] by which some early translators lured by the power of the Chinese ideograph were captivated, but Gautier may have anticipated her practice.

Although Gautier claims that she has "rigorously corrected" the poems carried over from the 1867 edition of *The Book of Jade*, most of her "corrections" consist of only slight changes to punctuation—the addition of commas and capitalization—and some compression of the lineation (if that indeed was her decision), with only two of the seventy-one poems undergoing significant revisions. One is the poem by Du Fu that she had titled "To eight great poets who drank together," which becomes, in a closer approximation of the original title, "The eight immortal drinkers" ("Les huit Buveurs immortels"). In 1902 the poem itself is much transformed and, as translation, greatly improved. Perhaps this time choosing to consult Hervey-Saint-Denys's version, Gautier corrects names of drinkers that were wrong in 1867 and provides new versions of the poems' sections that are both more accurate and more concise. What had been the opening of the paean to Li Bo—"Li Taibo, you raise your cup, and before putting it back on the table you've made 100 poems," for example, now reads "Li Taibo: one measure of wine, and instantly 100 poems!" ("Li-Taï-Pé: une mésure de vin, et aussitôt, cent poëmes!"). A closer translation of the original line, it is both crisper and more effective than Hervey-Saint-Denys's less economical version.[37]

The second is "The jade staircase," to which the changes are even more dramatic. For the 1867 volume she had already tinkered with the spacing and lineation of the poem from its first appearance in *L'Artiste* the year before, but in 1902 she took a closer look at the text for a version that is no longer simply "after Li Bo":

L'escalier de Jade est tout scintillant de rosée. Lentement, par cette longue nuit, la souveraine le remonte; laissant la gaze de ses bas et la traîne du vêtement royal, se mouiller, aux gouttes brillantes.	The Jade staircase glistens completely with dew. Slowly, through this long night, the sovereign ascends it again, letting the gauze of her stockings and the train of her regal gown be moistened by brilliant drops.

Sur le seuil du pavillon, éblouie, elle s'arrête, puis baisse le store de cristal, qui tombe, comme une cascade, sous laquelle on voit le soleil.	On the threshold of the tower, dazzled, she stops, then lowers the crystal blind, that falls like a cascade under which one sees the sun.
Et, tandis que s'apaise le clair cliquetis, triste et longuement rêveuse, elle regarde, à travers les perles, briller la lune d'automne.[38]	And, as the light tinkling subsides, sad and dreaming for a long time, she gazes through the pearls at the gleaming autumn moon.

In Gautier's hands the protagonist of this poem remains a "sovereign" rather than the neglected courtesan of Li Bo's quatrain, and while the woman's specific situation is still undefined, the addition of the word "sad" diminishes the evocative understatement of the original. But Gautier brings this version closer to its source in reducing it to four blocks rather than seven (1866) and then five (1867). All of them, particularly the opening, have been "corrected" to correspond more closely to Li's text. She restores the dampened stockings in line 2, which in Li Bo's poem tell the story of the courtesan's fruitless wait on the steps, and she reduces the description of the gown that she had added; the unfolding crystal blind and the woman's gazing at the moon now appear in correct order. The poem still displays her typical descriptive embellishments, but most curious is an addition to line 3, which in the original simply reads "Then she lowers the crystalline blind." Gautier's rendition includes this basic action but adds new information about location ("the threshold of the tower") and also describes the blind as falling "like a cascade under which one sees the sun." Here we see her again succumbing to the lure of the ideograph as a means of enriching the visual interest of the poem, focused here on the binome for "crystal," which consists of the graphs for water (*shui* 水) and crystalline (*jing* 晶); the latter comprises the graph for sun (*ri* 日) repeated three times. While acknowledging in her translation that *shui jing* means crystal, she also unpacks it to add that the lowering blind looks like a sun seen through a waterfall. A gratuitous addition, perhaps, but the simile allows her "to evoke, albeit with a lesser economy of means, both the movement of the unrolling blind and the play of water and light that the Chinese poem actually allows us to witness."[39]

The 1902 edition still consisted primarily of "variations" that in 1867 had harbored no ambitions to be bona fide translations, and the imagistic appeal and companionable cadence of her poems remained. A new scholarly impulse may have led her to insert foreign names for places and persons that she would have omitted in the first edition, and it certainly motivated her decision to include the Chinese characters for the poets' names. As persnickety sinologists could quickly point out, it also proved problematic.

Gautier herself had realized that there were errors of attribution in 1867 that needed to be corrected. Four poems had been "after" a poet named "Tché-Tsi," but the romanization "Tché" is not easily correlated to any Chinese name. Perhaps having recognized this problem, in 1902 Gautier changed the author of two of those poems to "Ouan-Tsi," with the characters for Wang Ji 王績 (585–644), a Sui-dynasty poet who certainly didn't write them. The other two are now by "Tchang-Tsi," but the Chinese characters for him read Li Wei 李巍, which is not the name of any Tang poet. One of the poems is unidentifiable, but the other, "Autumn evening," is by Qian Qi. In originally associating this poem with "Tché-Tsi," Gautier was thus not terribly wrong—Qian is within striking distance of Tché in pronunciation—although Qian Qi did not write the other poems associated in 1867 with "Tché-Tsi."

To complicate matters further, in addition to "Autumn evening," now assigned to Tchang-Tsi, although with characters for Li Wei, and actually written by Qian Qi, and the second unidentifiable poem once "after Tché-Tsi," two other erstwhile "Tché-Tsi" poems are now attributed to "Tchang-Tsi" in the 1902 edition. But for them, confoundingly, the Chinese characters provided by Gautier read Zhang Yue 張說, an early Tang figure who did not write these poems. One of them, "The virtuous wife," discussed earlier, was composed by the mid-Tang poet Zhang Ji 張籍 and is thus correctly identified, albeit with the wrong characters. As for the second, a look back to the 1867 edition is illuminating, for there Gautier attributes the poem to a "Tchan-Oui." The Yue 說 of 1902 was probably a misrepresentation of a similar character Wei 謂, in which case we have the possibility of a new author, the High Tang poet Zhang Wei 張謂 (711–780). Though identified as by Tchang-Tsi in 1902, Gautier's "In the middle of the river" ("Au milieu du fleuve") is in fact based on Zhang Wei's song "Written while drinking on the lake" ("Hu shang dui jiu zuo" 湖上對酒作), which Hervey-Saint-Denys had also conveniently translated.[40] Gautier had been right about the authorship the first time.

Now that everything's perfectly clear, one might wonder at Gautier's audacity in even seeking to provide such scholarly accoutrements to her compositions. It certainly provides an index of her level of confidence in the undertaking, however unwarranted some doubters might want to consider it. Thirty-five years had passed since her first efforts: Had any of her notes survived? And even for the scholars, as Hervey-Saint-Denys had observed, "The task is perilous, and painful as well." One could also wonder why modern scholars try to track down her sources. There's a certain satisfaction in the successful hunt and, for the less charitable, in pointing out her errors. But even as we recognize that adaptation was her primary mode and translation involved taking liberties, it is helpful to understand what her starting point might have been to understand the reasons behind her presumptive choices.

THE COURT

The Court, a newly added section to the 1902 edition, contains six titles. Not surprisingly, four of them focus on the plight of women at court. The authorship of two of those is "unknown," but a third is attributed to Yan-Ta-Tchen (or Yang Taizhen), another way of referring to the Tang emperor Xuanzong's favorite consort Yang Guifei. Titled "Oath of love" ("Voeu d'amour"[41]), it consists of the final lines of a renowned and much longer poem about the ill-fated relationship by a later poet, Bo Juyi 白居易 (772–846). Yang would eventually be held partly responsible for the rebellion launched in 755 that trapped Du Fu in the capital and led to the downfall of Xuanzong's reign; she was killed by government soldiers when the couple fled the capital in 756. Bo Juyi's much admired "Song of enduring regret" ("Chang hen ge" 長恨歌) tells the tragic story of their relationship, ending with the distraught emperor's attempt to reach his deceased beloved through the intercession of a Daoist priest. Yang's response through him to Xuanzong recalls a summer night together when they pledged their unending love, and Gautier's poem is based on the section of Bo Juyi's poem that contains her message. In a sense, therefore, her attribution to Yang was not far off the mark.

The fourth identifiable poem depicting women at court had been included in Gautier's "Prelude" as part of her discussion about Chinese poetic prosody. Titled "In the palace" ("Dans le palais") and attributed to Thou-Sin-Yu, it is a translation of a heptasyllabic quatrain titled "Palace song" ("Gong zhong ci" 宮中詞) by the mid-Tang poet Zhu Qingyu 朱慶餘 (ca. 825):

Quel calme sévère! Quel solennel silence!... Toutes les portes sont closes, et les parterres de fleurs embaument, discrètement;	What grave calm! What solemn silence!... All gates are closed, and the flowerbeds are subtly fragrant;
Deux femmes, appuyées l'une à l'autre, se tiennent debout, au bord de la terrasse, à balustrade de marbre rouge.	Two women, leaning against each other, stand on the edge of the terrace by the red marble balustrade.
L'une d'elles voudrait parler, confier à sa compagne, le chagrin secret qui meurtrit son coeur.	One of them would like to speak, to confide to her companion the secret grief that breaks her heart.
Elle jette un regard anxieux vers les feuillages immobiles, et à cause d'un perroquet, aux ailes chatoyantes, perché sur une branche voisine, elle soupire, et ne parle pas.[42]	She casts an anxious look toward the unmoving foliage, and because of a parrot with shimmering wings perched on a nearby branch, she sighs in silence.

寂寂花時閉院門	In deep stillness as flowers bloom the courtyard gates are shut.
美人相並立瓊軒	The lovely ladies stand leaning toward each other by the fine red balustrade.
含情欲說宮中事	Stifling their feelings they'd love talk about matters within the palace,
鸚鵡前頭不敢言	But with the parrot in front of them they dare not utter a word.

Like "The jade staircase," this poem depicts the plight of courtesans who have lost the emperor's favor and whose sadness can be expressed neither by the women themselves nor the poet. The reader can only infer it from details like the eerie silence and closed gates of a courtyard that in springtime should be abuzz with activity, or from the secretly harbored grief that cannot risk transmission by a parrot. Gautier respects the substance and reticence of the original even as her version displays the more ample rhythms and details of prose that she has always favored.

The two remaining new titles in this section describe a different part of life at court—that of its bureaucrats—and attest to Gautier's greater understanding of the importance of government service in the lives of poets. They are both by Du Fu and had been previewed in the 1901 articles. Du Fu's official career was less than he had hoped it would be, with his one major stint affording direct access to the emperor occurring when he was appointed as "Reminder" in the chancellery in 757. This could be a risky job since it involved "reminding" the ruler of things he might have overlooked. Du Fu's poem titled "Spending a spring night in the chancellery" ("Chun su zuo sheng" 春宿左省) describes what he sees and imagines hearing as he endures a sleepless night in the office while awaiting his appearance before the emperor at dawn the next day. (He may have taken his obligation a bit too seriously and lost his job temporarily as a consequence.) Gautier's version gets straight to the point with its title "Insomnia" ("Insomnie") and follows Du Fu's original fairly closely.[43]

The most impressive addition to this section was composed when Du Fu had left the court, a sequence of eight poems written in 766 while he was staying in the city of Kuizhou, on the Yangzi River in Sichuan, far from the capital of Chang'an. Titled "Autumn Evocations" ("Qiu xing" 秋興), and drawing upon the emotions and memories conjured by the season that is traditionally associated with melancholy, the sequence of eight poems moves back and forth between contemporary scenes in Kuizhou, Du Fu's recollections of life at court, the past glories of the government and his career, and the currently much diminished state of both. The series skillfully intertwines his personal history with that of the country in a painfully poignant manner and has "a strong claim to be the greatest poems in the Chinese language," producing "an extended meditation on the relationship of time and memory to the poetic art."[44] The dense syntax and ambiguous, allusive language of its heptasyllabic regulated verse also present significant challenges to any aspiring translator.

Hervey-Saint-Denys had translated the series as a "Song of autumn" ("Chant d'automne"), so this was one of the few additions to the 1902 volume that could benefit from his example. Gautier no doubt based her versions, which she titles "Autumn's rise: a poem in eight songs" ("Montée d'automne: poème en huit chants") on his explication and untangling of its complex linguistic webs. Her rendition of the first poem in Du Fu's sequence hews remarkably closely to the original, which begins the series with a description of autumn in Kuizhou, the second one he has spent there:

Le jade du givre, blesse et flétrit les tendres platanes de la forêt.	The hoarfrost's jade wounds and withers the tender plane trees in the woods.
Par les montagnes de Vou, par les gorges de Vou, l'air court, et bruit tristement dans les feuillages.	Through Wu peaks, through Wu gorges, the air rushes and rustles sadly through the foliage.
À l'horizon, le fleuve agité, roule le ciel dans ses flots.	On the horizon, the roiled river rolls the sky up in its waves.
Et, des hautains sommets, le vent rabat les nuages, tisse leur ouate avec la gaze des brumes de la terre.	And, from lofty peaks, the wind bats the clouds, weaving their wadding with the gauze of mists on the ground.
En cet exil, voici deux fois, déjà, que je vois, à travers mes larmes, fleurir les luxuriants chrysanthèmes!...	In this exile, it's already twice that I've seen, through my tears, the luxuriant chrysanthemums bloom!...
Je suis comme un barque, retenue par une chaîne au rivage: je ne peux voguer vers l'enclos regretté....	I am like a bark, restrained by a chain to the shore: I cannot sail toward the garden I long for....
De tous côtés, on se hâte de couper et de mesurer des habits d'hiver, en prévision du froid qui vient.	Everywhere they rush to cut and measure winter clothes, preparing for the coming cold.
Et, tout en regardant s'éteindre le jour, j'entends monter, vers la ville de Pé-Ty-Tchan, le son du claquement précipité des battoirs.[45]	And, while watching the daylight fall, I hear urgent clapping sounds of washing blocks rise toward the city of Baidishan.

玉露凋傷楓樹林	Jade dew withers and wounds the forest of maple trees.
巫山巫峽氣蕭森	From Wu Mountain and Wu Gorge the air whistles and wails.
江間波浪兼天湧	Within the river waves and billows join with the sky, surging;
塞上風雲接地陰	Above the pass winds and clouds touch the earth in darkness.
叢花兩開他日淚	Clustered flowers have twice opened: another day's tears;
孤舟一繫故園心	The lonely boat for once ties up a homeward-bound heart.
寒衣處處催刀尺	For winter clothes everywhere knives and rulers are pressed;
白帝城高急暮砧	In White Emperor City on high evening washing blocks hurry.

Gautier in many ways improves on Hervey-Saint-Denys's version:

Les feuilles se détachent, flétries sous les cristaux de la gelée blanche;	The leaves drop off, withered by the crystalline white frost;
Un vent froid suit la vallée des Vou-chan, soufflant et bruissant dans les arbres.	A cold wind follows the Wu Mountain valley, blowing and rustling through the trees.
Rapides et agités, les flots toujours croissant du grand fleuve semblent vouloir monter jusqu'au ciel.	Swift and tossed, the still surging waves of the great river seem to rise up to the sky.
Les nuages de la montagne s'unissent et se confondent avec les brumes de la prairie.	Clouds on the mountain gather and merge with mists on the plain,
Aujourd'hui fleurissent les chrysanthèmes; demain les dernières fleurs seront tombées.	Today the chrysanthemums are blooming; tomorrow the last blossoms will have fallen.

Je suis comme un frêle bateau qu'une chaîne retient à la rive; mes pensées reviennent seules vers mon pays.	I am like a frail boat held to the bank by a chain; my thoughts return alone to my homeland.
De tout côté je vois tailler des habits chauds pour l'hiver qui s'approche;	Everywhere I see warm clothes being cut for the approaching winter;
J'entends monter de la vallée le bruit des coups que frappent les laveuses, pressées d'accomplir leur tâche avant le rapide déclin du jour.[46]	I hear rising from the valley the sound of the blows pounded by laundresses rushing to finish their task before the swiftly dying day.

Unlike him, she retains more directly the opening metaphor of the damage inflicted by gem-like dew—jade, of course—on the forest's trees, the repetition of Wu mountains and Wu gorges in the second line, and the desolate quality of the wind. Her description of the river as "rolling" the sky up in its waves aptly conveys the sense of the merging of sky and water. And her inventive image of the clouds whose "wadding" becomes interwoven with the "gauze" of terrestrial mists or shadows is an effectively vivid representation of their intermingling. Gautier's treatment of the third couplet of the poem, which offers multiple interpretations,[47] is especially deft. Although she follows Hervey-Saint-Denys in reading the boat in line 6 as a simile for the poet, which is less likely than seeing it as an image to which his hopes for returning home are tied, and paradoxically tied down, she conveys more accurately the point of the fifth line, that this is his second autumn in the region, and she manages to incorporate the tears—which could also suggest dew on the flowers—as well. Also, her last line retains the specificity of the reference to Baidishan, or White Emperor Mountain, a city located on the hilltop above Kuizhou, where the sounds of preparations for winter have become more urgent.

Du Fu's sequence of "Autumn evocations" moves through the evening and then the following morning in Kuizhou, jumping in the fourth poem to his visions and memories of the capital of Chang'an and happier times—when he was privileged to be in the emperor's presence—to moments and monuments even further back in history from the Han dynasty, the last great empire before the Tang. Gautier tracks both the content and the emotional arc of the series, ending, as does Du

Fu, by lamenting the failures of his career, the decline of the government, and the fragility of his poetic talents. Where once his "skillful brush" had traced "a thousand new forms of joyful poetry, / Today my head is white and I can only sing painfully, my forehead bent towards the earth" (Mon habile pinceau, traçait alors, en mille forms nouvelles, d'heureux poèmes. / Aujourd'hui, ma tête est blanche et je ne sais plus chanter que douloureusement, le front courbé vers la terre).[48] Readers familiar with the Chinese originals may admire the fidelity of her renditions, but one might also wonder how accessible they were to the uninitiated. The poems become increasingly more allusive, with references to figures and places from both the Han and the Tang dynasties, for which Gautier—unlike in 1867—uses only transliterated Chinese names. Hervey-Saint-Denys and modern-day translators typically annotate the sequence heavily to unpack the allusions, which Gautier does not do.

HER SISTER IN SONG

Contemporary readers had no such problem appreciating the most significant additions to the 1902 volume, Gautier's translations of six song lyrics attributed to the Song-dynasty poet Li Qingzhao, or Li Yi'an. One of them had appeared in June 1901 in her "Chinese Poems," and the other five in December in "Some Great Chinese Poets." Li's pedigree was at least as distinguished as Gautier's. The well-educated daughter of an eminent man of letters whose mother was also an accomplished poet and descendant of a statesman, in 1101 she married a minor official, Zhao Mingcheng 趙明誠 (1081-1129), whose father served as minister of state to the Song-dynasty emperor. When northern invaders forced the Song court to relocate to southern China in 1127, they also fled separately, and Zhao died of illness shortly thereafter.

Li was best known for her *ci* 詞 or "song lyrics," a genre that emerged at the beginning of the eighth century but flourished during the Song. The dominant poetic forms (*shi* 詩) plied by Tang poets were composed in end-stopped lines of equal numbers of syllables—generally five or seven—and without stanza breaks, and if "regulated" consisted of only four or eight lines with one rhyme. Song lyrics, by contrast, were verses in irregular line lengths, often stanzaic, because they were originally set to music, and could vary in the number of lines and rhymes. Poets didn't "write" lyrics, they "filled them in" (*tian* 填) to preexisting tunes, many of which came into China from Central Asian cultures. Although most of the music was soon lost, the lyrics were still known by the title of the original song responsible for setting the pattern of tones, line lengths, and number of lines to which the words were obliged to conform, but the title generally had little to do with the content. Early song lyrics were composed to be performed by courtesans and musicians; some were also part of a courtly repertoire. As interactions between professional entertainers and literati flourished, song lyric forms that had once been largely of unknown authorship or composed by the singers themselves came gradually to be appropriated by educated officials for their own purposes. Typically written in a woman's voice and often employing more colloquial diction than *shi*, they were often performed by women at social gatherings, and sometimes for the very men who had composed them. Thus developed a conventional repertoire of expressions of desire and longing, usually situated in the boudoir and as imagined by men. Although song lyrics were considered a literary form of lower status than *shi*, respected scholars plied them with pleasure.

The traditional use of a female persona made it easy to read Li's song lyrics autobiographically, as authentic expressions of her own experiences and emotions, charting the contrast between the blissful early years of her marriage and the later sorrows of solitary widowhood. Very few of her lyrics, however, can be dated securely at all, and the instability of her collection and distinctive features of her style prompted many imitations. But for Gautier, as for most premodern commentators, there was no question about the seamless connection between the lyrics and Li's life. Thus the discussion of Li Qingzhao in which Gautier embeds her five translations in "Some Great Chinese Poets," which she then incorporates into her "Prelude" to the 1902 *Book of Jade*, describes her predecessor's work as "very personal" and presenting "the autobiography of a heart of a woman." Given the equally compelling resonance with her own unhappy love life, those lyrics imbued with the heartbreak of loss and loneliness—whenever they might have been composed—must have been of irresistible appeal to her; notably, she translates none of the pieces in different veins, whether lighthearted, political, or historical, that can also be found in Li's corpus. For Gautier it was clear that "Li Yi'an only deals with one subject: The incurable wound of a heart bleeding in solitude. The solitude, reclusion, the impotence of the Chinese woman in the face of action are expressed in her poems poignantly without her saying a single word about them." Gautier seems not in fact to have been aware of Zhao Mingcheng's existence, for she imagines that whoever has inspired the love "devouring this

Chinese Sappho" is oblivious to it: "Perhaps he's never even seen her, and she makes no effort to present herself or attract him: her situation as a woman, customs, conventions, don't permit that. One might say she's a flower in the clutches of a bird, without voice or wings, only able to breathe, while dying, her soul perfumed with love."[49]

How much of herself did Gautier see in Li? Her contemporaries likened the two because of their shared talent, but had they known more about the Chinese poet the similarities as well as the differences would have been striking. Judith Gautier and Li Qingzhao were both exceptional women married to men who in disparate ways did not live up to them. As an individual Catulle Mendès never proved worthy of the frustrated hopes and desires that fueled Gautier's readings of Chinese poetry, and his life and career after their separation left little trace on hers. She never looked back. Zhao Mingcheng was an exemplar of Confucian probity and dedication to government service who had spent his few years together with Li assembling and documenting a massive collection of precious artifacts that included rubbings of inscriptions on bronze vessels and stone steles. Both the collection and his catalogue of the inscriptions were largely lost, stolen, or destroyed when Li, who had been left responsible for them, fled with them to the south. Researching and savoring their books and treasures had been a shared delight, but as Li hints in an afterword to Zhao's *Records on Metal and Stone* (*Jin shi lu hou xu* 金石錄後序) that she wrote after his death, his devotion to the collection had bordered on an obsession more powerful than his concern for his wife's fate. The account is remarkable for its candor and emotional power, and it also reveals less helplessness in dealing with increasingly desperate straits than Gautier might have imagined, with a tinge of reproach as well.[50]

There was more about Li's biography unknown to Gautier that would have made it even more resonant for her, like her constant worries as a young, childless widow about her finances and her later remarriage to, lawsuit against, and subsequent divorce from an abusive man, in connection with which she was briefly imprisoned.[51] However romanticized and incomplete her view of Li may have been, Gautier saw in Li the same tragic figure that generations of Chinese readers had constructed. As she writes in her commentary, Li "connects her grief with the world in which she lives, the nature she sees all around her and discovers from her window; the seasons changing are the only events, the objects decorating her room are the only witnesses to her life, frozen in a single thought."[52] Her selections are crafted to maintain this image, but her translations follow the originals surprisingly closely, with minimal revision or augmentation.[53] The wild geese that in Chinese poetry were seen as messengers to or reminders of absent loved ones are replaced in more than one piece by wild swans more familiar to French readers, for example, but Gautier also retains, and even annotates, references to traditional Chinese holidays. What entrances her is the "light and perfect touch" of the tableau from which the image of a young woman clearly emerges, as in the following lyric, which she titles "Springtime chill" ("Froideur printanière"): "We see her languidly leaning against the jade railing watching the fragrant smoke rising from the incense burner. This light mist from which she seems to weave her dream is the only thing that slightly stirs around the recluse absorbed in a mysterious grief that she can only partially express."[54]

Dans l'enclos mélancolique,	In the melancholy courtyard,
Le vent penche, et entraîne les fils de la pluie mince.	The wind bends and sweeps the threads of light rain.
Il est bon que la double porte reste fermée.	It's good that the double door stays closed.
La grâce des saules, la délicatesse des fleurs subissent le temps capricieux qui règne vers cette époque des *aliments froids*.	The graceful willows and delicate flowers endure the changeable weather typical of Cold Food Festival.
Mais quel que soit le temps, il est toujours difficile de trouver la juste harmonie des rimes.	But whatever the weather, it's always hard to find the right rhymes.
Cependant voici que la poésie est terminée.	Nevertheless, now the poetry is done.

II

Qui donc soutient et console celui qui se réveille de l'ivresse?... de l'ivresse des poètes, qui est autre que celle du vin?...	Who then supports and consoles the one who awakens tipsy... from the tipsiness of poets, which is different from that of wine?...

Voici que les cygnes sauvages ont fini de passer.
Ah! J'ai dans le coeur mille choses douloureuses que je voulais confier à ces messagers rapides!...

Now the wild swans have all passed by.
Ah! there are a thousand painful things in my heart that I wanted to confide to those speedy messengers!...

III

En ces jours, le froid printanier se fait sentir, à l'étage supérieur.
Des quatre côtés les stores du pavillon sont baissés devant les fenêtres.
Je suis trop nonchalante pour venir m'appuyer à la balustrade de jade...
La couverture est froide,... le parfum est consumé...
Je m'éveille de mon dernier rêve!
...
Oh! pourquoi n'est-il pas interdit de rêver à ceux qui ont une grande douleur....
Les perles de la rosée se fondent en eau.
De nouveau les arbres vont reverdir.
Et beaucoup se réjouissent de voir ce retour du printemps.
Le soleil monte, le brouillard s'envole... Il me faut regarder, encore, le beau temps d'aujourd'hui!...

These days the springtime chill can be felt on the upper story.
On all four sides the pavilion's shades are drawn before the windows.
I feel too languid to come and lean on the jade balustrade....
The coverlet is cold,... the incense has been spent...
I've awakened from my last dream!
...
Oh! why isn't dreaming forbidden for those who suffer from great pain?...
The pearls of dew melt into water.
Once again the trees will be verdant.
And many rejoice to see the return of spring.
The sun rises, the fog disappears... I must look once again at today's fine weather!

"Springtime chill" is a translation of a lyric Li composed to the tune "Remembering her charms" ("Nian nu jiao" 念奴嬌):

蕭條庭院	Desolate is the courtyard,
又斜風細雨	And there's slanting wind and light rain.
重門須閉	The double doors must be closed.
寵柳嬌花寒食近	Favorite willows and fetching flowers: Cold Food Festival is nigh.
種種惱人天氣	So many ways this season can grate:
險韻詩成	But the poem with challenging rhymes is finished.
扶頭酒醒	I hold my head, sobering up from wine,
別事閑滋味	To leisure's flavor of a different sort.
征鴻過盡	The migrating geese have passed by,
萬千心事難寄	But my myriad cares are hard to convey.
樓上幾日春寒	On the upper story how many days of springtime chill?
簾垂四面	Shades hang down on all four sides.
玉闌干慵倚	On the jade balustrade just too languid to lean,
被冷香消新夢覺	The coverlet cold, incense spent, awake from the latest dream.
不許愁人不起	One can't expect someone grieving not to get up.
清露晨流	The clear dew flows at dawn,
新桐初引	New paulownia buds are just emerging.
多少遊春意	How right the mood for a springtime stroll!
日高煙斂	The sun is rising and haze dispersing,
更看今日晴未 [55]	So I'll look again to see if today will be clear or not.

This is one of Li's several lyrics set during a traditional Chinese holiday, in this case the Cold Food festival in early spring when ancestors were venerated; Gautier even provides a footnote to explain that. Her speaker does not explain the reasons for the irritation aroused by the weather, although holidays are meant to be celebrated with family, and she is presumably separated from loved ones she wishes the wild geese could send a message to. Nonetheless, she has succeeded in finding the correct and challenging rhymes to finish a poem and is sobering up from too much wine, and though resentful that her sadness won't allow her to stay in bed, seems curious at the end about whether clear skies will allow her to go outside.

In Gautier's hands most of the elements of Li's lyric have been incorporated, although the two stanzas have become three (she breaks the first into two), and her speaker, in contrast to Li's, laments the fact that she can't help sleeping and dreaming, despite her sadness. She does not seem to share with others the delightful prospect of a spring outing but will remain secluded, "absorbed in a mysterious grief which she can only partially express," although the final line offers promise for a change of mood. About reticence of expression Gautier is right, as she was correct in recognizing Li's pride in her poetic talents, something that appears in other lyrics as well. With those talents she no doubt identified, as she might have seen in the *nonchalante* ("languid" or "indifferent") figure leaning on a jade balustrade an image of herself. "Nonchalant" was in fact one of the most commonly deployed adjectives to describe Gautier herself by those who knew her.

Li Qingzhao knew well the work of other practitioners of the song lyric, and her "Discussion of the Lyric" ("Ci lun" 詞論) was one of the earliest critical essays on the genre, demonstrating both her awareness of its distinctiveness and her fearless critique of others' shortcomings. She was extremely conscious of her craft, and of her determination "to write in this form and to do so as well or better than any man."[56] Gautier knows that Li was recognized as "a superior mind" well versed "in all the minutiae and difficulties of poetic art," and that she was notable for her disarming expression, startling imagery, striking rhythms, and unexpected diction, "unusual innovations that she realizes with a skill that makes one forgive and admire her audacity."[57] Indeed, Li's unconventional style was as remarkable in her time as Gautier's own bold formal innovations in *The Book of Jade* were in hers. Li's poem to the tune "Sound after sound, a long song" ("Shengsheng man" 聲聲慢) is a recognized tour de force, which Gautier's translation, "Despair" ("Désespoir") captures remarkably well:

Appelle! Appelle! Implore! implore!	Appeal! Appeal! Implore! Implore!
Stagne! stagne! Rêve! rêve!	Stop! stop! Dream! dream!
Pleure! pleure! Souffre! souffre! ...	Weep! weep! Suffer! suffer!
Toujours! toujours!	Forever! forever!
A peine fait-il chaud que la saison du froid revient!	It's hardly turned warm when the season of cold returns!
Ah! qu'il est accablant d'exister!	Ah, how overwhelming it is to exist!

Deux ou trois tasses de faible vin,
Ne suffisent pas, pour faire sup-
  porter l'âpre vent de l'aurore.

Two or three cups of insipid wine
Don't suffice to protect against the
  biting wind of dawn.

II

Les cygnes sauvages repassent
  déjà.
Ah! que mon coeur est cruelle-
  ment blessé!
Il y a longtemps que je les connais,
  pour les voir ainsi passer et
  repasser...
Les chrysanthèmes foisonnent,
  partout sur la terre, en une
  exubérance somptueuse.
Mais la fleur qui s'étiole ici,
Qui donc voudrait la cueillir?

The wild swans have already
  passed by.
Ah! how cruelly wounded is my
  heart!
I've known them for so long, to see
  them pass by again and
  again...
Chrysanthemums pile up everywhere on the ground, richly
  luxuriant.
But the flower that withers here,
Who would want to pluck it?

III

Ne suis-je pas la sempiternelle gar-
  dienne de cette fenêtre?
Quand donc cette journée
  s'éteindra-t-elle dans
  l'obscurité?...
Une pluie fine mouille les larges
  feuilles des paulownias,
Le crépuscule vient lentement;
  l'obscurité tombe, tombe,
  goutte à goutte.
Le voici complète, maintenant, la
  nuit, et rien n'est changé
  pour moi...

Am I not the sempiternal keeper
  of this window?
When will this day be extin-
  guished by the darkness?

A light rain dampens the large
  paulownia leaves.
Twilight comes slowly; darkness
  falls, falls, drop by drop.

Now it's finally here, the night,
  and nothing has changed
  for me...

Oh! comment pourrait-on détruire, à jamais, le mot: *désespoir?* …	Oh! how might one destroy forever the word "despair?" …

尋尋覓覓	Seeking, seeking, searching, searching,
冷冷清清	Cold, cold, chill, chill,
悽悽慘慘戚戚	Mournful, mournful, anguished, anguished, fretful, fretful.
乍暖還寒時候	This season of sudden warmth, then cold again:
最難將息	Hardest of all is finding rest.
三杯兩盞淡酒	Two or three cups of insipid wine:
怎敵他	How can they fend off
晚來風力	That late wind's force?
雁過也	The geese passed by.
正傷心	Just wounding my heart,
卻是舊時相識	Yet I recognized them from before.
滿地黃花堆積	Yellow flowers cover the ground in heaps:
憔悴損	I'm wan and haggard,
如今有誰忺摘	So who will enjoy plucking them now?
守著窗兒	I keep by the window
獨自怎生得黑	Alone, how did it become so dark?
梧桐更兼細雨	On the paulownias still the fine rain
到黃昏	Until dusk goes
點點滴滴	Drip, drip, drop, drop.
這次第	One thing after another:
怎一箇愁字了得[58]	How can one word "sorrow" express it all?

"Sound after sound" was Li Qingzhao's best-known lyric, primarily because of its technical audacity: the unprecedented and plangent repetitions take the genre far beyond its conventional boudoir boundaries. By breaking up common disyllabic compounds and then duplicating each character, Li creates the mood of restless desperation from unnamed causes—only the wild geese/swans suggest that she has been separated from loved ones, and for some time—that pervades both the scene and temper of the entire piece, reinforced by another set of duplicatives at the end. Although Gautier's translations of the terms are free at best, she replicates and recognizes Li's method: "The cries of distress at the beginning are uttered in contravention of all rules. Nonetheless, the effect in Chinese is so energetic, so poignant, that even the most severe scholar on the verge of annoyance is obliged to admire it."[59] Gautier must have been aware that even the sounds of Li's poem in Chinese—with its repeated, often fricative consonants and preponderance of tones in the harsher "deflected" category—intensify its mood of fretful anguish. Her repeated questions, like Li's, convey the futility that suffuses the poem, an ennui read through the dense legacy of Baudelaire and Mallarmé. And while we might wonder at her rendering of the last line, her choice of the word "despair" summarizes aptly the work's emotional tenor.

Gautier describes these strophes as ones in which Li "reveals at once her great talent and her great sorrow. She lived cloistered in her suffering, wanting neither to be distracted nor cured, and she named in advance the volume that posterity would form of her scattered poems *The Debris of My Heart* (*Le débris de mon coeur*)."[60] This is a puzzling statement, for the printed collection of Li's song lyrics that circulated during her lifetime, although all copies were subsequently lost, was titled the *Collection of Jades for Rinsing* (*Shu yu ji* 漱玉集), which "derived from an old saying about rinsing one's mouth in a stream that flows over stones (to purify it), with 'jades' substituted for 'stones.'"[61] Since it is hard to imagine that Gautier would have passed up an opportunity to highlight more jades, it is likely that whoever introduced her to Li Qingzhao's work mistakenly appropriated the title of a collection of poetry attributed to another woman contemporary, Zhu Shuzhen 朱淑貞, *Collection of a Broken Heart* (*Duan chang ji* 斷腸集), with a preface dated 1182. Although wildly contradictory biographical information ranging over two centuries has led modern scholars to doubt Zhu's historical existence, suspecting that she may have been a fabrication of male writers, her collection did survive.[62] It would have been easy to confuse details about the two most famous woman poets of the twelfth century—Zhu Shuzhen was said to have lived an equally tragic life, having been married off unhappily by her parents and died young—and the title of her collection no doubt made perfectly good sense to Gautier as belonging to Li.

Gautier is silent about who, if anyone, may have worked with her on the second edition of *The Book of Jade*, and in particular on her translations of Li Qingzhao. To the contrary, she concludes her essay framing "Some Great Chinese Poets and the Poetess Li Yi'an" by claiming sole credit, writing that "for my part, it is with tender admiration that I've deciphered the verse of this lofty and moving poetess, and I am delighted to be the first, I think, to sound the melodious name of Li Yi'an outside the Celestial Empire."[63] Ham Nghi, as we have seen, had demurred for lack of expertise. Perhaps one of the Chinese emissaries she befriended introduced her to Li's work and provided some translation assistance. Or possibly, as has been suggested, it was a diplomat and scholar named George Soulié de Morant (1878-1955).[64]

The two met when his family was spending the summer on the Breton coast near Gautier's house at St. Énogat. According to one account, in the summer of 1886 a young boy could be seen "diligently tracing patterns in the sand" which "did not lack for originality. Only an informed eye would have been able to recognize in them Chinese ideograms: the young Georges Soulié was busy repeating the lessons taught by 'Théophile Gautier's Chinese man.'"[65] Soulié's biographers mistakenly believe that Ding Dunling lived with Gautier and have therefore concluded that it was he who introduced the boy to the rudiments of the language. We know that Ding lived with patrons elsewhere and had, moreover, been ill for some time and would die later that year. But whoever Soulié's first tutor may have been, Gautier certainly encouraged his studies of the language and culture.

Having embarked on a career in finance at age nineteen, Soulié demonstrated a facility in Chinese that led his employer to send him to a post abroad in 1901. Soulié spent most of the next two decades in the country, serving in various capacities as interpreter and then consul for the French diplomatic service. While in China he was the first European to become interested in acupuncture—he had witnessed its therapeutic powers during a 1905 cholera epidemic—and his efforts over the course of the next thirty years to instruct and persuade the French medical establishment of its efficacy after his return to the country were so successful that he was nominated for the Nobel Prize in Medicine in 1950.

In addition to numerous books and articles on acupuncture Soulié was also the author of almost forty works on subjects ranging from Mongolian grammar to Chinese literature, history, law, and culture; he also produced translations, biographies, and novels.[66] Gautier never hesitated to take credit for his interest, writing to one of his senior diplomatic colleagues that she was responsible for Soulié's successful career in China: "It's I who gave him the taste for things Chinese, who discovered his extraordinary aptitude for a language so difficult to learn that he knows so well."[67] And he never passed up an opportunity to return the favor, acknowledging both her support and her own accomplishments. On arriving in China, for example, he wrote to her that "One sees again with every step *The Imperial Dragon*,"[68] pointing to the accuracy of her descriptions. His 1912 *Essay on*

Chinese Literature cites her translation of a famous poem by the Han-dynasty emperor Wu and praises her *Book of Jade* as "the most precise and most poetic translation one could possibly achieve." Translating poetry is a challenge: "All the effects of rhythm and sonority disappear; only the poetic idea remains. But in order to understand it, beyond total familiarity with texts, one must already be a poet: to model it anew, one must also be a great poet and as perfectly literary as the author one translates. That is why we know only one beautiful translation of Chinese poems, the *Book of Jade* of Mme Judith Gautier, who, to conscientiousness and fidelity of translation, knew how to join the poetic expression of feeling: she saw and could make visible everything beautiful and delicate in the poems."[69] In the introduction to his own 1923 anthology of Song-dynasty poetry he recognizes her as the first French translator of any works from that era, noting especially that the name and lyrics of Li Qingzhao "were revealed to Europe for the first time by Madame Judith Gautier."[70]

There's no question about the linguistic fluency Soulié de Morant acquired after several years in China. He visited Gautier frequently in both Paris and St. Énogat when on home leave from China and was delighted that she once spoke to her Chinese manservant with an accent so impeccable that the latter introduced him as a "Chinese gentleman."[71] His sinological expertise was eventually broader and deeper than hers as well, but certainly not before his departure for China in early 1901—the timing of which in any case would have made it difficult if not impossible for him to collaborate on the Li Qingzhao translations she worked on that year.[72]

Did Gautier receive help from some of the many Chinese she came to know, in addition to the ambassadors? In a letter to Soulié she refers to someone named "Tcheu" (Zhi), "a new Chinese friend who is the best educated and most intelligent of them all. . . . Tcheu wrote a poem to me, another Chinese who came from America did the same, and I've hung them all in my living room, very proudly. You see that rather than countries I explore friends, and I am more than ever in China. Last Monday I took five Chinese to the Louvre. It was a spectacle worth seeing. Next Tuesday, I'm taking them in caravans to the National Library."[73] But she never mentions any of them as collaborators on this project.

Gautier's own command of Chinese had clearly advanced beyond the level she possessed when she undertook her first translation efforts a scant year after beginning the study of Chinese in 1863. In most of the "variations" in the 1867 volume of *The Book of Jade*, which were only loosely associated with authors, she rarely aspired to produce faithful versions of the sources; she dispensed with the original titles, replaced specific references with generic terms, chose to translate only a few lines of a poem, and added explanations of allusions to obviate the need for annotation. But it is also true that she knew more than most have suspected. The few examples of relatively straightforward translation suggest that Gautier's deviations from standard scholarly practice derived as much from aesthetic choice as from a failure of understanding—something that consulting Hervey-Saint-Denys's volume could have remedied, had she wished to. By 1902 she opted for greater fidelity more consistently, and the definitive attributions of authorship reflect her greater confidence with the language. There is little reason to doubt that she tackled most of the poems newly added to *The Book of Jade*, and especially those of Li Qingzhao, on her own.[74] While the liberties taken with the 1867 variations had not in fact been "rigorously corrected" at all, the 1902 "translations" fully merited the name, and hers as their author.

CHAPTER 8

"Radiated beyond the scholarly world"

An Extraordinary Afterlife

The 1902 edition of *The Book of Jade* quickly sold out, and its publisher Félix Juven reissued it in 1908. In addition to deleting the Chinese characters, he also cut the prefatory material except for Gautier's "Prelude" and her translation of Yu Geng's improvisational epigraph. This would provide the basis for all subsequent complete editions. Most French readers of *The Book of Jade* cared little about her fidelity to original Chinese sources; they recognized the groundbreaking nature of her publication and its unusually broad appeal. As one critic wrote, "Despite their unusual character and distant origins, these exquisite works have not remained confined to a circle of mandarins, they have radiated beyond the scholarly world and deserve a place in every anthology."[1] And, indeed, the book's impact was palpable in several literary domains from the turn of the century onward—in French letters, among Anglo-American modernist poets, in the larger international history of translation and retranslation, and across the other arts.[2]

THE BOOK OF JADE AND CONTEMPORARY POETRY

By unsettling prevailing prosodic conventions, Gautier's *Book of Jade* left its mark on the history of French poetry. Théophile Gautier had linked his daughter's work with the newly developed prose poem, likening her "Jade staircase" to Baudelaire's well-known "The blessings of the moon," and to works by the pioneer of the genre, Aloysius Bertrand. In many ways the differences are striking: her pieces are shorter and more clearly patterned by repetition, parallelism, and refrain than the typically long paragraphs of their works. The proliferation of commas, especially in the 1902 edition, creates an internal rhythm of pauses within each line. Her lines are not only longer than typical French verse but also unmetered and unrhymed, and she often reduces poems to uneven numbers of lines—three, five, seven—that reject the dictates of conventional prosody. In her memoir she herself recalls complaining to her father, who was encouraging her to write poetry, that it forced her to be "preoccupied with rhyme and measure ... but I have nothing to measure!" By contrast, when reading Persian poetry in unmetered translation, which her suitor Mohsin-Khan had introduced her to, she found a typical short piece by writers like [Omar] Khayyam, Hafiz, or Saadi [Shirazi] to be "perfect and complete, like a pearl or a diamond. Even through prose and the awkwardness of word for word you understand what it must be like."[3] And her family's literary orbit included not only Baudelaire but also the first publisher of his prose poems, Catulle Mendès.[4]

Often using the term "prose poem" interchangeably with *vers libre*, or free verse, other poets recognized the importance of Gautier's *Book of Jade* in the lineage of both.[5] In discussing what Baudelaire had described as "the miracle of a poetic prose, musical but without rhythm and rhyme," Mallarmé acknowledged that the Peruvian exile Nicanor della Rocca de Vergalo (1848–1919) and the Polish-born Marie Krysinska (1857–1908) were innovators in the form; the latter was even referred to as the "St. John the Baptist of free verse." But like his friend Mendès, he much preferred "*The Book of Jade* of Judith Gautier to the pale productions of the immigrant."[6] His fellow Symbolist Arthur Rimbaud (1854–1891) also likely "drew his first inspiration" from her volume for his own prose poems.[7] Verlaine's praise of *The Book of Jade* in his 1867 review compares it favorably to her forerunner: "I know of no analogue to this book in our literature other than the *Gaspard of the Night* of our late lamented Aloysius Bertrand. And moreover, if asked to choose I would much prefer *The Book of Jade* for its greater originality, its purer form, a poetry that is both more real and more intense."[8] And, indeed, Gautier's influence "is palpable in Verlaine's next collection," whose "restraint and descriptive precision" owe much to her example.[9]

Other contemporaries agreed with Verlaine that Gautier had composed prose poems and referred to them as such. Catulle Mendès stakes a different claim for his ex-wife as the most important early practitioner of *vers libre*, which he distinguishes from the prose poem. After dismissing the role of both Della Rocca de Vergalo and Marie Krysinska, he also argues that the earlier authors of prose poems like Bertrand and Baudelaire were not in fact writing verse. In speaking of the origins of *vers libre* one should therefore "take into consideration ... above all *The Book of Jade* of Mme Judith Gautier, with its exquisitely sonorous and melodiously measured stanzas."[10] Mendès uses the word "stanzas" to distinguish Gautier's block-lines of poetry from the prose poet's much longer paragraphs. But whether her "stanzas" that often comprised more than one sentence should be considered *vers libre* has been debated, and consensus opinion has associated her translations more closely with the prose poem tradition. The line between the two was obviously often unclear, reflecting "the tendency of the *fin-de-siècle* generation to view artistic prose, the prose poem, and even the new 'prosaic' verse form, *vers libre*, as barely distinguishable phenomena."[11] But what they did share was a rejection of rhyme, meter, and strict lineation, an origin in France, and the mark of innovation.

The Book of Jade also played a role in the story of how translations of Chinese poetry influenced modern English verse. As many have noted, in the late nineteenth and early twentieth centuries translations "were a site of experimentation and poems in their own right."[12] If Gautier's adaptations departed from conventional French verse, they also bore little formal resemblance to the Chinese originals that inspired them, for which rules governing rhyme, meter, and parallelism were even more restrictive than those of French poetry. Her idiomatic cadence contrasts markedly with the often highly compressed syntax and relatively short, end-stopped lines of Chinese regulated verse. Her translations as well as her prosody were "free." But the relative conciseness and restraint of her poems honored her sources and stimulated further innovation. Her fondness for poems featuring unrequited love may have betrayed the sentimentality appropriate to her age and the frustrations of her forbidden marriage, but readers recognized that her style provided a concrete model of how not to write like a French Romantic poet. Similarly, it suggested to poets working in English how to avoid the "periphrastic verbosity"[13] of their Victorian or Edwardian counterparts. Influences from poets writing across the Channel had already been important sources of innovation—"one had, in the late eighties and early nineties, to be preposterously French."[14] But a related source of inspiration was the insight into Chinese poetic methods that Gautier managed to provide, despite her many liberties, which Anglo-American writers explored in their own poetry and translations.

Indeed, she was described as the first European to suspect that "there might be in Chinese modes of poetry never so much as intuited by the West."[15] As the Imagist poet John Gould Fletcher (1886-1950) recalled, "if French Symbolism be taken for the father of Imagism, Chinese poetry was its foster-father," and Gautier was part of this lineage. He wrote that her work was more inspirational to him than the translations of the renowned sinologist James Legge (1815-1897), of whom he wrote that a "more than Scotch matter-of-factness, as well as his utter inability to appreciate any poetical qualities in the Chinese written character, repelled me."[16] Kenneth Rexroth (1905-1982) declared that "all the Imagists were familiar with Judith Gautier's *Livre de Jade*—that precious minor classic of French letters. From it they got their first intimation of Chinese poetry—a poetry which fulfilled and surpassed the Imagist Manifesto beyond the abilities or dreams of even the best of the Imagists." She inspired several to undertake their own translations from the Chinese, which are "in each case incomparably their author's best work." Gautier, who Rexroth believed did not know Chinese and worked with a "Thai informant," "provided the Imagists with her special interpretations of Chinese poetry—a mood of exquisitely refined weariness and excruciating sensibility."[17]

Most discussions about the influence of translations from the Chinese have rightly focused on Ezra Pound (1885-1972), who, through the work of the American scholar of Japanese art and culture, Ernest Fenollosa (1853-1908), discovered in the Asian tradition a lyric that proved instrumental in the rediscovery of concision and directness in Anglo-American poetry. The dynamics of this impact were shaped by the limited and in some ways mistaken view of both Chinese literature and its language that Pound extracted from notes entrusted to him by Fenollosa's widow on studies of Chinese poetry with Japanese scholars. His volume of translations published as *Cathay* in 1915 gives us good reason to think of him, as T. S. Eliot famously did, as the "inventor of Chinese poetry for our time,"[18] whose "misunderstanding of Chinese proved indispensable" to coping with a contemporary crisis of Western poetry.[19] Gautier's *Book of Jade* already "had invented Chinese poetry for her era"[20] and played a generally unacknowledged role in the one dominated by Pound.[21]

If Fenollosa's notebooks provided Pound with important theoretical inspiration and philological information, the formally innovative poems in Gautier's *Book of Jade* modeled the suggestive power of a reliance on concrete imagery, rhetorical restraint, and modulated emotions characteristic of the Chinese originals. Pound was familiar with the volume,[22] and three of the fifteen poems in his *Cathay*, all by Li Bo—whom Pound refers to by the Japanese Rihaku—overlap with her selections in the 1902 edition. While his own translations would distill and extend the lessons of Chinese poetry even further, readers have noticed the kinship between one of his most celebrated translations, "The Jewel Stairs' Grievance," and her "Jade staircase":

> The jewelled steps are already quite white with
> dew,
> It is so late that the dew soaks my gauze stockings,
> And I let down the crystal curtain
> And watch the moon through the clear autumn.

> NOTE—Jewel stairs, therefore a palace. Grievance, therefore there is something to complain of. Gauze stockings, therefore a court lady, not a servant who complains. Clear autumn, therefore he has no excuse on account of weather. Also she has come early, for the dew has not merely whitened the stairs, but has soaked her stockings. The poem is especially prized because she utters no direct reproach.[23]

Pound was prompted to append this note because, as he wrote later, he "never found any occidental who could 'make much' of that poem in one reading. Yet upon careful examination we find that everything is there, not merely by 'suggestion' but by a sort of mathematical process of reduction."[24] The most available previous translation into English, "From the Palace" by Herbert Giles in his *Chinese Poetry in English Verse*, respects the terseness but—thanks to its sing-song rhymes closer to limerick than lyric—certainly not the mood:

> Cold dews of night the terrace crown,
> And soak my stockings and my gown;
> I'll step behind
> The crystal blind,
> And watch the autumn moon sink down.

This was "the kind of pat versification that Pound was trying to blast out of favor forever."[25] Small wonder that, as Rexroth argues, Gautier's *Book of Jade* and, to a lesser degree, Hervey-Saint-Denys's *Poetry of the Tang Dynasty* were both of far greater value to English and American poets than those of English scholars like Giles, whose work was "practically worthless, because of the doggerel verse in which they were rendered."²⁶ Pound's version has radically condensed Gautier's unrhymed prose poem by extracting her explanatory additions—which she herself reduced in 1902—and moving them to the note, but he retains her typical use of the conjunction "and" to juxtapose elements of the poem unemotionally and without comment. By "glossing nearly every element of Gautier's translation that he removed, Pound's poem and annotation taken together appear more like a translation of, or at least an explicit response to, Gautier's translation."²⁷

Even more closely related are Pound's translation of Li Bo's famous "Farewell to a friend" and Gautier's "Departure of a friend," seen earlier:

TAKING LEAVE OF A FRIEND

Blue mountains to the north of the walls,
White river winding about them;
Here we must make separation
And go out through a thousand miles of dead grass.
Mind like a floating wide cloud.
Sunset like the parting of old acquaintances
Who bow over their clasped hands at a distance.
Our horses neigh to each other
    as we are departing.²⁸

Pound's version benefits in fidelity from not having been distracted by the "character-splitting" fallacy that led Gautier astray in the final line of the poem, where she hears a bird responding to the horse's whinny. While pointing this out, George Steiner also noticed years ago that though "Judith Gautier's 'Le Départ d'un ami' in *Le Livre de Jade* (1867) differs from Pound's 'Taking Leave of a Friend' in verbal detail, the conventions of melancholy and cool space are precisely analogous." Here, however, the kinship derives not so much, as Steiner argues, from the fact that they both knew so little about the Chinese but from the fact that they both correctly intuit so much and can convey remarkably faithfully the dispassionate "emotional register" of the original poem. And this register, expressed with linguistic economy in a concrete, imagistic style, became the hallmark of translations of Chinese poetry.²⁹

PROSE PASTELS

Anglo-American writers who had not read *The Book of Jade* in the original French had already been introduced to Gautier's work by the American poet Stuart Merrill (1863-1915).[30] Merrill had spent much of his childhood in France, thanks to his father's diplomatic appointment, and studied French with, among others, Mallarmé. After returning briefly to the States he began writing poetry—Rexroth described him as "the best American poet until the end of the First World War, with the exception of Carl Sandburg"[31]—and he published his translations of several French prose poems into English in 1890, in a volume titled *Pastels in Prose,* which modestly did not include examples of his own work in the genre. The three retranslations into German, Italian, and Portuguese of selections from *The Book of Jade* that were published around that time by Böhm, Massarani, and Feijó had all reverted to rhyme and meter in their renditions, unlike Gautier herself. For Merrill, however, it was precisely the absence of those features that was key: they were *prose* poems, and in his introduction to *Pastels in Prose* the writer and critic William Dean Howells (1837-1920) articulates additional distinguishing characteristics of the form.

Howells opens by declaring the prose poem to be "a peculiarly modern invention," although he grants that certain books of the Bible, and perhaps the entire scripture, could be viewed as exemplars of "poetical prose." But the selections in Merrill's book are defined by something different, "the beautiful reticence which characterizes them, as if the very freedom which the poets had found in their emancipation from the artificial trammels of verse had put them on their honor, as it were, and bound them to brevity, to simplicity." Most notably, he adds, "What struck me most was that apparently none of them had abused his opportunity to saddle his reader with a moral." The refusal to burden the prose poem with an argument, he concludes, creates a delicacy, if not fragility, that "is happily expressed in the notion of 'Pastels.'"[32] This concision, delicacy, rejection of didacticism, and resistance to definitive closure are precisely the characteristics about Gautier's works that had struck Verlaine and other readers as well and distinguish them from the style of earlier nineteenth-century poets in both France and England.

In Merrill's anthology we find the recognized luminaries of the prose poem form, beginning with thirteen pieces from Bertrand and moving on to eight of Baudelaire's best-known examples, including "The blessings of the moon." Mendès and Mallarmé even provide him with versions of works "from the final proof-sheets of their new volumes."[33] But the centerpiece of the volume is the group of fourteen poems from Gautier's *Book of Jade*, by far the greatest number of any author. Several of the pieces we have discussed make their appearance—Ding Dunling's "The shadow of the orange leaves," Li Bo's "The mysterious flute" and "The sages dance," and Du Fu's "The house in the heart" are all there—and they would remain favorites of later retranslators. Merrill's translations hew closely to Gautier's originals, rendering them in plain, unrhymed English and retaining her emotional and verbal restraint and reliance on simple juxtapositions of images and sentences without commentary.

Pastels in Prose was well received in the United States. The *New York Times* praised this "Dainty Volume" for exemplifying what Howells had called the "beautiful reticence" of the modern French prose poem, and it singled out one of Gautier's poems as "the truest poetry of prose." The reviewer advised readers to savor the collection slowly—it "has to be sipped with little tastings"—and appreciate it as "indicative of the coming of a better period of taste."[34]

RETRANSLATIONS AND MORE

Many readers of Merrill's *Pastels in Prose* not only "savored" his translations of Gautier's translations but also tried their hand at new English versions based on her original French. In 1918 the American James Whitall (1888–1954) published a selection of thirty poems, *Chinese Lyrics from the Book of Jade*, which includes a translation of the "Prelude"—"after Judith Gautier"—as well. His versions opted for verse lineation of her unrhymed stanzas and proved very popular, going into multiple printings. That same year Edward Powys Mathers (1892–1939), a British "self-professed second-hand translator of Oriental literature" who worked mostly from French texts,[35] published a volume titled *Coloured Stars: Versions of Fifty Asiatic Love Poems*, which assembled retranslations of poems from sources purportedly ranging from Turkish, Arabic, and Sanskrit to Manchu, Mongolian, and Japanese. Eight of the Chinese poems are based on Gautier's work, and Mathers's preface notes that versions "of some of the Chinese poems given here will be found in the incomparable *Livre de Jade* of Mme Judith Gautier."[36] A much larger anthology of "Asiatic love poems" he compiled two years later includes eleven poems based on her translations but without this acknowledgment.[37]

More recently, Kenneth Rexroth, who had pointed to the debt owed by Imagist poets to Gautier, chose to follow their lead in undertaking his own translations of Asian poetry. In a letter to James Laughlin, his editor at New Directions Press, he wrote: "I am working on the Chinese & Japanese poetry book—I think we will have an incomparably better book than anyone else. I plan to translate from [Judith] Gautier (use [Stuart] Merrill for her)." That he did, although he also went back to her French. Rexroth subsequently forgot about having revealed this plan and was therefore chagrined when, "poking around in his library one day," Laughlin came across some French translations "which seemed very familiar. I read them against Kenneth's translations and discovered that he had drawn them from the French of Judith Gautier. Nothing wrong with that."[38]

That there was indeed "nothing wrong with that" is evidenced by the profusion of other retranslations, and retranslations of the retranslations, of poems from Gautier's *Book of Jade* by writers with no knowledge of Chinese during the several decades spanning the turn of the century. This boom in "second-hand" translations may have been linked to the larger expansion of the market for translations in European countries from the 1870s spurred by the increased literacy generated by expanded systems of compulsory education. With more readers looking for books, imports from abroad helped to meet demand. Paris had already established itself as the center of a "culture of translation in Europe," with French the preferred "medium of exchange between other languages" and French books "sold everywhere."[39] Her volume was not alone in inspiring offspring, but it was distinctive for the number and variety of versions it spawned and the circuitous paths they followed. *The Book of Jade* left an astonishing wake across multiple countries and languages.

We've already glimpsed one chain of derivations in Jordan Stabler's English reworkings of Antonio Feijó's Portuguese adaptations. A version in Danish appeared, and at least two sets of retranslations into Italian, one titled *The Jade Moon*, were based on Tullo Massarani's 1882 *Il Libro di giada*.[40] In Russia the poet Nikolai Gumilev (1886-1921) looked to Gautier for inspiration in distilling the aims of Acmeism, a modernist poetic school that he founded and led. His debt is clear in the title of the slim volume *Farforovyi pavil'on* (*The porcelain pavilion*) published in 1918, which was illustrated with Chinese characters and Asian woodblocks from the University of Petrograd's collection. The first half of the book begins with eleven retranslations into Russian verse from *The Book of Jade*, leading off with Gautier's "Porcelain pavilion." Gumilev found the poem particularly appealing because it expressed to him "the ideals of art for art's sake and leisurely creativity, themes that resonated deeply with the anti-utilitarian views espoused in Acmeist circles."[41] Gautier's collection served as source text for Latin American writers as well, including the Mexican modernist Jose Juan Tablada (1871-1945), who—without mentioning his debt—translated several poems from *The Book of Jade* for his 1920 volume titled *Li Po and Other Ideographic Poems* (*Li-Po y otras poemas ideograficos*).[42]

For their part, French writers also saw "nothing wrong" with basing their own retranslations "from the Chinese" on Gautier's *Book of Jade*, as well as other sources. The poet Émile Blémont (1839-1927) published several adaptations of poems translated from other languages, and his 1887 *Poems of China* (*Poèmes de Chine*) offered rhymed versions of works primarily drawn from both *The Book of Jade* and Hervey-Saint-Denys's *Poetry of the Tang Dynasty*. Each was dedicated to a friend, including Gautier herself. Paul Arène, who fifteen years earlier had ridiculed the Parnassians' infatuation with things Chinese in his anonymous *Contemporary Parnassicle*, was now finding much to admire in a lengthy preface he contributed to his friend's volume. A minority voice in the chorus of praise for Gautier's eschewal of prosody, he lauded Blémont's ability to conserve the genius of Chinese poetry in proper French verse—for having, through a "miracle of patience and ingenuity," and "without letting its aroma evaporate, decanted into the crystal of the French strophe this pure oriental essence of such a volatile exoticism."[43]

Even more widely read was a collection of translated poems in prose published by Franz Toussaint (1879-1955) in 1920, titled *The Jade Flute: Chinese Poems* (*La Flute de jade: Poésies chinoises*) and extravagantly decorated, with the Chinese characters for the title (*yu di* 玉笛) printed on every page in some editions. He would become known for his translations from multiple languages and, as a contemporary noted, even though he had "never taken the trouble to learn Arabic, Persian, or Chinese" he was passionate about "Arabic, Persian, Chinese, Japanese literatures. He reads them in translations done by specialists. Through intuition, he himself writes in a French that provides an image of these languages whose spirit he captures so well."[44] Toussaint dedicated his volume to "the memory of Tsao-Chang-Ling, who went to sleep in the Garden of Nine Springs after entrusting to me the responsibility of presenting to French readers these illustrious poems, chosen and translated by him."[45] Tsao has never been identified and was presumed by some to be a Chinese scholar, but the provenance of the 169 pieces in Toussaint's volume appears to have been rather Hervey-Saint-Denys's *Poetry of the Tang Dynasty* and even more extensively Gautier's *Book of Jade*. One scholar wondered with good reason how, if he in fact existed, Tsao had managed to secure "the nonexistent Chinese text" of the several poems attributed to Du Fu in her volume;[46] "The house in the heart" would be among the most notable of these. The unacknowledged debt to Gautier is evident not only in Toussaint's choice to translate into prose but in several other selections ("The porcelain pavilion" is there), which not only replicate some of her original inventions and errors but also introduce new ones. For example, one of the quatrains Gautier had extracted from the seventh-century Tang poet Zhang Ruoxu's "Spring, river, flower, moon, night," which she titled "A woman before her mirror" ("Une femme devant son miroir"), is retranslated by Toussaint, but he gives the author's dates as 1426 to 1473. Ding Dunling's poem "The shadow of the orange leaves" also reappears here, but he is identified as a poet who lived from 772 to 845. Toussaint's *Jade Flute* was enormously successful, and some 131 editions were published between 1920 and 1958, with partial new editions as recently as 2002 and 2009.[47] It was quickly retranslated into other languages like Polish and Spanish—and into English prose poems as well,[48] and it provided the basis for song cycles and often lavishly illustrated multimedia print publications.

Gautier's *Book of Jade* also went on to inspire a small volume of poetry by the noted author Paul Claudel (1868-1995), who spent time in China as diplomatic consul from 1895 to 1909. For a 1937 lecture on "French poetry and the Far East," Claudel prepared seventeen versions of poems from her volume, which he had read before first departing for China. That he chose to rely on her work of seventy years prior, now in its fifth (1933) edition, when many other more authoritative texts were available, indicates how evocative he found it. While making a variety of changes to prosody and diction, he nonetheless seems especially to have appreciated her emphasis on themes, of which love and the moon predominate in his own choices.[49]

Retranslations into German flourished as well. In 1905 Hans Heilmann (1859-1930) published a substantial collection of unrhymed prose adaptations titled *Chinese Lyrics* (*Chinesische Lyrik*), with an ambitious scope that ranges, as his subtitle declares, "from the twelfth century B.C. to the present" (the earliest poems actually date from the sixth-century B.C. *Book of Songs*; the latest is based on Gautier's translation of a poem by the Qing statesman Li Hongzhang). He arranges the selections in roughly chronological order and provides a long introduction and elaborate annotations. Not counting himself, as he writes in the short foreword to the translations, "among the lucky four hundred in Europe and America who can enjoy Chinese poetry in the original," Heilmann had consulted scholarly works in German, French, and English, in addition to Gautier's *Book of Jade*, but the "rhythmic prose" of his German takes its cue from her example. Apologizing for not being able to produce German poetry worthy of the name, he argues that prose versions nonetheless offer "the most faithful images possible of the intellectual and emotional elements of the Chinese poems and of the parallelism of their structure."[50]

In the introduction to his collection Heilmann reproduces the diamond-shaped image of "The porcelain pavilion" that had appeared in Gottfried Böhm's 1873 *Chinese Songs from the Book of Jade*, praising his precursor's ability to represent typographically the poem's celebration of "art mirrored in a self-created nature," with the young men drinking in the pavilion seen as representatives of ideal artists themselves.[51] He helped thereby to disseminate Böhm's stroke of visual ingenuity more widely. This poem continued to live an especially robust afterlife in subsequent German collections of what were now explicitly labeled as "adaptations" (*Nachdichtungen*, literally "after-poems") of Chinese poetry. In 1921 Otto Wolfgang produced a limited edition in Vienna of fifteen pieces, each illustrated by an original lithograph by the artist Viktor Leyrer (1893-1959), with every poem also hand-engraved by him in "oriental" lettering. Titled *The Porcelain Pagoda* (*Die Porzellanpagode*), this slim volume of course features its version of the poem "The porcelain pavilion" ("Der Porzellanpavillon"), which is printed in the shape of a diamond.[52] A subsequent set of adaptations by Max Fleischer chooses, as had the Russian Gumilev, *The Porcelain Pavilion* as its title. Not only does Fleischer, like Gumilev, lead off with his own version of Gautier's poem, he also inserts its putative author, Li Bo, into the center of the poem itself: "In this pavilion sits Li Taibo / with his friends cheered by wine" (In diesem Pavillon sitzt Li-Tai-Pe / mit seinen Freunden wohlgelaunt beim Wein). Twelve of the forty-eight poems in the volume are attributed to Li Bo, based on translations from the Chinese from Gautier and other sources; her "Mysterious flute" is there, as is Ding Dunling's "The shadow of the orange leaves."[53]

Well-known German poets like Richard Dehmel (1863-1920) and Arno Holz (1863-1929) also tried their hand at adaptations of Chinese poems, with works by Li Bo particularly popular. Alfred Henschke (1890-1928), writing under the pseudonym Klabund, was especially prolific, and Gautier's *Book of Jade* was one of his most important sources. His volumes did spectacularly well on the market.

A collection of forty-one versions of Li Bo poems he published in 1916, for example, with an initial print run of 10,000 copies, by 1959 had been issued in a total of eleven editions and 97,000 copies.[54] Indeed, adaptations of Li's poetry published in German became so popular that in 1928 the critic Robert Neumann (1897-1975) published an exasperated critique of the practice in an article entitled "Li-Tai-Po: A German Poet."[55] The Chinese poet even made it to the stage: Clemens von Franckenstein (1875-1942) composed an opera titled *Li Tai Pe, the Emperor's Poet (Li Tai Pe der Kaisers Dichter)* that was produced in 1920 in Heidelberg and in 1924 in Munich.[56]

The most influential collection of *Nachdichtungen* into German had been published in 1907 by the poet Hans Bethge (1876-1946) and was titled *The Chinese Flute (Die chinesische Flöte)*. The first of his several volumes of retranslations from Chinese, Japanese, Arabic, Turkic, and other languages, this was by far his most successful; some 78,000 copies had been sold by 1941 in eighteen reprintings. It was in turn retranslated into English, Danish, and Dutch.[57] The book was elegantly produced, with "Chinese-style" silk strings binding the folded pages together and an illustration by the influential book designer Emil Rudolf Weiss of a young Chinese woman playing the flute on its title page.[58] Bethge follows Heilmann in claiming to span more than one millennium; the eighty-three selections range from the *Book of Songs* to the Qing dynasty, but the majority are from the Tang, with Li Bo and Du Fu most amply represented. He does include, notably, two of Li Qingzhao's lyrics, which Heilmann had not retranslated and which attest to his direct consultation of the French source. Bethge's adaptations are mostly, but not entirely, unrhymed, but unlike Heilmann's they are metered and definitively lineated.

At the end of his postface Bethge acknowledges having based his work on Heilmann, Gautier, Hervey-Saint-Denys, and English prose sources for nineteenth-century poems, but the opening account of his first encounter with the poetry makes it clear that the style of Gautier's versions left an especially deep impression: "When lyric poems after the Chinese first came before my eyes, I was totally enchanted. What a lovely lyrical art I had encountered! I sensed an anxious, fleeting tenderness of lyrical sound, I glimpsed an art of words replete with images that illuminated melancholy and the puzzles of existence, I felt a delicate, lyrical trembling, swelling with symbolism, something tender, fragrant, moonlit, a floral charm of emotion." Bethge goes on to sketch a brief history of Chinese poetry that calls attention to the enduring nature of the tradition, the respect accorded to poets, and the complexity of its prosody. Like his predecessors he singles out Li Bo and Du Fu as the greatest poets during the greatest age of poetry—the Tang—but in his opinion "Li Taibo is the more gifted of the two. He put into poetry the fleeting, drifting, inexpressible beauty of the world, its eternal grief and sorrow and the puzzle of all existence. Rooted deep in his breast was the entire brooding melancholy of the world, and even in moments of greatest joy he cannot free himself from the earth's shadows." And Bethge's postface conclusion laments the imminent influence of European civilization, which will transform China into a modern state that will "lose the sweet pollen of its ancient and great culture, including that of poetry."[59]

In his hands Gautier's renditions of gentle laments exude a philosophical Weltschmerz that attracted a readership already inclined, like Bethge, to view the East as both an object of nostalgia and an agent of modernity. "On this Chinese flute," his publisher announced, "one can hear the cheerful and melancholy tunes of the great poets of the Middle Kingdom.... There is hardly a poetry from another country that can compare in power and depth with the Chinese, who can boast of the great Li Taibo, and as ancient as Chinese poetry is, it will seem modern to us today."[60] One contemporary recalled that *The Chinese Flute* was especially popular among "romantically inclined schoolgirls of the period" and attributed its appeal to "the irresistible combination of the 'Orient' and highly charged sentiment, but that may be to do Bethge an injustice."[61] Indeed, the best known reader of Bethge's volume was no fainting adolescent but rather the composer Gustav Mahler (1860-1911), who was sent a copy by a friend, Theobald Pollak (1855-1912), shortly after its publication in 1907.

GUSTAV MAHLER'S *SONG OF THE EARTH*

The Chinese Flute deeply affected Mahler at a moment in his life when, having suffered multiple blows—the death of his daughter, his own diagnosis of a heart condition, and a career setback—he was especially susceptible to the mixture of laments over human mortality and acceptance of nature's permanence that Bethge's adaptations conveyed: "their melancholy accorded perfectly with his mood at the time."[62] Scholars agree that there can be no "serious doubt that here were texts with a special resonance, of immediate relevance to [Mahler] as man and artist," and that while Bethge's style was "perfervid in a way that the Chinese poets were not, ... who knows, if Mahler had encountered cool, authentic versions of the texts, [the experience] might have left him—musically speaking—correspondingly cold."⁶³ Having already read the volume and while on a conducting tour in the United States, Mahler also met Friedrich Hirth (1845-1927), a German-trained scholar who had spent time in China and was appointed as the first professor of Chinese at Columbia University in 1902. "One can imagine" that their several conversations in the spring of 1908 were for Mahler "of exceptional importance and that he questioned [Hirth] at length about that distant country which had always particularly stimulated the imagination of Westerners."⁶⁴

Rather than being left "cold" later that year Mahler thus began reworking seven of the poems in Bethge's *Chinese Flute* into a cycle of six songs for voice and orchestra which, though it differed from other song cycles he had composed and possessed many symphonic characteristics, he was reluctant to label as what it would have been, his ninth symphony. Beethoven, Schubert, and Bruckner had all died after completing theirs, the famous "curse of the ninth." He first intended to call the piece *The Jade Flute* (*Die Flöte von Jade*)—the same title Franz Toussaint would later choose for his anthology—thus combining the titles of Gautier's and Bethge's collections, but eventually settled on *The Song of the Earth*, with a subtitle referring to it as an unnumbered symphony for orchestra and two voices and acknowledging his source (*Das Lied von der Erde, eine Symphonie für eine Tenor- und eine Alt- [oder Bariton] Stimme und Orchester [nach H. Bethges "Die chinesische Flöte"]*). Once Mahler had completed his next symphony, he labeled *The Song of the Earth* his ninth, but it is not generally considered as such.⁶⁵

Completed in 1909, the *Song of the Earth*'s six songs are based on four poems by Li Bo, one by Qian Qi, and two poems about leave-taking by Wang Wei and Meng Haoran 孟浩然 (689-740) that Mahler combines in his sixth song, "The farewell" ("Der Abschied"). The first, fourth, and fifth songs—"The drinking song of earth's sorrow" ("Das Trinklied vom Jammer der Erde"), "Of beauty" ("Von der Schönheit"), and "The drunkard in spring" ("Der Trunkene im Frühling")—were all based on translations of poems by Li Bo included in Hervey-Saint-Denys's *Poetry of the Tang Dynasty* that had been redone by Heilmann and then Bethge. (Gautier also had produced a version of the fourth poem that was not, however, the basis of the two German retranslations.) The original texts for these three and the sixth were not difficult to identify early on. But the second and third songs both derive from poems in Gautier's *Book of Jade* whose Chinese sources eluded identification for decades. It was only the painstaking detective work of

Mahler scholars and devotees in consultation with sinologists that succeeded in answering questions about the lineage of the texts that had truly become "curiouser and curiouser" and were discussed earlier. The second song, "The lonely one in autumn" ("Der Einsame im Herbst") was finally determined to have been based on Gautier's "Autumn evening" ("Le soir d'automne"), for which the task of identifying the author as Qian Qi had been stymied by her truncated version of the original text and faulty romanization of his name ("Tché-Tsi" in 1867, who became "Tchang-Tsi" but with characters for "Li Wei" in 1902). Qian's poem depicts a young woman weaving and weeping alone at her loom, whom Gautier envisions as hoping that the "sun of marriage" will dry her tears. Mahler transforms the young woman into a solitary man now longing for the "sun of love." And the third song, "Of youth" ("Von der Jugend") turns out to have been based, by way of Gautier's "Porcelain pavilion," on Li Bo's "Banqueting at the Tao family pavilion."[66]

Music historians have noted the echoes of the pentatonic scale that resonate throughout the song cycle, as well as other features that indicate Mahler's certain familiarity with the conventions of Chinese music while composing *The Song of the Earth*, but one of the more interesting musical reflections of Mahler's distant sources occurs in this third song, whose orchestration has long been considered one of the most "Chinese" in any case. The repeated ascending and descending—arch-like—sequences of notes seem to mimic "The porcelain pavilion's" own preoccupation with arches and recalls the diamond-shaped image in which Gottfried Böhm printed his version of the poem, reprinted by Heilmann in his introduction. "Böhm's visual rendering of the poem rather precisely represents in diagrammatic form the 'shape' of the music. It is not at all probable that Mahler would have known anything of Böhm or Heilmann, but that does nothing to lessen the intrinsic interest of the musico-literary parallel, coincidence though it may have been."[67]

How Mahler incorporated aspects of Asian music and the themes of Chinese poetry and philosophy that he was able to discern from texts multiply removed from original sources is a story that has been explored extensively by musicological experts. *The Song of the Earth* "crowns a comparative cultural chain of rare complexity,"[68] one that derives from both Hervey-Saint-Denys and Gautier. It was not the only orchestration of her poems. Gautier knew that the composer Gabriel Fauré (1858–1921) had put ten of her songs to music for voice and piano between 1905 and 1908; she would not know that in 1951 John Haussermann composed a song cycle to five of her poems as retranslated into English by James Whitall.[69]

But it is certainly the most renowned. There is no indication that she ever learned about what she had helped to inspire in German, although *The Song of the Earth* was first performed in Munich in November of 1911, six months after Mahler's death but six years before hers.

HONORED AT LAST

By that time Gautier had become something of a celebrity herself. In 1904 she had been invited to join the jury for a new literary prize created by the editor of the women's magazine titled *Happy Life* (*Vie heureuse*). This group of women writers, called the Academy of Ladies (Académie des Dames), would award—to either a man or a woman—the Prix Femina of 5,000 francs provided by the publishers Hachette. The Comtesse Anna de Noailles (1876-1933) chaired the panel and recalled "the emotion with which I saw for the first time Mme Judith Gautier: the face of a tranquil goddess, the daughter of an illustrious poet, and the inspiration for Victor Hugo's only, divine sonnet. She dazzled my heart. I read with enchantment *The Book of Jade* where, through the miracle of her talent, the brevity of poetry unfurls so sumptuously."[70] But an even greater recognition came six years later when Gautier was elected to membership in the Académie Goncourt.

The academy had been founded in 1900 with an 1896 bequest by Edmond de Goncourt in honor of his brother Jules, who had died in 1870. Unlike the Académie Française, founded in 1635, it highlighted literary achievement exclusively, and Goncourt stipulated that it could not select anyone belonging to the older organization. Its ten lifetime members met monthly over a restaurant meal, awarded the Goncourt Prize of 5,000 francs to what they judged the best work of prose that year, and received an annual stipend of 4,000 francs themselves. Gautier's election in October 1910 as the first woman (and over Paul Claudel) made front page news, with headlines trumpeting "A Female Victory" in the selection of "A Female Academician," and even "A Female Academician—Finally!"[71] (Not until 1944 did a second woman, the writer Colette, follow her.) The headline on the first page of the *New York Times* hailed the "Honor for Judith Gautier: First woman to be elected to the Goncourt Academy," although the announcement flanked her—as always—by the two men in her life:

> Madame Judith Gautier, daughter of the novelist and poet, Theophile Gautier, and at one time wife of the late Catulle Mendes, has been elected to the Goncourt Academy of Letters.
>
> She is the first woman to be thus honored.[72]

Some press articles referred to the "junior" status of the Goncourt Academy, but to other eyes it was to be respected for being "less politicized, less worldly, more literary, and more impartial."[73] Years after her death its president recalled that Gautier had been elected "in recognition of her artistic talent, her poetic imagination that created a Far East to which she never traveled except in her dreams, and her delicate manner, both pictorial and musical, of writing about art and life." The nine other academicians also admired her courageous defense of Wagner and the "delightful anecdotes" in her memoirs. She was an "*évocatrice*," someone who could conjure other worlds and a genial colleague as well, "a Chinese woman poet, inspired by music, and the daughter of the great Théo carrying within the flame of her father's heritage."[74] Indeed, to many her election served to redress the injustice suffered by Théophile Gautier, who despite several attempts had never been elected to the Académie Française. That honor, Gautier's brother-in-law Émile Bergerat later pointed out in his obituary of her, was not open to women during her lifetime. Had that not been the case, as Gaston Boissier, the permanent secretary of the august body, declared to him, "she would have joined us long ago," adding, with a smile, "because she is perhaps the masterpiece of her father."[75]

Gautier accepted the accolade with her typical equanimity. She published a short note of thanks to those "friends known and unknown" who had climbed the five floors to her "ivory tower" perch to congratulate her, acknowledging both her honor and her happiness, despite the "assault" on her habitual solitude.[76] In another interview Gautier writes of the "veritable invasion of books and letters" into her garret, thanks to her work on both the Femina and Goncourt juries, which she jokes has made her "a very important lady." When asked if she has a favorite, she replies with a comment that acknowledges the extraordinary transformation sparked by the tutelage of Ding Dunling: "*I am a Chinese woman*. I have no literary salon and I live on my own. So I have an open mind, and my vote will go simply to the volume that I've found the best. Independent I've lived, independent I've grown old, and independent I'll die. I will be for my entire life a sort of Far Eastern woman detached from the things and times around her. That's lasted for forty years, and I don't see it changing now."[77] Thus she answers

8.1 Judith Gautier in her Paris apartment.
BnF Gallica

definitively those skeptics who had once asked of her and her *Book of Jade*: "How can one be Chinese?" A photo of Gautier in her Paris apartment with her beloved pets taken a few years earlier also shows us how.

Although "A Female Victory" opens by proclaiming that "champions of the feminist cause are rubbing their hands gleefully" at the news of Gautier's election, she herself observes, with a smile: "I am not a feminist, at least in the exaggerated sense of the word. Nevertheless, I'm happy to have successfully broken down the prejudice that says that a woman of letters cannot be part of a literary or scholarly institution." About feminism Gautier was content to maintain her characteristic indifference, while living a life that challenged traditional norms. She also retained her sense of humor when dealing with anyone unable to imagine a woman capable of her accomplishments. To one young unknown admirer, one of many who wrote to her as "Monsieur Judith Gautier," she penned a letter that opened: "M. Judith Gautier died a long time ago, so long ago that I don't remember when; I don't even remember where he is buried. Please allow his widow, who has continued his literary affairs, to respond to you."[78]

On January 1, 1911, Gautier was honored again when she was named a Chevalier of the Legion of Honor, as had been the sinologist Hervey-Saint-Denys. She kept writing—the Goncourt stipend had not alleviated her financial woes—and churned out more novels, plays, children's books on China and Japan and, as an advertising stunt for the chocolate shop La Marquise de Sévigné, an elegantly decorated book of letters purportedly by the seventeenth-century writer describing her experiences upon returning to twentieth-century France, which include visiting the store itself.[79] There was no doubt that she was famous. As one contemporary critic opens his 1913 acidulous profile of Gautier, "Ever since the Goncourt Academy everyone is talking about her. Those who know her a little speak of her as an old friend, and those who've never known her act as if they always have." Newspapers and magazines clamor for photos and articles. "Judith Gautier is in fashion! And since fashion is a quintessentially French epidemic, everyone wants to read Judith Gautier." Which means "a few more chinoiseries for French literature."[80]

Perhaps the most elegant "chinoiserie" connected to Gautier, which broadcast her recent accolade prominently on its title page, had been published two years earlier. In 1911 a significantly abridged edition of her anthology appeared in England, issued by the Eragny Press, which had been cofounded in 1894 by Lucien Pissarro (1863-1944; the Impressionist painter Camille's older son) and his wife Esther, and which was named after the village northwest of Paris where the family had lived. Modeled on the Kelmscott Press of William Morris as part of the Arts and Crafts movement, Eragny aimed to produce small-scale artisanal publications for the bibliophile audience featuring the distinctive use of colored wood engravings.

Lucien and Esther Pissarro had written to Judith Gautier the year before requesting her permission to publish a selection of her translations, which they envisioned as a "'pot-boiler,' an album of stunning engravings with very little text."[81] Other writers on their list ranged from Villon to Milton, Keats, Flaubert, and Browning; they also published two books from the Bible. Gautier concurred, and Pissarro selected seven pieces from the 1902 edition for an *Album of Poems Drawn from the* Book of Jade (*Album de poèmes tirés du* Livre de jade), producing, as he had for other imprints, several wood engravings in rich colors with generous use of gold leaf and gold powder. He printed the poems in gray rather than black ink to harmonize with the colors of the engravings and assembled the pages "Japanese style," folded and printed on only one side and sewn along the spine. The volume, which now could be advertised as the work of "Judith Gautier, of the Académie Goncourt," was bound in green kidskin, with a stamped image of a gold emblem on the front cover. The print run for the volume consisted of 125 copies for sale, with 5 more for museums; 10 of these used Roman vellum and the rest Japanese vellum. It cost over £103 to produce, one of Eragny's most expensive books, and the press made no profit on it.[82] As rare book aficionados have observed, the cover alone "can still be appreciated as a remarkable statement about the simple, yet richly expressive poetry it holds," maintaining "an exquisite balance between purity and luxury, creating a book that in itself suggests a life lived well but with restraint."[83]

Diana White (1868-1950), an Impressionist artist and translator who was a good friend of Esther Pissarro and had also published a volume with Eragny, introduces the poems, which include three lyrics by Li Qingzhao, two of Li Bo's translations, the palace quatrain by Zhu Qingyu, and a poem attributed to Du Fu. All of them feature figures of women desolate in their solitude. What White finds especially striking about Gautier's translations is how "the emotion and the observed fact are combined with the utmost grace in a salient line of extraordinary charm." She notes an attention to visual detail that evokes a deeper significance, embodying the "unity and complexity of decorative purpose, founded upon the closest study of Nature, that underlie all forms of Chinese art."[84]

Judith Gautier found the Pissarros' *Album* "well composed and of a remarkable perfection," perhaps because the relatively ample use of white space surrounding the type and engravings resonated with the typographical format of her own volume.[85] The book was hailed as "one of the five masterpieces of the Eragny Press" and "monumental in their use of color and design." The collector L. W. Hodson considered it "the most beautiful little book of recent times. Seldom has the sympathetic 'study of appearance' so perfectly allied itself to the literature it clothes."[86]

The year 1911 also saw the publication of six "Unedited poems from *The Book of Jade*," three of which are attributed to Chinese poets and the others to recent envoys from China. Now decades removed from her original research, Gautier erroneously attributes a poem by Li Bo to Du Fu, which remains nonetheless identifiable because of the fidelity of her rendition. She also translates a poem written for her by Sun Baoqi, who served as ambassador to France from 1902-1905. Sun expresses his delight at having met a true poet who understands Chinese civilization enough to appreciate the superiority of Du Fu. Poetry is their common heritage: "Is poetic inspiration not heaven's echo? / In Europe and Asia scripts may differ but thoughts have the same origin.... How could I, loving poetry so profoundly, not be pleased to have met you?" (L'inspiration poétique n'est-elle pas un

8.2 and 8.3 Cover and title page of Judith Gautier, *Album de Poèmes tirés du Livre de jade* (The Brook, Hammersmith, London: The Eragny Press), 1911.
From the British Library Collection: 11094.a.56

JUDITH GAUTIER
DE L'ACADÉMIE GONCOURT.

ALBUM DE POEMES TIRES DU LIVRE DE JADE

THE ERAGNY PRESS, THE BROOK,
HAMMERSMITH, LONDON, W.
M.D.CCCC.XI.

écho du ciel? / D'Europe et d'Asie, les écritures diffèrent mais les pensées des hommes ont la même origine.... / Comment ne serais-je pas heureux de vous connaître, moi qui aime si profondément la poésie?).[87]

Gautier published her own tribute to Sun Baoqi in a volume of her poetry that also appeared in 1911. The eclectic collection includes a sonnet sent to Wagner on his birthday, poems to friends like Suzanne Meyer-Zundel, Ham Nghi, and Robert de Montesquiou, and a three-act opera. Unlike *The Book of Jade* that had brought her such renown, these pieces were all composed in classical French meters, somewhat to the disappointment of her first biographer, who found it "regrettable that in her own poems Judith didn't follow the Chinese and Japanese models that she had so admirably manipulated and reproduced. She abandons the colorful, unexpected, graceful images, the light strokes of the brush that create effortlessly and delicately the rarest of gems."[88] But three pieces remind us of the abiding passion that had first expressed itself in *The Book of Jade*. Her poem to Sun Baoqi celebrates in alexandrines the China of the Tang dynasty that remains for her, as it was in her 1878 essay on Chinese poetry, "The paradise of poets" ("Le Paradis des poètes") whose capital Chang'an was "a palace of dreams" where the emperor Minghuang "bowed his majesty" before the sages (... Tchann-Gann, palais de rêve! / Où les sages avaient l'empereur pour élève, / Car Minn-Hoang devant eux courbait sa majesté, ...) And so, as the poem concludes:

Li-Taï-pé, Thou-Fou, merveilleuses étoiles,	Li Taibo, Du Fu, marvelous stars,
Sur vous le morne oubli n'a pu tisser ses toiles,	Dreary oblivion has not woven its shroud on you;
Vous traversez les temps d'un rayonnement tel	You transcend time so radiantly that
Qu'illuminé par lui, Minn-Hoang est immortel.	Minghuang, illuminated, is immortal.[89]

A second poem, titled "Chinese evening" ("Soir de Chine") and dedicated to Liu Shixun 劉式訓, ambassador to France from 1905 to 1911), presents in sonnet form images and motifs that Gautier had first adumbrated in "The porcelain pavilion" and "The mysterious flute." She sketches a tall tower, whose roof resembles "the wing of a black dragon" (l'aile d'un dragon noir) reflected in the mirror of the lake below, toward which a willow bends "for a better view" (pour mieux voir). Floating on a small boat, a man with slender fingers plucks a sandalwood *pi-pa* and sings in a plangent voice that "sends crystalline cries to the sky" (Jette au ciel des cris de cristal).⁹⁰

Most personally poignant is a third poem written to Sun's predecessor, Yu Geng, who had provided the epigraph to her 1902 *Book of Jade*. Gautier had kept in touch with him after his departure from Paris, and this piece, written after his death, expresses the enduring sense of dislocation—one might call it disorientation—that led her to consider herself "a Chinese woman." Interestingly, she recalls what the Persian general Mohsin-Khan had observed about her decades earlier: "You are like a plant born by chance in foreign soil."

À FEU S. E. YU-KENG, MINISTRE DE CHINE, POUR LE REMERCIER D'UN POÈME	TO HIS EXCELLENCY THE LATE YU GENG, MINISTER FROM CHINA, TO THANK HIM FOR A POEM
Comme une graine au vent, jetée Par une ragale emportée J'ai fleuri loin du ciel natal,	Like a grain in the wind, thrown And carried by a gale I blossomed far from my native skies
Sous le brouillard occidental.	Under the occidental fog.
Mais dans mon ennui nostalgique Toujours vers l'Orient magique Mon rêve, au tournesol pareil Se tourne vers le vrai soleil.	But in my nostalgic melancholy Forever for the magical East My dream, like a sunflower Turns toward the true sun.
Loin de la glorieuse aïeule, Je me sens orpheline et seule, Et dans mon coeur jamais lassé Veille le culte du passé.	Far from my glorious forebears I feel orphaned and alone, And in my never weary heart Abides reverence for the past.
Ô Yu-Keng! illustre poète, Par vous la Chine me fait fête	Oh, Yu Geng! illustrious poet, China welcomes me through you

Et, comblant mon plus cher souhait,	And fulfilling my most cherished wish
Pour son enfant me reconnaît.[91]	Recognizes me as her child.

Gautier would never visit the country that had animated and peopled her dreams. After her one venture abroad to visit Ham Nghi and his family in Algeria in 1914, she spent the last three years of her life at Birds' Meadow, her home on the Breton coast, at greater remove than Paris from the war that erupted three months after her return. Gautier had been chagrined to see her godson Siegfried Wagner's signature on the "Manifesto of the 93" signed in October 1914 by prominent intellectuals in support of the German cause and to realize that the country of his revered father was at war with hers again, but she nonetheless taught a rescued blackbird to whistle three tunes from Wagner's operas.[92] She may have been independent, but she was not alone, with Suzanne Meyer-Zundel her companion and Louis Benedictus her loyal friend until the end. She urged the much younger woman to refer to her as godmother (Marraine), an "intimate but respectful" appellation, but Meyer-Zundel eventually chose to call her Maya, the Sanskrit term for illusion, a name other friends used as well.[93] Writing became increasingly difficult, but always penurious she kept at it, and she started the fourth but never published volume of her memoirs.

Judith Gautier died of a coronary thrombosis on December 26, 1917. As requested, Meyer-Zundel buried her in the small St. Énogat cemetery a block away from her house and arranged to have two Chinese inscriptions incised on the gravestone. On the upper right, the somewhat cryptic phrase "the [sun]light comes from heaven" (ri lai tian 日來天), was probably devised by Gautier herself; her nephew's widow later recalled that the characters were painted in gold on the vermilion lacquered walls of the fifth-floor Paris walk-up.[94] Ham Nghi translated the phrase for Meyer-Zundel and added a tribute of his own, engraved on the lower left of the gravestone, and reading from right to left: "Here lies my Maya / before whom Tu Xuan bows down," or, more literally "My Maya / Tu Xuan bows" (wo ma yi jia / zi chun bai 我麻依嘉 / 子春拜). The three characters ma yi jia transcribe the name Maya in Vietnamese pronunciation; Tu Xuan was the name Ham Nghi used for his French friends.[95] The grave is now adorned with a ceramic bouquet, perhaps as enduring as the flowers of her collection.

8.4 Judith Gautier's gravestone, St. Énogat.
Author's photograph

Meyer-Zundel remained at Gautier's Birds' Meadow until her own death in 1971, when she was buried on the same site. The story goes that she saved the house from being appropriated by the German forces occupying the area during World War II by declaring to the commandeering officer that it had been owned by a great friend of Wagner's and pointing out the numerous photographs and scores of the composer scattered around the living room, some of which were signed. Gautier had even been the godmother of Wagner's son Siegfried! The officer retreated in the face of the multiple testimonies of a friendship with the "god of Bayreuth," and thus, "by a miraculous and mysterious return, Richard Wagner had preserved and saved the last earthly retreat of the woman who had idolized him."[96] In 2017, on the centenary of Gautier's death, a local chocolatier (not La Marquise de Sévigné) created a new confection in her honor, a dark chocolate bonbon called Birds' Meadow and flavored, appropriately, with ginger and lemongrass. It was embossed with the Chinese character for "sunlight" imprinted on her gravestone.[97]

Epilogue

"One of the most original talents in contemporary literature"

Both the 1902 and 1908 editions of *The Book of Jade* had long sold out by the time of Gautier's death and were thus "impossible to find," according to a critic reviewing her last set of writings in 1918.[1] A fourth edition was published in 1928 by Jules Tallandier and a fifth in 1933 by the Librairie Plon. In 2004 the Imprimerie nationale issued a sixth edition, granting extraordinary longevity to a book that has been called "the most unusual anthology in the history of Chinese poetry anthologies."[2] The many obituaries written on her death, and at regular intervals over the years, brought renewed tributes to the author and her collection, "these delicately crafted jewels iridescent with a mysterious glow," "the precious reliquary" where Gautier had "fixed, as in a coffer of rare jewels and fine stones, the dreams of her young imagination in search of carefully chosen ecstasies," which "in fact opened one's mind to infinite meditations."[3] She was "one of the most original talents in contemporary literature."[4] Many also remembered Ding Dunling, now "Judith Gautier's Chinese man," her "professor of the dialect of the Celestial Empire" whom everyone in Paris had recognized, whose poems were now as renowned as those of Li Bo and Du Fu, and whom Théophile Gautier defended from accusations of petty thievery by describing him as "a scholar in exile among barbarians."[5]

Not everyone agreed. Émile Poiteau, in a collection of essays about writers of his time, believed that the degree of her talent was "arguable," despite the "consecration" of the Goncourt Academy, because of her "incomprehensible" love of China. She "threw herself headlong into the study of the Orient. She saturated her soul with exotic impressions, and that is why her style trudges painfully through Chinese images and sentences. It is deliberately sober, cadenced, heavy, often monotonous." Prose poems do not provide a "comfortable" home for real ideas, and her suggestive restraint of expression was inimical to the national spirit, for "the French genius loves lucidity and precision. It doesn't fit well into obscure forms that come to us from another race and within which Judith Gautier seeks to imprison them." As far as he was concerned, "we should leave to the Chinese their customs, their beliefs, their literature, and their gibberish. But let us be proud of our race; preserve the purity of the French language!"[6]

Théophile Gautier, by contrast, was for Poiteau "a very French poet"; he had preserved that purity, embodied "an entire literary epoch," and was responsible for her "lively imagination linked to a mind and heart almost masculine" and thus her success.[7] When Judith Gautier was alive, there was only one way to introduce her—in the way Anatole France opens his biographical sketch: "She is the daughter of the poet." Her father would remain the source and standard of her talent, however original it proved: "she had her own style, a calm and confident style, rich and placid, like that of Théophile Gautier, less robust, less rich, but fluid and light in a different way."[8] Others discerned no differences: "she has, like him, an Olympian beauty, a poetic soul, and all the riches of imagination and mind. It's the same intuition, the same impeccable scholarship, the same magnificence and boldness of style linked to a precision that nothing can disrupt: the same ability to animate all beings and to evoke the most beautiful sights of the visible and invisible worlds."[9] The Italian writer Gabriele d'Annunzio (1863-1938) even paid tribute to her by inscribing a copy of his 1910 novel with the same epithet (appropriately altered for gender) with which Baudelaire had honored her father in the dedication of his *Flowers of Evil*: "the perfect magician of letters" (la parfaite magicienne ès lettres).[10]

Obituaries continued to define her in his terms. One article lamented that "in losing her it seemed we were losing her father for the second time."[11] But those who most admired her insisted on her distinctiveness. As Henri de Régnier writes in his reminiscences, "Judith Gautier added to the paternal glory an extension that continued it without being confused with it. Her works were in no way a replica of her father's. She had her own virtues."[12] Her studies with Ding Dunling had given her the opportunity to define herself and forge a path her father could never have followed, even if he had made it all possible by sheltering the Chinese refugee. One obituary observes that she lived "in an Orient more oriental than the one her father had known," a passion fueled by "the old Chinese books that one can only read in the National Library."[13] Yet another gave her credit for something more: "Infatuated with China to the point of studying its impenetrable language, Judith Gautier, by dint of hard work and intuition, ended by mastering the scholarship of a mandarin. She lived in the intimacy of the Chinese classics." And her *Book of Jade* succeeded, better than the versions of the scholar Hervey-Saint-Denys, in translating for the world of European letters "the fragile marvels" of Tang poets.[14]

Something more than "intuition" grounded Gautier's work—and it was certainly more informed than what guided Franz Toussaint in his many retranslations. In a 1910 essay on "Chinese poets," André de Fouquières relies heavily on her "Prelude" to the 1902 *Book of Jade* and counts her among "the pious enthusiasts" thanks to whom "the most beautiful Chinese poems" have been "faithfully transmitted to us." "Madame Judith Gautier," he writes, "to whom we are indebted for the most precious translations, teaches us how the glory of the likes of Li Taibo and Du Fu was established." She has, moreover, "become what would be called a Chinese scholar. She writes the classical language and speaks the vernacular."[15] Gautier's first biographer also declared confidently that she "translated the Chinese poets with a rigorous precision," citing Rémy de Gourmont's observation that it "annoyed her to suggest that the translator had added the slightest detail to the grace of the original."[16] Even more recently she was described as "an informed sinologist, having acquired a rare competence in the history, art, and literature of several countries in the Orient, without having traveled there except in her imagination." In an age when exoticism was "all the rage," she blazed a path toward one that was "solidly documented."[17]

Gautier never called herself a sinologist and insisted that her only contribution had been to be "a faithful interpreter. It's difficult to believe this; nonetheless one must because it's true."[18] It is also true that although most of the newly added poems in 1902 observed traditional conventions of translation, the liberties taken in 1867 had not been "rigorously corrected" at all, and those poems make up most of the collection. Small wonder, then, that specialists within the world of sinology have taken issue with how "solidly documented" her work actually was. The Russian French scholar Basile Alexéiev, for example, castigated Gautier in 1926 for producing "false" translations that betray for the sake of "novelty" the translator's duty to "be exact"; they are simply "would-be translations" in which "fantasy reigns."[19] Four decades later the noted sinologist Paul Demiéville, in his otherwise comprehensive history of the discipline in France, mentions Gautier only in passing—and primarily as the daughter of Théophile and the mistress of Wagner—in a paragraph on the contribution of career diplomats who had spent time in China. He describes her versions of the song lyrics by Li Qingzhao as "freely adapted with the aid of Chinese scholars who arrived in Paris with the first Chinese legation in France" and mistitles her collection *The jade flute* (*La flûte de jade*).[20] Meanwhile the eminent Du Fu scholar William Hung credits her "pseudo translations" of the poet as apparently the earliest, though of the fourteen poems attributed to him he recognizes but two as "rather garbled translations of genuine poems." "The rest can be said to represent only the creative imagination of a talented French lady at twenty-two."[21] David Lattimore also criticizes her versions as "pseudo-translations," examples of an exoticized, antiquated, and quaint chinoiserie.[22]

Not all critics with knowledge of Chinese were so harsh. George Soulié de Morant praised her work as both beautiful and faithful. Another friend and regular guest at her salon, Eugène-Albert de Pourvourville (1861–1939), who spent years in China and became an authority on Daoism, published an obituary after her death in 1917 that pointed to *The Book of Jade* as evidence that Gautier had subjected "her brain to the same discipline as her imagination. . . . Each sentence, each line of this singular collection is replete with the gentle philosophy, resigned and a bit disdainful, of those magnificent sages of the Middle Kingdom, who judge humanity by its real value, don't ask much of it, and don't hope for more."[23]

Two years later Arthur Waley included *Le Livre de jade* in the "Bibliographical Notes" to one of his compilations and remarked:

> It has been difficult to compare these renderings with the original, for proper names are throughout distorted or interchanged. . . . Such mistakes are evidently due to faulty decipherment of someone else's writing. Nevertheless, the book is far more readable than that of [Hervey-]St. Denys, and shows a wider acquaintance with Chinese poetry on the part of whoever chose the poems. Most of the credit for this selection must certainly be given to Ting Tun-ling, the *literatus* whom Théophile Gautier befriended. But the credit for the beauty of these often erroneous renderings must go to Mademoiselle Gautier herself.[24]

In a review the same year of an English translation of poems from *The Book of Jade*, Waley began rather less charitably: "The story of how Théophile Gautier rescued the starving Ting Tun-ling and made him Judith's tutor is well known; how much she ever succeeded in learning from him is less certain." He criticizes the "wildly mutilated form" in which proper names appear, the unwarranted expansion of the "epigrammatic" form of the originals, and he declares that "many of the poems are simply wrong from start to finish." And yet, he admits:

> It is very difficult for anyone familiar with Chinese poetry to judge how far the "Livre" is successful simply as literature. Mistranslation seems a strange way of arriving at beauty; yet it was those yellow pages of half-intelligible ideographs, studied with Ting at the Bibliothèque, which fired Mlle. Gautier's imagination. If she had been able to translate them correctly, her book would not have become a classic; for the originals abound in references to customs, traditions and places unfamiliar to Western readers.[25]

In his history of European scholarship on the Orient Raymond Schwab observed that Gautier's translations displayed the very virtues that he thought most philologists sought assiduously to avoid: they were simple, clear, and intelligible.[26] Roy Edward Teele praised both Gautier and Hervey-Saint-Denys for their notable "choice of fine examples of T'ang poetry and for the fluent prose they used in their translations. English translators were not to show either such fine taste or such ease of manner in translating for more than a quarter of a century."[27] And the distinguished scholar and translator David Hawkes stated quite unequivocally that "nothing... could conceivably have interested a Western poet [in Chinese verse] until the publication of the *Livre de jade*."[28]

Indeed, as one contemporary scholar has asked, why focus on Gautier's errors "when most faithful translations have fallen into oblivion while a great many French poets came to know Chinese poetry thanks to *The Book of Jade*?"[29] Perhaps, as Waley suspected, it was "the wide difference between the unbridled imagery of the Parisian girl and the decorous fancy of the T'ang poet" that helped to account for the volume's astounding popularity. It may be telling that some of the poems most remote from any Chinese original, like "The house in the heart" attributed to Du Fu, elicited the most enthusiastic responses among European readers. For many, both admirers and detractors, the China depicted by someone like her who had never journeyed there could only be the stuff of imagination and dream, something created, as Anatole France writes, "in the soul of a young woman, a silent soul, a sort of deep mine where the diamond forms itself amidst the shadows." The great sinologists, of course, had never set foot in the country either. Gautier herself would have agreed with Agnès de Noblet's characterization of her as a "sedentary Orientalist," declaring proudly in an interview that "I could never regret very much not having visited the Far East. For I've never visited it. I came to know it precisely and delightfully through its poets, its history, its scholars. What could I hope for that might be superior to the notion that I conceived of it? And I've never wanted to run the risk of returning disenchanted." But she also insisted, in another interview, that she had an equally real basis for her knowledge and her love of the country: "I could not know the Chinese better nor love them more than I do now. I am surrounded here by their music, their literature and religion and I am in touch continuously both personally and by correspondence with the finest of their people."[30]

In her heart, as in her poem to Yu Geng, Gautier believed herself a Chinese woman. More than a century later we may file this under cultural appropriation and the sins of orientalism. But if, as Anatole France continues, Gautier had only "invented an immense Orient in order to lodge her dreams there," her spirit was one of generosity rather than cooptation, of openness rather than violence. As Hugh Kenner wrote of Ezra Pound's "invention" of Chinese poetry, "if his model was mythical, if it was created thanks to a plausible misunderstanding of Chinese poetry, we ought next to reflect that Chinese poetry is after all undamaged. . . . It remains what it was. It easily survives that necessary half-century of misunderstanding."[31] And there was understanding and great insight as well.

Indifferent to fame, Judith Gautier became a celebrity. Denying feminist ambitions she charted a path no woman had walked before. Abhorring travel she proved a remarkably effective ambassador and cultural mediator. Judith Gautier composed her Chinese songs in a French key, a register that would be accessible to her readers, first as adaptations inspired by the original poems and then as hard-won translations, all of them presented in new forms that sparked further innovation. She drew admiring readers in France and Europe who knew nothing of the originals and among the Chinese who did. That Chinese poetry suffered no real damage in her hands is evidenced by the appreciation and recognition on the part of those Chinese who could read French. Chen Jitong considered her volume "a masterpiece" comprising the best of Chinese poetry and "worthy of the admiration of all the literati in the world." Ambassador Yu Geng praised her for having clasped "the poems of [his] country to her heart." And Rémy de Gourmont testified that "those Chinese who know French rediscover in this anthology the stanzas they know by heart that are the timeless exemplars of their poetry."[32]

Gautier succeeded in reaching a broad readership who, encountering Chinese poetry for the first time, felt that they had crossed a previously impenetrable barrier of understanding. For every Émile Poiteau dismayed by an infiltration of Chinese aesthetics into the long-honored "lucidity" of the French language, there was a multitude of admirers for whom a door had been opened. As Paul Souday wrote after her death, "These poems translated by Mme Judith Gautier are all very short. Almost all are lovely. You find there the eternal themes also treated by Western lyrics and elegies, old and new: the brevity of life, the irreparable passage of time, the impossible return of the past, love, wine, country, the sadness of exile, etc.... This commonality of poetic themes between distant races that do not know one another is perhaps the best proof of the unity of humankind." As the contemporary editor of her complete works points out, she "took care to highlight the distance that separates the Occident from Chinese poetry but never led anyone to believe that it could not be bridged."[33]

It had been a most unusual collaboration, between Judith Gautier, "the most Chinese Parisian,"[34] and Ding Dunling, who had been called "the most Parisian Chinese," one embedded in the history of multiple intersections—of cultures, worlds, languages, and arts, of the scholarly and amateur, military and missionary, letters and music, China and France—and multiple circuits of knowledge and influence. As one contemporary noted, no one before her "had penetrated the charm of China and Japan, and no one has known better than she how to make it accessible to our minds and our sensibility." And of her many books, none succeeded so well at this as Gautier's *Book of Jade*, "a kind of miracle in the history of French literature"[35] that brought Chinese poetry to nineteenth-century Europe.

Acknowledgments

This book has been almost half a century in the making, so there are many people to thank, even as I take full responsibility for its oversights and flaws. The late Herbert Lindenberger, founder of the Comparative Literature Program at Stanford where I did my doctorate, first planted the idea of a project on Judith Gautier in my head as I was finishing my degree. I dutifully wrote it down and promptly forgot about it. Thirty years later I was unpacking the last boxes from a recent move—files from graduate school days that somehow had never been discarded—and came across the slip of paper with Gautier's name and some other scribbles about French, German, Chinese, and Mahler. William Boltz of the University of Washington had just invited me to give the Andrew Markus Memorial Lecture, and this seemed as good an idea to explore as any. It meant a great deal to me that distinguished sinologists in attendance like Bill, his wife Judy, and David Knechtges urged me to pursue it.

That exploration could only proceed at an embarrassingly dilatory pace, however, thanks to my full-time job as president of the American Council of Learned Societies, although I appreciated Vice President Steve Wheatley's always gracious interest and encouragement. Thankfully, two more invitations to speak—from Harriet Stone to deliver the William H. Matheson Lecture at Washington University and from Paul Kroll to celebrate the thirtieth anniversary of the Department of Asian Languages and Civilizations at the University of Colorado—helped to move it along. Colleagues in an informal medieval court cultures workshop who heard a brief presentation about the project also provided a welcome audience, as did good friends like Sheila Biddle, Kate Stimpson, and Jean Strouse, with whom many a dinner conversation about Judith Gautier were shared during the past two decades.

To several individuals I owe a special debt of thanks. My graduate student at UCLA, Wendy Swartz, now an accomplished professor at Rutgers University, has offered invaluable support of all kinds; I never fail to learn from her, and I treasure her friendship. Steve West of Arizona State University has provided technical assistance whenever I've needed it, and Ron Egan of Stanford University tracked down references in his office when the pandemic kept me from the library. John Finlay in Paris, once my undergraduate student at Columbia, provided good company and useful advice on my occasional research trips to the city. Neil Parker, an excellent physician (mine!) and equally superb photographer, helped make many of the images in the book publishable; I'm very grateful for his eleventh-hour assistance. Reference librarians at the Bibliothèque Nationale de France, the British Library, and Columbia University were unfailingly helpful. And speaking of libraries, I thank Eileen Gillooly for ensuring that I'd have access to Columbia's exceptional library resources by appointing me a Senior Scholar of the Heyman Center for the Humanities.

I've never met the rare book dealer Jonathan Chiche, but I will always be grateful to him for sending me his essay on Gautier and Victor Hugo out of the blue, which not only brought to my attention several sources of which I'd been unaware but also convinced me that there was a book to be written about *Le Livre de jade*. To Ted Widmer I am equally thankful for his enthusiasm for the project and for persuading me I might aspire to a larger audience for that book than the usual handful of scholars who read academic publications; he read through several versions of my proposal to help me shape it. I am indebted as always to my friend Bob Moeller, who surely didn't know that years ago, when he inherited my faculty office at the University of California Irvine, he would also end up being one of the best critics of anything I've written since then. And I thank the anonymous readers of the manuscript for their extraordinarily helpful comments and suggestions.

My deepest gratitude goes to my husband Scott Waugh, without whose love and support I truly cannot imagine having been able to bring this to completion. An enthusiastic companion on pilgrimages to Gautier's homes and gravesite, he fetched library books when I was marooned at home with orthopedic mishaps and cheerfully served as photographer, tech guru, and thoughtful reader, even while deeply immersed in his own research in medieval British history. His dedication to that work has been inspiring, and his company a joy. I could not ask for a better partner in writing and in life.

Notes

1. "AN ELEGANT AND ORIGINAL VOLUME" BY "THE MOST SINGULAR OF WOMEN": INVENTION OR TRANSLATION?

1. Eugen Weber, *France, Fin de Siècle* (Cambridge, MA: Harvard University Press, 1986), 92.
2. Judith Gautier, *Le Collier des jours. Souvenirs de ma vie* (Paris: Félix Juven, 1902; rpt. Paris: Christian Pirot, 1994), 185-87, and *Le Second Rang du collier: Souvenirs littéraires* (Paris: Félix Juven, 1903; rpt. Paris: L'Harmattan, 1999), 38.
3. Charles Baudelaire, *Correspondance*, vol. 2 (mars 1860-mars 1866), ed. Claude Pichois and Jean Ziegler (Paris: Gallimard, 1973), 352-53. See also Judith Gautier, *Le Second Rang du collier*, 67-68.
4. Judith Gautier, *Le Second Rang du collier*, 69.
5. According to Bettina Knapp, *Judith Gautier: Writer, Orientalist, Musicologist, Feminist. A Literary Biography* (Lanham, MD: Hamilton Books, 2004), 55, "A priest from Colmar attacked her article on *Eureka* in one of his sermons, claiming it was antireligious, and would have written an article denouncing it had he not been persuaded otherwise, after learning of the young age of the offender—not even old enough to wear long skirts."
6. As noted by the editor of the 2004 edition of the collection. Yvan Daniel, "Présentation: *Le Livre de Jade*, un rêve de Judith Gautier," in Judith Gautier, *Le Livre de Jade*, ed. Yvan Daniel (Paris: Imprimerie nationale, 2004), 7.
7. For the same point made by a distinguished Chinese critic, see Qian Zhongshu, *Tan yi lu*, rev. ed. (Hong Kong: Zhonghua shuju, 1986), notes to page 48 on 372.
8. After railing about the contemporary critical obsession with morality and utility, Gautier makes his point in his typically memorable fashion:

   Nothing that is beautiful is indispensable to life.—If one eliminated flowers, the world would not suffer materially; but who would want there to be no flowers? . . .

   What use is the beauty of women? . . .

   What good is music? What good is painting? . . .

   There is nothing truly beautiful except what is of no use; everything useful is ugly because it's the expression of some need, and those of man are despicable and disgusting, like his poor, infirm nature.—The most useful spot in a house is the latrine.

   From the preface in Théophile Gautier, *Mademoiselle de Maupin* (Paris: Charpentier et Cie, 1869), 21. The novel first appeared in 1835.

9. Letter of May 9, 1867. Charles-Marie Leconte de Lisle, *Lettres à José-Maria de Heredia* (Paris: Honoré Champion, 2004), 36-37.
10. Charles-Louis de Montesquieu, *Lettres persanes* (Paris: Garnier-Flammarion, 1964), letter 30, 66.
11. Paul Verlaine, *Oeuvres en prose complètes* (Paris: Gallimard, 1972), 622-23. The review first appeared in *L'Étendard* on May 11, 1867.
12. Anon., "Causerie de la semaine," *Le Jockey: Journal de sport / Journal des chasseurs* (May 21, 1867): 3.
13. It is something of a challenge, given Gautier's uncertain transcription, to decipher the characters with which she renders Hugo's name; her translation of them is equally inventive, but what she meant to convey in her choice of its five characters was this phrase. See the discussion of the inscription by the rare book dealer who provides important background on the volume for sale in his catalogue: Jonathan Chiche, "La Déesse et l'Archange," *L'Express de Bénarès*, 2020, accessed April 13, 2020, http://lexpressdebenares.com/Catalogues/VH-Judith.pdf. The Chinese transliteration of her own name, Judith (Yu-di-de 俞第德, which she took to mean "graceful and primordial virtue") had, according to a fragment from her memoir collected by Suzanne Meyer-Zundel, been suggested by "a Chinese official passing through Paris." Hugo's name was devised in collaboration with her tutor Ding Dunling. See Suzanne Meyer-Zundel, *Quinze ans auprès de Judith Gautier* (Porto: Tipografia Nunes, 1969), 245-46.
14. Victor Hugo, *Correspondance*. Ancienne collection. 4 vols., ed Louis Barthou (Paris: Albin Michel, 1947-1952), 3: 48.
15. Orlando Figes, *The Europeans: Three Lives and the Making of a Cosmopolitan Culture* (New York: Henry Holt Metropolitan Books, 2019), 409.
16. Suzanne Meyer-Zundel, *Quinze ans*, 246.
17. François Coppée, "*Le Livre de jade* par Mme Judith Walter," *Le Moniteur universel*, October 5, 1867, 7.
18. Anon., "Chinese Poetry," *The Albion, A Journal of News, Politics and Literature* (June 8, 1867): 274. "Bluestocking" is an often derogatory term for an intellectual woman. This unidentified Parisian woman evidently knew Gautier personally and alludes to the influence of Chinese taste in the interior decoration of the author's home. For commentary on this cross-Atlantic dissemination see Laura Lauth, " 'Strange and Absurd Words': Translation as Ethics and Poetics in the Transcultural U.S. 1830-1915" (PhD diss., University of Maryland, 2011), 139-41.
19. Robert de Bonnières, "Madame Judith Gautier, samedi, 29 décembre 1883," in *Mémoires d'aujourd'hui*, 3 vols. (Paris: Paul Ollendorff, 1883), 1: 307.
20. Anatole France, "Judith Gautier," *La Vie littéraire*, 4 vols. (Paris: Calmann-Lévy, 1897), 4: 141-42.
21. Anatole France, "Judith Gautier," 134; André de Fouquières (1874-1959), "Les Poètes chinois," in *De l'art, de l'élégance, de la charité* (Paris: Fontemoing et Cie, 1910), 44; Rémy de Gourmont (1858-1915), *Judith Gautier* (Paris: Bibliothèque Internationale d'Édition, 1904), 17.
22. Rémy de Gourmont, *Judith Gautier*, 5.
23. Sylvie Camet and Anne Geisler-Szmulewicz both note that the dubious chronology of certain events recounted in Gautier's memoirs seems quite purposeful: "The resolution of these uncertainties can only point to one thing: until her death, Judith Gautier wanted to mystify her public about her real age; she claimed to have been born in 1850, thus rejuvenating herself by five years." Anne Geisler-Szmulewicz, "Mémoires enchevétré.e.s.: *Le Collier des jours* et *Le Second Rang du collier*," in *Gautier: Judith & Théophile, Bulletin de la Société Théophile Gautier*, ed. Anne Geisler-Szmulewicz and Marie-Hélène Girard, 40 (2018): 44n41. She cites Sylvie Camet, *Parenté et creation: Familles d'artistes, de la relation personnelle à la production collective* (Paris: L'Harmattan, 1995), 123n34.
24. Rémy de Gourmont, *Judith Gautier*, 17.

25. As recorded in Suzanne Meyer-Zundel, *Quinze ans*, 163: "Ce que j'écrivis avec le plus de Plaisir, me disait Judith, c'est le *Livre de Jade*."
26. Letter to Pierre Lôti (1850–1923) from 1890, cited in M. Dita Camacho, *Judith Gautier: Sa vie et son oeuvre* (Paris: Librairie E. Droz, 1939), 177.
27. Anatole France (Camille d'Ivry), "Judith Mendès [June 25, 1869]," in *Croquis féminins*, included in Michael Pakenham, ed., *Portraits littéraires*, vol. 32 of *Textes littéraires*, ed. Keith Cameron ([Exeter]: University of Exeter, 1979), 11.
28. Anon., "Judith Gautier," *La Petite Presse*, November 22, 1904, 5.
29. Joanna Richardson, *Judith Gautier: A Biography* (London: Quartet Books, 1986). Biographies of Judith Gautier by Camacho and Knapp are noted above. The literary discussions cited are William Leonard Schwartz, *The Imaginative Interpretation of the Far East in Modern French Literature, 1800–1925* (Paris: Honoré Champion, 1927); Muriel Détrie, "*Le Livre de Jade* de Judith Gautier: Un livre pionnier," *Revue de littérature comparée* 633 (1989): 301-24; Ferdinand Stocès, "*O Livro de Jade* de Judith Gautier: Caracteristicas gerais das edições de 1867 e de 1902," *Revue Oriente* 7 (2003): 3-20; Ferdinand Stocès, "Sur les sources du *Livre de Jade* de Judith Gautier (1845–1917) (Remarques sur l'authenticité des poèmes)," *Revue de littérature comparée* 319 (2006): 335-50; Ferdinand Stocès, "*Le Livre de Jade* de Judith Gautier (Caractéristiques générales des éditions de 1867 et de 1902)," *Neige d'Août* 14 (Spring 2006): 35-54; Ferdinand Stocès, "Le mystère du *Livre de Jade* de Judith Gautier," *Histoires littéraires* 26 (April-June 2006): 49-76; Min Ling, "Première rencontre poétique entre la France et la Chine: traduction et réception de la poésie classique chinoise en France au XIXème siècle" (PhD diss., University Paris-Sorbonne, 2013); Yu Wang, *La Réception des anthologies de poésie chinoise classique par les poètes français (1735–2008)* (Paris: Classiques Garnier, 2016); Anne Geisler-Szmulewicz and Marie-Hélène Girard, eds., *Gautier: Judith & Théophile*; Yvan Daniel and Martine Lavaud, eds., *Judith Gautier*, Collection "Interférences" (Rennes: Presses universitaires de Rennes, 2020); Judith Gautier, *Oeuvres complètes*, ed. Yvan Daniel, 2 vols. (Paris: Gallimard, 2011-); Meng Hua, "'Bu zhong de mei ren': Lue lun Zhudite Gediye de Han shi 'fanyi'": *Dong fang fan yi* 4 (2012): 49-58; Richard Serrano, *Neither a Borrower: Forging Traditions in French, Chinese and Arabic Poetry*. Legenda: Studies in Comparative Literature 7 (Oxford: European Humanities Research Centre, 2002); Barbara Jessome-Nance, "The Passionate Pursuit of Beauty: The Literary Career of Judith Gautier (1845-1917)" (PhD diss., University of Virginia, 1988); Laura Lauth, "'Strange and Absurd Words'"; Pauline Yu, "'Your Alabaster in This Porcelain': Judith Gautier's *Le livre de jade*," *PMLA* 122, no. 2 (March 2007): 464-82; and Pauline Yu, "Judith Gautier and the Invention of Chinese Poetry," in *Reading Medieval Chinese Poetry: Studies in Text, Context, and Culture*, ed. Paul Kroll (Leiden: E. J. Brill, 2014), 251-88.

2. "GOING TO CHINA IS LIKE GOING TO THE MOON": FRANCE ENCOUNTERS CHINA

1. Letter of August 4, 1869, in Victor Hugo, *Correspondance*. Ancienne collection. 4 vols., ed. Louis Barthou (Paris: Albin Michel, 1947-1952), 3: 213. Hugo was thanking her for sending him a copy of her first novel, *Le Dragon impérial*, which was set in China; it had been published serially in 1868 and appeared in hard cover in 1869.
2. Yvan Daniel, *Littérature française et Culture chinoise (1846–2005)* (Paris: Les Indes savantes, 2010), 77.
3. Edward Schafer, "What and How Is Sinology?" *T'ang Studies* 8-9 (1990-1991): 28.
4. Arnold H. Rowbotham, "A Brief Account of the Early Development of Sinology," *The Chinese Social and Political Science Review* 7 (1923): 127.

2. France Encounters China

5. Theodore N. Foss, "Reflections on a Jesuit Encyclopedia: Du Halde's Description of China (1735)," *Appréciation par l'Europe de la tradition chinoise à partir du XVIIe siècle*. Actes du IIIe Colloque international de sinologie. Centre de recherches interdisciplinaires de Chantilly, September 11-14, 1980 (Paris: Les belles lettres, 1983): 68-71.
6. Paul Demiéville, "Aperçu historique des études sinologiques en France," in *Acta Asiatica* (Tokyo: The Tōhō Gakkai, 1966), 67.
7. Jean-Pierre Abel-Rémusat, "Lettre au rédacteur, sur l'état et le progrès de la littérature chinoise en Europe," *Journal asiatique* 1, no. 7-12 (1822): 279, as cited by Yu Wang, *La Réception des anthologies de poésie chinoise classique par les poètes français (1735–2008)* (Paris: Classiques Garnier, 2016), 59n7.
8. Yu Wang, *La Réception des anthologies*, 76-77, 83; and Marie-Claire Bergère, "Introduction: L'Enseignement du chinois à l'École des langues orientales du XIXe au XXIe siècle," in Marie-Claire Bergère and Angel Pino, eds., *Un siècle d'enseignement du chinois à l'École des langues orientales 1840–1945* (Paris: L'Asiathèque, 1995), 13-26.
9. De Guignes's solution to these impediments was to crib from an older Chinese-Latin dictionary published by a Dominican cleric, Father Basilio Brollo de Gemona (1648-1704)—whose name is often erroneously spelled Glemona—and raided from the Vatican by Napoleon's armies. Isabelle Landry-Deron, "Les outils d'apprentissage du chinois en France au moment de l'ouverture de la chaire d'études chinoises du Collège Royal (1814) et les efforts de Jean-Pierre Abel-Rémusat pour les améliorer," in *Jean-Pierre Abel-Rémusat et ses successeurs: Deux cent ans de sinologie française en France et en Chine*, ed. Pierre-Étienne Will and Michel Zink (Paris: Académie des Inscriptions et Belles-Lettres, 2020), 38-39. See also William Leonard Schwartz, *The Imaginative Interpretation of the Far East in Modern French Literature, 1800–1925* (Paris: Honoré Champion, 1927), 16. On his father Joseph's claims in a work titled *Mémoire dans lequel on prouve que les Chinois sont une colonie égyptienne*, see Isabelle Landry-Deron, "L'ombre portée par l'ouvrage de Du Halde sur les premiers sinologues français non-missionnaires," in Michel Cartier, ed., *La Chine entre amour et haine*. Actes du VIIIe colloque de sinologie de Chantilly, *Variétés sinologiques*, No. 87 (Paris: Desclée de Brouwer, 1998), 36.
10. Nathalie Monnet, "Abel-Rémusat (1788-1832): Un autodidacte et ses livres," in Will and Zink, eds, *Jean-Pierre Abel-Rémusat et ses successeurs*, 77.
11. Isabelle Landry-Deron, "Les outils," 17-18.
12. Isabelle Landry-Deron, "Les outils," 39.
13. Pierre-Étienne Will, "Abel-Rémusat l'orientaliste," in Will and Zink, eds., *Jean-Pierre Abel-Rémusat*, 3.
14. Knud Lundbaek, "The Establishment of European Sinology 1801-1815," in *Cultural Encounters: China, Japan, and the West*, ed. Søren Clausen, Roy Starrs, and Anne Wedell-Wedellsborg (Aarhus: Aarhus University Press, 1995), 38.
15. Henri Wallon, "Notice sur la vie et les travaux de M. Aignan-Stanislas Julien, membre ordinaire de l'Académie," *Comptes rendus des séances de l'Académie des Inscriptions et Belles-Lettres*, 19e année 4 (1875): 392, accessed September 13, 2014, http://www.persée.fr/web/revues/home/prescript/article/crai_0065-0536_1875_num_19_4_68273.
16. André Mangin, "Stanislas Julien: Orientaliste et sinologue orléanais (1797-1873)," *Bulletin de la Société archéologique et historique de l'Orléanais*, Nouvelle Série 18, no. 143 (1er trimestre 2005): 11.
17. Gustave Flaubert, *L'Éducation sentimentale: Histoire d'un jeune homme* (Paris: Gallimard, 1965), 45. As noted by Hung Cheng Fu, *Un siècle d'influence chinoise sur la littérature française (1815–1930)* (Paris: Les éditions Domat-Montchrestien, 1934), 125. Also cited by William Leonard Schwartz, *The Imaginative Interpretation*, 31n1.
18. Paul Demiéville, "Aperçu," 81.

19. Angel Pino, "Stanislas Julien et l'École des langues orientales à travers quelques documents," in Bergère and Pino, eds., *Un siècle d'enseignement*, 55n5; and Demiéville, "Aperçu," 81.
20. André Mangin, "Notice sur la vie," 14, 15.
21. Léon Bertin (Paul Perny), *Le Charlatanisme littéraire dévoilé ou la vérité sur quelques professeurs de langues étrangères à Paris* (Versailles: Imprimerie G. Beaugrand et Dax, 1874), 14–15.
22. Jenny Huangfu Day, *Qing Travelers to the Far West: Diplomacy of the Information Order in Late Imperial China* (Cambridge: Cambridge University Press, 2018), 93.
23. André Lévy, *Nouvelles lettres édifiantes et curieuses d'Extrême-Occident par des voyageurs lettrés chinois à la Belle Époque 1866–1906* (Paris: Éditions Seghers, 1986), 78.
24. Diary entry from *Hanghai shuqi* 航海述奇 of April 12, 1866, quoted in André Lévy, *Nouvelles lettres*, 91.
25. Leon Bertin (Paul Perny), *Le Charlatanisme littéraire*, 16.
26. See, for example, Clément Fabre, "La sinologie est un sport de combat: L'affaire Paul Perny et les querelles sinologiques à Paris au XIXe siècle," *Genèses* 1, no. 110 (2018): 12–31, accessed June 9, 2024, https://www.cairn.info/revue-geneses-2018-1-page-12.htm.
27. Henri Cordier, *Les Études chinoises (1891–1894)* (Leiden: E. J. Brill, 1895), 15, 18.
28. Jenny Huangfu Day, *Qing Travelers to the Far West*, 38-39. Binchun's diary entry is from his *Cheng cha biji* 乘槎筆記 (Jingu liulichang eryou tang, 1868), 21. See also André Lévy, *Nouvelles lettres*, 94.
29. Edmond and Jules de Goncourt, *Journal des Goncourt: Mémoires de la vie littéraire* (January 27, 1886), ed. Robert Ricatte, 4 vols. (Paris: Flammarion, 1956), 3: 528. Unless otherwise noted, all references to the Goncourts' *Journal* are to this edition.
30. Angel Pino, "Abrégé dûment circonstancié de la vie de Marie Jean Léon le Coq, baron d'Hervey, marquis de Saint-Denys, professeur au Collège de France et membre de l'Institut, sinologue de son état, onironaute à ses heures: Une enquête à l'usage, non exclusif, des futurs biographes," in Bergère and Pino, eds., *Un siècle d'enseignement*, 114. Pino writes that Louise was the model for both the princess of Orvillers and the princess of Nassau. The former, who like Charlus appears in the second volume of the Pléiade edition of *Sodom and Gomorrah*, possesses "a sweet and charming gaze" and "a delicious, throbbing, and weary breast," and the latter, who is featured later in the third volume, *Time Regained* (*Le Temps retrouvé*), is described as "a Marie-Antoinette with an Austrian nose, and a delicious, preserved, embalmed gaze thanks to a thousand delightfully applied layers of make-up which gave her a lilac face." See Betty Schwartz, "Le Marquis d'Hervey de Saint-Denys: Rêves et réalités," in Olivier de Luppé, Angel Pino, Roger Rippert, and Betty Schwartz, eds., *D'Hervey de Saint-Denys, 1822–1892* (Île Saint-Denis: Éditions Oniros, 1995), 40, 43.
31. Félix Ribeyre, *Cham: Sa vie et son oeuvre* (Paris: Librairie Plon, 1884), between 154 and 155.
32. Anon., "Essai de biographie d'Hervey de Saint-Denys," in *Les Rêves et les moyens de les diriger*, preface by Robert Desoille, in *Bibli du Merveilleux*, ed. Claude Tchou (Paris: L'Imprimerie Blanchard, 1964), 47. The anonymous author of this essay details the surprising difficulty of extracting much biographical information about Hervey-Saint-Denys from the archives of the Collège de France, the Académie des Inscriptions et Belles-Lettres, to which he had not only been elected but also named president, and from local city records. One of the problems, as will become clear, was that little consensus exists about what to call him. His name was Marie-Jean-Léon Lecoq, and his title by birth the Baron d'Hervey. Upon the death of his mother in 1844 he was adopted by her brother, the Marquis de Saint-Denys. The Archives of the Seine filed notice of his death under the surname Lecoq, which momentarily stymied this biographer because the Marquis is elsewhere always referred to, variously, as d'Hervey, d'Hervey-de-Saint-Denys (or Denis), Hervey-de-Saint-Denys, or Hervey-Saint-Denys. Anon., "Essai de biographie," 48–50.

33. Angel Pino, "Abrégé," in Bergère and Pino, eds., *Un siècle d'enseignement*, 101.
34. See Raymond Schwab, *The Oriental Renaissance: Europe's Rediscovery of India and the East, 1680–1880*, trans. Gene Patterson-Black and Victor Reinking (New York: Columbia University Press, 1984), 45.
35. They could be called "sinologues" or "philologues en chambre." See, for example, José Frèches, *La Sinologie. Que sais-je?* No. 1610 (Paris: Presses universitaires de France, 1975), 67.
36. Jean-Louis de Négroni, *Souvenirs de la campagne de Chine: Détails sur la collection* (Paris: Imprimerie Renou et Maulde, 1864), 48.
37. For a detailed description of the Yuanmingyuan and its artifacts see Louise Tythacott, "The Yuanmingyuan and its Objects," in Louise Tythacott, ed., *Collecting and Displaying: China's "Summer Palace" in the West: The Yuanmingyuan in Britain and France* (New York: Routledge, 2018), 3–24.
38. [Georges-Louis Le Rouge, ed.], *Jardins de l'Empéreur de la Chine* (Paris: G. L. Le Rouge, 1786), based on 1745 woodcuts of the emperor's album. For a discussion of the album, see John Finlay, "Henri Bertin (1720–1792) and Images of the Yuanmingyuan in Eighteenth-Century France," in Louise Tythacott, ed., *Collecting and Displaying*, 123–37.
39. D'Hérisson, Le Comte Maurice d'Irisson, *Journal d'un interprète en Chine*, 14th ed. (Paris: Paul Ollendorff, 1886), 306.
40. Lt. Col. G.-J. Wolseley, *Narrative of the War with China in 1860* (London: Longman Green, Longman and Roberts, 1862), 224, 227.
41. Jean-Louis de Négroni, *Souvenirs*, 54, 56.
42. James Hevia points out that the word "loot" derives from Hindi and Sanskrit words meaning to rob, and it entered common usage between the two Opium Wars. See James Hevia, "Looting Beijing: 1860, 1900," in *Tokens of Exchange: The Problem of Translation in Global Circulations*, ed. Lydia H. Liu (Durham, NC: Duke University Press, 1999), 192; and James Hevia, *English Lessons: The Pedagogy of Imperialism in Nineteenth-Century China* (Durham, NC: Duke University Press, 2003), 75.
43. James Hevia, *English Lessons*, 107.
44. Jean-Louis de Négroni, *Souvenirs*, 54.
45. Louise Tythacott, "The Yuanmingyuan and Its Objects," 12. I have benefited from her summary of events as well as from the précis and analyses presented in Greg M. Thomas, "The Looting of Yuanming and the Translation of Chinese Art in Europe," *Nineteenth-Century Art Worldwide* 7, no. 2 (Autumn 2008), accessed February 13, 2022, www.19thc-artworldwide.org/index.php/autumn08/93-the-looting-of-yuanming-and-the-translation-of-chinese-art-in-europe; and by Erik Ringmar, *Liberal Barbarism: The European Destruction of the Palace of the Emperor of China* (New York: Palgrave Macmillan, 2013), 69ff.
46. Edmond and Jules de Goncourt, *Journal* (December 10, 1860), 1: 848.
47. Victor Hugo, letter of November 25, 1861, "Au capitaine Butler," in *Oeuvres complètes de Victor Hugo: Actes et paroles pendant l'exil, 1852–70* (Paris: J. Hetzel, 1880), 267–70. See the discussion of this letter in Petra ten-Doesschate Chu, "Victor Hugo and the Romantic Dream of China," in *Beyond Chinoiserie: Artistic Exchange between China and the West during the Late Qing Dynasty (1796–1911)*, ed. Petra ten-Doesschate Chu and Jennifer Milam (Leiden: Brill, 2019), 148–77. In another intriguing discussion of this letter, Zenghou Cheng points out that William Frances Butler (1838–1910) was only a lieutenant, not captain, in 1861 and does not appear in Hugo's calendar as a visitor until 1866; he was also not promoted to captain until 1872. Cheng suggests, therefore, that Hugo may not have written, or finished editing, the letter until 1866 or even much later; it was not published until a collection of his works from exile was issued in 1875. See Zenghou Cheng, "Qui est le capitaine Butler? A propos d'une lettre de Victor Hugo sur le Palais d'Été," *Revue d'histoire littéraire de la France* 111, no. 4

(2011): 891–903, accessed June 6, 2022, https://www.cairn.info/revue-d-histoire-litteraire-de-la-france-2011-4-page-891.htm.
48. Erik Ringmar, *Liberal Barbarism*, 208n119.
49. Described in Colombe Samoyault-Verlet, Jean-Paul Desroches, Gilles Béguin, and Albert Le Bonheur, eds., *Le Musée chinois de l'impératrice Eugénie* (Paris: Réunion des musées nationaux, 1994).
50. See Louise Tythacott, "Exhibiting and Auctioning Yuanmingyuan ("Summer Palace") Loot in 1860s and 1870s London: The Elgin and Negroni Collections," *Journal for Art Market Studies* 2, no. 3 (2018): 1–15, accessed February 13, 2022, https://eprints.soas.ac.uk/26149/on.
51. Jean-Louis de Négroni, *Souvenirs*, 7–8.
52. The first auction of his collection took place in Paris in May 1864, and the catalogue is available in the New York Public Library: https://digitalcollections.nypl.org/collections/catalogue-of-captain-de-negronis-collection-of-porcelain-jade-jewels-c#/?tab=about. The catalogue does not mention the Yuanmingyuan provenance of the items, although his memoirs make it explicit, and it was clearly no secret. See Léa Saint-Raymond, "Tracing Dispersal: Auction Sales from the Yuanmingyuan loot in Paris in the 1860s," *Journal for Art Market Studies*, Forum Kunstmark Cologne (2018): 11, accessed April 30, 2022, https://hal.archives-ouvertes.fr/hal-02986360. Louise Tythacott, "Exhibiting," 5–6, writes that the exhibitions initially did tend to inflate the prospective value of the collection, but that when it was finally put up for auction in England, starting in 1866, the hammer prices were significantly lower than had been anticipated. Moreover, in 1868 Négroni's French creditors sued him for inflating his collection's value; he was convicted of fraud and swindling, served a one-month prison sentence and paid a fine of 3,000 francs.
53. Louise Tythacott, "The Yuanmingyuan and Its Objects," 14.
54. Judith Walter, "Collection chinoise de M. Négroni," *L'Artiste: journal de la littérature et des beaux-arts* (April 15, 1864): 188–89.
55. According to E. Feydeau, Théophile Gautier: *Souvenirs intimes*, chap. 34, as noted by William Leonard Schwartz, *The Imaginative Interpretation of the Far East*, 20; and Joanna Richardson, *Théophile Gautier: His Life and Times* (London: Max Reinhardt, 1958), 186.
56. On the risotto, see Judith Gautier, *Le Second Rang du collier: Souvenirs littéraires*. Preface by Agnès de Noblet (Paris: Félix Juven, 1903; rpt. Paris: L'Harmattan, 1999), 189. On the number of publications, Joanna Richardson, *Théophile Gautier*, 283.
57. Edmond and Jules de Goncourt, *Journal* (May 12, 1857), 1: 349.
58. Charles Baudelaire, *Les Fleurs du mal*, ed. A. Adam (Paris: Garnier Frères, 1961), 3. The full dedication reads:

AU POÈTE IMPECCABLE
AU PARFAIT MAGICIEN ÈS LETTRES FRANÇAISES
À MON TRÈS CHER ET TRÈS VÉNÉRÉ
MAÎTRE ET AMI
THÉOPHILE GAUTIER
AVEC LES SENTIMENTS
DE LA PLUS PROFONDE HUMILITÉ
JE DÉDIE
CES FLEURS MALADIVES
C.B.

To the impeccable poet
To the perfect magician of French letters
To my dearest and most revered

Master and friend
Théophile Gautier
With sentiments
Of the most profound humility
I dedicate
These sickly flowers.
C. B.

59. Published in Théophile Gautier, *La Comédie de la mort* (Paris: Desessart, 1838), 333-34.
60. Gustave Flaubert, letter to Madame Sandeau of November 1859 published on July 15, 1919, in *Revue de Paris* and cited in William Leonard Schwartz, *The Imaginative Interpretation*, 30n5.
61. William Leonard Schwartz, *The Imaginative Interpretation*, 17. Schwartz discusses the influence of Gautier's interest in China on Parnassian poets on pp. 38-46.
62. Judith Gautier, *Le Second Rang du collier*, 161. Antoine-Pierre-Louis Bazin (1799-1863) was a student of both Abel-Rémusat and Julien and translated several Yuan-dynasty plays. In 1843 he was appointed as the first occupant of the chair in Chinese at the School of Vernacular Oriental Languages.
63. Henri David, "Théophile Gautier: 'Le Pavillon sur l'eau,'" part I, in *Modern Philology* 13, no. 7 (November 1915): 89.
64. Pauthier had published the first section of his *Chine moderne, ou Description historique, géographique et littéraire de ce vaste empire d'après des documents chinois* in 1837; see Yvan Daniel, *Littérature française et Culture chinoise (1846–2005)* (Paris: Les Indes savantes, 2010), 57. The second volume was a collaboration with Bazin, and the two were included in a series called *L'Univers pittoresque* (Paris: Firmin Didot frères, 1837-1853). Angel Pino and Isabelle Rabut, "Bazin aîné et la création de la chaire de chinois vulgaire à l'École des langues orientales: Relation historique accompagnée d'une bibliographie exhaustive des oeuvres du savant professeur," in Bergère and Pino, eds., *Un siècle d'enseignement*, 50.

For a description of Pauthier, who had been a Romantic poet before delving into sinology, as Gautier's "Chinese muse" see M. Marc Chadourne, "Le Parnasse à l'école de la Chine," *Cahiers de l'Association internationale des études françaises* 13 (June 1961): 14.

For an extensive discussion of the relationship between Gautier's story and his Chinese sources, see the two-part article by Henri David, "Théophile Gautier: 'Le Pavillon sur l'eau,'" in *Modern Philology* 13, no. 7 (November 1915): 391-416, and 13, no. 11 (March 1916): 647-68.

On Gautier's incorporation of Chinese garden design and other themes not in the original story, see Jingwen Liu, "From *chinoiserie* to *à la manière chinoise*: Théophile Gautier's 'Le pavillon sur l'eau,'" *The French Review* 94, no. 3 (March 2021): 151-66. Project Muse, accessed June 6, 2022.

65. Judith Gautier, *Le Second Rang du collier*, 244-45, recounts how a swimming party and picnic on the Seine in July [1865] and Théophile Gautier's infatuation with Marguerite Dardenne de la Grangerie prompted the composition of this sonnet. The group included her family, the Gautiers, and a Persian general named Mohsin-Khan. Stephan von Minden notes that this account differs entirely from the documented story of the poem's genesis as a "precious bouquet" from Gautier to thank Marguerite for hosting a dinner party whose various dishes on the menu had been inspired by his works. Stephan von Minden, "Une expérience d'exotisme vécu: 'Le Chinois de Théophile Gautier,'" *L'Orient de Théophile Gautier. Bulletin de la Société Théophile Gautier* 12 (1990): 41. The poem was first published on August 1, 1865, in the *Journal des Postes* and was included the following year in the first collection of the Parnassian poets: Catulle Mendès and Louis-Xavier de Ricard, eds., *Le Parnasse contemporain: Recueil de vers nouveaux* (Paris: Alphonse Lemerre, 1866), 5.

66. According to *The Illustrated London News*, July 29, 1848, 63. See L. Cassandra Hamrick, "Entre barbare et civilisé ou pour aller en Chine avec Gautier," *Études littéraires* 42, no. 3 (2011): 51–52.
67. Théophile Gautier, "En Chine," in *L'Orient* (Paris: G. Charpentier, 1884), 229–30; originally published in *Caprices et zigzags* (Paris: Hachette, 1856). Hamrick notes that the "Hereford Suspension Bridge" is the Hungerford Foot Bridge, 49n1.
68. Théophile Gautier, "En Chine," 235–37.
69. M. Marc Chadourne, "Le Parnasse," 14.
70. Edmond and Jules de Goncourt, *Journal* (Friday, July 17, 1863), 1: 1300; (Thursday, March 27, 1862), 1: 1044; (August 31, 1862), 1: 1127.
71. Edmond and Jules de Goncourt, *Journal* (July 7, 1872), 2: 906.
72. Jacques Brosse, *La Découverte de la Chine* (Paris: Bordas, 1981), 98.
73. As noted by Kimiko Kanazawa, "Le Japon paru dans les oeuvres de Théophile et Judith Gautier," *Kyoyo ronsyu (Liberal Arts Review)* 8 (December 1990): 74.
74. Judith Gautier, *Le Second Rang du collier*, 132–34.
75. Raoul Aubry, "Promenades et visites: Un début chez les Goncourt," *Le Temps*, November 25, 1910, 3.
76. Muriel Détrie, "L'image du Chinois dans la littérature occidentale au XIXe siècle," in Michel Cartier, ed., *La Chine entre amour et haine*, 412.
77. Grison, "Tin-Tun-Lin," *Le Figaro*, December 29, 1917, 3.
78. Judith Gautier, *Le Second Rang du collier*, 159–63. According to an unedited letter of September 14, 1863, from Judith Gautier's mother, Ernesta Grisi, to Charles Clermont-Ganneau, Théophile Gautier tried unsuccessfully to find employment for Ding in the Chinese museum, now part of the Chateau Fontainebleau, that Empress Eugénie filled with plunder from the Yuanmingyuan. Bibliothèque de l'Institut, ms 4109, f. 281, as cited in the notes to Catulle Mendès, "Ting-Tun-Ling," *Figurines des poètes*, in Michael Pakenham, ed., *Portraits littéraires*, vol. 32 of *Textes littéraires*, ed. Keith Cameron ([Exeter]: University of Exeter, 1979), 89.
79. Theodore Bean, "A Chat with Judith Gautier," *Theatre Magazine* 18 (August 1913): 59.
80. Armand Silvestre, "Tin Tun Ling," In *Portraits et souvenirs, 1866–1891* (Paris: Charpentier, 1891), 188.
81. L. Cassandra Hamrick, "Entre barbare et civilisé ou pour aller en Chine avec Gautier, 66n71, cites an extract from one of Gautier's letters to his daughter Estelle: "No one has mentioned anything about the Chinese man to me.—Has this amiable *magot* returned to the country of folding screens and porcelains?" Letter written from Russia and dated July 29, 1865, in Théophile Gautier, *Correspondance générale*, ed. Claudine Lacoste-Veysseyre (1995), 9: 92. It may be worth noting that *magot* literally meant Barbary ape and came, by extension, to mean a grossly ugly person and then a rotund Asian figurine.
82. As noted in Anon., "'Le Chinois de Gautier,'" *Le Gaulois*, November 16, 1886, 1, and in *Le Voleur*, November 1886, 748.
83. Ding's "Préface: Au public français" is printed on the first page of Tin-Tun-Ling, *La Petite Pantoufle (Thou-Sio-Sié): Roman chinois (The Stolen Little Slipper: Tou xiao xie 偷小鞋: Chinese novel)*, trans. M. Charles Aubert (Paris: Librairie de l'eau-forte, 1875).

3. "ONE OF THE MOST INTERESTING CHARACTERS OF HIS TIME": PROFESSOR, BARON, BARNUM, OR RAKE?

1. Similar epithets abound in the newspaper articles about Ding throughout his life. The first of these three is from Sifflet, "L'Aventure de Tin-Tun-Ling," *Le Gaulois*, April 21, 1881, 3, and the second two from Anon., "Le Chinois de Théophile Gautier," *L'Éclair*, April 27,

1902, 2; repr. as "Théophile Gautier et le Chinois," *Le Journal du dimanche*, May 25, 1902, 6. As was the case with Hervey-Saint-Denys, we will encounter considerable variation in the nineteenth-century romanization of his name: Tin-Tun-Ling, Ting-Tun-Ling, Tin-ton-ling, Tun-Tin-Ling, etc.

2. Anon., "Le Chinois de Théophile Gautier," *L'Intermédiare des chercheurs et curieux. Notes et quéries français: Questions et réponses, communications diverses à l'usage de tous, littérateurs et gens du monde, artistes, archéologues, généalogistes, etc.*, ed. M. Carle de Rash, year 68, vol. 95, no. 1776 (Paris: October 15, 1932): 729.

3. The account appears in her memoir, Judith Gautier, *Le Second Rang du collier: Souvenirs littéraires*. Préface by Agnès de Noblet (Paris: Félix Juven, 1903; rpt. Paris: L'Harmattan, 1999), 159-63. The report of the trial was published as Anon., "Les deux mariages du chinois Tin-Tun-Ling," Cour d'assises de la Seine, Présidence de M. Bondurand, Audience du 11 juin, *Gazette des tribunaux*, June 12, 1875, 564.

4. Émile Bergerat, "Le Chinois de Gautier," in *Souvenirs d'un enfant de Paris. Les Années de Bohème troisième mille* (Paris: Bibliothèque-Charpentier, 1911), 368.

5. The first report of the trial does not provide a precise date of birth, but an article published on the same date specifies his birthdate as May 15, 1831; see Fernand de Rodays, "Gazette des tribunaux, Cour d'assises: L'affaire du Chinois Tin-Tun-Ling," *Le Figaro*, June 12, 1875, 2-3. Yichao Shi, "La Formation de Judith Gautier au chinois et à la culture chinoise (1863-1905)," *Revue d'histoire littéraire de la France* 3 (July-Sept. 2020): 640, accepts this date, but Liu Zhixia, "Ding Dunling de Faguo suiyue," *Shu cheng zazhi* (September 2013): 40, offers May 17. That is the date Ding himself provides on his marriage certificate, included in Olivier Jacquot, "Paul Jean Baptiste Marie Tin-Tun-Ling (Ding Dunling), lecteur chinois de la Bibliothèque impériale," *Carnet de la recherche à la Bibliothèque nationale de France*, October 23, 2023, 18, accessed May 28, 2024, https://doi.org/10.58079/m40h. Both Shi and Liu write that the Chinese date of his birth would be June 22, 1831, by Western reckoning, which, however, corresponds to May 13, 1831, on the Chinese lunar calendar.

6. For the belief that Ding must have "certainly been compromised in the Taiping revolt and thus risked execution if he returned to China" see Muriel Détrie, "*Le Livre de jade* de Judith Gautier: Un livre pionnier," *Revue de littérature comparée* 633 (1989): 301n1.

7. "La Légende de Tie-Ouang, l'empéreur des Taepings," signed "Walter," in *Le Moniteur du soir*, October 17, 1864, 4, cited in Jean Claude Fizaine, "Un Portrait de Judith en impératrice chinoise," *Bulletin de la Société Théophile Gautier* 14 (1992): 149.

8. For the classic history see Joseph-Marie Callery, *Li Ki ou Mémorial des Rites* (Paris: Benjamin Duprat, 1853); the coauthored history was titled *L'Insurrection en Chine depuis son origine jusqu'à la prise de Nankin* (Paris, 1853). The city of Nanjing was captured by the Taiping insurgents in 1853 and was declared capital of their "Heavenly Kingdom." See the bibliography of Callery's works as compiled by Giuliano Bertuccioli, "Giuseppe Maria Calleri: Un Piemontese al servizio della Francia in Cina," *Pubblicazioni di "Indologica Taurinensia," Collana di Biografie e Saggi diretta da Oscar Botto* (Torino: Instituto de indologia, 1986), 21-23.

9. Marie-Claire Bergère, "Introduction: L'enseignement du chinois," in Marie-Claire Bergère and Angel Pino, eds., *Un siècle d'enseignement du chinois à l'École des langues orientales 1840-1945* (Paris: L'Asiathèque, 1995), 17. Kleckzkowski's argument did not prevail, for the "armchair sinologist" Antoine-Pierre-Louis Bazin was the first appointee to this chair in 1843, succeeded by Stanislas Julien in 1863, and then, finally, by Kleckzkowski—a Chinese speaker—himself in 1871.

10. Joseph-Marie Callery, "Préface," in *Li-Ki ou Mémorial des Rites*, xix.

11. "Indication sommaire des principales questions relatives à la politique & au commerce actuels de la Chine," *Archives de la Courneuve*, 393QO/710. Cited by Clément Fabre, "La sinologie est un sport de combat: L'affaire Paul Perny et les querelles sinologiques à Paris au XIXe siècle," *Genèses* 1, no. 110 (2018): 21, https://www.cairn.info/revue-geneses-2018-1-page-12.htm.

12. Guilliano Bertuccioli, "Giuseppe Maria Calleri," 17-19.
13. This interesting tidbit is provided in the account of the defense attorney's concluding statement at the trial in Fernand de Rodays, "Gazette des tribunaux, Cours d'assises: L'affaire du Chinois Tin-Tun-Ling," 3.
14. Georges Grison, "Tin-Tun-Lin," *Le Figaro*, December 29, 1917, 3.
15. In the opinion of Liu Zhixia, "Ding Dunling de Faguo suiye," 45.
16. Angel Pino, "Trois répétiteurs indigènes: Ly Hong-fang, Ly Chao-pée et Ting Tun-Ling, 1869-1870," in Bergère and Pino, eds., *Un siècle d'enseignement*, 278, includes a copy of the title page of the volume, signed by Ding as calligrapher.
17. In a brief essay titled "Free Masonry in China," de Rosny writes that he served as interpreter for Ding's initiation, during which the Chinese man "found himself as at home as a European on entering the Temple. Monsieur Ting Tun-ling accomplished the tasks demanded of initiates and demonstrated vivid satisfaction upon earning the modest apron of an Apprentice." Ding suggests to de Rosny that secret societies similar to Masonic lodges also existed in China though he was never a member of them. Another Chinese informant leads de Rosny to believe that the reference may have been to the Taiping revolutionaries, who adopted a syncretic Christianity. Léon de Rosny, *La Franc-Maçonnerie chez les Chinois* (Paris: Alexandre Lebon, 1864), 3-4, 6. See also Angel Pino, "Trois répétiteurs," in Bergère and Pino, eds., *Un siècle d'enseignement*, 279.
18. Angel Pino, "Trois répétiteurs," 272ff. Ding Dunling identifies himself as a drill instructor at the more prestigious Collège de France (rather than the School of Vernacular Oriental Languages) in one version of Tin-Tun-Ling (Ding Dunling), "Le jour de l'an chinois," *Le Monde illustré*, January 6, 1872, 14. It is no wonder that it has become difficult to keep the facts straight.
19. Raoul Aubry, "Promenades et visites: Un début chez les Goncourt." *Le Temps*, November 25, 1910, 3. Georges Grison, "Tin-Tun-Lin," 3, mentions this contretemps as well.
20. Fernand de Rodays, *Gazette des tribunaux*, 3.
21. As reported in *Le Figaro*, September 6, 1873, 1; and cited in Olivier Jacquot, "Paul Jean Baptiste Marie Tin-Tun-Ling," 7.
22. Edmond and Jules de Goncourt, *Journal: Mémoires de la vie littéraire* (July 17, 1863), ed. Robert Ricatte, 4 vols. (Paris: Flammarion, 1956), 1: 1300. Although it therefore seems reasonable to concur with Yichao Shi, "La Formation de Judith Gautier," 641, that Ding first met the Gautier family on July 16, 1863, some sources do not agree. M. Marc Chadourne, "Le Parnasse à l'école de la Chine," *Cahiers de l'Association internationale des études françaises* 13 (June 1961): 15, gives 1861 as the year in which "the refugee from the Great Wall rang their doorbell," but this is unlikely since Ding was still employed by Callery at that time. Michael Pakenham writes that the first reference to Tin-Tun-Ling as "le Chinois de Gautier" is found in the Goncourt *Journal* on December 29, 1862, but there is no entry for that date in any edition of the diaries. See note to Catulle Mendès, "Ting-Tun-Ling," in *Figurines des poètes*, included in Michael Pakenham, ed., *Portraits littéraires*, vol. 32 of *Textes littéraires*, ed. Keith Cameron. [Exeter]: University of Exeter, 1979, 89.
23. Edmond and Jules de Goncourt, *Journal* (April 21, 1864), 2: 38.
24. Edmond and Jules de Goncourt, *Journal* (May 4, 1865), 2: 158. Flaubert, letter to his niece Caroline dated Friday, May 5, 1865, in Gustave Flaubert, *Correspondance*, vol. 3 (Paris: Gallimard, 1991), 436. As noted, among others, by Yichao Shi, "La Formation de Judith Gautier," 642.
25. On Bouilhet's commitment to learning Chinese, see Judith Gautier, *Le Second Rang du collier*, 269. The Goncourt entry is from Edmond and Jules de Goncourt, *Journal* (May 22, 1863), 1: 1274. The reference from Yriarte appears in Charles Yriarte, "Louis Bouilhet," *Le Monde illustré*, July 24, 1869, 53. On Bouilhet's interest in writing Chinese poems, see William

Leonard Schwartz, *The Imaginative Interpretation of the Far East in Modern French Literature, 1800–1925* (Paris: Honoré Champion, 1927), 33-34; and Henri David, "Les Poésies chinoises de Bouilhet," *Modern Philology* 15, no. 11 (March 1918): 663-72. Francis Steegmuller in *Flaubert and Madame Bovary: A Double Portrait* (New York: New York Review of Books, 2005), 251, 263, tells a slightly different story, writing that it was only after his conversation "with an exiled mandarin who was teaching young Mademoiselle Gautier Chinese" that Bouilhet was "inspired" to buy a Chinese grammar and teach himself the language. But he dates the first encounter to the period after the publication of *Miloenis* in 1851, which is clearly erroneous.

26. Edmond and Jules de Goncourt, *Journal* (June 29, 1866), 2: 267.
27. Edmond and Jules de Goncourt, *Journal* (December 28, 1873), 2: 958.
28. These photographs were also taken by Potteau; the engravings appear in Armand de Quatrefages (1810-1892), *Histoire générale des races humaines; introduction à l'étude des races humaines* (Paris: Hennuyer, 1889), 430-31. Included by Olivier Jacquot, "Paul Jean Baptiste Marie Tin-Tun-Ling," 13. Jacquot also provides three 1874 images of Ding taken by the most renowned society photographer in Paris, Gaspard-Félix Tournachon (1820-1910), known as Nadar, 12.
29. Lancelot, "Échos de partout," *La Liberté*, June 25, 1878, 3. Perhaps because this was written after Ding's trial for bigamy, Lancelot adds that he would not defame Ding by saying he's not a serious man of letters. The other "scholar" was Ly-Chao-Pé, who preceded Ding as drill instructor for Hervey-Saint-Denys. An earlier article notes that Ding was among "ten to twelve Chinese" currently in Paris. Anon., "Les Tribunaux: Cours d'assises de la Seine: L'affaire Tin-Tun-Ling," *La Liberté*, June 13, 1875, 3.
30. G. P. V., "Causerie parisienne: La Colonie chinoise à Paris," *Le Radical*, May 15, 1882, 2.
31. The author writes that soon there may only be one because Chinese like Ding, fearing recriminations as an enemy at war, have taken to identifying themselves as something other than Chinese, in his case "Tartar." Anon., "Déchinoisement," *Gil Blas*, August 30, 1884, 1-2.
32. Un sportsman [alias], "Le grand prix de Paris et la question des courses," *La Question* 17 (June 23, 1878): 114; cited by Olivier Jacquot, "Paul Jean Baptiste Marie Tin-Tun-Ling," 15.
33. Armand Silvestre, "Tin Tun Ling," in *Portraits et souvenirs, 1886–1891* (Paris: Charpentier, 1891), 190.
34. Catulle Mendès, "Ting-Tun-Ling," in Michael Pakenham, ed., *Portraits littéraires*, 16. "Kin-jen" probably refers to *jin shi* 進士, the highest degree in the civil service examination system, which Ding definitely did not obtain; his cap displayed the button of the lowest title. Louis Belmontet (1799-1879) was a largely forgotten Bonapartist and poet (see Pakenham's note, 89).
35. Émile Bergerat, "Le Chinois de Gautier," 367, 369-71.
36. In, for example, three different issues of *La Petite Presse*: December 29, 1866, 4; January 8, 1876, 2; and January 1, 1882, 1; in *La Science pittoresque*, June 10, 1867, 27-29; and in *Le Monde illustré*, January 6, 1872, 14.
37. See M. Marc Chadourne, "Le Parnasse à l'école de la Chine," 18.
38. Yriarte's announcement appears in the issue of October 19, 1867, 234. The four installments of Ding's work appeared in Tin-Tun-Ling (Ding Dunling), "La Justice du fils du ciel," *Le Monde illustré*, June 13, 1868, 379; June 20, 1868, 391-92; June 27, 1868, 406-07, 410; and July 4, 1868, 7, 10.
39. Judith Gautier, *Le Second Rang du collier*, 208.
40. William Butcher, "The Tribulations of a Chinese in China: Verne and the Celestial Empire," *Journal of Foreign Languages* 5 (September 2006): 69, 71.

41. The poem appeared in the issue of March 29, 1868, 21.
42. Anon., "Revue des théâtres," *Le Petit Journal*, May 23, 1874, 3; "Courrier des théâtres," *Le XIXe Siècle*, May 23, 1874, 4.
43. Jules Prével, "Courrier des théâtres," *Le Figaro*, May 21, 1874, 3. Note that he mentions Ding as the "Chinese man" of Judith Gautier's husband, Catulle Mendès, and that the word for spring has been misromanized as "Tchu" rather than "Tchun."
44. Anon., "L'Actualité," *L'Événement*, July 6, 1874, 1; Bixiou, "Matinée chinoise," *Le Gaulois*, July 7, 1874, 1; Gaston Vassy, "La Représentation chinoise à Passy," *Le Figaro*, July 7, 1874, 3.
45. Anon., "Soirée de bienfaisance," *La Petite Presse*, August 2, 1874, 3-4.
46. Anon., "Informations," *Le Figaro* July 13, 1875, 2.
47. Anon., "Poignée d'informations," *La Petite Presse*, January 29, 1878, 3. The matinee took place the day before.
48. Anon., "Échos de Paris," *L'Événement*, April 12, 1880, 1.
49. Lancelot, "Échos de partout," *La Liberté*, June 30, 1878), 3.
50. Zhang Deyi, entry for February 15, 1869, in his *Hanghai shu qi* 航海 述 奇. As cited by Qian Zhongshu, *Tan yi lu*, rev. ed. (Hong Kong: Zhonghua shuju, 1986), 372.
51. The British translator of this diary acknowledges the difficulty of identifying many French and English surnames by the Chinese characters used to denote them in the text and simply renders him as an unknown Frenchman named "Augien." Simon Johnstone, trans., *Diary of a Chinese Diplomat: Zhang Deyi* (Beijing: Panda Books, 1992), 227.
52. In this two-page note to a one-sentence passage, he omits the reference to "Ou Jian's" mother and daughter. Qian Zhongshu, *Tan yi lu*, 372-373.
53. Liu Zhixia, "Ding Dunling de Faguo suiye," 49; and Yichao Shi, "La Formation de Judith Gautier," 643.
54. For versions of these stories, see Maurice Dreyfous, *Ce que je tiens à dire: Un demi-siècle de choses vues et entendues, 1862–1872*, 5th ed. (Paris: Librairie Paul Ollendorff, 1912), 100-02; Armand Silvestre, "Tin Tun Ling," 190-92, and Arnold Mortier, *Les Soirées parisiennes de 1876* (Paris: E. Dentu, 1877), 65-66. According to Dreyfous and Mortier, Ding's volunteer defense lawyer was Léon Gambetta (1838-1882), soon to become a noted republican politician but now pleading his first case; he was known for his glass eye.
55. Some newspaper articles report the date as February 6. Olivier Jacquot provides a copy of Ding's marriage certificate, where he is identified as a "professor of Oriental languages" and which he signs "Baron Tin-Tun-Ling." Olivier Jacquot, "Paul Jean Baptiste Marie Tin-Tun-Ling," 18.
56. Devéria would later teach at the School of Vernacular Oriental Languages, from 1889-1899. Laurent Galy, "Entre sinologie pratique et sinologie savante: Les interprètes-professeurs de l'École des langues orientales vivantes, 1871-1930," in Bergère and Pino, eds., *Un siècle d'enseignement*, 141.
57. For an interesting tidbit to the story—that eight years later Liégeois's name appeared in American newspapers in connection with yet another lawsuit, this time to seek living expenses from her American boyfriend, see Liu Zhixia, "Ding Dunling de Faguo suiyue," 46.
58. Maurice Dreyfous, *Ce que je tiens à dire*, 103. Elzéar appears, wearing a top hat, in Henri Fantin-Latour's famous group portrait of eight poets and politicians (including Verlaine and Rimbaud), *The Corner of the Table* (*Un coin de table*), which is held by the Musée d'Orsay in Paris.
59. According to one obituary published after his death, Ding had also proved fearless when standing down two Prussian soldiers who saw him and declared that "it would be better if that Chinese man were in Peking." To which Ding "simply replied in his gentle voice: 'And you

270   3. Professor, Baron, Barnum, or Rake?

in Berlin! Good day, sirs.'" Anon., "Échos du 'Courrier,'" *Le Courrier du soir*, November 29, 1886, 4.

60. Anon., "Les deux mariages de Tin-Tun-Ling." Cour d'assises de la Seine, Présidence de M. Bondurand, Audience du 11 juin. *Gazette des tribunaux*, June 12, 1875, 564–65.

61. Anon., "Paris au jour le jour," *Le Figaro*, June 17, 1875, 2. At about this time the highest paid French laborer, a Parisian mechanic, barely earned 1,500 francs per year; see Angel Pino, "Stanislas Julien et l'École des langues orientales à travers quelques documents," in Bergère and Pino, eds., *Un siècle d'enseignement*, 77n52.

62. Olivier Jacquot, "Tin-Tun-Ling, a Chinaman," *Carnet de la recherche à la Bibliothèque nationale de France*, October 1, 2023, accessed May 28, 2024, https://doi.org/10.t8079/m3zv.

63. "Monsieur et Mesdames Tin-Tun-Ling," cartoon by Henri Meyer, *Le Sifflet*, June 20, 1875, cover, Bibliothèque nationale de France–l'Arsenal. Included in Stephan von Minden, "Une expérience de l'exotisme vécu: 'Le Chinois de Théophile Gautier.'" *L'Orient de Théophile Gautier. Bulletin de la Société Théophile Gautier* 12 (1990): 39.

64. Originally published in the *Daily News* and included in Andrew Lang, "A Chinaman's Marriage," *Lost Leaders* (New York: Longmans, Green, and Co., 1889), 31–37.

65. On Charles Aubert, see Michael Pakenham, "La République des lettres de Catulle Mendès et Adelphe Froger," in *Catulle Mendès et la République des lettres*, ed. Jean-Pierre Saïdah. Rencontres 26, Série Études dix-neuviémistes dirigée par Pierre Glaudes 11 (Paris: Classiques Garnier, 2011), 28. The description of Lesclide comes from Charles Monselet, "Causerie littéraire," *L'Événement*, July 22, 1875, 1.

66. Tin-Tun-Ling (Ding Dunling), "Tin-Tun-Ling au public français," *La Petite Pantoufle (Thou-Sio-Sié): Roman chinois*, trans. M. Charles Aubert (Paris: Librairie de l'eau-forte, 1875), [1].

67. Brévannes, "Bibliographie," *Le Tintamarre*, July 18, 1875, 6.

68. Anon., "Chronique," *Le Temps*, August 1, 1875, 2.

69. Joë Bengali, "Semaine dramatique et littéraire," *Le Parti ouvrier*, December 31, 1889, 3.

70. "La Semaine," *Paris à l'eau-forte*, July 25, 1875, 89–90. The book was reissued twice, in 1887 and 1889, according to Liu Zhixia, "Ding Dunling de Faguo suiyue," 47.

71. Anon., "À travers Paris," *Le Figaro*, November 16, 1886, 1. Paul de Cassagnac (1842–1904) was a journalist and well-known duelist and, in politics, a conservative Bonapartist. He is the subject of one of Adolphe Racot's *Portraits-cartes*, included in Michael Pakenham, ed., *Portraits littéraires*, 48.

72. Joanna Richardson, *Judith Gautier: A Biography* (London: Quartet Books, 1986), 24. Richardson cites Suzanne Meyer-Zundel, *Quinze ans auprès de Judith Gautier* (Porto: Tipografia Nunes, 1969), 159, who, however, does not refer to the funeral expenses. Stephan von Minden, "Une expérience de l'exotisme vécu," 53n75, notes that there is no gravestone with Ding's name on it in St-Ouen cemetery. This could be because Ding was buried rather in the cemetery of the Batignolles church where his funeral took place. His patrons, Gabriel Dumas (presumably the "P. Dumas" referred to earlier) and his wife, erected a granite monument over his grave stating: "Here lies the baron Tun-Tin-Lin [sic] / Chinese scholar / dead at the age of 56 years." Anon., "Le Parisien de Pékin," *Le Voltaire*, April 9, 1887, 2. His grave can no longer be found there either: Batignolles cemetery records indicate that the plot was reclaimed on July 2, 1980. Olivier Jacquot, "Paul Jean Baptiste Marie Tin-Tun-Ling," 16.

73. Lucien Valette, "Un Chinois de Paris: Tin-Tun-Ling et Th. Gautier," *Le Voltaire*, November 18, 1886, 1–2.

74. Anon., "Le Chinois de Gautier," *Le Gaulois*, November 16, 1886, 1.

75. Anon., "Le Commerce de la France," *Le Temps*, November 17, 1886, 1.

76. Émile Bergerat, *Vie et aventures de sieur Caliban 1884–1885* (Paris: E. Dentu, 1886), 76.

4. "FOR A WOMAN THE WORD 'IMPOSSIBLE' NO LONGER EXISTS": THE CHALLENGES OF CHINESE POETRY

1. Judith Gautier, *Le Second Rang du collier: Souvenirs littéraires* (Paris: Félix Juven, 1903; rpt. Paris: L'Harmattan, 1999), 38, 195-203.
2. Judith Gautier, *Le Second Rang du collier*, 203.
3. Judith Gautier, *Le Second Rang du collier*, 203. Earlier she explains that the dictionary had been a gift of the family's friend Olivier de Gourjault, 90.
4. Paul Demiéville, "Aperçu historique des études sinologiques en France," in *Acta Asiatica* (Tokyo: The Tōhō Gakkai, 1966), 75-76.
5. Judith Gautier, *Le Second Rang du collier*, 203.
6. Quoted in Suzanne Meyer-Zundel, *Quinze ans auprès de Judith Gautier* (Porto: Tipografia Nunes, 1969), 244-45. The "214 keys" refer to the word roots or radicals used to organize Chinese words in a dictionary.
7. For a translation and introduction to this anthology, see Arthur Waley, trans., *The Book of Songs: The Ancient Chinese Classic of Poetry*, new edition by Joseph R. Allen, foreword by Stephen Owen (New York: Grove, 1997).
8. For a discussion about the context and methods of court poetry, see "How to Write a Court Poem in 708: Forms, Genres, and Subgenres" and "Poetry in the Life of the Court," in Stephen Owen, *The Poetry of the Early T'ang* (New Haven, CT: Yale University Press, 1977), 234-55, 256-73. James J. Y. Liu, *The Art of Chinese Poetry* (Chicago: University of Chicago Press, 1962) provides a concise introduction to classical Chinese poetry. See also Zong-qi Cai, ed., *How to Read Chinese Poetry: A Guided Anthology* (New York: Columbia University Press, 2008); Zong-qi Cai, ed., *How to Read Chinese Poetry in Context: Poetic Culture from Antiquity Through the Tang* (New York: Columbia University Press, 2018); and Michael Fuller, *An Introduction to Chinese Poetry: From the Canon of Poetry to the Lyrics of the Song Dynasty* (Cambridge, MA: Harvard University Press, 2017).
9. Arthur Waley, "The Limitations of Chinese Literature," in *One Hundred and Seventy Chinese Poems* (New York: Knopf, 1919), 19.
10. For an introduction to Tang poetry, see Stephen Owen, *The Great Age of Chinese Poetry: The High T'ang* (New Haven, CT: Yale University Press, 1981).
11. For an extensive analysis of this poem as an example of regulated verse, see Zong-qi Cai, "Recent-Style Shi Poetry: Pentasyllabic Regulated Verse (*Wu yan lü shi*)," in *How to Read Chinese Poetry: A Guided Anthology*, 162-72.
12. Fathers Pierre-Martial Cibot (1727-1780) and Jean Joseph Marie Amiot (1718-1793), in the compendium of their writings, *Mémoires concernant l'histoire, les sciences, les arts, les moeurs, les usages &c . . . des Chinois, par les Missionnaires de Pékin*, 16 vols. (Paris: Nyon, 1776-1814), 4: 168. As cited by Yu Wang, *La Réception des anthologies de poésie chinoise classique par les poètes français (1735–2008)* (Paris: Classiques Garnier, 2016), 59n10.
13. Father Cibot, in *Mémoires* 13: 46. As cited by Muriel Détrie, "Translation and Reception of Chinese Poetry in the West," *Tamkang Review* 22 (1991): 46.
14. From the preface to his translation of *Yu-jiao-li*, quoted in Anon., *Notice sur les travaux de M. D'Hervey de Saint-Denys relatifs aux études chinoises* (Paris: J. Claye, n.d.), 3.
15. From Stanislas Julien, "Preface," *Hoeï-lan-ki, ou l'Histoire du cercle de craie: Drame en prose et en vers* (London: L'imprimerie de Cox père et fils, 1832), xxviii-xxix.
16. For an account of these efforts see Yu Wang, *La Réception*, 47-81.
17. The lecture was subsequently published as Sir John Francis Davis, *The Poetry of the Chinese* (London: Asher and Co., 1870). His translations include, without identification, the "Farewell

4. The Challenges of Chinese Poetry

to spring" attributed to Wang Wei, trans. Judith Gautier as "Pour oublier ses pensées" (see chapter 5), and Du Fu's "Enjoying the rain on a spring night," trans. Hervey-Saint-Denys (see note 29 below); Davis, 43-45.

18. Léon d'Hervey-Saint-Denys, *Poésies de l'époque des Thang, précédé de L'art poétique et la prosodie chez les Chinois* (Paris: Amyot, 1862; rpt. Éditions Champ Libre, 1977). While this volume was in press, Hervey-Saint-Denys published a preview of two poems from it in his article "Poésies chinoises composées sous la dynastie des Thang (Li-Taï-pé; Thou-fou)," *Revue orientale et américaine* 2 (Paris: Challamel Aîné, 1859): 285-88. As noted by Yu Wang, *La Réception*, 55.

19. Léon d'Hervey-Saint-Denys, "L'Art poétique et prosodique chez les Chinois," in *Poésies*, 108-09.

20. Léon d'Hervey-Saint-Denys, "L'Art poétique," in *Poésies*, 96.

21. Léon d'Hervey-Saint-Denys, *Poésies*, 182-83.

22. Charles de Labarthe, review in *Journal asiatique* 6, no. 6 (August-September 1865): 281-88. See Angel Pino, "Léon d'Hervey Sinologue: Repères bio-bibliographiques (1849-1894)," in Olivier de Luppé, Angel Pino, Roger Rippert, and Betty Schwartz, eds., *D'Hervey de Saint-Denys* (Île Saint-Denis: Éditions Oniros, 1995), 166.

23. Anon., *Notice sur les travaux*, 3.

24. Muriel Détrie, "Translation and Reception," 48. Paul Demiéville, "Aperçu historique," 82, agrees with this assessment.

25. Paul Demiéville, "Aperçu historique," 82.

26. Paul Demiéville, "Aperçu historique," 82; Paul Pelliot, "Bulletin critique: *Fir-Flower tablets, poems translated from the Chinese* par Mme Florence Ayscough, 'english version' de Mlle Amy Lowell," *T'oung Pao*, Second Series 21, no. 2/3 (May-July 1922): 242.

27. Émile Montégut, "La poésie d'une vieille civilisation," *Revue des Deux-Mondes* (March 15, 1863): 435; Mary Lafon, "Li-Taï-Pé et Thou-Fou," *Revue britannique* (September 1863): 134; and Barthélemy Saint-Hilaire, "De la poésie chinoise," *Journal des savants* (October 1864): 597. As cited by Yu Wang, *La Réception des anthologies*, 138, 133, 138.

28. This appears in the entry for January 21, 1866, in some editions of the journal, for example, in vol. 3 (1866-1870) of Edmond and Jules de Goncourt, *Journal des Goncourt: Mémoires de la vie littéraire*, 9 vols. (Paris: G. Charpentier and E. Fasquelle, 1887-1896), 14. It is not included in any of the four volumes of the Robert Ricatte edition, which I cite unless otherwise noted.

29. Entry for August 3, 1876, in Edmond and Jules de Goncourt, *Journal des Goncourt: Mémoires de la vie littéraire*, ed. Robert Ricatte. 4 vols. (Paris: Flammarion, 1956), 2: 1142-43. He is quoting the first line ("Oh! la bonne petite pluie qui sait si bien quand on a besoin d'elle!" [hao yu zhi shi jie 好雨知時節]) of the translation of Du Fu's "La pluie de printemps," in Léon d'Hervey-Saint-Denys, *Poésies de l'époque des Thang*, 192. The poem in Chinese is titled "Enjoying the rain on a spring night" ("Chun ye xi yu" 春夜喜雨), in Qiu Zhaoao, ed., *Du shi xiang zhu*, 2 vols. (1767; rpt. Taipei: Wenshizhe chubanshe, 1973), 1: 510.

30. M. Marc Chadourne, "Le Parnasse à l'école de la Chine," *Cahiers de l'Association internationale des études françaises* 13 (June 1961): 19; Marcellin Berthelot (1827-1907) was a distinguished chemist. Edmond and Jules de Goncourt, *Journal*, June 20, 1864, 2: 58. Years earlier Renan had dismissed Chinese language itself as too "inorganic and incomplete" to be capable of anything more than "a trivial literature of inferior quality," in Ernest Renan, *De l'origine du langage*, 2nd ed. (Paris: Michel Lévy Frères, 1858), 195-96, cited by Angel Pino and Isabelle Rabut, "Bazin aîné et la création de la chaire de Chinois vulgaire," in Marie-Claire Bergère and Angel Pino, eds., *Un siècle d'enseignement du chinois à l'École des langues orientales 1840-1945* (Paris: L'Asiathèque, 1995), 33.

31. L. Letellier, *Louis Bouilhet, 1821–1869, sa vie et ses oeuvres d'après des documents inédits* (Paris: Hachette, 1919), 244. As cited by William Leonard Schwartz, *The Imaginative Interpretation of the Far East in Modern French Literature, 1800–1925* (Paris: Honoré Champion, 1927), 33. See also Henri David, "Les poésies chinoises de Bouilhet," *Modern Philology* 15, no. 11 (March 1918): 663–72.
32. Yu Wang, *La Réception des anthologies*, 43n81.
33. Betty Schwartz, "Le Marquis d'Hervey de Saint-Denys: Rêves et réalités," in Olivier de Luppé et al., eds., *D'Hervey de Saint-Denys, 1822–1892*, 17.
34. Judith Gautier, *Le Second Rang du collier*, 204–05.
35. Undated letter from Judith Gautier to Catulle Mendès (Collection Lovenjoul, C502, quater f. 19), cited in Michael Pakenham, ed., *Portraits littéraires*, 89n.
36. Judith Gautier, *Le Second Rang du collier*, 240–41.
37. The second and third memos are dated February 9 and 10, respectively. Items 138-40 in Madeleine Cottin, ed., *Théophile Gautier: 1811–1872. [Exposition]* (Paris: Bibliothèque nationale, 1961), 44, a catalogue of an exhibit at the library on Théophile Gautier that ran from December 1961 to March 1962. The catalogue does not include Taschereau's response in full and this important qualification, which is discussed by Juliette Delobel, "Judith Gautier, érudite intuitive," *Revue de la BNF* 60 (January 2020): 165. All three memos are reproduced in Olivier Jacquot, "Judith Gautier, lectrice de la Bibliothèque impériale," *Carnet de recherche* of the BnF, accessed September 8, 2024, https://doi.org/10.58079/m40f.
38. For information about the holdings of the Bibliothèque and their acquisition see Maurice Courant, *Catalogue des livres chinois, coréens, japonais, etc.* (Paris: Ernest Leroux, 1902). I am grateful to Nathalie Monnet, head curator of the Oriental Division, for kindly confirming dates of acquisition of some of these texts, in a personal communication of July 21, 2005. The two anthologies of Tang poetry Hervey-Saint-Denys consulted, which Gautier also read, were both compiled in the eighteenth century: Wang Yaoqu 王堯衢, ed., *Gu Tang shi he jie jian zhu* 古唐詩合解箋註 (Compiled explications of ancient and Tang poetry with annotations and commentaries), and Liu Wenwei 劉文薇, ed., *Tang shi he xuan xiang jie* 唐適合選詳解 (Compiled selections of Tang poetry with detailed explications). As mentioned in part in Léon d'Hervey-Saint-Denys, *Poésies de l'époque des Thang*, 107. In addition, the library held two other eighteenth-century Tang anthologies: *Shan man lou jian zhu Tang shi qi yan lü* 山滿樓箋註唐時七言律 (Shanmanlou edition of Tang seven-syllable regulated verse, with annotations and commentaries, ed. Zhao Chenyuan 趙臣瑗), and *Tang shi guan zhu jian shi* 唐詩貫珠箋釋 (Linked pearls of Tang Poetry, with commentaries, ed. Hu Yimei 胡以梅), also seven-syllable regulated verse and mostly dating from the late Tang.

Hervey-Saint-Denys notes having made use of two eighteenth-century editions of the collected writings of the two most renowned Tang dynasty poets: *Li Taibo wen ji ji zhu* 李太白文集輯註 (Li Taibo's [Li Bo's] collected writings with commentaries, by Wang Qi 王琦); and *Du Shaoling quan ji xiang zhu* 杜少陵全集詳註 (Du Fu's complete works with commentaries, by Qiu Zhaoao 仇兆鰲), the latter mentioned in note 29 above with its modern title. Two other editions of the two poets' works were also in the library: *Chong kan fen lei bu zhu Li shi quanji* 重刊分類補註李詩全集 (New edition of the classified complete works of Li Taibo [Li Bo], ed. Yang Qixian 楊齊賢 and Xiao Shiyun 蕭士贇 during the Yuan dynasty) and *Chong kan qian jia zhu Du shiwen quanji* 重刊千家註杜詩文全集 (New edition of the complete works of Du Fu with several commentaries, a sixteenth-century edition of Huang He 黃鶴 and Liu Chenweng 劉辰翁).

The library also held five editions of the earlier sixth-century anthology, the *Zhao ming wen xuan* 昭明文選 (Selections of refined literature). Though Hervey-Saint-Denys did not translate any works from this collection, he was clearly familiar with it; Gautier may have perused it as well. She certainly consulted the *Wang Shi he zhu Su Dongpo shi quanji* 王施合註蘇東坡詩全集 (Complete poetry of Su Dongpo with commentaries by Wang [Shipeng 王十朋 1112-1171] and Shi [Yuanzhi 施元之 jin shi 1154]) for her several renditions of his poems in her volume.

This was in fact the first volume Gautier borrowed, on February 15, 1866; on March 5, 1866, her mother Ernesta Grisi signed out the first three of the four Tang anthologies mentioned above. She kept them for several months, and in one case almost two years. See Olivier Jacquot, "Judith Gautier, lectrice de la Bibliothèque impériale," *Carnet de la recherche à la Bibliothèque nationale de France*, October 18, 2023, https://doi.org/10.58079/m40f, which reproduces the records of her loans.

39. Judith Gautier, *Le Second Rang du collier*, 205.
40. Emphasis mine. Judith Walter, "Variations sur des thèmes chinois d'après les poésies de Li-taï-pé, Thou-fou, Than-jo-su, Houan-tchan-lin, Haon-ti," *L'Artiste: journal de la littérature et des beaux-arts* (January 15, 1864): 38. Louis Figuier (1819-1894) was a scientist who wrote several illustrated works for the public, including *The World Before the Deluge* (*La Terre avant le deluge*) (1863) and *The World and Its Oceans* (*La Terre et ses mers*) (1864). Gautier's first publication, also for *L'Artiste*, was a witty and lively piece arguing that books are a more durable New Year's gift for children than toys and recommending Figuier's second book as an excellent complement to the first. Judith Walter, "Livres d'Étrennes, II: L'Oraison dominicale, de Lorenz Frolich. La Terre et les mers, de Louis Figuier," *L'Artiste: Revue de l'art contemporain* (December 15, 1863): 262-63.
41. Judith Walter, "Variations sur des thèmes chinois d'après des poésies de Su-tchou, Sou-ton-po, Thou-fou, Li-taï-pé et Kouan-tchau-lin," *L'Artiste: Journal de la littérature et des beaux-arts* (June 1, 1865): 261. Gautier provides a footnote that translates literally the characters in the poets' names, which confirms the identification of Wang Changling but not "Su-tchou."
42. Judith Walter, "Soirs de lune: Petits poèmes chinois," *Revue du XIXe siècle* 6 (April 1866): 338-40. Joanna Richardson omits this publication in her otherwise comprehensive bibliography of Gautier's works.
43. Judith Walter, "Variations," *L'Artiste* (January 15, 1864): 37.
44. Included in Wang Yaoqu, *Gu Tang shi he jie* (Rpt. Taipei: Wenhua tushu gongsi, 1968), 1: 97-98 and Liu Wenwei, *Tang shi he xuan* (Rpt. Guangxi: Guangxi renmin chubanshe, 1988), 190.
45. Andrea S. Thomas makes some of these points in "Judith Gautier, *Vers Libre*, and the Faux East," *Symposium: A Quarterly Journal in Modern Literatures* 72, no. 2 (2018): 77-81. The distinction between "domesticating" and "foreignizing" translations derives from one made by Friedrich Schleiermacher (1768-1834) and is developed by Lawrence Venuti in *The Translator's Invisibility: A History of Translation* (New York: Routledge, 1995). As Thomas notes, Gautier "domesticates" the content of poems, but her innovative prose format was actually "foreignizing." James J. Y. Liu, "Polarity of Aims and Methods: Naturalization or Barbarization?" *Yearbook of Comparative and General Literature* 24 (1975): 60-68, anticipates Venuti's distinction.
46. As one critic famously put it, "the words come to an end but the meaning is inexhaustible" (yan you jin er yi wu qiong 言有盡而意無窮). Yan Yu (fl. 1180-1235), *Canglang shihua jiaoshi*, ed. Guo Shaoyu (Beijing: Renmin wenxue chubanshe, 1961), 24.
47. Judith Gautier, *Le Second Rang du collier*, 233. 39. Suzanne Meyer-Zundel includes much of the account of this meeting in her own memoir but erroneously attributes it to the first volume of Gautier's memoir, *Le Collier des jours: Souvenirs de ma vie*. Suzanne Meyer-Zundel, *Quinze ans*, 84-86.

48. Judith Gautier, *Le Second Rang du collier*, 331-34. Mohsin-Khan and Gautier remained good friends, and she dedicated her 1888 novel *Iskender*, which was set in Persia, to him. He was at the time serving as minister of justice, and when his ruler the shah read the book, which Gautier had asked her friend to give him, he was so moved that he sent her a diamond from his treasury. Suzanne Meyer-Zundel, *Quinze ans*, 184-85.
49. On Pasdeloup, see Alex Ross, *Wagnerism: Art and Politics in the Shadow of Music* (New York: Farrar, Straus and Giroux, 2020), 84; and Maurice Dreyfous, *Ce que je tiens à dire: Un demi-siècle de choses vues et entendues, 1862–1872*. 5th ed. (Paris: Librairie Ollendorff, 1912), 84-88.
50. On Judith Gautier's beauty, see Maurice Dreyfous, *Ce que je tiens à dire*, 84; and Robert de Bonnières, "Madame Judith Gautier, samedi 29 décembre 1883," in *Mémoires d'aujourd'hui*, 3 vols. (Paris: Paul Ollendorff, 1883), 3: 303-04.
51. On Mendès's appearance, see Robert de Bonnières, "Catulle Mendès, samedi 18 novembre 1882," in *Mémoires d'aujourd'hui*, 184; and Théodore de Banville, "Catulle Mendès," in *Camées parisiens*, Deuxième série (Paris: Librairie Richelieu, 1866), 49-50. For "blond Christ," see J.-H. Rosny, *Torches et Lumignons*, 194-95, cited by Joanna Richardson, *Judith Gautier: A Biography* (London: Quartet Books, 1986), 30.
52. Joanna Richardson, *Judith Gautier*, 29-30. In his second of four lectures on the group Mendès describes how the poets were linked by their enthusiasm for Wagner. Catulle Mendès, *La Légende du Parnasse contemporain*, 4 lectures (Bruxelles: Auguste Brancart, 1884), lecture 2: 97.
53. They met on Tuesdays, according to Yann Mortelette, "Catulle Mendès et le Parnasse," in *Catulle Mendès: L'Énigme d'une disparition*, ed. Patrick Besnier, Sophie Lucet, and Nathalie Prince (Rennes: Presses universitaires de Rennes, 2005), 16; and Yann Mortelette, *Histoire du Parnasse* ([Paris]: Fayard, 2005), 26, 231. Joanna Richardson, *Judith Gautier*, 29, writes that the gatherings occurred on Wednesdays.
54. Mendès's coeditor, Louis-Xavier de Ricard (1843-1911) was the nephew of the sinologist Guillaume Pauthier. Catulle Mendès and Louis-Xavier de Ricard, eds., *Le Parnasse contemporain: Recueil de vers nouveaux* (Paris: Alphonse Lemerre, 1866), 38n1. Mendès was chagrined that they became known as Parnassians, for they had "never dreamed of encumbering themselves with that burlesque name." Catulle Mendès, *La Légende*, lecture 1: 5.
55. M. Dita Camacho, *Judith Gautier: Sa vie et son oeuvre* (Paris: Librairie E. Droz, 1939), 41-42.
56. M. Dita Camacho, *Judith Gautier*, 57, therefore concludes that she was a Parnassian "in name only." See also Yvan Daniel, "Présentation: *Le Livre de jade*, un rêve de Judith Gautier," in Judith Gautier, *Le Livre de jade*, ed. Yvan Daniel (Paris: Imprimerie nationale, 2004), 20-22; and Yu Wang, *La Réception des anthologies*, 184-87.
57. Suzanne Meyer-Zundel, *Quinze ans*, 254-55.
58. Catulle Mendès and Louis-Xavier de Ricard, eds., "Épilogue," *Le Parnasse contemporain: Recueil de vers nouveaux*, 170.
59. Richard Serrano, *Neither a Borrower: Forging Traditions in French, Chinese and Arabic Poetry*. Legenda: Studies in Comparative Literature 7 (Oxford: European Humanities Research Centre, 2002), 218.
60. M. Marc Chadourne, "Le Parnasse à l'école de Chine," 16.
61. Paul Arène (1843-1896) et al., eds., "Une séance littéraire à l'Hôtel du Dragon bleu," *Le Parnassiculet contemporain: Recueil de vers nouveaux*, 2nd ed. (Paris: Librairie centrale, 1872), 9-20. Also discussed by William Leonard Schwartz, *The Imaginative Interpretation*, 40-41.
62. Eugène Vermersch (1845-1878), "Les Hommes du jour," Première série, no. 12, 1867, pub. in *Le Hanneton*, August 12, 1866, in Michael Pakenham, ed., "Introduction," *Portraits littéraires*, x.
63. Vance Thomas, "The Last of the Parnassians: Catulle Mendès," in *French Portraits* (Boston: Richard G. Badger and Co., 1900), 83.

276   4. The Challenges of Chinese Poetry

64. Yann Mortelette, "Catulle Mendès," 14-15.
65. As recounted by Maurice de Waleffe, *Quand Paris était un paradis: Mémoires 1900–1939* (Paris: Société des éditions Denoël, 1947), 42.
66. Judith Gautier's recollection, as recorded by Suzanne Meyer-Zundel, *Quinze ans*, 65.
67. On the rumors, Joanna Richardson, *Théophile Gautier: His Life and Times* (London: Max Reinhardt, 1958), 206; on Wilde, see Julian Barnes, *The Man in the Red Coat* (New York: Knopf, 2020), 202.
68. Holmès was the goddaughter of the writer Alfred de Vigny, who may in fact have been her father. She was also rumored to have been romantically involved with both Franz Liszt and Richard Wagner. Judith Richardson, *Judith Gautier*, 35-36. For her attendance at the concerts, see Maurice Dreyfous, *Ce que je tiens à dire*, 87.
69. On Augusta Holmès's income, see Edmond and Jules de Goncourt, *Journal* (August 25, 1895), 4: 838. Even she failed to maintain Mendès's interest; after separating from her around 1885, having drained her coffers, he would go on to father a child with a third woman and to marry, briefly, a fourth, after his divorce from Gautier. Joanna Richardson, *Judith Gautier*, 164, 168.
70. Robert de Bonnières, *Mémoires d'aujourd'hui*, 193-94, citing first an essay by Guy de Maupassant in *Gil Blas*.
71. Maurice Dreyfous, *Ce que je tiens à dire*, 91.
72. Edmond and Jules de Goncourt, *Journal* (April 9, 1866), 3: 257.
73. Maurice Dreyfous, *Ce que je tiens à dire*, 84; Suzanne Meyer-Zundel, *Quinze ans*, 83.
74. Suzanne Meyer-Zundel, *Quinze ans*, 69-70.
75. Suzanne Meyer-Zundel, *Quinze ans*, 73, 76, 77, 78, 79. The letters appear on pp. 70-80. Some extracts from them are also included in Richard and Cosima Wagner, *Lettres à Judith Gautier*, ed. Léon Guichard ([Paris]: Gallimard, 1964), 375-79. For a summary of this "episode" see Joanna Richardson, *Judith Gautier*, 28-48. For an account of Judith's triumphant demeanor in her costume at the dance, hosted by Marguerite Dardenne de la Grangerie, which suggests that she and her mother had finally managed to overcome Théophile Gautier's objection to the marriage, see Maurice Dreyfous, *Ce que je tiens à dire*, 92.
76. Suzanne Meyer-Zundel, *Quinze ans*, 79, 76.
77. Olivio (Catulle Mendès), four "Lettres d'amour," dated November 26, 27, 28, and 29, 1865, appeared in *L'Art*, November 30, 1865, 7-8. Three more, dated December 4, 4, and 5, 1865, appeared in *L'Art*, December 8, 1865, 5-6.
78. Joanna Richardson, *Théophile Gautier*, 210; and M. Dita Camacho, *Judith Gautier*, 47.
79. Maurice Dreyfous, *Ce que je tiens à dire*, 93-94.
80. Joanna Richardson, *Judith Gautier*, 108-12.
81. Maurice de Waleffe, *Quand Paris était un paradis*, 41.
82. Maurice Dreyfous, *Ce qui'il me reste à dire: Un demi-siècle de choses vues et entendues, 1848–1900*, 3rd ed. (Paris: Librairie Paul Ollendorff, [1913]), 301.
83. Suzanne Meyer-Zundel, *Quinze ans*, 69.

5. "THE CELESTIAL EMPIRE UNFURLS COMPLETELY THROUGHOUT THIS BOOK": THE 1867 *BOOK OF JADE*

1. Meredith Marrin, "Staging China, Japan, and Siam at the Paris Universal Exhibition of 1867," in Petra ten-Doesschate Chu and Jennifer Milam, eds., *Beyond Chinoiserie: Artistic Exchange between China and the West during the Late Qing Dynasty (1796–1911)* (Leiden: Brill, 2019), 124.

2. Meredith Martin, "Staging China," 126. Jules's brother Ferdinand is known as the founding director of the Suez Canal Company. For a detailed discussion of Hervey-Saint-Denys's involvement with the exhibit, see Meng Hua, "Faguo Hanxue jia De Liwen de Zhongguo qingjie: Dui 1867 nian Bali shijie bolanhui Zhongguo guan chengbai de wenhua sikao," in *Zhong Fa wenxue guanxi yanjiu* (Shanghai: Fudan, 2011), 256-57.
3. Raoul Ferrère, "Le Jardin chinois à l'Exposition," in *L'Exposition universelle de 1867 illustrée*, ed. François Ducuing, 2 vols. (Paris: Imprimerie Générale Ch. Lahure, 1867), 1: 134. See also Greg M. Thomas, "The Looting of Yuanming and the Translation of Chinese Art in Europe," *Nineteenth-Century Art Worldwide* 7, no. 2 (Autumn 2008), www.19thc-artworldwide.org/index.php/autumn09/93-the-looting-of-yuanming-and-the-translation-of-chinese-art-in-europe; and Angel Pino, "Léon d'Hervey sinologue: Repères bio-bibliographiques (1849-1894)," in *D'Hervey de Saint-Denys*, ed. Olivier de Luppé, Angel Pino, Roger Ripert, and Betty Schwartz (Île Saint-Denis: Éditions Oniros, 1995), 167. John Finlay believes Chapon's model may have been in the eighth view of the Yuanmingyuan, "Above and below the heavenly light" (*Shang xia tian guang* 上下天光); personal communication.
4. Angel Pino, "Léon d'Hervey sinologue," 167; Meredith Martin, "Staging China," 129.
5. Edmond and Jules de Goncourt, January 16, 1867, *Journal des Goncourt: Mémoires de la vie littéraire*, ed. Robert Ricatte. 4 vols. (Paris: Flammarion, 1956), 2: 317.
6. Meredith Martin, "Staging China," 129.
7. Raoul Ferrère, "Le Jardin," 135, 138.
8. Gustave Duchesne de Bellecourt (1817–1881), "La Chine et le Japon à l'Exposition universelle," *Revue des deux mondes* (1829-1871), seconde période 70, no. 3 (August 1, 1867): 720, 713.
9. Tribunal de commerce de la Seine, *Note pour M. le marquis d'Hervey contre MM. Penon Frères* (Paris: Imprimerie centrale des chemins de fer. A Chaix et Cie, 1868), 13, 17-18.
10. Angel Pino, "Léon d'Hervey sinologue," 168.
11. Général Tcheng-Ki-Tong, in *Les Plaisirs en Chine* (Paris: Charpentier et Cie, 1890), 229.
12. Judith Walter, "Chine-Japon-Siam," *Le Moniteur universel*, November 12, 1867, 6.
13. The poem is titled "The peach blossom" ("La fleur de pêcher," attributed to Tse-Tié), in Judith Walter, *Le Livre de jade* (Paris: Alphonse Lemerre, 1867), 13-14. Théophile Gautier, "Chinois et Russes: À l'Exposition universelle de Paris, 1867," *Le Moniteur universel*, May 19, 1867, 3.
14. Information about these holdings is provided by Maurice Courant, *Catalogue des livres chinois, coréens, japonais, etc.* (Paris: Ernest Leroux, 1902), 333-35. Gautier did not take the *Linked Pearls* home, but she could have consulted it onsite.
15. I owe this suggestion to the thesis of Jin Yun Chow, "Franco-Chinese Poetic Dialogues in the 19th Century: Judith Gautier's *Le livre de jade*" (Princeton University, 2017), which her advisor, Professor Anna Shields, kindly shared with me.
16. Arthur Waley, "The Limitations of Chinese Literature," in *One Hundred and Seventy Chinese Poems* (New York: Knopf, 1919), 18, 20; James J. Y. Liu, *The Art of Chinese Poetry* (Chicago: University of Chicago Press, 1962), 57.
17. Li Bo, "Wu ye ti," in Liu Wenwei, *Tang shi he xuan* (Rpt. Guangxi: Guangxi renmin chubanshe, 1988), 80-81; also in Wang Yaoqu, *Gu Tang shi he jie* (Rpt. Taipei: Wenhua tushu gongsi, 1968) 1: 54.
18. Léon d'Hervey-Saint-Denys, *Poésies de l'époque des Thang précédé de L'art poétique et la prosodie chez les Chinois* (Paris: Amyot, 1862; rpt. Éditions Champ Libre, 1977), 170.
19. Judith Walter, *Le Livre de jade*, 19-20.
20. For more on the story of Su Hui, see Wilt Idema and Beata Grant, *The Red Brush: Writing Women of Imperial China* (Cambridge, MA: Harvard University Press, 2004), 127-31. The comment on their deepened love is on 129.

21. Judith Walter, *Le Livre de jade*, 31-32.
22. Stephen Owen, *The Making of Early Chinese Classical Poetry* (Cambridge, MA: Harvard University Press, 2006), 224.
23. Wang Yaoqu, *Gu Tang shi he jie*, 2: 122. Léon d'Hervey-Saint-Denys, *Poésies de l'époque des Thang*, 27-28, alludes to the work in the preface.
24. Judith Walter, *Le Livre de jade*, 11-12; Léon d'Hervey-Saint-Denys, *Poésies de l'époque des Thang*, 316. Liu Wenwei, *Tang shi he xuan*, 124-25; Wang Yaoqu, *Gu Tang shi he jie*, 1: 64.
25. Shen Deqian 沈德潛 (1673-1769), cited in Liu Wenwei, *Tang shi he xuan*, 125.
26. Judith Walter, *Le Livre de jade*, 7-8.
27. Judith Walter, *Le Livre de jade*, 35-36. An earlier version was included in Judith Walter, "Variations sur des thèmes chinois d'après les poésies de Li-taï-pé, Thou-fou, Than-jo-su, Houan-tchan-lin, Haon-ti," *L'Artiste: Journal de la littérature et des beaux-arts* (January 15, 1864): 38.
28. Du Fu, "A song about autumn winds destroying my thatched roof" ("Mao wu wei qiu feng suo po ge" 茅屋為秋風所破歌), in Qiu Zhaoao, ed., *Du shi xiang zhu*, 2 vols. (1767; rpt. Taipei: Wenshizhe chubanshe, 1973), 1: 527.
29. Alain Bosquet, *Les cent plus beaux poèmes du monde* (Paris: Édition Saint Germain des Près, 1979), quoted by Ferdinand Stocès, "O Livro de Jade de Judith Gautier: Caracteristicas gerais das edições de 1967 e de 1902," *Revue Oriente* 7 (2003): 18.
30. The four poems titled "Yue xia du zhuo" 月下獨酌 are included in Wang Qi, ed., *Li Taibo quanji* (rpt. Taipei: Heluo tushu, 1976), 515-16. Gautier would have found the quatrain "Sitting alone before Jingting Mountain" ("Du zuo jing ting shan" 獨坐敬亭山) in Wang Yaoqu, *Gu Tang shi he jie*, 1: 73; and Liu Wenwei, *Tang shi he xuan*, 141.
31. Du Fu, "Ye wang," in Wang Yaoqu, *Gu Tang shi he jie*, 1: 151; and Liu Wenwei, *Tang shi he xuan*, 332-33.
32. Judith Walter, *Le Livre de jade*, 53-54. An earlier version was included in Judith Walter, "Soirs de lune: Petits poèmes chinois," *Revue du XIXe siècle* 6 (April 1866): 339.
33. These five poems can be found in Judith Walter, *Le Livre de jade*, 43-44; 49-50; 51-52; 55-56; and 59-60. Earlier versions appeared in Judith Walter, "Soirs de lune," 310. Zhang Ruoxu's poem was included in Wang Yaoqu, *Gu Tang shi he jie*, 1: 41-43; Liu Wenwei, *Tang shi he xuan*, 77-80.
34. Li Bo, "Yu jie yuan," in Wang Yaoqu, *Gu Tang shi he jie*, 1: 72-73; Liu Wenwei, *Tang shi he xuan*, 139-40.
35. Judith Walter, "Soirs de lune," 338. Version below in Judith Walter, *Livre de jade*, 47-48.
36. "À Arsène Houssaye," in Charles Baudelaire, *Petits poèmes en prose*, ed. Robert Kopp (Paris: Librairie José Corti, 1969), 8.
37. Judith Gautier, *Le Second Rang du collier: Souvenirs littéraires*. Préface by Agnès de Noblet (Paris: Félix Juven, 1903; rpt. Paris: L'Harmattan, 1999), 58-60. The poem has not been preserved.
38. Judith Gautier, *Le Second Rang du collier*, 205-06.
39. In a later version of Baudelaire's prose poem, published in the *Revue nationale et étrangère* on September 14, 1867, "la lune" is no longer capitalized. See Charles Baudelaire, *Petits poèmes en prose*, 114n1. "Les Bienfaits de la lune" appears on 14-15.
40. Andrea S. Thomas, "Judith Gautier, *Vers Libre*, and the Faux East," *Symposium: A Quarterly Journal in Modern Literatures* 72, no. 2 (2018): 84.
41. Henri Céard, "Chine littéraire," *L'Événement*, 29 June 1900. Cited by Yu Wang, *La Réception des anthologies de poésie chinoise classique par les poètes français (1735-2008)* (Paris: Classiques Garnier, 2016), 168n136.
42. Judith Walter, *Le Livre de jade*, 79-80.

43. Included in Wang Yaoqu, *Gu Tang shi he jie*, 1: 89. Cui was a poet active in the first half of the eighth century who earned the highest examination degree in 726. He was known for poems inspired by folk songs that often centered on lonely women. Translations appear, respectively, in Hervey-Saint-Denys, *Poésies*, 355-56; and Judith Walter, *Le Livre de jade*, 85-86.
44. Yu Wang argues that one cannot "unequivocally" show that Gautier "knew of the existence of *Poésies de l'époque des Thang*" until 1876, when she refers to the scholar in her popular works on China, and that it is "highly probable" that she consulted Hervey-Saint-Denys's work only while preparing the second edition of *The Book of Jade*. This example suggests otherwise. Similarly, this discussion should make clear that there are significantly more than the "half-dozen" poems in common between the two anthologies that Muriel Détrie detects. See Muriel Détrie, "*Le Livre de jade* de Judith Gautier: Un livre pionnier," *Revue de littérature comparée* 633 (1989): 309. Ferdinand Stocès believes that "one quarter" of Gautier's seventy-one poems overlap with those in Hervey-Saint-Denys's volume and goes on to discuss some of her likely debts to his work, but by my count there may be as many as twenty-seven; Ferdinand Stocès, "*Le Livre de Jade* de Judith Gautier (Caractéristiques générales des éditions de 1867 et de 1902)," *Neige d'Août* 14 (Spring 2006): 43. Stephan von Minden counts seven poems in common but concludes after comparing the two sets of examples that Gautier had not seen Hervey-Saint-Denys's book; see Stephan von Minden "Une experience d'exotisme vécu: 'Le Chinois de Théophile Gautier,'" *L'Orient de Théophile Gautier. Bulletin de la Société Théophile Gautier* 12 (1990): 51n50.
45. Judith Walter, *Le Livre de jade*, 69-70.
46. Léon d'Hervey-Saint-Denys, *Poésies de l'époque des Thang*, 351-52; Wang Yaoqu, *Gu Tang shi he jie*, 1: 63; Liu Wenwei, *Tang shi he xuan*, 122-23.
47. Judith Walter, *Le Livre de jade*, 93-94. The 160 folk songs in *The Book of Songs* are arranged according to the Zhou-dynasty state from which they were putatively collected, and it is possible that the attribution to "Sao-Nan" refers to the second chapter, which contains the airs of Shao Nan 召南, South of Shao, one of the states associated with the Zhou-dynasty ruling house. But Gautier's poem is clearly based on the first stanza of the well-known song titled "Big rat," which is poem 113 in the anthology from a later chapter of songs from the state of Wei 魏. In Arthur Waley, trans., *The Book of Songs*, new edition by Joseph R. Allen (New York: Grove, 1997), 88-89.
48. Judith Walter, *Le Livre de jade*, 91-92. Wang Yaoqu, *Gu Tang shi he jie*, 1: 72; and Liu Wenwei, *Tang shi he xuan*, 137.
49. Léon d'Hervey-Saint-Denys, "L'Art poétique et la prosodie chez les Chinois," in *Poésies de l'époque des Thang*, 51. For a discussion of the poem's afterlife, see Joseph R. Allen, "From Literature to Lingerie: Classical Chinese Poetry in Taiwan's Popular Culture," in *Popular Culture in Taiwan: Charismatic Modernity*, ed. Marc L. Moskowitz (London: Routledge, 2010), 65-85.
50. Judith Walter, *Le Livre de jade*, 107-08.
51. Wang Yaoqu, *Gu Tang shi he jie*, 1: 71. The Qing-dynasty editor of Wang Wei's collected works places the poem in an appendix and notes that some anthologies attribute it to Wang Ya 王涯 or Zhang Zhongsu 張仲素. Zhao Diancheng, *Wang Youcheng ji jian zhu* (rpt. Taipei: Heluo tushu, 1975), 274. As Richard Serrano rightly points out, "Porcelain cups have no place in a Chinese wine-drinking poem"—wooden vessels or gourds would have been more likely—but they "are perfectly appropriate to nineteenth-century French chinoiserie." Richard Serrano, *Neither a Borrower: Forging Traditions in French, Chinese and Arabic Poetry*. Legenda: Studies in Comparative Literature 7 (Oxford: European Humanities Research Centre, 2002), 187.
52. Léon d'Hervey-Saint-Denys, *Poésies de l'époque des Thang*, 210-12; Wang Yaoqu, *Gu Tang shi he jie*, 1: 46-47; and Liu Wenwei, *Tang shi he xuan*, 89-91.

53. Judith Walter, *Le Livre de jade*, 119-20.
54. Judith Walter, *Le Livre de jade*, 113-14.
55. Wang Qi, ed., *Li Taibo quanji*, 460.
56. Fusako Hamao suggests that Gautier was inspired by the porcelain panels on the Chinese pavilion at the International Exposition, but the manuscript for *The Book of Jade* was already at the publisher when the fair opened in April 1867. Fusako Hamao, "The Sources of the Texts in Mahler's 'Lied von der Erde,'" *19th-Century Music* 19 (1995): 95. Gautier may have been thinking of her father's story, "The Waterside Pavilion," in which the reflection of the lovers in the water plays a key role in the plot.
57. Gottfried Böhm, *Chinesische Lieder aus dem Livre de jade von Judith Mendès* (Munich: Ackermann, 1873), 82.
58. Arthur Waley, trans., *The Book of Songs* (London: Allen and Unwin, 1937), 110-57, who organized the poems by theme, included thirty-five poems—more than one-tenth of the collection—in his section called "Warriors and Battles."
59. Judith Walter, *Le Livre de jade*, 131-32.
60. Judith Walter, *Le Livre de jade*, 133-34.
61. Judith Walter, *Le Livre de jade*, 129-30. She would have found this poem in Liu Wenwei, *Tang shi he xuan*, 34-37. See Léon d'Hervey-Saint-Denys, *Poésies de l'époque des Thang*, 207-09, for his version.
62. Judith Walter, *Le Livre de jade*, 127-28.
63. Wang Yaoqu, *Gu Tang shi he jie*, 1: 100; and Liu Wenwei, *Tang shi he xuan*, 195.
64. Judith Walter, *Le Livre de jade*, 135-36. An earlier version appeared in Judith Walter, "Variations," *L'Artiste* (January 15, 1864): 38.
65. Judith Walter, *Le Livre de jade*, 151-52 and 153-54. An earlier version of "Indifference" was included in Judith Walter, "Variations," *L'Artiste* (January 15, 1864): 38.
66. Denise Brahimi, *Théophile et Judith vont en orient* (Paris: La Boîte aux Documents, 1990), 124.
67. Judith Walter, *Le Livre de jade*, 157-58.
68. Kong Fanli, ed., *Su Shi shi ji* (Beijing: Zhonghua shuju, 1982), 3: 877.
69. Michael A. Fuller, *The Road to East Slope: The Development of Su Shi's Poetic Voice* (Stanford, CA: Stanford University Press, 1990), 224-25.
70. Wang Yaoqu, *Gu Tang shi he jie*, 1: 56-57; and Liu Wenwei, *Tang shi he xuan*, 82-84; also translated in Léon d'Hervey-Saint-Denys, *Poésies de l'époque des Thang*, 125-26.
71. Judith Walter, *Le Livre de jade*, 143-44.
72. This anecdote from the *Lie zi* 列子 is included in A. C. Graham, *The Book of Lieh-tzu: A Classic of the Tao* (New York: Columbia University Press, 1990), 45.
73. Judith Walter, *Le Livre de jade*, 143-44. An earlier version appeared in Judith Walter, "Variations," *L'Artiste* (June 1, 1865): 261.
74. Wang Yaoqu, *Gu Tang shi he jie*, 1: 57.
75. Judith Walter, *Le Livre de jade*, 161-62. It appeared earlier in Judith Walter, "Variations," *L'Artiste* (June 1, 1865): 261. Included in Wang Yaoqu, *Gu Tang shi he jie*, 1: 149; and Liu Wenwei, *Tang shi he xuan*, 317-18.
76. Qiu Zhao'ao, ed., *Du shi xiang zhu*, 1: 8, 70-71.
77. Judith Walter, *Le Livre de jade*, 163-64.
78. There is no obvious source in Li Bo's corpus for this poem. Ling Min suggests that it may have been inspired by passages from Stanislas Julien's translation of the Yuan dynasty play *The Orphan of Zhao* (Zhao shi gu er 趙氏孤兒), though that is traveling rather far afield for material whose invention could more simply have been prompted by ideas and images running through the poet's work. Ling Min, "Première rencontre poétique: Traduction et réception de la poésie classique chinoise en France au XIXème siècle" (PhD diss., University of

Paris-Sorbonne, 2013), 61-62. George Soulié de Morant, a scholar who much admired Gautier's volume, silently corrected what he must have thought was her error when quoting the poem in his study of Chinese literature. He attributes it to the statesman Li Hongzhang 李鴻章 (1823-1901), but Gautier could not have had access to his writings in 1867. George Soulié de Morant, *Essai sur la littérature chinoise* (Paris: Plon, 1912), 309-10.

79. Judith Walter, *Le Livre de jade*, 165-66.

6. "BRUSHING UP AGAINST THE FAMOUS": JUDITH GAUTIER'S ARTISTIC CONNECTIONS

1. Anatole France, "Judith Gautier," in *La vie littéraire*, 4 vols. (Paris: Calmann-Lévy, 1897), 4: 142.
2. Judith Gautier, *Richard Wagner et son oeuvre poétique depuis Rienzi jusqu'à Parsifal* (Paris: Charavay Frères, 1882), 7; Anon., "Judith Gautier," *La petite presse*, November 22, 1904, 5.
3. All references from *La Liberté* (March 23, April 2, May 27, 1868) cited by M. Dita Camacho, *Judith Gautier: Sa vie et son oeuvre* (Paris: Librairie E. Droz, 1939), 68. The novel ran from April 11 to May 27.
4. Kong Shangren's 孔尚任 (1648-1718) *Peach Blossom Fan* (*Taohua shan* 桃花扇). As noted by Yvan Daniel, *Littérature française et Culture chinoise (1846-2005)* (Paris: Les Indes savantes, 2010), 37. Daniel also surmises that the missionary Régis-Evariste Huc's popular account, *The Empire of China* (*L'Empire de Chine*) (Paris: Imprimerie impériale, 1854) served as an important historical source for Gautier, 35.
5. Although William Schwartz believed that her extensive description of Beijing was "impossible to collate with" historical maps, Yichao Shi argues that most of Gautier's descriptions "are exact and well located." William Leonard Schwartz, *The Imaginative Interpretation of the Far East in Modern French Literature, 1800–1925* (Paris: Honoré Champion, 1927), 51; Yichao Shi, "Voyager dans un monde de rêve: La reconstruction du temps et de l'espace dans *Le Dragon Impérial*," *Loxias-Colloques*, 15, *Traversez l'espace*, accessed December 5, 2019, http://revel.unice.fr/symposia/actel/index.html?id=1427.
6. Stéphane Mallarmé, "Lettre à Henri Cazalis," in *Correspondance choisie* of *Oeuvres complètes* (Paris: Gallimard, 1998), 1: 747; and Villiers de l'Isle-Adam, "*Le Dragon impérial* par Madame Judith Mendès," *La Vogue Parisienne*, August 13, 1868; both cited in Yvan Daniel, *Littérature française et Culture chinoise*, 35-36.
7. Anatole France, "Judith Gautier,"136.
8. Rémy de Gourmont, *Judith Gautier* (Paris: Bibliothèque Internationale d'Édition, 1904), 8, 11.
9. Edmond and Jules de Goncourt, April 5, 1868, and February 7, 1872, in *Journal: Mémoires de la vie littéraire*, ed. Robert Ricatte. 4 vols. Paris: Flammarion, 1956, 2: 422; and 2: 871.
10. Anon., "L'Ambassade chinoise," *L'Indépendant des Basses-Pyrénées*, January 29, 1869, 4; first published in *Le Journal officiel du soir (Moniteur)*. This visit appears to have occurred earlier than the one mentioned previously and recounted by Zhang Deyi in his diary entry of February 15, 1869—the dinner party which Ding Dunling, and perhaps Gautier, attended and which lasted well past midnight.
11. Joanna Richardson, *Judith Gautier: A Biography* (London: Quartet Books, 1986), 290, includes the full list of twelve articles in her bibliography.
12. Judith Gautier, "Les Chinois: Poésie et poëtes," in *Les Peuples étranges* (Paris: Charpentier, 1879), 43-44.
13. Judith Gautier, "Les Chinois: Poésie et poëtes," 53, where she also credits the work of Hervey-Saint-Denys and repeats the dates he provides for Li Bo and Du Fu. The poetry contest is

recounted on p. 62. For the transcription error, see pp. 64-65, where Hervey-Saint-Denys's "Tchang-hio" becomes "Tan-jo-su," a romanized name Gautier also used to denote Ban Jieyu and Zhang Ruoxu.

14. Jean-Marc Hovasse describes her as a "hyphen" between the two men in "Chantiers sur l'océan? Poétique du vieil Hugo," a lecture of January 28, 2020, at the Collège de France, cited by Jonathan Chiche in "La Déesse et l'archange," L'Express de Bénarès, 2020, http://lexpressdebenares.com/Catalogues/VH-Judith.pdf. For the most extensive examinations of the implications of the father-daughter relationship, see Denise Brahimi, Théophile et Judith vont en orient (Paris: La Boîte aux Documents, 1990); and Denise Brahimi, "Judith Gautier, ses pères, sa mère, son oeuvre," Romantisme 77 (1992): 55-60; as well as Sylvie Camet, Parenté et création: Familles d'artistes, de la relation personnelle à la production collective (Paris: L'Harmattan, 1995). On the many women in Victor Hugo's life, see, for example, Paul Bouchon, ed., Pages d'amour de Victor Hugo pour Adèle Faucher, Juliette Drouet, Madame Biard, Judith Gautier et quelques autres (Paris: Éditions Albin-Michel, 1949); and Raymond Escholier, Un amant de génie. Victor Hugo. Lettres d'amour et carnets intimes (Paris: Fayard, 1953). On Wagner, see Louis Barthou, La vie amoureuse de Richard Wagner (Paris: Flammarion, 1925); and Dietrich Mack, Wagners Frauen (Berlin: Insel, 2013).

    Gautier signs a letter to Hugo "your faithful disciple"; cited in Joanna Richardson, Judith Gautier, 102, and one of September 14, 1871, to Wagner as "your best disciple"; included in the unpaginated front matter of Richard and Cosima Wagner, Lettres à Judith Gautier, ed. Léon Guichard ([Paris]: Gallimard, 1964). Of course, both letters were written when she was still married to Mendès. For the subtitle referring to Gautier as the muse of both Hugo and Gautier, see Anne Danclos, La vie de Judith Gautier: Égérie de Victor Hugo et Richard Wagner (Paris: Éditions Fernand Lanore, 1996).

15. Letter of June 16, 1867, in Victor Hugo, Correspondance, 4 vols. (Paris: Albin-Michel, 1947-1952), 3: 48. Cited by Joanna Richardson, Judith Gautier, 57.

16. In Marie Letourneur, ed., Les cent plus beaux sonnets de la langue française (Paris: Le Cherche-midi Éditeur, 1982), 59. Interestingly, Letourneur also includes a sonnet by Judith Gautier titled "The Peony" ("La Pivoine"), 92, referring to her as Judith Mendes (no accent) even though the poem was written long after Gautier's separation from Catulle Mendès.

17. Included in Paul Bouchon, ed., Pages d'amour de Victor Hugo, 282-85.

18. Joanna Richardson, Judith Gautier, 98, citing Raymond Escholier, "Victor Hugo, l'homme," Les Oeuvres libres (May 1952): 138. He develops the argument further in Raymond Escholier, Un amant de génie: he believes that the relationship was consummated on July 11, 1872, when she offered "her young and splendid body" to him; Hugo wrote the sonnet to her the next day (16, 497). Bettina Knapp writes that the affair began as early as March 4, 1872, when Hugo writes an "O" in his journals standing for Oscula, Latin for "kiss," referring to a moment alone with Gautier in his library when she and her family had come to dinner. See Bettina Knapp, Judith Gautier: Writer, Orientalist, Musicologist, Feminist. A Literary Biography (Lanham, MD: Hamilton Books, 2004), 120, based on Raymond Escholier, Un amant de génie, 493. See also Jean Savant, La Vie sentimentale de Victor Hugo, Livret 6 (Paris: Jean Savant, 1985); and Geneviève Franc, "Nivea non frigida: Les amours de Judith Gautier," Bulletin de la Société Théophile Gautier 20 (1998): 142-64.

19. Raymond Escholier, Un amant de génie, 505.

20. Joanna Richardson, Judith Gautier, 108, speculates that an affair with Hugo "was perhaps a factor in ending Judith's marriage to Mendès." She certainly had other good reasons for wishing to leave him.

21. Joanna Richardson, Judith Gautier, 140-41.

22. Richard and Cosima Wagner, *Lettres à Judith Gautier*, notes, 288. Joanna Richardson, *Judith Gautier*, 79, makes virtually the same statement.
23. Hugo writes in a notebook entry of July 30, 1872, that Gautier came to visit him with her dog Grimace. "This dog plays the piano, lies down when one says 'Ponsard' and rises up when one says 'Victor Hugo.' " François Ponsard (1814-1867) was a playwright who rejected Hugo's romantic style. A similar entry appears in fall 1873, when Hugo went to visit Gautier with his granddaughter Jeanne. Jonathan Chiche, "La Déesse et l'archange"; and Raymond Escholier, *Un amant de génie*, 503. As for Wagner, in one of her few preserved letters to the German composer, on September 14, 1871, Gautier writes "I have a new dog named Grimace who already jumps up for 'Wagner.' " Richard and Cosimo Wagner, *Lettres à Judith Gautier*, 302.
24. Laurent Tailhade, "Judith Gautier," in *Quelques fantômes de jadis* (Paris: L'édition française illustrée, 1919), 169.
25. Raoul Aubry, "Promenades et visites: Un début chez les Goncourt." *Le Temps*, November 25, 1910, 3; and Stuart Henry, "Judith Gautier," in *French Essays and Profiles* (London: J. M. Dent and Sons, 1922), 252.
26. Judith Gautier, *Le Troisième Rang du collier* (Paris: Félix Juven, 1909), 27, 33, 219.
27. Judith Gautier, *Le Second Rang du collier: Souvenirs littéraires*. Préface by Agnès de Noblet (Paris: Félix Juven, 1903; rpt. Paris: L'Harmattan, 1999), 172-76. She had earlier recorded this exchange in Judith Gautier, *Richard Wagner et son oeuvre poétique*, 16. Orlando Figues, among others, notes that the performance was a disaster and the whistling came primarily from members of the Jockey Club, who were displeased that Wagner had moved the obligatory ballet from the second to the first act of the opera, which required them to arrive on time to see their mistresses in the dance corps perform before going backstage for sex. Orlando Figues, *The Europeans: Three Lives and the Making of a Cosmopolitan Culture* (New York: Henry Holt Metropolitan Books, 2019), 316-17. See also Alex Ross, *Wagnerism: Art and Politics in the Shadow of Music* (New York: Farrar, Straus and Giroux, 2020), 76-77.
28. Judith Gautier, *Le Second Rang du collier*, 178.
29. "Théatre de Bade: *Lohengrin*, opéra en 3 actes, de Richard Wagner," *La Presse*, September 8, 1868, as cited by Richard and Cosima Wagner, *Lettres à Judith Gautier*, 12.
30. John Grand-Carteret, *Richard Wagner en caricatures* (Paris: Larousse [1892]), 211.
31. Wagner's letters are included in Richard and Cosima Wagner, *Lettres à Judith Gautier*, 39-41 and 46-47; for a selection of recollections and letters, see also Suzanne Meyer-Zundel, *Quinze ans auprès de Judith Gautier* (Porto: Tipografia Nunes, 1969), 114-29 and 219-28. On the rumors concerning Wagner's living situation and unsociability, see Judith Gautier, *Le Troisième Rang du collier*, 7.
32. She published it first in serial form in *La Revue de Paris* and then as the third volume of her memoirs, *The Third Strand of the Necklace* (*Le Troisième Rang du collier*). It was published in English as Effie Dunreith Massie, trans., *Wagner at Home* (London: Mills and Boon, 1910), with an American edition published in 1911 in New York by John Lane Company. On the five editions, see Joanna Richardson, *Judith Gautier*, 287n29. Gautier had published some of her reminiscences years earlier in Judith Gautier, *Richard Wagner et son oeuvre poétique*.
33. On the "Trinity," see letter of March 25, 1870, in Richard and Cosima Wagner, *Lettres à Judith Gautier*, 48. The other quotes are scattered throughout Judith Gautier, *Le Troisième Rang du collier*, especially 2-3, 11-12, 18, 39, 41, 48, 56, 65-66.
34. According to Suzanne Meyer-Zundel, *Quinze ans*, 69. Gautier remained, however, eternally grateful for Benedictus's devotion, which was demonstrated by his willingness to accompany her, "half-dead," back to Paris from Vienna when she caught cholera during an epidemic in 1873. She and Mendès had gone there for work, but her husband ignored her plight,

284   6. Judith Gautier's Artistic Connections

35. having recently installed Augusta Holmès in a nearby apartment. Suzanne Meyer-Zundel, *Quinze ans*, 68.
35. According to a letter of October 1, 1877, from Richard Wagner, *Lettres à Judith Gautier*, 60. Gautier did try studying German, but Cosima's French was excellent.
36. Léon Guichard, "Introduction," in Richard and Cosima Wagner, *Lettres à Judith Gautier*, 20.
37. Suzanne Meyer-Zundel, *Quinze ans*, 121.
38. So Guichard concludes, "prudently"; see commentary by Léon Guichard, the editor of Richard and Cosima Wagner, *Lettres à Judith Gautier*, 23ff. Henri de Régnier, who was a regular at her salons, recalls that Gautier vigorously denied yielding to overtures from the composer that went as far as a proposal to elope and offered reasons for her refusal "that it would seem to me indiscreet to reveal," but he suspected that there might be something in their correspondence "that would give to their relationship a character rather different from the one Judith Gautier acknowledged." As recounted by Henri de Régnier, "Judith Gautier," in *Nos Rencontres* (Paris: Mercure de France, 1931), 70. Also excerpted in Vincent Laisney, "Témoignages sur le 'salon' de Judith Gautier," in Yvan Daniel and Martine Lavaud, eds. *Judith Gautier*, Collection "Interférences" (Rennes: Presses universitaires de Rennes, 2020), 73. Gautier's letters have not survived to tell the tale, but Dietrich Mack cites an excerpt from Cosima's diary (February 12, [1878]) that suggests that she may have been distressed by something Gautier wrote; he states that Cosima forbade her husband from further communication with the French woman and that "Wagner obeyed." Indeed, in Wagner's last letter to Gautier, dated February 15, 1878, he writes rather formally that he has asked his wife to take charge of all future "commissions" from Paris. Dietrich Mack, *Wagners Frauen* (Berlin: Insel, 2013), 123.
39. On the Eastern ambience, see Alex Ross, *Wagnerism: Art and Politics in the Shadow of Music* (New York: Farrar, Straus and Giroux, 2020), 91. On the text, see Willi Schuh, *Die Briefe Richard Wagners an Judith Gautier. Mit einer Einleitung, "Die Freundschaft Richard Wagners mit Judith Gautier"* (Erlenbach-Zürich: Rotapfel Verlag, [1936]), 90.
40. Richard Ormond, "Sargent and the Arts," in Richard Ormond with Elaine Kilmurray, eds., *Sargent: Portraits of Artists and Friends* (London: National Portrait Gallery, 2015), 12. Charles Mount, "John Singer Sargent and Judith Gautier," *The Art Quarterly* 18 (1955): 137, referred to her as the Wagnerians' "high priestess."
41. For a discussion of Gautier's lifelong fascination with creating and presenting marionettes, some of which even featured articulated joints, see Raphaële Fleury, "Entre divertissement de société et recherche de l'oeuvre d'art totale: Les 'marionnettes' de Judith Gautier," in Yvan Daniel and Martine Lavaud, eds., *Judith Gautier*, 223–51. As Fleury notes on 223, Théophile Gautier wrote about marionettes and was believed to have introduced the word "marionnettiste" into the French language.
42. Von der Vogelweide was the inspiration for a singer named Walther in *Die Meistersinger von Nürnberg* who claimed that he had learned his art by studying the works of the medieval poet and by listening to the songs of birds, and he is a major character himself in *Tannhäuser*.
43. Brigitte Koyama-Richard, ed., *Le Japon et la Chine dans les oeuvres de Judith Gautier*, 5 vols. (Tokyo: Édition Synapse, 2007), 1: xii; and Elaine Brody, "Letters from Judith Gautier to Chalmers Clifton," *The French Review* 58, no. 5 (April 1985): 672.
44. Vincent Laisney, "Le temple des souvenirs," in Yvan Daniel and Martine Lavaud, eds., *Judith Gautier*, 57. See also Vincent Laisney, "Témoignages sur le salon de Judith Gautier," 61–73. For the "pagoda," see Alice Théo Bergerat, "Il y a trente ans mourait Judith Gautier," *L'Époque*, December 26, 1946, included in *Recueil factice d'articles de presse et références concernant Wagner et Judith Gautier*, BnF RO-7020. For a detailed description of the apartment in Judith's

obituary, which refers to "Judith Gautier's palace," see Maurice Verne, "La fille de Théophile Gautier vient de mourir," *Le Dimanche littéraire*, January 7, 1918, in *Recueil factice d'articles biographiques sur Judith Gautier*, BnF 8-RF-59973. See also Anne Danclos, *La Vie de Judith Gautier*, 128-29.

45. Maurice Guillemot, "Portrait de femme: Judith Gautier," *L'Événement*, July 14, 1887, 1. Maurice Guillemot, "La Marchande de sourires," *Le Figaro*, April 21, 1888, 1-2, includes much of this portrait in his review the next year of Gautier's play based on Japanese history. On Baudry and Parsifal, see Stuart Henry, "Judith Gautier," 252.

46. Judith Gautier, "Le Salon," *Le Rappel*, May 1, 1884, 1.

47. Judith Gautier, "Le Salon," *Le Rappel*, May 1, 1888, 1.

48. See Richard Ormond and Elaine Kilmurray, *John Singer Sargent: The Early Portraits; Complete Paintings I* (New Haven, CT: Yale University Press, 1998), 80-85. In the "Iconographie" appended to his biography of Gautier, Rémy de Gourmont provides yet a different list, which includes a second watercolor and a third sepia, both of which he owned and which have not been traced; he seems to refer to *A Gust of Wind* as "a large sketch." Rémy de Gourmont, *Judith Gautier*, 33. These two famous oils of Gautier both sold for impressive sums (10,700 francs for the interior portrait and 18,000 francs for the beach scene, respectively), in 1934 as reported in Anon., "Sargent Portrait and Landscape Sold at Drouot," *Chicago Daily Tribune*, January 19, 1934, 2.

In his "Chronologie" of Gautier's life Yvan Daniel writes that *A Gust of Wind* was painted in 1887, several years after *Judith Gautier*; see Judith Gautier, *Oeuvres complètes*, 2 vols., ed. Yvan Daniel (Paris: Gallimard, 2011), 1: 11. This later date was proposed by Warren Adelson, "John Singer Sargent and 'The New Painting,'" in *Sargent at Broadway: The Impressionist Years*, ed. Stanley Olson, Warren Adelson, and Richard Ormond (New York: Universe / Coe Kerr Gallery, 1986), 26, 46, 50, because its setting and style seem indebted to that of Claude Monet, whom Sargent visited at Giverny in the summer of 1887, but Ormond and Kilmurray do not find it dispositive, 81. Charlotte Ribeyrol suggests that Gautier's use of the future tense when musing about a choice of portraitist in her 1888 review above may argue for a later date for the more formal interior painting, but the consensus for 1883 and 1884 has prevailed. Charlotte Ribeyrol, "John Singer Sargent and the *fin de siècle* Culture of Mauve," *Visual Culture in Britain* 19, no. 1 (2018): 20n11.

49. This is evident from a cache of letters from Sargent to Allouard-Jouan, according to Elaine Kilmurray, "Judith Gautier," no. 103, in *Forging a Modern Identity: Masters of American Painting Born after 1847. American Paintings in the Detroit Institute of Arts*, ed. James W. Tottis, 3 vols. (Detroit and London: D. Giles, 2005), 3: 230.

50. R. A. M. Stevenson, "J. S. Sargent," *The Art Journal* 50 (March 1888): 69.

51. For "conjectures" about Gautier's relationship with Pozzi—yet another rumored lover—see Deborah Davis and Elizabeth Oustinoff, "Madame X Speaks," *The Magazine Antiques* (November 2003): 125n18; and Julian Barnes, *The Man in the Red Coat* (New York: Knopf, 2020), 252. Gautier and Pozzi certainly traveled in the same circles. In one of her three accounts of social events involving the Chinese envoys to Paris, two at the embassy and one at the home of Pierre Loti, Gautier notes the presence of "professor Pozzi." Judith Gautier, "Le Prince Tsaï-tché à Paris," in *Les Parfums de la pagode* (Paris: Charpentier, 1919), 157-62. See also "Une fête chinoise chez Pierre Loti" (141-49) and "Le premier jour de l'an à l'ambassade chinoise" (151-55) in the same volume.

52. Marc Simpson, "Sargent in Paris, 1874-85: The Omnivore's Delight," in Richard Ormond with Elaine Kilmurray, eds., *Sargent: Portraits of Artists and Friends*, 29; and Richard Ormond, "Sargent and the Arts," 12.

53. Marc Simpson, "Sargent in Paris," 29. Charles Mount, "John Singer Sargent and Judith Gautier," 143, speculates that Gautier found Sargent "tall and strong, young and capricious enough to be interesting and a good lover."
54. John Singer Sargent, *Judith Gautier*, photo Tokyo University of the Arts / DNPartcom, reprinted with permission from the Museum of the Tokyo University of the Arts. Florence Rionnet, "Judith Gautier, 'Vous êtes un marbre, habité par une étoile,' la muse inspiratrice et la femme sculpteur," in Yvan Daniel and Martine Lavaud, eds., *Judith Gautier*, 309, dates the sketch without hesitation to the summer of 1883.
55. Kimiko Kanazawa, "Le Japon paru dans les oeuvres de Théophile et Judith Gautier," *Kyoyo ronsyu* (*Liberal Arts Review*) 8 (December 1990): 78, states that the portrait is of Judith Gautier. However, it bears little resemblance to her, and the Museum of the Tokyo University of the Arts, which holds the painting, identifies it only as *Portrait of a Western Woman*.
56. See Erika Takashina, "East-West Cultural Exchange in Art—France and the Orient in the 1880s (Part 5)," *Japan Spotlight* (January-February 2004): 54-56.
57. William Leonard Schwartz, *The Imaginative Interpretation*, 52n5.
58. Kimiko Kanazawa, "Le Japon paru," 77.
59. William Leonard Schwartz, *The Imaginative Interpretation*, 52; and Jan Walsh Hokenson, *Japan, France, and East-West Aesthetics* (Madison, NJ: Fairleigh Dickinson University Press, 2004), 115.
60. From Philippe Burty's review of the book on May 22, 1885, in *La République française*, cited by Joanna Richardson, *Judith Gautier*, 151.
61. Kimiko Kanazawa, "Le Japon paru," 77.
62. See Jan Walsh Hokenson, *Japan, France, and East-West Aesthetics*, 110-19.
63. Judith Gautier, *Poëmes de la libellule: Traduits du japonais d'après la version littérale de M. Saionzi, Conseiller d'État de S.M. l'Empereur du Japon. Illustrés par Yamamoto* (Paris: Gillot, 1885).
64. Philippe Jullian, *Robert de Montesquiou: Un prince 1900* (Paris: Libr. Académique Perrin, [1965]), 110. See also Ursula Link-Herr and Eva Erdmann, "Robert de Montesquiou und die ideographischen Zeichen: Jugendstil, *japonisme* und preziöze Lyrik," in *Ostasienrezeption zwischen Klischee und Innovation: Zur Begegnung zwischen Ost und West um 1900*, ed. Walter Gebhard (Munich: Iudicium Verlag, 2000), 294. As noted earlier, fukusas are silk squares used for wrapping or in the tea ceremony; netsukes are small sculptures of precious stone or wood worn on the kimono belt; kakemonos are painted folding screens.
65. Ursula Link-Herr and Eva Erdmann, "Robert de Montesquiou," 295.
66. Philippe Jullian, *Robert de Montesquiou*, 72.
67. Julian Barnes, *The Man in the Red Coat*, 11.
68. Philippe Jullian, *Robert de Montesquiou*, 73-74.
69. Stéphane Guégan, "Le Miroir à deux faces," in *Joris-Karl Huysmans: De Degas à Grunewald*, ed. Stéphane Guégan and André Guyaux (Paris: Gallimard, 2019), 82. Jullian writes that *Against Nature* introduced Moreau to the public, and that Moreau and Huysmans may have met through Gautier; see Philippe Jullian, *Robert de Montesquiou*, 82, 85. She first reviewed Moreau's work with admiration as early as 1865, but more substantial articles began appearing when he returned to salon exhibitions after several years' absence in 1876. About Moreau's *Salomé*, for example, she wrote that "it is of a surprising beauty, more beautiful than a poet's dream might have been able to imagine it." Judith Gautier, "Le Salon: Salomé," *Le Rappel*, May 6, 1876, 3, included in "Critiques d'art de Judith Gautier," in *Théophile Gautier / Gustave Moreau: "Le rare, le singulier, l'étrange,"* ed. Marie-Cécile Forest, Samuel Mandin, Aurélie Peylhard, and Pierre Pinchon (Paris: Musée Gustave Moreau, 2011), 87. Moreau was also Flaubert's favorite living painter, as noted by Julian Barnes, *The Man in the Red Coat*, 103.

70. Philippe Jullian, *Robert de Montesquiou*, 75, 78.
71. See Anne Danclos, "À Dinard avec ses animaux," in *La Vie de Judith Gautier*, 154-158. Alice Théo Bergerat, "Il y a trente ans," recalls the "Wagnerian blackbird" Fidi as "a winged tenor" who could whistle some of Siegfried's lines "because he'd had the patient Judith as his professor."
72. Joris-Karl Huysmans, *À Rebours* (Paris: G. Charpentier et Cie, 1884), 265. For previous references: walls and windows, 21-22; "sustainer," 234-35; nutritional enema, 279-80; "mouth organ," 62; Moreau's *Salomé*, 71; turtle, 55-61, 68; Baudelaire's "Anywhere out of the world," 22; *Book of Jade*, 263. Huysmans discusses des Esseintes's library throughout chapter 14, 234-66.
73. Böhm deletes one poem by Li Bo, "Chanson sur le fleuve," for reasons that are unclear, and one by Su Shi, "Le poète monte la montagne enveloppée de brouillard" (*Le Livre de jade*, 155-58), presumably because of its resemblance—and inferiority—to the poet's "Le poète se promène sur la montagne enveloppée de brouillard."
74. Tullo Massarani, *Il Libro di Giada: Echi dell'Estremo Oriente recati in versi italiani secondo la lezione di Mma J. Walter* (Florence: Successori le Monnier, 1882).
75. Jordan Herbert Stabler, "Introduction," in *Songs of Li-Tai-Pè from the "Cancionerio [sic] Chines" of Antonio Castro Feijo: An Interpretation from the Portuguese* (New York: Edgar H. Wells and Co., 1922), 4-5. Based on Antonio Feijó, *Cancioneiro Chinez* (Porto: Magalhães and Moniz, 1890).
76. Jordan Herbert Stabler, *Songs of Li-Tai-Pè*, 22. "Impossible to believe if not seen," as commented on long ago by Roy Earl Teele, *Through a Glass Darkly: A Study of English Translations of Chinese Poetry* (Ann Arbor: N.p., 1949), 118.
77. Catherine Yeh, "The Life-Style of Four *Wenren* in Late Qing Shanghai," *Harvard Journal of Asiatic Studies* 57, no. 2 (December 1997): 436. See also Ke Ren, "Fin-de-siècle Diplomat: Chen Jitong and Cosmopolitan Possibilities in the Late Qing World," PhD diss., John Hopkins University, 2014; and Ke Ren, "Chen Jitong, *Les Parisiens peints par un Chinois*, and the Literary Self-Fashioning of a Chinese Boulevardier in Fin-de-siècle Paris," *L'Esprit Créateur* 56, no. 3 (Fall 2016): 90-103.
78. Tcheng Ki-Tong, "Avant-propos," *Les Chinois peints par eux-mêmes* (Paris: Calmann Lévy, 1884), vii; the book was translated by James Millington as *The Chinese Painted by Themselves* (London: Field and Tuer [1885]). As both Catherine Yeh and Ke Ren point out, Chen appropriated the title and format of an earlier compilation titled *Les Français peints par eux-mêmes: Encyclopédie morale du dix-neuvième siècle* (Paris: L. Curmer, 1841), an example of the "panoramic," sociological "literature of physiologies" that was popular over the course of the century. Catherine Yeh, "The Life-Style," 440-41; Ke Ren, "Chen Jitong," 93-94.
79. Général Tcheng Ki-Tong, "Préface," *Les Plaisirs en Chine* (Paris: Charpentier and Co., 1890), ii (i-iii). The book was translated by R. H. Sherard as *Bits of China* (London: Trischler and Co., 1890) and also as *Chin-Chin, or the Chinaman at Home* (London: A. P. Marsden, 1895).
80. Tcheng Ki-Tong [Chen Jitong], "Préface," in Antonio Feijó, *Cancioneiro Chinez*, ix-xiv. As Ke Ren, "Chen Jitong," 100, notes, a utopian "hope for universal reconciliation between Europe and China based on scientific progress and mutual understanding" appears frequently in Chen's writings."
81. On Chen Jitong and Anatole France, see Catherine Yeh, "The Life-Style," 439. For a discussion of Chen's translation of Chinese tales, *Contes chinois*, in a chapter of the same title, see Anatole France, *La vie littéraire*, 3: 79-91. On Ding and Gautier, see Ke Ren, "Fin-de-siècle Diplomat," 98n224 and 99. The novel was *Le Fleuve des perles* (*L'Araignée rouge*), which had been serialized "with great success" in 1873 and was reissued in book form with Tcheng-Ki-Tong's preface years later (Paris: E. Dentu, [1890]). Pont-Jest willingly acknowledged that

Ding had indeed provided him with "a half-dozen illegible pages" based on a story from a Chinese feuilleton, for which he received 300 francs. But he was outraged to learn that during the bigamy trial Ding's lawyers credited their client with the authorship of the serialized novel, an error that Pont-Jest vigorously corrects in a letter to the editor: René de Pont-Jest, "Boîte aux lettres," *Le Gaulois*, April 22, 1881, 3.

82. From Zeng's diplomatic diaries: Zeng Jize, 曾紀澤, *Chu shi Ying Fa E Guo riji* 出使英法俄國日記, *Zou xiang shijie congshu* 走向世界叢書 (Changsha: Yuelu shushe, 1985), 425. As cited in Yichao Shi, "La Formation de Judith Gautier au chinois et à la culture chinoise (1863-1905)," *Revue d'histoire littéraire de la France* 3 (July-September 2020): 639-50: 644.

83. Montclair, "Silhouettes féminines: Mme Judith Gautier," included in the *Recueil factice d'articles biographiques sur Judith Gautier*, BnF 8-RF-59973, 2.

84. Rémy de Gourmont, *Judith Gautier*, 12. "Li Yi-an" refers to the Song dynasty woman poet Li Qingzhao 李清照 (1084-ca. 1150), whom—as we shall see—Gautier translated for the second edition of *The Book of Jade*. For the two quotes from de Noblet, see Agnès de Noblet, *Un univers d'artistes: Autour de Théophile et Judith Gautier* (Paris: L'Harmattan, 2003), 436, and Agnès de Noblet, "Un ami de Judith Gautier: George Soulié de Morant," *Les carnets de l'exotisme: Orient-extrêmes* 15-16 (1995): 26.

7. "GREATLY ENLARGED AND RIGOROUSLY CORRECTED": *THE BOOK OF JADE*, 1902

1. See Yu Wang, *La Réception des anthologies de poésie chinoise classique par les poètes français (1735-2008)* (Paris: Classiques Garnier, 2016), 161; and Yvan Daniel, "De l'authenticité des poèmes du *Livre de jade*: Histoire d'une reception polémique (1867-1917)," in Yvan Daniel and Martine Lavaud, eds., *Judith Gautier*, Collection "Interférences" (Rennes: Presses universitaires de Rennes, 2020), 112.

2. In Suzanne Meyer-Zundel, *Quinze ans auprès de Judith Gautier* (Porto: Tipografia Nunes, 1969), 245.

3. Yu Wang, *La Réception des anthologies*, 157, provides a chart that shows how the new poems were distributed: in addition to the twenty-five going to the Lovers section, four were added to Autumn, two to Poets, one each to War and Travelers, and six to The Court.

4. Amandine Dabat, *Hàm Nghi: Empereur en exil, artiste à Alger* (Paris: Sorbonne Univ. Presses, 2019), 320, includes a letter of June 12, 1901, from Gautier to her friend Ham Nghi, in which she writes that the book is due out in autumn. On Félix Juven, see Martine Reid, "*Le Collier des jours* et les choix singuliers de Judith Gautier," in Yvan Daniel and Martine Lavaud, eds., *Judith Gautier*, 30.

5. The insert did not survive in many editions of the volume; for example, the one digitized by the HathiTrust does not contain it. It is, however, in the Bibliothèque Nationale's version on Gallica.

6. Charlotte Ribeyrol, "John Singer Sargent and the *fin-de-siècle* Culture of Mauve," *Visual Culture in Britain* 19, no. 1 (2018): 12, 19.

7. "Annam" was never the term preferred by the Vietnamese to refer to their country. It means "pacified south," which is the name China gave to its province previously known as Nan Yuę after quelling a series of revolts in the seventh century. The French conquered Vietnam in three stages and insisted on maintaining the administrative separation of each section, with Annam denoting central Vietnam. D. R. SarDesai, *Vietnam: Past and Present* (Boulder, CO: Westview Press, 1998), 2-3.

8. Robert Aldrich, *Banished Potentates: Dethroning and Exiling Indigenous Monarchs under British and French Colonial Rule, 1815–1955* (Manchester: Manchester University Press, 2018), 129.
9. The poem (no. 303 in the anthology) is "Dark bird" ("Xuan niao" 玄鳥), whose penultimate line reads "Yin received a charge that was all good [entirely proper]" 殷受命咸宜. In Arthur Waley, trans., *The Book of Songs*, ed. Joseph R. Allen, foreword by Stephen Owen (New York: Grove, 1997), 320. For a discussion of Ham Nghi's Vietnamese names, see Amandine Dabat, *Hàm Nghi*, 19-20.
10. On the role of Pierre Louÿs, see Suzanne Meyer-Zundel, *Quinze ans*, 105. Amandine Dabat, *Hàm Nghi*, refers to Gautier's devotion to Ham Nghi as a "desperate love," 295, and the four acrostics (Buddha, Teu Soune, Ham Nghi, and Prince D'Annam) appear on 296, 297, 314, and 506, respectively. For the most extensive discussion of their relationship and correspondence, see Amandine Dabat, "Judith Gautier: L'amie fidèle (1900-1917)," in *Hàm Nghi*, 289-330; as well Amandine Dabat, "Judith Gautier et le prince d'Annam (1871-1944): Une amitié artistique," in Yvan Daniel and Martine Lavaud, eds., *Judith Gautier*, 325-39.
11. Amandine Dabat, *Hàm Nghi*, 324.
12. Judith Gautier, "Les Chinois: Poésie et poëtes," in *Les Peuples étranges* (Paris: Charpentier, 1879), 43-81; and Judith Gautier, "Prélude," *Le Livre de jade* (Paris: Félix Juven, 1902), ix-xi.
13. Léon d'Hervey-Saint-Denys, "Li-taï-pé," in *Poésies de l'époque des Thang, précédé de L'art poétique et la prosodie chez les Chinois* (Paris: Amyot, 1862, rpt. Éditions Champ Libre, 1977), 115-18; Judith Gautier, "Prélude," xi-xv.
14. Léon d'Hervey-Saint-Denys, "Thou-fou," in *Poésies de l'époque des Thang*, 182-83; Judith Gautier, "Prélude," xv.
15. Judith Gautier, "Prélude," xii-xiii, xvi. Léon d'Hervey-Saint-Denys, "Thou-fou," in *Poésies de l'époque des Thang*, 181, had pointed to this same series of poems in likening the Chinese poet to Ovid in exile.
16. Judith Gautier, "Prélude," xxi.
17. Xingling's is titled "Separation" ("Séparation"), dated Peking 1898, and the two poems by Xunling are "Don't forget me" ("Ne m'oubliez pas"), dated Tokyo 1891, and "Morning dew" ("Rosée matinale"), Peking, March 1901, in Judith Gautier, *Le Livre de jade* (1902), 99-100, 95-98.
18. Judith Gautier, *Le Livre de jade* (1902), 1-3.
19. The goddess of the Xiang River, sometimes represented as two sisters, figures in the "Nine songs" ("Jiu ge" 九歌) of the "Songs of Chu" ("Chu ci" 楚辭) attributed to Qu Yuan, and with their zithers in the poem "The far-off journey" ("Yuan you" 遠遊). See David Hawkes, *Ch'u Tz'u: The Songs of the South* (Boston: Beacon Press, 1962), 37-39, 81-87.
20. Rémy de Gourmont, *Judith Gautier* (Paris: Bibliothèque Internationale d'Édition, 1904), 27-28, includes Yu Geng's praise of her unpublished essay on a Chinese philosophical text: "Like a sublime dragon, Judith Gautier has understood the secret of birth and death and reconciled good and evil. One listens to her voice as to the wind in the pines. She will reach into the future and will be listened to forever.". For a brief discussion of Yu Geng and Gautier, see also Yichao Shi, "La Formation de Judith Gautier au chinois et à la culture chinoise (1863-1905)," *Revue d'histoire littéraire de la France* 3 (July-September 2020): 645-46.
21. A later edition of *Le Livre de jade* published in a series titled "Beautiful Illustrated Texts" would include seven illustrations reproduced by photogravure of works by unnamed "masters of Chinese printing." Judith Gautier, *Le Livre de jade. Les Beaux Textes illustrées* (Paris: Librairie Plon, Éditions d'histoire et d'art, 1933).

22. Judith Gautier, "Poëmes chinois de tous les temps," *La Revue de Paris* (June 15, 1901): 805-20; and Judith Gautier, "Quelques grands poètes chinois et la poétesse Li Yi'an," *La Grande Revue* (December 1, 1901): 543-53.
23. Judith Gautier, "Poëmes chinois," 806. Yu Wang, *La Réception des anthologies*, 153, writes that the poems Gautier added from the *Book of Songs* "had almost all already been cited in the excellent introduction to *Poetry of the Tang Dynasty*," but in fact of the several poems Hervey-Saint-Denys mentions from the classic, only one of them, which becomes Gautier's "Vengeance," overlaps with her selection. The *Book of Songs* was the one Chinese text that Jules Taschereau of the Bibliothèque Nationale encouraged her to take home because the library owned multiple copies. Gautier would also have been able to consult a recent translation of the classic by the Jesuit missionary Séraphin Couvreur (1835-1919), *Cheu King: Texte chinois avec une double traduction en français et en latin, une introduction et un vocabulaire* (Ho kien Fou: 1896).
24. Judith Gautier, "Poëmes chinois," 806-07; Judith Gautier, *Le Livre de jade* (1902), 9-10.
25. Léon d'Hervey-Saint-Denys, *Poésies de l'époque des Thang*, 20.
26. Yvan Daniel, "Présentation: *Le Livre de jade*, un rêve de Judith Gautier," in Judith Gautier, *Le Livre de jade*, ed. Yvan Daniel (Paris: Imprimerie nationale, 2004), 17.
27. While serving as Chinese ambassador to Russia, Li passed through Paris on a European tour in July 1896. Lung Chang, *La Chine à l'aube du XXe siècle: Les relations diplomatiques de la Chine avec les puissances depuis la guerre sino-japonaise jusqu'à la guerre russo-japonaise* (Paris: Nouvelles Éditions Latines, 1962), 130. Noted by Yu Wang, *La Réception*, 155n83.
28. These are poems 2, 7, 8, 10, 12, and 13 in Judith Gautier, "Poëmes chinois"; "Montée d'automne" in Judith Gautier, "Quelques grands poètes chinois"; and Li Bo's "Strophes improvisées devant l'empereur Ming-Hoang et sa belle favorite Taï-Tsun," Judith Gautier, *Le Livre de jade* (1902), 33-36.
29. Yvan Daniel, "De l'authenticité des poèmes du *Livre de Jade*," 114.
30. According to the count in Ferdinand Stocès, "Sur les sources du *Livre de Jade* de Judith Gautier (1845-1917) (Remarques sur l'authenticité des poèmes)," *Revue de littérature comparée* 319 (2006): 345.
31. "Some good luck on the path" is based on Li Bo's "Given to a beautiful woman on the path" ("Mo shang zeng mei ren" 陌上贈美人), included in Wang Yaoqu, *Gu Tang shi he jie* (Rpt. Taipei: Wenhua tushu gongsi, 1968), 1: 98; Judith Gautier, "Poëmes chinois," 811, and *Le Livre de jade* (1902), 19-20. "Youth" is based on his "Song of youth" ("Shao nian xing" 少年行), in Wang Yaoqu, *Gu Tang shi he jie*, 1: 93; Judith Gautier, "Quelques grands poètes," 545, and *Le Livre de jade* (1902), 31-32. "Forbidden flower" is based on Li Bo's poem written to the "Song of clear water" ("Lü shui qu" 淥水曲), where the lotus flower is not "forbidden" but rather so beautiful that the person in the boat is envious and saddened beyond measure. Judith Gautier, "Quelques grands poètes," 545, and *Le Livre de jade* (1902), 29-30; Wang Yaoqu, *Gu Tang shi he jie*, 1: 72; and Liu Wenwei, *Tang shi he xuan* (Rpt. Guangxi: Guangxi renmin chubanshe, 1988), 137. Li Bo's "Song of clear water" was also the likely source for Gautier's 1867 "Near the mouth of the river" ("Près de l'embouchure du fleuve"), published in the first volume, Judith Walter, *Le Livre de jade* (Paris: Alphonse Lemerre, 1867), 57-58; (1902), 105-06.
32. "Drunkenness of love" is based on Li Bo's poem composed to the title "Song of roosting crows" ("Wu qi qu" 嗚棲曲); Judith Gautier, "Poëmes chinois," 811, and *Le Livre de jade* (1902), 21-22; Léon d'Hervey-Saint-Denys, *Poésies de l'époque des Thang*, 164-65; Wang Yaoqu, *Gu Tang shi he jie*, 1: 54. Li Bo's series of three "Strophes" was written to "Clear and calm tunes" ("Qing ping diao" 清平調). Taizhen 太真 was the title briefly given to Yang by the emperor, who named her as a Daoist nun to facilitate her transition from her previous status as his son's wife. Léon d'Hervey-Saint-Denys, *Poésies de l'époque des Thang*, 138-41, describes both the circumstances and the skill of their composition after his translation of the sequence. Judith Gautier, *Le Livre de jade* (1902), 33-36; Wang Yaoqu, *Gu Tang shi he jie*, 1: 92-93; Liu Wenwei, *Tang shi he xuan*, 185-87.

33. Judith Gautier, "Poëmes chinois," 812, and *Le Livre de jade* (1902), 123-24.
34. Wang Yaoqu, *Gu Tang shi he jie*, 1: 142; Liu Wenwei, *Tang shi he xuan*, 284 .
35. Florence Ayscough and Amy Lowell, *Fir-Flower Tablets: Poems Translated from the Chinese* (Boston: Houghton, 1921), lxxxix-xcii.
36. A. C. Graham, *Poems of the Late T'ang* (Baltimore, MD: Penguin Books, 1965), 39. Gautier's fascination with the graphic components of characters is illustrated in a passage of her memoirs which recounts her explication of some examples to Louis Bouilhet, who himself was interested in "decomposing them to give them a mystical meaning." Judith Gautier, *Le Second Rang du collier: Souvenirs littéraires*. Préface by Agnès de Noblet (Paris: Félix Juven, 1903; rpt. Paris: L'Harmattan, 1999), 269. Ling Min believes a third example of Gautier's graphic deconstruction can be found in the second line of her "River song," discussed in chapter 5. In its source, Li Bo's "River song," the poem's third line, reads "Fine wine in goblets is poured by thousands of barrels," which Gautier transforms "Like the plant that removes a stain on silk fabric, wine erases discord in one's heart" (Comme la plante qui enlève une tache sur une étoffe de soie, le vin efface la dispute dans le coeur); Judith Walter, *Le Livre de jade* [1867]), 111. Ling proposes to explain this curiosity by analyzing the components of "goblet" (*zun* 樽) and "barrel" (*hu* 斛): "The left part of 樽 signifies plant. And the right part of 斛 signifies discord. By uniting these two elements, Judith Gautier is tapping into an effect of wine, which can 'erase' sadness." Ling Min, "Première rencontre poétique: Traduction et réception de la poésie classique chinoise en France au XIXème siècle" (PhD diss. University of Paris-Sorbonne, 2013), 120-21. This example is less compelling than the other two because the right part of *hu* 斛, which literally means ten pecks, or one hundred pints, is *dou* 斗, which means one peck, or ten pints, and not, as Ling Min surmises, *dou* 鬥, which means discord. The former is only a modern simplified version of the latter.
37. Judith Walter, *Le Livre de jade* (1867), 122; Judith Gautier, *Le Livre de jade* (1902), 198; Léon d'Hervey-Saint-Denys, *Poésies de l'époque des Thang*, 211. See Yu Wang, *La Réception des anthologies*, 167-68 for a brief discussion.
38. Judith Gautier, "Quelques grands poètes," 545, and *Le Livre de jade* (1902), 103-04.
39. Muriel Détrie, "*Le Livre de Jade* de Judith Gautier: Un livre pionnier," *Revue de littérature comparée* 633 (1989): 321.
40. Her translation, "In the middle of the river," can be found in Judith Gautier, *Le Livre de jade* [1902], 189-90. Zhang Wei's song, "Written while drinking on the lake," is in Liu Wenwei, *Tang shi he xuan*, 122. The scholar's version of the poem is in Léon d'Hervey-Saint-Denys, *Poésies de l'époque des Thang*, 350.
41. Judith Gautier, *Le Livre de jade* (1902), 147-48.
42. Judith Gautier, "*Poëmes chinois*," 816, and *Le Livre de jade* (1902), 139-40; Wang Yaoqu, *Gu Tang shi he jie*, 1: 123. The characters for Zhu's name in the 1902 volume are in Gautier's own calligraphy.
43. Judith Gautier, "*Poëmes chinois*," 815, and *Le Livre de jade* (1902), 143-44; Wang Yaoqu, *Gu Tang shi he jie*, 1: 147.
44. Stephen Owen, *The Great Age of Chinese Poetry: The High T'ang* (New Haven, CT: Yale University Press, 1981), 214.
45. Judith Gautier, "*Quelques grands poètes chinois*," 546, and *Le Livre de jade* (1902), 149-150; Wang Yaoqu, *Gu Tang shi he jie*, 2: 48.
46. Léon d'Hervey-Saint-Denys, *Poésies de l'époque des Thang*, 236.
47. As discussed by A. C. Graham, *Poems of the Late T'ang*, 20-22.
48. Judith Gautier, "*Quelques grands poètes chinois*," 549 (the entire series appears on 546-49), and *Le Livre de jade* (1902), 161-62 (series 149-62), with the number of each poem indicated in Chinese in Gautier's calligraphy.

49. Judith Gautier, "*Quelques grands poètes chinois*," 550, and "Prélude," *Le Livre de jade* (1902), xvii. Others have noted the reasons behind Li's special appeal to Gautier, including Yvan Daniel, "Présentation," 25, and Rémy de Gourmont, *Judith Gautier*, 12.
50. For discussions of the "Afterword," see Stephen Owen, "The Snares of Memory" in *Remembrances: The Experience of the Past in Classical Chinese Literature* (Cambridge, MA: Harvard University Press, 1986), 80-98; and Ronald Egan, "The 'Afterword,'" in *The Burden of Female Talent: The Poet Li Qingzhao and Her History in China* (Cambridge, MA: Harvard University Press, 2013), 191-212. Ronald Egan, *The Works of Li Qingzhao* (Boston: DeGruyter, 2019) provides a bilingual translation of all of Li's writings.
51. Discussed by Ronald Egan, *The Burden of Female Talent*, 145-62.
52. Judith Gautier, "*Quelques grands poètes chinois*," 550, and *Le Livre de jade* (1902), xviii.
53. In addition to the two poems discussed below, three other translations can be linked to originals by Li Qingzhao: "The messengers" ("Les messagers") in "*Quelques grands poètes chinois*," 551, which she retitles "The wild swans" ("Les Cygnes sauvages") in *Le Livre de jade* (1902), 79-80, is based on Li's lyric to the tune "Waves wash the sand" ("Lang tao sha" 浪淘沙), in Wang Zhongwen, ed., *Li Qingzhao ji jiao zhu* (Beijing: Renmin wenxue chubanshe, 1979), 85. Gautier's "Holiday of poets" ("La Fête des poètes"), "*Quelques grands poètes chinois*," 552, further specified as "The ninth day of the ninth month" ("Le 9e jour du 9e mois") in *Le Livre de jade* (1902), 81-82, is based on Li's lyric to the tune of "Drunk in the flower's shadow" ("Zui hua yin" 醉花陰), in Wang Zhongwen, *Li Qingzhao*, 34-35. And "My staring eyes" ("Mes yeux fixes"), in *Le Livre de jade* (1902), 69-72, is based on Li's lyric to the tune "Atop Phoenix Tower, remembering the playing of the flute" ("Fenghuangtai shang yi chui xiao" 鳳凰臺上憶吹簫), in Wang Zhongwen, *Li Qingzhao*, 20. Only "The red lotus ("Le Lotus rouge"), "*Quelques grands poètes chinois*," 552, and *Le Livre de jade* (1902), 73-74, appears to have no obvious counterpart in Li's collection, although it is a pastiche of many motifs and devices common to her lyrics. It is not clear what sources Gautier consulted for her Chinese texts. The library held Zeng Zao's 曾慥 *Yue fu ya ci* 樂府雅詞, but not all of the works by Li that Gautier translated were in it.
54. Judith Gautier, "*Quelques grands poètes chinois*," 551, and *Le Livre de jade* (1902), xviii.
55. Judith Gautier, "*Quelques grands poètes chinois*," 550-51, and *Le Livre de jade* (1902), 75-78, whose slightly altered lineation and stanzaic breaks have been followed here; Wang Zhongwen, *Li Qingzhao*, 49.
56. Ronald Egan, *The Burden of Female Talent*, 76.
57. Judith Gautier, "*Quelques grands poètes chinois*," 550, and *Le Livre de jade* (1902), xvii.
58. Wang Zhongwen, *Li Qingzhao*, 64-65; Judith Gautier, "*Quelques grands poètes chinois*," 553, and *Le Livre de jade* (1902), 83-86.
59. Judith Gautier, "*Quelques grands poètes chinois*," 553.
60. Judith Gautier, "*Quelques grands poètes chinois*," 553, and *Le Livre de jade* (1902), xviii.
61. Ronald Egan, *The Burden of Female Talent*, 91.
62. Wilt L. Idema, "Male Fantasies and Female Realities: Chu Shu-chen and Chang Yü-niang and Their Biographers," in *Chinese Women in the Imperial Past: New Perspectives*, ed. Harriet T. Zurndorfer (Leiden: Brill, 1999), 19-25; and Ronald Egan, *The Burden of Female Talent*, 32-36.
63. Judith Gautier, "*Quelques grands poètes chinois*," 553. Denise Brahimi believes that Ting Tun-ling must have introduced Gautier to Li's song lyrics, having realized that the genre's "melancholy and languorous mode" of expression was well suited to his student's sensibility as a young woman herself in love at the time she was working on the 1867 edition of *Le Livre de jade*. But given that immediate resonance, it seems unlikely that she would not have tried her

hand at rendering them into French as soon as she first encountered them. Denise Brahimi, *Théophile et Judith vont en orient* (Paris: La Boîte aux Documents, 1990), 123.

64. This proposal comes from one of the firmest skeptics of Gautier's ability to translate on her own: Ferdinand Stocès, "Sur les sources du *Livre de Jade* de Judith Gautier," 346, and "*Le Livre de Jade* de Judith Gautier," *Histoires littéraires* 26 (April-June 2006): 40.

65. Agnès de Noblet, "Un ami de Judith Gautier: George Soulié de Morant," *Les carnets de l'exotisme: Orients-extrêmes* 15-16 (1995): 25. The connection to Ding Dunling was first drawn by Jeannine Jacquemin, "George Soulié de Morant: Sa vie, son oeuvre d'écrivain et de sinologue," *Histoire des sciences médicales* 20, no. 1 (1986): 33. There is, however, no evidence that Ding spent time in Brittany with Gautier during this period. Soulié de Morant chose to anglicize his first name by dropping the "s."

66. For a comprehensive bibliography of his works, see Jean Choain, "George Soulié de Morant," *Méridiens* (*Revue de l'association scientifique des Médecins acupuncteurs de France*) 43-44 (1978): 28-31.

67. A letter (undated, perhaps from 1910) to Philippe Berthelot (1866-1934), a senior diplomat in the Ministry of Foreign Affairs, cited by Agnès de Noblet, "Un ami de Judith Gautier," 28.

68. As recounted by Suzanne Meyer-Zundel, *Quinze ans*, 49.

69. George Soulié de Morant, *Essai sur la littérature chinoise* (Paris: Mercure de France, 1912), 161, 199.

70. George Soulié de Morant, *Florilège des poèmes Song* (Paris: Plon, 1923), "Introduction," i, and "La poétesse Li Tsring-Tchao," 3. Soulié translates seven of Li's lyrics, none of which duplicates Gautier's.

71. Jeannine Jacquemin, "George Soulié de Morant," 38; Agnes de Noblet, "Un ami de Judith Gautier," 29.

72. Agnes de Noblet, "Un ami de Judith Gautier," 26, cites a letter of April 18, 1901, in which Gautier refers to having waited impatiently for news of his journey to China.

73. Cited by Agnes de Noblet, "Un ami de Judith Gautier," 26.

74. Yu Wang, *La Réception des anthologies*, 170, also takes exception to Stocès's assertion that Soulié de Morant assisted Gautier in her translations and "corrections" for her 1902 volume, pointing out that Gautier's Chinese was much better in 1902 than in 1867. The following year Gautier did work with an informant while collaborating with Pierre Loti (1850-1923) on a play that Sarah Bernhardt had requested she write for her, which was published in 1911 as *The Daughter of Heaven* (*La Fille du ciel*) but never performed by the actress. A letter to Ham Nghi reports on the project and notes that "a young Chinese from the embassy came to spend more than a month with me and was very helpful," although she still insists that the exiled ruler himself "could have given me real information." Letter of September 24, 1903, Amandine Dabat, "Judith Gautier et le prince d'Annam," 335.

8. "RADIATED BEYOND THE SCHOLARLY WORLD": AN EXTRAORDINARY AFTERLIFE

1. C. LeSenne, "Judith Gautier est morte," December 29, 1917, *Recueil factice d'articles biographiques sur Judith Gautier*, BnF 8-RF-59973, 47.

2. Interestingly, Gautier was also mistaken as the author of a volume in English titled *The Book of Jade*, a collection by a young Harvard graduate: David Park Barnitz [1878-1901], *The Book of Jade* (New York: Doxey's at the Sign of the Lark, ca. 1901). The morbid themes of his poems, with titles like "Requiem," "The Grave," and "Corpse," do not suggest any influence of her work, and Barnitz committed suicide shortly after his book's publication. An unlikely

confusion, one would think, but the catalogue of Harvard's Widener Library identified Judith Gautier as the author of Barnitz's *The Book of Jade* until I pointed out the error several years ago.

3. Judith Gautier, *Le Second Rang du collier: Souvenirs littéraires*. Préface by Agnès de Noblet (Paris: Félix Juven, 1903; rpt. Paris: L'Harmattan, 1999), 282.

4. As noted by Junko Yoshikawa, "*Le Livre de Jade* de Judith Gautier, traduction de poèmes chinois: Le rapport avec sa création du poème en prose," *Études de langue et littérature française* 96 (March 2010), accessed June 22, 2020, https://www.jstage.jst.go.jp/article/ellf/96/0/96 _KJ00007641735/_pdf.

5. In 1872 and 1873 she published a series of seven prose poems in issues of *La Renaissance littéraire et artistique* that were not translations, but they did not attract the same degree of recognition. See Junko Yoshikawa, "*Le Livre de jade* de Judith Gautier," 26; and Yu Wang, *La Réception des anthologies de poésie chinoise classique par les poètes français (1735–2008)* (Paris: Classiques Garnier, 2016), 160. The first poem she wrote, we may recall, "The return of the swallows," had also been a prose poem.

6. Henri Mondor, *Vie de Mallarmé* (Paris: Gallimard, 1943), 690. Jan Walsh Hokenson, *Japan, France, and East-West Aesthetics* (Madison, NJ: Fairleigh Dickinson University Press, 2004), 441n46, alludes to this comparison.

7. Enid Starkie, *Arthur Rimbaud* (New York: New Directions, 1961), 241-42. Starkie writes that "Judith Gautier deserves more recognition in the history of French poetry than she has yet received," and that her own original prose poems in French, published fourteen years before the more acclaimed works by Rimbaud, "have their own originality, and bear some resemblance to certain poems in *Illuminations*," 242.

8. Paul Verlaine, "*Le Livre de Jade* par Judith Walter," in *Oeuvres en prose complètes* (Paris: Gallimard, 1972, 623 [originally published in *L'Étendard*, May 11, 1867].

9. Verlaine's *Fêtes galantes* of 1869; Laura Lauth, " 'Strange and Absurd Words': Translation as Ethics and Poetics in the Transcultural U.S. 1830-1915" (PhD diss., University of Maryland, 2011), 135-37.

10. Catulle Mendès, *Le Mouvement poétique français de 1867 à 1900*. Rapport à M. le Ministre de l'Instruction publique et des beaux-arts, précédé de réflexions sur la personnalité de l'esprit poétique de France, suivi d'un dictionnaire bibliographique et critique et d'une nomenclature chronologique de la plupart des poètes français du XIXe siècle (Paris: Imprimerie nationale, 1903), 152-53. Given the time frame of the report and this generous praise, one might surmise that his starting point of 1867 had been set by the publication of *The Book of Jade*. Mendès was, however, just picking up from where his former father-in-law Théophile Gautier and his colleagues had left off in presenting their report to the government on "the progress of poetry" from 1848 to 1867 (*Rapport sur les progrès de la poésie* [Paris: Imprimerie nationale, 1868]).

11. Margueritte S. Murphy, *A Tradition of Subversion: The Prose Poem in English from Wilde to Ashbery* (Amherst: University of Massachusetts Press, 1992), 12. Muriel Détrie, "*Le Livre de Jade* de Judith Gautier: Un livre pionnier," *Revue de littérature comparée* 633 (1989): 314-15, argues against considering Gautier's poems as *vers libre* because they are often too long; it is only their layout that links them. But Gautier's rhythms and internal rhymes, assonances, and alliteration are less "the effect of chance" than Détrie perceives. As the subtitle of Junko Yoshikawa, "*Le Livre de Jade* de Judith Gautier, traduction de poèmes chinois: Le rapport avec sa création du poème en prose" ("the relationship [of her translations] to her creation of prose poems") suggests, the author argues for the association with that form. On the other hand, the title of Andrea S. Thomas, "Judith Gautier, *Vers Libre*, and the Faux East," argues for the other.

12. Annmarie Drury, *Translation as Transformation in Victorian Poetry* (Cambridge: Cambridge University Press, 2015), 31; as cited by Francesca Orsini, "From Eastern Love to Eastern Song: Re-translating Asian Poetry," *Comparative Critical Studies* 17, no. 2 (2020): 183.
13. Arthur E. Christy, "Chinoiserie and Vers Libre," *The Open Court* 43 (April 1929): 216.
14. Victor Plarr, *Ernest Dowson* (New York: Laurence J. Gomme, 1914), 22; cited by R. K. R. Thornton, *The Decadent Dilemma* (London: Edward Arnold, 1983), 15, and then by Margueritte S. Murphy, *A Tradition of Subversion*, 13.
15. Hugh Kenner, "The Poetics of Error," *MLN* 90, no. 6 (1975): 739.
16. John Gould Fletcher, "The Orient and Contemporary Poetry," in *The Asian Legacy and American Life*, ed. Arthur Christy (New York: Greenwood, 1968), 155-56, 149.
17. Kenneth Rexroth, "The Influence of French Poetry on American," in *World Outside the Window: The Selected Essays of Kenneth Rexroth*, ed. Bradford Morrow (New York: New Directions, 1987), 152. Rexroth mentions the "Thai informant" in his remarks in a presentation for a 1977 symposium; see Kenneth Rexroth, "Chinese Poetry and the American Imagination," in *The New Directions Anthology of Classical Chinese Poetry*, ed. Eliot Weinberger (New York: New Directions, 2003), 209.
18. In Ezra Pound, *Selected Poems*, ed. T. S. Eliot (London: Faber and Faber, 1928), 14.
19. Hugh Kenner, "The Poetics of Error," 738.
20. Steve Bradbury, "On the Cathay Tour with Eliot Weinberger's *New Directions Anthology of Classical Chinese Poetry*," *Translation Review* 66 (2003): 43. See also Pauline Yu, "Judith Gautier and the Invention of Chinese Poetry," in *Reading Medieval Chinese Poetry: Studies in Text, Context, and Culture*, ed. Paul Kroll (Leiden: E. J. Brill, 2014), 251-88. Timothy Billings agrees that "it would not be much of an exaggeration to say that Gautier was the "inventor of Chinese poetry for her time"; see Ezra Pound, *Cathay: A Critical Edition*, ed. Timothy Billings (New York: Fordham University Press), 2019), 113n45.
21. As Christopher Bush observes, one should perhaps not think of their relationship as one of influence; Gautier was part of a larger literary chain "that abounds in not only successors but also precursors and contemporaries." Christopher Bush, "Introduction: 'From the Decipherings,'" in Ezra Pound, *Cathay: A Critical Edition*, 5.
22. "We know that Pound had read Judith Gautier," writes Christopher Bush, "Introduction," 6. Timothy Billings, in Ezra Pound, *Cathay: A Critical Edition*, 113n45, explains how "Pound told Angela Jung-Palandri that he had read Judith Gautier's translations long before he had received the Fenollosa notebooks, which makes them interesting matter for comparison." Laura Lauth, " 'Strange and Absurd Words,'" 165, also cites Angela Jung Palandri as the source of the knowledge that Pound had read *Le Livre de jade* by 1913, if not earlier.
23. In Ezra Pound, *Cathay: For the Most Part from the Chinese of Rihaku, from the Notes of the Late Ernest Fenollosa, and the Decipherings of the Professors Mori and Ariga* (London: Elkin Matthews, 1915), 13. See also Ezra Pound, *Cathay: A Critical Edition*, 40. Steve Bradbury points to the family resemblance in "On the Cathay Tour," 45. The other two overlapping poems are Li Bo's "River song" (which I have argued Gautier had worked into two shorter poems, "River song" and "The sages dance") and his "Farewell to a friend."
24. In Ezra Pound, *Cathay: A Critical Edition*, 328, from "Chinese Poetry," *To-day* 3, no. 4 (April 1918): 54-57.
25. Herbert Giles, *Chinese Poetry in English Verse* (London: B. Quaritch, 1898), 72. Cited by Timothy Billings in Ezra Pound, *Cathay: A Critical Edition*, 135.
26. Kenneth Rexroth, "Chinese Poetry and the American Imagination," 209. In addition to his mistaken belief that Gautier worked with a Thai informant, Rexroth also errs in stating

that Hervey-Saint-Denys translated the eighteenth-century anthology *Three Hundred Poems of the Tang* (*Tang shi san bai shou* 唐詩三百首).

27. Andrea Thomas, "Judith Gautier, *Vers Libre*, and the Faux East," 82.
28. Ezra Pound, *Cathay*, 28-29. Also in Ezra Pound, *Cathay: A Critical Edition*, 50.
29. George Steiner, *After Babel: Aspects of Language and Translation* (New York: Oxford University Press, 1975), 359-60. Robert Kern, *Orientalism, Modernism, and the American Poem* (Cambridge: Cambridge University Press, 1996), 176ff, discusses how formally innovative French prose poems like Gautier's offered a "precognition of imagist lyric" that would, in turn, thanks to Pound's practice, establish expectations of what any future translations of Chinese poetry into English should look like.
30. The first translations into English of Gautier's poems appeared almost immediately in the article "Chinese Poetry" by the unidentified "fellow Parisienne" who insisted that Gautier's labors be taken seriously. Three poems are rendered into English, without rhyme or meter and thus resembling Gautier's originals in form. Laura Lauth, " 'Strange and Absurd Words,' " 139-41.
31. Kenneth Rexroth, "The Influence of French Poetry on American," in *World Outside the Window: The Selected Essays of Kenneth Rexroth*, ed. Bradford Morrow (New York: New Directions, 1987), 152.
32. William Dean Howells, "The Prose Poem," introduction to Stuart Merrill, ed., *Pastels in Prose* (New York: Harper & Brothers, 1890), v-viii.
33. "Translator's note," Stuart Merrill, ed., *Pastels in Prose*, ix.
34. Anon., "A Dainty Volume," *New York Times*, April 13, 1890, 19. Cited by Laura Lauth, 'Strange and Absurd Words,' " 145, who notes that the *Times* also reprinted an entire bookleaf from the volume.
35. Maddalena Italia, "Eastern Poetry by Western Poets: Powys Mathers' 'Translations' of Sanskrit Erotic Lyrics," *Comparative Critical Studies* 17, no. 2 (2020): 206.
36. Edward Powys Mathers, *Coloured Stars: Versions of Fifty Asiatic Love Poems* (Oxford: B. H. Blackwell, 1918), 5.
37. Edward Powys Mathers, *The Garden of Bright Waters: One Hundred and Twenty Asiatic Love Poems* (Boston: Houghton Mifflin Company, 1920).
38. Letter of September 20, 1948, in Lee Bartlett, ed., *Kenneth Rexroth and James Laughlin: Selected Letters* (New York: Norton, 1991), 121-22. Quoted in Emily Apter, "Translation with No Original: Scandals of Textual Reproduction," in *The Translation Zone: A New Comparative Literature* (Princeton, NJ: Princeton University Press, 2006), 282n20.
39. Orlando Figues, *The Europeans: Three Lives and the Making of a Cosmopolitan Culture* (New York: Henry Holt Metropolitan Books, 2019), 179, 400. James St. André, "Retranslation as Argument: Canon Formation, Professionalization, and International Rivalry in 19th Century Sinological Translation," *Cadernos de Tradução* 11 (2003): 59-93, discusses the slightly different type of "retranslation," beginning in the eighteenth century, among sinologists who chose to produce their own versions of previously translated works (primarily plays) rather than tackle something new.
40. William Hung writes that "Aage Matthison-Hansen, *Vandliljerne: En Samling Digte fra Dynastiet Tang's Tid* (Copenhagen: A. Anderson, 1903) contains several pieces that sound like Danish adaptations of Gautier's "pseudo translations of Tu Fu," in William Hung, *Tu Fu: China's Greatest Poet. A Supplementary Volume of Notes* (Cambridge, MA: Harvard University Press, 1952), 10. Guido Amedeo Vitale published two sets of selections that did not bother to name authors or source in "Poesia cinese," *Italia Coloniale* 2, no. 1 (1901): 5-12; and "Ombre cinesi," *Italia Coloniale* 2, no. 8 (1901): 35-39. Arturo Onofri's (1885-1928) retranslations in

The Jade Moon both credited Gautier as the ultimate source and—unlike most adaptations—also emulated her lyrical prose (*Lune di giada. Poesie cinese tradotte da Arturo Onofri*, ed. Carlo D'Alessi [Rome: Salerno, 1994]). As cited by Rosa Lombardi, "The Italian Reception of Chinese Literature in the Twentieth Century: An Analysis of the Earliest Translations of Chinese Poetry," in *The Translator as Author: Perspectives on Literary Translation*, ed. Claudia Buffagni, Beatrice Garzelli, and Serenella Zanotti. Proceedings of the International Conference, Università per Stranieri of Siena, May 28-29, 2009 (Berlin: Lit, [2011]), 234-36.

41. Maria Rubins, "Dialogues across Cultures: Adaptations of Chinese Verse by Judith Gautier and Nikolai Gumilev," *Comparative Literature* 54, no. 2 (Spring 2002): 153.
42. Adriana Garcia de Aldridge, "Some Chinese Influences on Latin-American Writers," *Tamkang Review* 10 (1971): 149. As cited by Laura Lauth, " 'Strange and Absurd Words,' " 178.
43. Paul Arène, "Préface" to Émile Blémont, *Poèmes de Chine* (Paris: Lemerre, 1887), iv, xiv. Cited in part by Yu Wang, *La Réception des anthologies*, 248.
44. Anon., "Orient ex Extrême-Orient," in *Nouvelles littéraires* (April 26, 1924), as cited by Yu Wang, *La Réception des anthologies*, 271. Wang provides some examples of Toussaint's revisions of Gautier, 274-77.
45. Franz Toussaint, *La Flûte de jade: Poésies chinoises* (Paris: L'Édition d'Art H. Piazza, 1922), 7.
46. William Hung, *Tu Fu: China's Greatest Poet*, 11.
47. Muriel Détrie, "*Le Livre de jade*," 302, and Yu Wang, *La Réception des anthologies*, 277.
48. Ts'ao Shang-ling, *Fletnia Chińska* (Warsaw: J. Mortkowicz, 1922); Ts'ao Shang-ling, *Cathay: Poemas orientales* (Bogotá: Camacho Roldan, 1929); Gertrude Laughlin Joerissen, *The Lost Flute* (London: T. F. Unwin, 1923, and New York: The Elf, 1929). As cited by William Hung, *Tu Fu: China's Greatest Poet*, 11.
49. Claudel's rewrites of Gautier were published as "Autres poèmes d'après le chinois" in *Conférencia* (March 15, 1938), as noted by Yu Wang, *La Réception des anthologies*, 301. Wang discusses how Claudel revises Gautier on pp. 301-21. For a discussion of Claudel's relationship to China, see Yvan Daniel, *Paul Claudel et l'empire du milieu* (Paris: Indes savantes, 2003).
50. Hans Heilmann, *Chinesische Lyrik vom 12. Jahrhundert v. Chr. bis zur Gegenwart* (Munich: Piper, 1905), "Vorwort zu den Übersetzungen," liv-lvi.
51. Hans Heilmann, "Einleitung," in *Chinesische Lyrik*, l.
52. Otto Wolfgang, *Die Porzellanpagode* (Vienna: Glorietteverlag, 1921).
53. Max Fleischer, *Der Porzellanpavillon: Nachdichtungen chinesischer Lyrik* (Berlin: Paul Zsolnay Verlag, 1927).
54. Kuei-Fen Pan-Hsu, *Die Bedeutung der chinesischen Literatur in den Werken Klabunds: Eine Untersuchung zur Entstehung der Nachdichtungen und deren Stellung im Gesamtwerk* (Frankfurt am Main: Peter Lang, 1990), 16, 54-55. Klabund's three volumes of adaptations from the Chinese (*Dumpfe Trommel und berauschtes Gong* [Leipzig: Insel, 1915], *Li-Tai-Pe* [Leipzig: Insel, 1916], and *Das Blumenschiff* [Berlin: Erich Reiss, 1921]) were brought together as the second volume of Klabund (Alfred Henschke), *Dichtungen aus dem Osten*, 3 vols. (Vienna: Phaidon-Verlag, 1929).
55. Robert Neumann, "Li-Tai-Po: Ein deutscher Dichter," *Die neue Bücherschau: Buchkritische Zeitschrift für Literatur, Kunst, Kulturpolitik* (Munich: Weimar Aufbau-Verlag, 1928), 77-81. Cited by Kuei-Fen Pan-Hsu, *Die Bedeutung der chinesischen Literatur*, 36-37.
56. Yimin Jiang, "*Die chinesische Flöte* von Hans Bethge und *Das Lied von der Erde* von Gustav Mahler: Vom Textverständnis bei der Rückübersetzung," in Walter Gebhard, ed., *Ostasienrezeption zwischen Klichee und Innovation: Zur Begegnung zwischen Ost und West um 1900* (Munich: Iudicium Verlag, 2000), 339.

298   8. An Extraordinary Afterlife

57. Yimin Jiang, "Die chinesische Flöte," 331. According to Ben Hutchinson, "The Echo of 'After-Poetry': Hans Bethge and the Chinese Lyric," *Comparative Cultural Studies* 17, no. 2 (2020): 306, the print run totaled "some 100,000 copies."
58. Ben Hutchinson, "The Echo of 'After-Poetry,' " 307, notes as well that Gautier's rendition of Li Bo's "The mysterious flute" most likely inspired the title of Bethge's anthology.
59. Hans Bethge, "Geleitwort," in *Die chinesische Flöte: Nachdichtungen chinesischer Lyrik* (Leipzig: Insel, 1907), 103-11.
60. Publication announcement from Insel Verlag, reprinted in Donald Mitchell, *Gustav Mahler: Songs and Symphonies of Life and Death* (Berkeley: University of California Press, 1985), 165.
61. Donald Mitchell, *Gustav Mahler*, 435.
62. Henri-Louis de La Grange, *Gustav Mahler: Chronique d'une vie*. Vol. 3: *Le génie foudroyé, 1907–1911* (Paris: Fayard, 1973), 90, 346.
63. Donald Mitchell, *Gustav Mahler*, 342, 351.
64. Henri-Louis de La Grange, *Gustav Mahler*, 301.
65. Henri-Louis de La Grange, *Gustav Mahler*, 347-48, 1123.
66. Henri-Louis de La Grange, *Gustav Mahler*, 1139, among others proposed Qian Qi's poem, via Gautier's "Autumn evening," as the source for Mahler's second song. But Donald Mitchell, *Gustav Mahler*, based on conflicting opinions from experts in Chinese literature, was skeptical; the epithet "curiouser and curiouser," 441, is his. In her discussion of the textual genealogies of both songs, Fusako Hamao, "The Sources of the Texts in Mahler's 'Lied von der Erde,' " *19th-Century Music* 19 (1995): 83-95, convincingly argues for both this attribution and the even more stunning identification of Li Bo's poem on the gathering at the Tao family pavilion as the basis for Gautier's "Porcelain pavilion."
67. Donald Mitchell, *Gustav Mahler*, 463n57. On Mahler's exposure to Chinese music, see Henri-Louis de La Grange, *Gustav Mahler*, 340-41, 1143.
68. Ben Hutchinson, "The Echo of 'After-Poetry,' " 304.
69. Gabriel Fabre, *Poèmes de jade* (Paris: Heugel et Cie, 1905-1908); John Haussermann, *On the River* (New York: The Composers Press, 1951). André de Fouquières, "Les Poètes chinois," 66, writes that when he heard Fabre's compositions performed, "they offered us a profound impression of the Chinese soul, graceful, amiable, and melancholy."
70. Christian Melchior-Bonnet, "À la mémoire de Judith Gautier," *Le Gaulois*, January 6, 1923, 1. Included in *Recueil factice d'articles critiques sur Judith Gautier*, BnF 8-RF-59975. Also recounted in Joanna Richardson, *Judith Gautier: A Biography* (London: Quartet Books, 1986), 199.
71. Anon., "Une victoire féminine"; Émile Vedel, "Une académicienne"; and Anon., "Une académicienne: Enfin!" Clippings included in the *Recueil factice d'articles biographiques sur Judith Gautier*, BnF 8-RF-59973.
72. Anon., "Honor for Judith Gautier: First Woman to be Elected to the Goncourt Academy," *New York Times*, October 29, 1910, 1.
73. Paul Souday, "Autour des prix littéraires," *Paris-midi*, December 24, 1910, 3. The second sentence of Anon., "Une victoire féminine" announces that "A woman, Mme Judith Gautier, daughter of the exquisite poet of Émaux et Camées, is since yesterday an academician, not, evidently, academician with a capital A, but academician of the Goncourt academy." And the subtitle of Anon., "Une académicienne: Enfin!" reads "It is, to be true, the Goncourt that names her."
74. M. Gustave Geffroy, quoted in Christian Melchior-Bonnet, "À la mémoire de Judith Gautier," 1. Paul Verlaine, "Deux poètes français," *Oeuvres en prose complètes* (Paris: Gallimard, 1972), 952, also referred to her obliquely as "the illustrious *évocatrice* of China" in his discussion of Robert de Montesquiou.

75. Émile Bergerat, "Judith Gautier," *Le Figaro*, January 8, 1918, 1. Unable to elect her, Bergerat adds, the Académie had at least "crowned" her works with their approbation in 1898. Joanna Richardson, *Judith Gautier*, 226, gives the date of the "crowning" as 1892.
76. Judith Gautier, "L'académicienne est heureuse: Remerciements d'une solitaire," *Recueil factice d'articles biographiques*, BnF 8-RF-59973.
77. Emphasis mine. Raoul Aubry, "Promenades et visites: Un début chez les Goncourt." *Le Temps*, November 25, 1910, 3.
78. P. Dollfus, "Erreur de sexe," *Le Cri de Paris*, January 13, 1918, 10.
79. Judith Gautier, *Lettres inédites de Madame de Sévigné*, recueillies par Judith Gautier et illustrées par Madeleine Lemaire (Paris: À la Marquise de Sévigné, 1913).
80. Émile Poiteau, "Judith Gautier," in *Quelques écrivains de ce temps* (Paris: Bernard Grasset, 1913), 189.
81. Letter of Lucien to Esther Pissarro of May 10, 1910, in Marcella Genz, *A History of the Eragny Press 1894–1914* (London: Oak Knoll Press and the British Library, 2004), 105, 118n110. Gautier provided Pissarro with several other unpublished translations, but he chose not to include them because he considered the volume to be "an experimental work and if it did not succeed he did not want her previously unpublished work to be in something that might be badly done," 226.
82. Juliette Delobel, "Judith Gautier, érudite intuitive," *Revue de la BNF* 60 (January 2020): 165; and Marcella Genz, *A History of the Eragny Press*, 66; the book was priced at £4, 225.
83. Alice H. R. H. Beckwith, *Illustrating the Good Life: The Pissarros' Eragny Press, 1894–1914. A Catalogue of an Exhibition of Books, Prints & Drawings Related to the Work of the Press* (New York: The Grolier Club, 2007), 54. Beckwith provides illuminating examples of the multiple series of drawings, prints, and woodblocks behind each illustration, 33-35.
84. Diana White, "Préface," *Album de poèmes tirés du Livre de Jade* (London: The Eragny Press, 1911), 3-6.
85. Letter to Lucien Pissarro, December 6, 1911, in Marcella Genz, *A History of the Eragny Press*, 226. As Genz notes, French book design, in contrast to English and American practice, "still advocated abundant white spaces on text pages," 106. Laura Lauth, " 'Strange and Absurd Words,' " 168, also observes that the Pissarros had "made Gautier's experiments with the compositional units of page, space, and typography more explicit than ever before."
86. Marcella Genz, *A History of the Eragny Press*, 134; and L. W. Hodson, letter of January 21, 1913, in Marcella Genz, *A History of the Eragny Press*, 226.
87. Li Bo's poem, said to be "after Du Fu," is his "Song of roosting crows" ("Wu qi qu" 烏棲曲), which Gautier had included, correctly attributed to Li Bo, as a new addition to her 1902 edition of *Le Livre de jade*, 21–22. As noted in chapter 7, that version of the poem is much truncated and bears a title that obscures the source, "Drunkenness of love" ("Ivresse d'amour"), whereas the 1911 version translates the Chinese title accurately. Sun's poem is titled "Strophes written by His Excellency Sun Baoqi, minister from China to Paris, for Madame Judith Gautier" ("Strophes écrites par S. E. Soueng-Pao-Ki, ministre de Chine à Paris pour Madame Judith Gautier"). Judith Gautier, "Poèmes inédits du *Livre de Jade*," *La Dépêche coloniale illustrée* 23-24 (December 15 and 31, 1911): 289.
88. M. Dita Camacho, *Judith Gautier: Sa vie et son oeuvre* (Paris: Librairie E. Droz, 1939), 54.
89. Judith Gautier, "Le Paradis des poètes: A. S. E. Soueng-Pao-Ki," in *Poésies* (Paris: Bibliothèque-Charpentier, 1911), 87-90.
90. Judith Gautier, "Soir de Chine," in *Poésies*, 82-83.
91. Judith Gautier, *Poésies*, 85-86.
92. M. Dita Camacho, *Judith Gautier*, 182, 187.

93. Suzanne Meyer-Zundel, *Quinze ans auprès de Judith Gautier* (Porto: Tipografia Nunes, 1969), 36; and Joanna Richardson, *Judith Gautier*, 189.
94. Alice Théo Bergerat, "Il y a trente ans mourait Judith Gautier," *L'Époque*, December 26, 1846, n.p. Meyer-Zundel wrote a note to Robert de Montesquiou on November 26, 1918, referring to this phrase as "an idea that [Gautier] had written in Chinese characters in her bedroom and for which the Prince of Annam just sent a translation 'The light comes from heaven.'" See Joanna Richardson, *Judith Gautier*, 283n58. In Suzanne Meyer-Zundel, *Quinze ans*, 218, however, she writes (much later) that a Vietnamese visitor to the cemetery discovered—to his great surprise and delight—Gautier's grave with its Chinese characters, sought her friend out and insisted on painting the phrase on the wall. More recently Meng Hua has suggested that the "heaven" in the phrase might refer to the "Heavenly" or "Celestial Kingdom" (*tian guo* 天國), or China, the source of Gautier's most enduring and illuminating inspiration. Meng Hua, "'Bu zhong de mei ren': Lue lun Zhudite Gediye de han shi 'fanyi,'" *Dongfang fanyi* 4 (2012): 50. That is not, however, how Gautier's surviving friends understood it.
95. Amandine Dabat, "Judith Gautier et le prince d'Annam (1871–1944): Une amitié artistique," in *Judith Gautier*, ed. Daniel and Lavaud, 332. Dabat slightly mistranscribes the placement of the Chinese characters.
96. Pierre Descaves, "Richard Wagner: 'Protecteur de Judith Gautier,'" *La France au Combat*, August 29, 1946, in *Recueil. Articles sur Judith Gautier. 1943–1946*, BnF 8-RSUPP-3458.
97. Anon., "Hommage chocolaté à la Dinardaise Judith Gautier," accessed June 23, 2017, http://www.ouest-france.fr/bretagne/dinard-35800/hommage-chocolate-la-dinardaise-judith-gautier-4673888.

EPILOGUE

1. Paul Souday, "Les Livres," *Feuilleton du Temps*, January 19, 1918, *Recueil factice d'articles critiques sur Judith Gautier*, BnF 8-RF-59975.
2. Yu Wang, *La Réception des anthologies de poésie chinoise classique par les poètes français (1735–2008)* (Paris: Classiques Garnier, 2016), 142.
3. C. LeSenne, "Judith Gautier est morte," December 29, 1917, *Recueil factice d'articles biographiques sur Judith Gautier*, BnF 8-RF-59973, 47; G. D. [Gaston Deschamps], "Nécrologie: Judith Gautier," *Le Temps*, December 29, 1917, *Recueil factice d'articles biographiques sur Judith Gautier*, BnF 8-RF-59973; Christian Melchior-Bonnet, "À la mémoire de Judith Gautier," *Le Gaulois*, January 6, 1923, 1. *Recueil factice d'articles critiques sur Judith Gautier*, BnF 8-RF-59975.
4. Anatole France, "Judith Gautier," in *La Vie littéraire*, 4 vols. (Paris: Calmann-Lévy, 1897), 4: 141–42.
5. As in Anon., "Le Chinois de Judith Gautier," January 5, 1918, unsigned and unsourced article in *Recueil factice d'articles biographiques*, BnF 8-RF-59973. For use of the same phrase see Georges Grison, "Tin-tun-ling," *Le Figaro*, December 29, 1917, 3.
6. Émile Poiteau, "Judith Gautier," in *Quelques écrivains de ce temps* (Paris: Bernard Grasset, 1913), 191, 194–95.
7. Émile Poiteau, "Judith Gautier," 190–91.
8. Anatole France, "Judith Gautier," 133, 135.
9. Théodore de Banville, "Iskender: À Paul Ginisty," *Gil Blas*, June 4, 1806, 1; cited by, among others, Rémy de Gourmont, *Judith Gautier* (Paris: Bibliothèque Internationale d'Édition, 1904), 27; and Christian Melchior-Bonnet, "À la mémoire de Judith Gautier."
10. As recalled by Christian Melchior-Bonnet, "À la mémoire de Judith Gautier." The novel is *Forse che si, forse che no* (Maybe yes, maybe no).

11. Paul Souday, "Les Livres."
12. Henri de Régnier, "Judith Gautier," in *Nos Rencontres* (Paris: Mercure de France, 1931), 66.
13. G. D. [Gaston Deschamps], "Nécrologie: Judith Gautier."
14. Laurent Tailhade, "Les Morts: Judith Gautier," in *La médaille qui s'efface: Mémoires d'écrivains et d'artistes* (Paris: Les Éditions G. Crès et Cie, 1924), 232.
15. André de Fouquières, "Les poètes chinois," *De l'art, de l'élégance, de la charité* (Paris: Fontemoing et Cie, 1910), 42, 44. His last statement repeats verbatim comments from Rémy de Gourmont, *Judith Gautier*, 12.
16. M. Dita Camacho, *Judith Gautier: Sa vie et son oeuvre* (Paris: Librairie E. Droz, 1939), 51.
17. Agnès de Noblet, "Préface" in Judith Gautier, *Le Second Rang du collier: Souvenirs littéraires* (Paris: Félix Juven, 1903; rpt. Paris: L'Harmattan, 1999), ix.
18. Rémy de Gourmont, *Judith Gautier* (Paris: Bibliothèque Internationale d'Édition, 1904), 13.
19. Basile Alexéiev, "La littérature chinoise et son lecteur," in *La littérature chinoise: Six conférences au Collège de France et au Musée Guimet* (Paris: Librairie Orientaliste Paul Geutner, 1937), 110–12.
20. Paul Demiéville, "Aperçu historique des études sinologiques en France," in *Acta Asiatica* (Tokyo: The Tōhō Gakkai, 1966), 86.
21. William Hung, *Tu Fu: China's Greatest Poet. A Supplementary Volume of Notes* (Cambridge, MA: Harvard University Press, 1952), 10.
22. David Lattimore, "Discovering Cathay," *Parnassus: Poetry in Review* 2 (1975): 8.
23. Eugène-Albert de Pourvourville, "Judith Gautier," *Le Gaulois*, December 29, 1917. Also cited by Yu Wang, *La Réception des anthologies*, 196.
24. Arthur Waley, *A Hundred and Seventy Chinese Poems* (New York: Knopf, 1919), 35.
25. Arthur Waley, "Chinese Lyrics," review of James Whitall, trans., *Chinese Lyrics from The Book of Jade* (London: Erskine Macdonald [1919]), *Times Literary Supplement* 917 (August 14, 1919): 436.
26. Félix Lacôte criticized Alexandre Langlois's translation of the Rig Veda (published in *Monuments littéraires de l'Inde*, 1837) for precisely these characteristics. It was judged "indisputably deficient: simple, clear, intelligible—these were its greatest shortcomings." Félix Lacôte, "L'Indianisme," in *Société asiatique: livre du centenaire* (Paris: La Société asiatique, 1922), 219–49. Quoted in Raymond Schwab, *The Oriental Renaissance: Europe's Rediscovery of India and the East, 1680–1880*, trans. Gene Patterson-Mack and Victor Reinking (New York: Columbia University Press, 1984), 45.
27. Roy E. Teele, *Through a Glass Darkly: A Study of English Translations of Chinese Poetry* (Ann Arbor: N.p., 1949), 74.
28. David Hawkes, "Chinese Poetry and the English Reader," in *The Legacy of China*, ed. Raymond Dawson (London: Oxford University Press, 1964), 91.
29. Yu Wang, *La Réception des anthologies*, 171.
30. Arthur Waley, "Chinese Lyrics," 437; Anatole France, "Judith Gautier," 135; Agnès de Noblet, "Préface," x; Raoul Aubry, "Promenades et visites"; Theodore Bean, "A Chat with Judith Gautier," 59.
31. Anatole France, "Judith Gautier," 135; Hugh Kenner, "The Poetics of Error," *MLN* 90, no. 6 (1975): 745.
32. Rémy de Gourmont, *Judith Gautier*, 13.
33. Paul Souday, "Les Livres"; Yvan Daniel, "Présentation: *Le Livre de Jade*, un rêve de Judith Gautier," in Judith Gautier, *Le Livre de jade*, ed. Yvan Daniel (Paris: Imprimerie nationale, 2004), 16.
34. Seymour de Ricci, "La Chine à Paris: une conférence de Mme Judith Gautier," *Gil Blas*, November 19, 1912, 1.

35. André Chevrillon, "Hommage à Madame Judith Gautier," *L'Action nationale* (February 1911), 14, quoted in Barbara Jessome-Nance, "The Passionate Pursuit of Beauty: The Literary Career of Judith Gautier (1845-1917)" (PhD diss., University of Virginia, 1988), 169; Jonathan Chiche, "La Déesse et l'archange," *L'Express de Bénarès*, 2020, http://lexpressdebenares.com/Catalogues/VH-Judith.pdf.

Works Cited

Unless otherwise noted, all French newspaper articles were accessed through Bibliothèque nationale de France Gallica (BnF Gallica), which has also digitized most nineteenth-century French books. References are provided only for sources personally consulted.

Adelson, Warren. "John Singer Sargent and 'The New Painting.'" In *Sargent at Broadway: The Impressionist Years*, ed. Stanley Olson, Warren Adelson, and Richard Ormond, 25-61. New York: Universe/Coe Kerr Gallery, 1986.

Aldrich, Robert. *Banished Potentates: Dethroning and Exiling Indigenous Monarchs under British and French Colonial Rule, 1815–1955*. Manchester: Manchester University Press, 2018.

Alexéiev, Basile. "La littérature chinoise et son lecteur." In *La Littérature chinoise: Six conférences au Collège de France et au Musée Guimet*, 78-124. Paris: Librairie Orientaliste Paul Geutner, 1937.

Allen, Joseph R. "From Literature to Lingerie: Classical Chinese Poetry in Taiwan's Popular Culture." In *Popular Culture in Taiwan: Charismatic Modernity*, ed. Marc L. Moskowitz, 65-85. London: Routledge, 2010.

Anon. "A Dainty Volume." *New York Times*, April 13, 1890.

——. "À travers Paris." *Le Figaro*, November 16, 1886.

——. "Causerie de la semaine." *Le Jockey: Journal de sport / Journal des chasseurs*, May 21, 1867.

——. "Chinese Poetry." *The Albion, A Journal of News, Politics and Literature* (June 8, 1867): 274-75.

——. "Chronique." *Le Temps*, August 1, 1875.

——. "Courrier des théâtres." *Le XIXe Siècle*, May 23, 1874.

——. "Déchinoisement." *Gil Blas*, August 30, 1884.

——. "Échos de Paris." *L'Événement*, April 12, 1880.

——. "Échos du 'Courrier.'" *Le Courrier du soir*, November 29, 1886.

——. "Essai de biographie d'Hervey de Saint-Denys." In *Les Rêves et les moyens de les diriger*, préface by Robert Desoille. In *Bibli du Merveilleux*, ed. Claude Tchou. Paris: L'Imprimerie Blanchard, 1964.

——. "Hommage chocolaté à la Dinardaise Judith Gautier." http://www.ouest-france.fr/bretagne/dinard-35800/hommage-chocolate-la-dinardaise-judith-gautier-4673888.

——. "Honor for Judith Gautier: First Woman to be Elected to the Goncourt Academy." *New York Times*, October 29, 1910.

——. "Informations." *Le Figaro*, July 13, 1875.

——. "Judith Gautier." *La Petite Presse*, November 22, 1904.

——. "L'Actualité." *L'Événement*, July 6, 1874.

——. "L'Ambassade chinoise." *L'Indépendant des Basses-Pyrénées*, January 29, 1869.

—. "La Semaine." *Paris à l'eau-forte*, July 25, 1875.

—. "Le Chinois de Gautier." *Le Gaulois*, November 16, 1886. Also in *Le Voleur*, November 25, 1886.

—. "Le Chinois de Judith Gautier." January 5, 1918. *Recueil factice d'articles biographiques sur Judith Gautier*, BnF 8-RF-59973.

—. "Le Chinois de Théophile Gautier," *L'Éclair*, April 27, 1902. Rpt. as "Théophile Gautier et le Chinois." *Le Journal du dimanche*, May 25, 1902.

—. "Le Chinois de Théophile Gautier." In *L'Intermédiare des chercheurs et curieux. Notes et quéries français: questions et réponses, communications diverses à l'usage de tous, littérateurs et gens du monde, artistes, archéologues, généalogistes, etc.*, ed. M. Carle de Rash, year 68, vol. 95, no. 1776 (Paris: October 15, 1932): 728-32.

—. "Le Commerce de la France." *Le Temps*, November 17, 1886.

—. "Le Parisien de Pékin." *Le Voltaire*, April 9, 1887.

—. "Les deux mariages du chinois Tin-Tun-Ling." Cour d'assises de la Seine, Présidence de M. Bondurand, Audience du 11 juin. *Gazette des tribunaux*, June 12, 1875.

—. "Les Tribunaux: Cours d'assises de la Seine: L'affaire Tin-Tun-Ling." *La Liberté*, June 13, 1875.

—. *Notice sur les travaux de M. D'Hervey de Saint-Denys relatifs aux études chinoises*. Paris: J. Claye, n.d.

—. "Paris au jour le jour." *Le Figaro*, June 17, 1875.

—. "Poignée d'informations." *La Petite Presse*, January 29, 1878.

—. "Revue des théâtres." *Le Petit Journal*, May 23, 1874.

—. "Sargent Portrait and Landscape Sold at Drouot." *Chicago Daily Tribune*, January 19, 1934.

—. "Soirée de bienfaisance." *La Petite Presse*, August 2, 1874.

—. "Une académicienne: Enfin!" *Recueil factice des articles biographiques sur Judith Gautier*. BnF 8-RF-59973.

—. "Une victoire féminine." *Recueil factice des articles biographiques sur Judith Gautier*. BnF 8-RF-59973.

Apter, Emily. "Translation with No Original: Scandals of Textual Reproduction." In *The Translation Zone: A New Comparative Literature*, 210-25. Princeton, NJ: Princeton University Press, 2006.

Arène, Paul. "Préface" to Émile Blémont, *Poèmes de Chine*, iii-xvi. Paris: Lemerre, 1887.

Arène, Paul, et al. "Une séance littéraire à l'Hôtel du Dragon bleu." In *Le Parnassiculet contemporain: Recueil de vers nouveaux*, 9-20. 2nd ed. Paris: Librairie centrale, 1872.

Aubry, Raoul. "Promenades et visites: Un début chez les Goncourt." *Le Temps*, November 25, 1910.

Ayscough, Florence, and Amy Lowell, trans. *Fir-Flower Tablets: Poems Translated from the Chinese*. Boston: Houghton, 1921.

Banville, Théodore de. "Catulle Mendès." In *Les Camées parisiens*. Deuxième série, 49-50. Paris: Librairie Richelieu, 1866.

Barnes, Julian. *The Man in the Red Coat*. New York: Knopf, 2020.

Barnitz, David Park. *The Book of Jade*. New York: Doxey's at the Sign of the Lark, ca. 1901.

Barthou, Louis. *La Vie amoureuse de Richard Wagner*. Paris: Flammarion, 1925.

Bartlett, Lee, ed. *Kenneth Rexroth and James Laughlin: Selected Letters*. New York: Norton, 1991.

Baudelaire, Charles. *Correspondance*. 2 vols., ed. Claude Pichois and Jean Ziegler. Paris: Gallimard: 1973.

—. *Les Fleurs du mal*, ed. A. Adam. Paris: Garnier Frères, 1961.

—. *Petits poèmes en prose*, ed. Robert Kopp. Rpt. Paris: Librairie José Corti, 1969.

Bean, Theodore. "A Chat with Judith Gautier." *Theatre Magazine* 18 (August 1913): ix, 59-60.

Beckwith, Alice H. R. H. *Illustrating the Good Life: The Pissarros' Eragny Press, 1894-1914. A Catalogue of an Exhibition of Books, Prints & Drawings Related to the Work of the Press*. New York: The Grolier Club, 2007.

Bengali, Joë. "Semaine dramatique et littéraire." *Le Parti ouvrier*, December 13, 1889.

Bergerat, Alice Théo. "Il y a trente ans mourait Judith Gautier." *L'Époque*, December 26, 1946. *Recueil factice d'articles de presse et références concernant Wagner et Judith Gautier*, BnF RO-7020.

Bergerat, Émile. "Judith Gautier." *Le Figaro*, January 8, 1918.

—. "Le Chinois de Gautier." In *Souvenirs d'un enfant de Paris. Les Années de Bohème troisième mille*, 365-73. Paris: Bibliothèque-Charpentier, 1911.

—. *Vie et aventures de sieur Caliban 1884–1885*. Paris: E. Dentu, 1886.

Bergère, Marie-Claire. "Introduction: L'Enseignement du chinois à l'École des langues orientales du XIXe au XXIe siècle," 13-26. In Bergère and Pino, eds., *Un siècle d'enseignement du chinois*.

Bergère, Marie-Claire, and Angel Pino, eds. *Un siècle d'enseignement du chinois à l'École des langues orientales 1840–1945*. Paris: L'Asiathèque, 1995.

Bertin, Léon (Paul Perny). *Le Charlatanisme littéraire dévoilé ou la vérité sur quelques professeurs de langues étrangères à Paris*. Versailles: Imprimerie G. Beaugrand et Dax, 1874.

Bertuccioli, Giuliano. "Giuseppe Maria Calleri: Un Piemontese al servizio della Francia in Cina," 1-29. *Pubblicazioni di "Indologica Taurinensia," Collana di Biografie e Saggi diretta da Oscar Botto* (Torino: Instituto de indologia, 1986).

Bethge, Hans. *Die chinesische Flöte: Nachdichtungen chinesischer Lyrik*. Leipzig: Insel, 1907.

Bixiou. "Matinée chinoise." *Le Gaulois*, July 7, 1874.

Böhm, Gottfried. *Chinesische Lieder aus dem Livre de jade von Judith Mendès*. Munich: Ackermann, 1873.

Bonnières, Robert de, "Catulle Mendès, samedi 18 novembre 1882." In *Mémoires d'aujourd'hui*, 3 vols. 1: 184. Paris: Paul Ollendorff, 1883.

—. "Madame Judith Gautier, samedi 29 décembre 1883." In *Mémoires d'aujourd'hui*. 3 vols. 3: 303-14. Paris: Paul Ollendorff, 1883.

Bouchon, Paul, ed. *Pages d'amour de Victor Hugo pour Adèle Faucher, Juliette Drouet, Madame Biard, Judith Gautier et quelques autres*. Paris: Éditions Albin-Michel, 1949.

Bradbury, Steve. "On the Cathay Tour with Eliot Weinberger's *New Directions Anthology of Classical Chinese Poetry*." *Translation Review* 66 (2003): 39-52.

Brahimi, Denise. "Judith Gautier, ses pères, sa mère, son oeuvre." *Romantisme* 77 (1992): 55-60.

—. *Théophile et Judith vont en orient*. Paris: La Boîte aux Documents, 1990.

Brévannes. "Bibliographie." *Le Tintamarre*, July 18, 1875.

Brody, Elaine. "Letters from Judith Gautier to Chalmers Clifton." *The French Review* 58, no. 5 (April 1985): 670-74.

Brosse, Jacques. *La Découverte de la Chine*. Paris: Bordas, 1981.

Bush, Christopher. "Introduction: 'From the Decipherings.'" In Ezra Pound, *Cathay: A Critical Edition*, 1-11, ed. Timothy Billings.

Butcher, William. "The Tribulations of a Chinese in China: Verne and the Celestial Empire." *Journal of Foreign Languages* 5 (September 2006): 63-78.

Cai, Zong-qi. "Recent-Style *Shi* Poetry: Pentasyllabic Regulated Verse (*Wu yan lü shi*)," 161-80. In Zong-qi Cai, ed., *How to Read Chinese Poetry: A Guided Anthology*.

Cai, Zong-qi, ed. *How to Read Chinese Poetry in Context: Poetic Culture from Antiquity Through the Tang*. New York: Columbia University Press, 2018.

—. *How to Read Chinese Poetry: A Guided Anthology*. New York: Columbia University Press, 2008.

Callery, Joseph-Marie. "Préface," xix. In *Li-Ki ou Mémorial des Rites*. Paris: Benjamin Duprat, 1853.

Camacho, M. Dita. *Judith Gautier: Sa vie et son oeuvre*. Paris: Librairie E. Droz, 1939.

Camet, Sylvie. *Parenté et création: Familles d'artistes, de la relation personnelle à la production collective*. Paris: L'Harmattan, 1995.

Cartier, Michel, ed. *La Chine entre amour et haine*. Actes du VIIIe colloque de sinologie de Chantilly. *Variétés sinologiques*, no. 87. Paris: Desclée de Brouwer, 1998.

Chadourne, M. Marc. "Le Parnasse à l'école de la Chine." *Cahiers de l'Association internationale des études françaises* 13 (June 1961): 11-23.

Chang, Lung. *La Chine à l'aube du XXe siècle: Les relations diplomatiques de la Chine avec les puissances depuis la guerre sino-japonaise jusqu'à la guerre russo-japonaise*. Paris: Nouvelles Éditions Latines, 1962.

Cheng, Zenghou. "Qui est le capitaine Butler? À propos d'une lettre de Victor Hugo sur le Palais d'Été." *Revue d'histoire littéraire de la France* 111, no. 4 (2011): 891-903. https://www.cairn.info/revue-d-histoire-litteraire-de-la-France-2011-4-page-891.htm.

Chiche, Jonathan. "La Déesse et l'Archange." *L'Express de Bénarès*, 2020. http://lexpressdebenares.com/Catalogues/VH-Judith.pdf.

Choain, Jean. "George Soulié de Morant." *Méridiens (Revue de l'association scientifique des Médecins acupuncteurs en France)* 43-44 (1978): 13-31.

Chow, Jin Yun. "Franco-Chinese Poetic Dialogues in the 19th Century: Judith Gautier's *Le livre de jade*." BA thesis, Princeton University, 2017.

Christy, Arthur E. "Chinoiserie and Vers Libre." *The Open Court* 43 (April 1929): 209-18.

Chu, Petra ten-Doesschate. "Victor Hugo and the Romantic Dream of China," 148-77. In Chu and Milam, eds., *Beyond Chinoiserie*.

Chu, Petra ten-Doesschatte, and Jennifer Milam, eds. *Beyond Chinoiserie: Artistic Exchange between China and the West during the Late Qing Dynasty (1796–1911)*. Leiden: E. J. Brill, 2019.

Coppée, François. "*Le Livre de jade* par Mme Judith Walter." *Le Moniteur universel*, October 5, 1867.

Cordier, Henri. *Les Études chinoises (1891–1894)*. Leiden: E. J. Brill, 1895.

Cottin, Madeleine, ed. *Théophile Gautier: 1811–1872*. [Exposition] Paris: Bibliothèque nationale, 1961.

Courant, Maurice. *Catalogue des livres chinois, coréens, japonais, etc*. Paris: Ernest Leroux, 1902.

D'Hérisson, Le Comte Maurice d'Irisson. *Journal d'un interprète en Chine*. 14th ed. Paris: Paul Ollendorff, 1886.

Dabat, Amandine. "Judith Gautier et le prince d'Annam (1871-1944): Une amitié artistique," 325-39. In Daniel and Lavaud, eds., *Judith Gautier*.

—. *Hàm Nghi: Empereur en exil, artiste à Alger*. Paris: Sorbonne Université Presses, 2019.

Danclos, Anne. *La Vie de Judith Gautier: Égérie de Victor Hugo et Richard Wagner*. Paris: Éditions Fernand Lanore, 1996.

Daniel, Yvan. "De l'authenticité des poèmes du *Livre de jade*: histoire d'une réception polémique (1867-1917)," 109-18. In Daniel and Lavaud, eds. *Judith Gautier*.

—. "Présentation: *Le Livre de jade*, un rêve de Judith Gautier." In Judith Gautier, *Le Livre de jade*, ed. Yvan Daniel, 7-33. Paris: Imprimerie nationale, 2004.

—. *Littérature française et Culture chinoise (1846–2005)*. Paris: Les Indes savantes, 2010.

—. *Paul Claudel et l'empire du milieu*. Paris: Les Indes savantes, 2003.

Daniel, Yvan, and Martine Lavaud, eds. *Judith Gautier*. Collection "Interférences." Rennes: Presses universitaires de Rennes, 2020.

David, Henri. "Les poésies chinoises de Bouilhet." *Modern Philology* 15, no. 11 (March 1918): 663-72.

—. "Théophile Gautier: 'Le Pavillon sur l'eau.'" Part I: *Modern Philology* 13, no. 7 (November 1915): 391-416. Part II: *Modern Philology* 13, no. 11 (March 1916): 647-68.

Davis, Deborah, and Elizabeth Oustinoff. "Madame X Speaks." *The Magazine Antiques* (November 2003): 116-25.

Davis, Sir John Francis. *The Poetry of the Chinese*. London: Asher and Co., 1870.

Day, Jenny Huangfu. *Qing Travelers to the Far West: Diplomacy of the Information Order in Late Imperial China*. Cambridge: Cambridge University Press, 2018.

Delobel, Juliette. "Judith Gautier, érudite intuitive." *Revue de la BNF* 60 (January 2020): 160-69.

Demiéville, Paul. "Aperçu historique des études sinologiques en France." In *Acta Asiatica*, 56-110. Tokyo: The Tōhō Gakkai, 1966.
Descaves, Pierre. "Richard Wagner: 'Protecteur de Judith Gautier.'" *La France au Combat*, August 29, 1946. Recueil. *Articles sur Judith Gautier. 1943–1946*, BnF 8-RSUPP-3458.
Détrie, Muriel. "L'Image du Chinois dans la littérature occidentale au XIXe siècle," 403-30. In Michel Cartier, ed., *La Chine entre amour et haine*.
——. "*Le Livre de Jade* de Judith Gautier: Un livre pionnier." *Revue de littérature comparée* 633 (1989): 301-24.
——. "Translation and Reception of Chinese Poetry in the West." *Tamkang Review* 22 (1991): 43-57.
Dollfus, P. "Erreur de sexe." *Le Cri de Paris*, January 13, 1918.
Dreyfous, Maurice. *Ce qu'il me reste à dire: Un demi-siècle de choses vues et entendues, 1848–1900*. 3rd. ed. Paris: Librairie Paul Ollendorff, [1913].
——. *Ce que je tiens à dire: Un demi-siècle de choses vues et entendues, 1862–1872*. 5th ed. Paris: Librairie Ollendorff, 1912.
Duchesne de Bellecourt, Gustave. "La Chine et le Japon à l'Exposition universelle." *Revue des deux mondes* (1829-1871), seconde période 70, no. 3 (August 1, 1867): 710-42.
Ducuing, François, ed. *L'Exposition universelle de 1867 illustrée*. Publication internationale autorisée par la Commission impériale. 2 vols. Paris: Imprimerie Générale Ch. Lahure, 1867.
Egan, Ronald. *The Burden of Female Talent: The Poet Li Qingzhao and Her History in China*. Cambridge, MA: Harvard University Press, 2013.
——. *The Works of Li Qingzhao*. Boston: De Gruyter, 2019.
Escholier, Raymond. *Un amant de génie. Victor Hugo. Lettres d'amour et carnets intimes*. Paris: Fayard, 1953.
Fabre, Clément. "La sinologie est un sport de combat: L'affaire Paul Perny et les querelles sinologiques à Paris au XIXe siècle." *Genèses* 1, no. 110 (2018): 12-31. https://www.cairn.info/revue-geneses-2018-1-page-12.htm.
Fabre, Gabriel. *Poèmes de jade*. Paris: Heugel et Cie, 1905-1908.
Feijó, Antonio. *Cancioneiro Chinez*. With preface by Chen Jitong. Porto: Magalhães and Moniz, 1890.
Ferrère, Raoul. "Le Jardin chinois à l'Exposition," 1: 134-38." In François Ducuing, ed., *L'Exposition universelle de 1867 illustrée*.
Figues, Orlando. *The Europeans: Three Lives and the Making of a Cosmopolitan Culture*. New York: Henry Holt Metropolitan Books, 2019.
Finlay, John. "Henri Bertin (1720-1792) and Images of the Yuanmingyuan in Eighteenth-Century France," 123-37. In Louise Tythacott, ed., *Collecting and Displaying China's "Summer Palace" in the West*.
Fizaine, Jean Claude. "Un Portrait de Judith en impératrice chinoise." *Bulletin de la Société Théophile Gautier* 14 (1992): 149-63.
Flaubert, Gustave. *Correspondance*, 4 vols. Paris: Gallimard, 1991.
——. *L'Éducation sentimentale: Histoire d'un jeune homme*. Paris: Gallimard, 1965.
Fleischer, Max. *Der Porzellanpavillon: Nachdichtungen chinesischer Lyrik*. Berlin: Paul Szolnay Verlag, 1927.
Fletcher, John Gould. "The Orient and Contemporary Poetry." In *The Asian Legacy and American Life*, ed. Arthur Christy, 145-74. New York: Greenwood, 1968.
Fleury, Raphaële. "Entre divertissement de société et recherche de l'oeuvre d'art totale: Les 'marionnettes' de Judith Gautier," 223-51. In Daniel and Lavaud, eds., *Judith Gautier*.
Foss, Theodore N. "Reflections on a Jesuit Encyclopedia: Du Halde's Description of China (1735)." *Appréciation par l'Europe de la tradition chinoise à partir du XVIIe siècle*. Actes du IIIe Colloque international de sinologie. Centre de recherches interdisciplinaires de Chantilly, 11-14 septembre 1980, 67-77. Paris: Les belles lettres, 1983.

Fouquières, André de. "Les Poètes chinois." In *De l'art, de l'élégance, de la charité*, 39-66. Paris: Fontemoing et Cie, 1910.

Franc, Geneviève. "*Nivea non frigida*: Les amours de Judith Gautier." *Bulletin de la Société Théophile Gautier* 20 (1998): 142-64.

France, Anatole (Camille d'Ivry). "Contes chinois" and "Judith Gautier." In *La Vie littéraire*. 4 vols. 3: 79-91; and 4: 133-44. Paris: Calmann-Lévy, 1897.

—. *Croquis féminins*, 3-17, 64-84. In Michael Pakenham, ed. *Portraits littéraires*.

—. "Judith Mendès [June 25, 1869]," 11-12. In *Croquis féminins*.

Frèches, José. *La Sinologie*. Que sais-je? No. 1610. Paris: Presses universitaires de France, 1975.

Fu, Hung Cheng. *Un siècle d'influence chinoise sur la littérature française (1815-1930)*. Paris: Les éditions Domat-Montchrestien, 1934.

Fuller, Michael A. *An Introduction to Chinese Poetry: From the Canon of Poetry to the Lyrics of the Song Dynasty*. Cambridge, MA: Harvard University Press, 2017.

—. *The Road to East Slope: The Development of Su Shi's Poetic Voice*. Stanford, CA: Stanford University Press, 1990.

G. D. [Gaston Deschamps]. "Nécrologie: Judith Gautier." *Le Temps*, December 29, 1917. *Recueil factice d'articles biographiques sur Judith Gautier*, BnF 8-RF-59973.

G. P. V. "Causerie Parisienne: La Colonie chinoise à Paris." *Le Radical*, May 15, 1882.

Galy, Laurent. "Entre sinologie pratique et sinologie savant: Les interprètes-professeurs de l'École des langues orientales vivantes, 1871-1930," 130-67. In Bergère and Pino, eds., *Un siècle d'enseignement*.

Gautier, Judith. "L'Académicienne est heureuse: Remerciements d'une solitaire." *Recueil factice d'articles biographiques sur Judith Gautier*, BnF 8-RF-59973.

—. *Le Collier des jours: souvenirs de ma vie*. Paris: Félix Juven, 1902; rpt. Paris: Christian Pirot, 1994.

—. *Le Livre de jade*. Les Belles Oeuvres littéraires. Paris: Éditions Jules Tallandier, 1928.

—. *Le Livre de jade*. Paris: Félix Juven, 1902.

—. *Le Livre de jade*. Les Beaux Textes illustrées. Paris: Librairie Plon, Éditions d'histoire et d'art, 1933.

—. *Le Livre de jade*, ed. Yvan Daniel. Paris: Imprimerie nationale, 2004.

—. "Le premier jour de l'an à l'ambassade chinoise," 151-55. In *Les Parfums de la pagode*.

—. "Le Prince Tsaï-tché à Paris," 157-62. In *Les Parfums de la pagode*

—. "Le Salon." *Le Rappel*, May 1, 1884.

—. "Le Salon: Salomé." *Le Rappel*, May 6, 1876. Included in "Critiques d'art de Judith Gautier." In *Théophile Gautier / Gustave Moreau*, ed. Marie-Cécile Forest, Samuel Mandin, Aurélie Peylhard, and Pierre Pinchon, 83-92. Paris: Musée Gustave Moreau, 2011.

—. *Le Second Rang du collier: Souvenirs littéraires*. Préface by Agnès de Noblet. Paris: Félix Juven, 1903. Rpt. Paris: L'Harmattan, 1999.

—. *Le Troisième Rang du collier*. Paris: Félix Juven, 1909.

—. "Les Chinois: Poésie et poëtes." In *Les Peuples étranges*, 43-81. Paris: Charpentier, 1879.

—. *Les Parfums de la pagode*. Paris: Charpentier, 1919.

—. *Lettres inédites de Madame de Sévigné*. Recueillies par Judith Gautier et illustrées par Madeleine Lemaire. Paris: À la Marquise de Sévigné, 1913.

—. *Oeuvres complètes*, ed. Yvan Daniel. 2 vols. Paris: Gallimard, 2011.

—. "Poèmes chinois de tous les temps." *La Revue de Paris* (June 15, 1901): 805-20.

—. *Poèmes de la libellule: Traduits du japonais d'après la version littérale de M. Saionzi, Conseiller d'État de S.M. l'Empereur du Japon*. Illustrées par Yamamoto. Paris: Gillot, 1885.

—. "Poèmes inédits du *Livre de Jade*." *La Dépêche coloniale illustrée* 23-24 (December 15 and 31, 1911): 289-90.

—. *Poésies*. Paris: Bibliothèque-Charpentier, 1911.

—. "Prélude." In Judith Gautier, *Le Livre de jade*, ix-xxi. Paris: Félix Juven, 1902.

—. "Quelques grands poètes chinois et la poétesse Ly-y-Hane." *La Grande Revue* (December 1, 1901): 543-53.

—. *Richard Wagner et son oeuvre poétique depuis Rienzi jusqu'à Parsifal*. Paris: Charavay Frères, 1882.

—. "Une fête chinoise chez Pierre Loti," 141-49. In *Les Parfums de la pagode*.

Gautier, Théophile. "Chinois et Russes: À l'Exposition universelle de Paris." *Le Moniteur universel*, May 19, 1867.

—. "En Chine." In *L'Orient*, 229-50. Paris: G. Charpentier, 1884.

—. *La Comédie de la mort*. Paris: Desessart, 1838.

—. *Mademoiselle de Maupin*. Paris: Charpentier et Cie, 1869.

Gebhard, Walter, ed. *Ostasienrezeption zwischen Klischee und Innovation: Zur Begegnung zwischen Ost und West um 1900*. Munich: Iudicium Verlag, 2000.

Geisler-Szmulewicz, Anne. "Mémoires enchevêtré.e.s.: *Le Collier des jours* et *Le Second Rang du collier*." In Anne Geisler-Szmulewicz and Marie-Hélène Girard, eds. *Gautier: Judith & Théophile. Bulletin de la Société Théophile Gautier* 40 (2018): 27-46.

Geisler-Szmulewicz, Anne, and Marie-Hélène Girard, eds. *Gautier: Judith & Théophile. Bulletin de la Société Théophile Gautier* 40 (2018): 1-155.

Genz, Marcella. *A History of the Eragny Press 1894-1914*. London: Oak Knoll Press and the British Library, 2004.

Goncourt, Edmond, and Jules de. *Journal des Goncourt: Mémoires de la vie littéraire*. 9 vols. Paris: G. Charpentier and E. Fasquelle, 1887-1896.

—. *Journal des Goncourt: Mémoires de la vie littéraire*, ed. Robert Ricatte. 4 vols. Paris: Flammarion, 1956.

Gourmont, Rémy de. *Judith Gautier*. Paris: Bibliothèque Internationale d'Édition, 1904.

Graham, A. C. *Poems of the Late T'ang*. Baltimore, MD: Penguin Books, 1965.

—. *The Book of Lieh-tzu: A Classic of the Tao*. New York: Columbia University Press, 1990.

Grand-Carteret, John. *Richard Wagner en caricatures*. Paris: Larousse, [1892].

Grison, Georges. "Tin-Tun-Lin." *Le Figaro*, December 29, 1917.

Guégan, Stéphane. "Le Miroir à deux faces." In *Joris-Karl Huysmans: De Degas à Grunewald*, ed. Stéphane Guégan and André Guyaux, 81-91. Paris: Gallimard, 2019.

Guillemot, Maurice. "La Marchande de sourires." *Le Figaro*, April 21, 1888.

—. "Portrait de femme: Judith Gautier." *L'Événement*, July 14, 1887.

Hamao, Fusako. "The Sources of the Texts in Mahler's 'Lied von der Erde.'" *19th-Century Music* 19 (1995): 83-95.

Hamrick, L. Cassandra. "Entre barbare et civilisé ou pour aller en Chine avec Gautier." *Études littéraires* 42, no. 3 (2011): 49-69.

Haussermann, John. *On the River*. New York: The Composers Press, 1962.

Hawkes, David. "Chinese Poetry and the English Reader." In *The Legacy of China*, ed. Raymond Dawson, 90-115. London: Oxford University Press, 1964.

—. *Ch'u Tz'u: The Songs of the South*. Boston: Beacon Press, 1962.

Heilmann, Hans. *Chinesische Lyrik vom 12. Jahrhundert v. Chr. bis zur Gegenwart*. Munich: Piper, 1905.

Henry, Stuart. "Judith Gautier." In *French Essays and Profiles*, 249-56. London: J. M. Dent and Sons, 1922.

Hervey-Saint-Denys, Léon d'. "L'Art poétique et prosodique chez les Chinois," 11-109. In *Poésies de l'époque des Thang*.

—. "Poésies chinoises composées sous la dynastie des Thang (Li-Tai-pé; Thou-fou)." *Revue orientale et américaine* 2. Paris: Challamel Aîné, 1859: 285-88.

—. *Poésies de l'époque des Thang, précédé de L'art poétique et la prosodie chez les Chinois*. Paris: Amyot, 1862. Rpt. Éditions Champ Libre, 1977.

Hevia, James. "Looting Beijing: 1860, 1900." In *Tokens of Exchange: The Problem of Translation in Global Circulations*, ed. Lydia H. Liu, 192–213. Durham, NC: Duke University Press, 1999.

———. *English Lessons: The Pedagogy of Imperialism in Nineteenth-Century China*. Durham, NC: Duke University Press, 2003.

Hokenson, Jan Walsh. *Japan, France, and East-West Aesthetics*. Madison, NJ: Fairleigh Dickinson University Press, 2004.

Howells, William Dean. "The Prose Poem." Introduction to *Pastels in Prose*, ed. Stuart Merrill, v–viii.

Hugo, Victor. *Correspondance*. Ancienne collection. 4 vols. ed. Louis Barthou. Paris: Albin Michel, 1947–1952.

———. *Oeuvres complètes de Victor Hugo: Actes et paroles pendant l'exil, 1852–70*. Paris: J. Hetzel, 1880.

Hung, William. *Tu Fu: China's Greatest Poet. A Supplementary Volume of Notes*. Cambridge, MA: Harvard University Press, 1952.

Hutchinson, Ben. "The Echo of 'After-Poetry': Hans Bethge and the Chinese Lyric." *Comparative Cultural Studies* 17, no. 2 (2020): 303–17.

Huysmans, Joris-Karl. *À Rebours*. Paris: G. Charpentier et Cie, 1884.

Idema, Wilt L. "Male Fantasies and Female Realities: Chu Shu-chen and Chang Yü-niang and Their Biographers." In *Chinese Women in the Imperial Past: New Perspectives*, ed. Harriet T. Zurndorfer, 19–52. Leiden: E. J. Brill, 1999.

Idema, Wilt, and Beata Grant, eds. *The Red Brush: Writing Women of Imperial China*. Cambridge, MA: Harvard University Press, 2004.

Italia, Maddalena. "Eastern Poetry by Western Poets: Powys Mathers' 'Translations' of Sanskrit Erotic Lyrics." *Comparative Critical Studies* 17, no. 2 (2020): 205–24.

Jacquemin, Jeannine. "George Soulié de Morant: Sa vie, son oeuvre d'écrivain et de sinologue." *Histoire des sciences médicales* 20, no. 1 (1986): 31–40.

Jacquot, Olivier. "Judith Gautier, lectrice de la Bibliothèque impériale." *Carnet de la recherche à la Bibliothèque nationale de France*, October 18, 2023. https://doi.org/10.58079/m4of

———. "Paul Jean Baptiste Marie Tin-Tun-Ling (Ding Dunling 丁敦齡), lecteur chinois de la Bibliothèque impériale." *Carnet de la recherche à la Bibliothèque nationale de France*, October 23, 2023. https://doi.org/10.58079/m4oh.

———. "Tin-Tun-Ling, a Chinaman." *Carnet de la recherche à la Bibliothèque nationale de France*, October 1, 2023. https://doi.org/10.58079/m3zv.

Jessome-Nance, Barbara. "The Passionate Pursuit of Beauty: The Literary Career of Judith Gautier (1845–1917)." PhD diss., University of Virginia, 1988.

Jiang, Yimin. "*Die chinesische Flöte* von Hans Bethge und *Das Lied von der Erde* von Gustav Mahler: Vom Textverständnis bei der Rückübersetzung," 331–54. In Walter Gebhard, ed., *Ostasienrezeption zwischen Klichee und Innovation*.

Joerissen, Gertrude Laughlin. *The Lost Flute*. London: T. F. Unwin, 1923; and New York: The Elf, 1929.

Johnstone, Simon, trans. *Diary of a Chinese Diplomat: Zhang Deyi*. Beijing: Panda Books, 1992.

Julien, Stanislas. *Hoeï-lan-ki, ou l'Histoire du cercle de craie: Drame en prose et en vers*. London: L'Imprimerie de Cox père et fils, 1832.

Jullian, Philippe. *Robert de Montesquiou: Un prince 1900*. Paris: Libr. Académique Perrin, [1965].

Kanazawa, Kimiko. "Le Japon paru dans les oeuvres de Théophile et Judith Gautier." *Kyoyo ronsyu (Liberal Arts Review)* 8 (December 1990): 71–80.

Kenner, Hugh. "The Poetics of Error." *MLN* 90, no. 6 (1975): 738–46.

Kern, Robert. *Orientalism, Modernism, and the American Poem*. Cambridge: Cambridge University Press, 1996.

Kilmurray, Elaine. "Judith Gautier." No. 103 in *Forging a Modern Identity: Masters of American Painting Born after 1847. American Paintings in the Detroit Institute of Arts*, 3: 230, ed. James W. Tottis. 3 vols. Detroit and London: D. Giles, 2005.

Klabund (Alfred Henschke). *Dichtungen aus dem Osten*. 3 vols. Vienna: Phaidon-Verlag, 1929.

Knapp, Bettina. *Judith Gautier: Writer, Orientalist, Musicologist, Feminist. A Literary Biography*. Lanham, MD: Hamilton Books, 2004.

Kong Fanli 孔凡禮. *Su Shi shi ji* 蘇軾詩集. Beijing: Zhonghua shuju, 1982.

Koyama-Richard, Brigitte, ed. *Le Japon et la Chine dans les oeuvres de Judith Gautier*. 5 vols. Tokyo: Édition Synapse, 2007.

La Grange, Henri-Louis de. *Gustav Mahler: Chronique d'une vie*. 3 vols. Vol. 3: *Le génie foudroyé, 1907–1911*. Paris: Fayard, 1973.

Laisney, Vincent. "Le Temple des souvenirs," 53–59. In Daniel and Lavaud, eds., *Judith Gautier*.

—. "Témoignages sur le 'salon' de Judith Gautier," 61–73. In Daniel and Lavaud, eds., *Judith Gautier*.

Lancelot. "Échos de Partout." *La Liberté*, June 25, 1878.

—. "Échos de partout." *La Liberté*, June 30, 1878.

Landry-Deron, Isabelle. "L'ombre portée par l'ouvrage de Du Halde sur les premiers sinologues français non-missionnaires," 33–41. In Michel Cartier, ed., *La Chine entre amour et haine*.

—. "Les outils d'apprentissage du chinois en France au moment de l'ouverture de la chaire d'études chinoises au Collège Royal (1814) et les efforts de Jean-Pierre Abel-Rémusat pour les améliorer," 15–47. In Will and Zink, eds., *Jean-Pierre Abel-Rémusat et ses successeurs*.

Lang, Andrew. "A Chinaman's Marriage." In *Lost Leaders*, 31–37. New York: Longmans, Green, and Co., 1889.

Lattimore, David. "Discovering Cathay." *Parnassus: Poetry in Review* 2 (1975): 5–26.

Lauth, Laura. "'Strange and Absurd Words': Translation as Ethics and Poetics in the Transcultural U.S. 1830–1915." PhD diss., University of Maryland, 2011.

[Le Rouge, Georges-Louis, ed.]. *Jardins de l'Empéreur de la Chine*. [Paris: G. L. Le Rouge, 1786.]

Leconte de Lisle, Charles-Marie. *Lettres à José-Maria de Heredia*. Paris: Honoré Champion, 2004.

LeSenne, C. "Judith Gautier est morte," December 29, 1917. *Recueil factice d'articles biographiques sur Judith Gautier*, BnF 8-RF-59973, 47.

Letourneur, Marie, ed. *Les cent plus beaux sonnets de la langue française*. Collection Espaces. Paris: Le Cherche-midi Éditeur, 1982.

Lévy, André. *Nouvelles lettres édifiantes et curieuses d'Extrême-Occident par des voyageurs lettrés chinois à la Belle Epoque 1866–1906*. Paris: Éditions Seghers, 1986.

Ling Min. "Première rencontre poétique entre la France et la Chine: Traduction et réception de la poésie classique chinoise en France au XIXème siècle." PhD diss., University of Paris-Sorbonne, 2013.

Link-Herr, Ursula, and Eva Erdmann. "Robert de Montesquiou und die ideographischen Zeichen: Jugendstil, *japonisme* und preziöse Lyrik," 283–304. In Walter Gebhard, ed., *Ostasienrezeption zwischen Klischee und Innovation*.

Liu, James J. Y. "Polarity of Aims and Methods: Naturalization or Barbarization?" *Yearbook of Comparative and General Literature* 24 (1975): 60–68.

—. *The Art of Chinese Poetry*. Chicago: University of Chicago Press, 1962.

Liu, Jingwen. "From *chinoiserie* to *à la manière chinoise*: Théophile Gautier's 'Le pavillon sur l'eau.'" *The French Review* 94, no. 3 (March 2021): 151–66.

Liu Wenwei 劉文薇. *Tang shi he xuan* 唐詩合選. Rpt. Guangxi: Guangxi renmin chubanshe, 1988.

Liu Zhixia. "Ding Dunling de Faguo suiyue" 丁敦齡的法國歲月. *Shu cheng za zhi* 書城雜誌 (September 2013): 39–49.

Lombardi, Rosa. "The Italian Reception of Chinese Literature in the Twentieth Century: An Analysis of the Earliest Translations of Chinese Poetry." In *The Translator as Author: Perspectives on Literary Translation*, ed. Claudia Buffagni, Beatrice Garzelli, and Serenella Zanotti, 233-45. Proceedings of the International Conference, Università per Stranieri of Siena, May 28-29, 2009. Berlin: Lit, [2011].

Lundbaek, Knud. "The Establishment of European Sinology 1801-1815." In *Cultural Encounters: China, Japan, and the West*, ed. Søren Clausen, Roy Staffs, and Anne Wedell-Wedellsborg, 5-54. Aarhus: Aarhus University Press, 1995.

Luppé, Olivier de, Angel Pino, Roger Rippert, and Betty Schwartz, eds. *D'Hervey de Saint-Denys. 1822–1892*. Île Saint-Denis: Éditions Oniros, 1995.

Mack, Dietrich. *Wagners Frauen*. Berlin: Insel, 2013.

Mangin, André. "Stanislas Julien: Orientaliste et sinologue orléanais (1797-1873)." *Bulletin de la Société archéologique et historique de l'Orléanais*, Nouvelle Série 18, no. 143 (1er trimestre 2005): 5-33.

Martin, Meredith. "Staging China, Japan, and Siam at the Paris Universal Exhibition of 1867," 122-48. In Chu and Milam, eds., *Beyond Chinoiserie*.

Massarani, Tullo. *Il Libro di Giada: Echi dell'Estremo Oriente recati in versi italiani secondo la lezione di Mma J. Walter*. Florence: Successori le Monnier, 1882.

Massie, Effie Dunreith, trans. *Wagner at Home*. London: Mills and Boon, 1910.

Mathers, Edward Powys. *Coloured Stars: Versions of Fifty Asiatic Love Poems*. Oxford: B. H. Blackwell, 1918.

——. *The Garden of Bright Waters: One Hundred and Twenty Asiatic Love Poems*. Boston: Houghton Mifflin Company, 1920.

Melchior-Bonnet, Christian. "À la mémoire de Judith Gautier." *Le Gaulois*, January 6, 1923. Recueil factice d'articles critiques sur Judith Gautier, BnF 8-RF-59975.

Mendès, Catulle. *Figurines des poètes*, 19-39, 84-98. In Michael Pakenham, ed., *Portraits littéraires*.

——. *La Légende du Parnasse contemporain*. 4 lectures. Bruxelles: Auguste Brancart, 1884.

——. *Le Mouvement poétique français de 1867 à 1900*. Rapport à M. le Ministre de l'Instruction publique et des beaux-arts, précédé de réflexions sur la personnalité de l'esprit poétique de France, suivi d'un dictionnaire bibliographique et critique et d'une nomenclature chronologique de la plupart des poètes français du XIXe siècle. Paris: Imprimerie nationale, 1903.

——. "Ting-Tun-Ling," 26-27, 89-91. In *Figurines des poètes*.

Mendès, Catulle, and Louis-Xavier de Ricard, eds. *Le Parnasse contemporain: Recueil de vers nouveaux*. Paris: Alphonse Lemerre, 1866.

Mendès, Judith (Judith Gautier). *Le Dragon impérial*. Paris: Alphonse Lemerre, 1869.

——. "Poëme chinois." Translation of Tin-Tung-Ling [sic], "Ié-man / La nuit triste." *Revue des lettres et des arts*, March 29, 1868, 21.

Meng Hua 孟華. "'Bu zhong de mei ren': Lue lun Zhudite Gediye de Han shi 'fanyi'" '不忠的美人: 略論朱迪特戈蒂耶的漢詩'翻譯.' *Dongfang fanyi* 東方翻譯 4 (2012): 49-58.

——. "Faguo Hanxuejia De Liwen de Zhongguo qingjie: Dui 1867 nian Bali shijie bolanhui Zhongguo guan chengbai de wenhua sikao" 法國漢學家德理文的中國情結: 對1867年巴黎世界博覽會中國館成敗的文化思考. In *Zhong Fa wenxue guanxi yanjiu* 中法文學關係研究, 256-75. Shanghai: Fudan, 2011.

Merrill, Stuart, ed. *Pastels in Prose*. New York: Harper and Brothers, 1890.

Meyer-Zundel, Suzanne. *Quinze ans auprès de Judith Gautier*. Porto: Tipografia Nunes, 1969.

Mitchell, Donald. *Gustav Mahler: Songs and Symphonies of Life and Death*. Berkeley: University of California Press, 1985.

Mondor, Henri. *Vie de Mallarmé*. Paris: Gallimard, 1943.

Monnet, Nathalie. "Abel-Rémusat (1788-1832): Un autodidacte et ses livres," 71-116. In Will and Zink, eds., *Jean-Pierre Abel-Rémusat*.

Monselet, Charles. "Causerie littéraire." *L'Événement*, July 22, 1875.
Montclair. "Silhouettes féminines: Mme Judith Gautier." *Recueil factice d'articles biographiques sur Judith Gautier*, BnF 8-RF-59973, 2.
Montesquieu, Charles-Marie de. *Lettres persanes*. Paris: Garnier-Flammarion, 1964.
Mortelette, Yann. "Catulle Mendès et le Parnasse." In *Catulle Mendès: L'énigme d'une disparition*, ed. Patrick Besnier, Sophie Lucet, and Nathalie Prince, 13-38. Rennes: Presses universitaires de Rennes, 2005.
———. *Histoire du Parnasse*. [Paris]: Fayard, 2005.
Mortier, Arnold. *Les Soirées parisiennes de 1876*. Paris: E. Dentu, 1877.
Mount, Charles. "John Singer Sargent and Judith Gautier." *The Art Quarterly* 18 (1955): 136-45.
Murphy, Margueritte S. *A Tradition of Subversion: The Prose Poem in English from Wilde to Ashbery*. Amherst: University of Massachusetts Press, 1992.
Négroni, Jean-Louis de. *Souvenirs de la campagne de Chine: Détails sur la collection*. Paris: Imprimerie Renou et Maulde, 1864.
Neumann, Robert. "Li-Tai-Po: Ein deutscher Dichter." *Die neue Bücherschau: Buchkritische Zeitschrift für Literatur, Kunst, Kulturpolitik*, 77-81. Munich: Weimar Aufbau-Verlag, 1928.
Noblet, Agnès de. "Préface." In Judith Gautier, *Le Second Rang du collier: Souvenirs littéraires*, i-xiii. Paris: Félix Juven, 1903. Rpt. Paris: L'Harmattan, 1999.
———. "Un ami de Judith Gautier: George Soulié de Morant." *Les carnets de l'exotisme: Orients-extrêmes* 15-16 (1995): 25-29.
———. *Un univers d'artistes: Autour de Théophile et Judith Gautier*. Paris: L'Harmattan, 2003.
Olivio (Catulle Mendès). "Lettres d'amour." *L'Art*, November 30, 1865, 7-8; and December 8, 1865, 5-6.
Ormond, Richard. "Sargent and the Arts," 9-21. In Ormond with Kilmurray, eds., *Sargent: Portraits of Artists and Friends*.
Ormond, Richard, and Elaine Kilmurray. *John Singer Sargent: The Early Portraits. Complete Paintings*, vol. 1 of 9. New Haven, CT: Yale University Press, 1998.
Ormond, Richard, with Elaine Kilmurray, eds. *Sargent: Portraits of Artists and Friends*. London: National Portrait Gallery, 2015.
Orsini, Francesca. "From Eastern Love to Eastern Song: Re-translating Asian Poetry." *Comparative Critical Studies* 17, no. 2 (2020): 183-203.
Owen, Stephen. "The Snares of Memory." In *Remembrances: The Experience of the Past in Classical Chinese Literature*, 80-98. Cambridge, MA: Harvard University Press, 1986.
———. *The Great Age of Chinese Poetry: The High T'ang*. New Haven, CT: Yale University Press, 1981.
———. *The Making of Early Chinese Classical Poetry*. Cambridge, MA: Harvard University Press, 2006.
———. *The Poetry of the Early T'ang*. New Haven, CT: Yale University Press, 1977.
Pakenham, Michael. "La République des lettres de Catulle Mendès et Adelphe Froger." In *Catulle Mendès et la République des lettres*, ed. Jean-Pierre Saïdah, 27-54. Rencontres 26, Série Études dix-neuviémistes dirigée par Pierre Glaudes 11. Paris: Classiques Garnier, 2011.
Pakenham, Michael, ed. *Portraits littéraires*. Vol. 32 of *Textes littéraires*, ed. Keith Cameron. [Exeter]: University of Exeter, 1979.
Pan-Hsu, Kuei-Fen. *Die Bedeutung der chinesischen Literatur in den Werken Klabunds: Eine Untersuchung zur Entstehung der Nachdichtungen und deren Stellung im Gesamtwerk*. Frankfurt am Main: Peter Lang, 1990.
Pelliot, Paul. "Bulletin critique: *Fir-Flower Tablets, poems translated from the Chinese* par Mme Florence Ayscough, 'english version' de Mlle Amy Lowell." *T'oung Pao* 21, no. 2/3 (May-July 1922): 232-42.
Pino, Angel. "Abrégé dûment circonstancié de la vie de Maris Jean Léon le Coq, baron d'Hervey, marquis de Saint-Denys, professeur au Collège de France et membre de l'Institut, sinologue en

son état, onironaute à ses heures: une enquête à l'usage, non exclusive, des futurs biographes," 95-129. In Bergère and Pino, eds., *Un siècle d'enseignement*.

—. "Léon d'Hervey sinologue: Repères bio-bibliographiques (1849-1894)," 155-229. In Luppé et al., eds., *D'Hervey de Saint-Denys, 1822–1892*.

—. "Stanislas Julien et l'École des langues orientales à travers quelques documents," 52-94. In Bergère and Pino, eds., *Un siècle d'enseignement*.

—. "Trois répétiteurs indigènes: Ly Hong-fang, Ly Chao-pée et Ting Tun-Ling, 1869-1870," 271-313. In Bergère and Pino, eds., *Un siècle d'enseignement*.

Pino, Angel, and Isabelle Rabut. "Bazin ainé et la création de la chaire de chinois vulgaire à l'École des langues orientales: relation historique accompagnée d'une bibliographie exhaustive des oeuvres du savant professeur," 29-51. In Bergère and Pino, eds., *Un siècle d'enseignement*.

Poiteau, Émile. "Judith Gautier." In *Quelques écrivains de ce temps*, 189-98. Paris: Bernard Grasset, 1913.

Pont-Jest, René de. "Boîte aux lettres." *Le Gaulois*, April 22, 1881.

Pound, Ezra. *Cathay: A Critical Edition*, ed. Timothy Billings. New York: Fordham University Press, 2019.

—. *Cathay: For the Most Part from the Chinese of Rihaku, from the Notes of the Late Ernest Fenollosa, and the Decipherings of the Professors Mori and Ariga*. London: Elkin Matthews, 1915.

—. *Selected Poems*, ed. T. S. Eliot. London: Faber and Faber, 1928.

Pourvourville, Eugène-Albert de. "Judith Gautier." *Le Gaulois*, December 29, 1917.

Prével, Jules. "Courrier des théâtres." *Le Figaro*, May 21, 1874.

Qian Zhongshu 錢鍾書. *Tan yi lu* 談藝錄. Rev. ed. Hong Kong: Zhonghua shuju, 1986.

Qiu Zhaoao 仇兆鰲, ed. *Du shi xiang zhu* 杜詩詳註. 2 vols. 1767. Rpt. Taipei: Wenshizhe chubanshe, 1973.

Quatrefages, Armand de. *Histoire générale des races humaines; introduction à l'étude des races humaines*. Paris: Hennuyer, 1889.

Racot, Adolphe. *Portraits-cartes*, 41-62, 99-114. In Michael Pakenham, ed. *Portraits littéraires*.

Recueil. Articles sur Judith Gautier. 1943–1946, BnF 8-RSUPP-3458.

Recueil factice d'articles biographiques sur Judith Gautier, BnF 8-RF-59973.

Recueil factice d'articles critiques sur Judith Gautier, BnF 8-RF-59975.

Recueil factice d'articles de presse et références concernant Wagner et Judith Gautier, BnF RO-7020.

Régnier, Henri de. "Judith Gautier." In *Nos Rencontres*, 63-72. Paris: Mercure de France, 1931.

Reid, Martine. "*Le Collier des jours* et les choix singuliers de Judith Gautier," 27-38. In Daniel and Lavaud, eds., *Judith Gautier*.

Ren, Ke. "Chen Jitong, *Les Parisiens peints par un Chinois*, and the Literary Self-Fashioning of a Chinese Boulevardier in Fin-de-siècle Paris." *L'Esprit Créateur* 56, no. 3 (Fall 2016): 90-103.

—. "Fin-de-siècle Diplomat: Chen Jitong and Cosmopolitan Possibilities in the Late Qing World." PhD diss., Johns Hopkins University, 2014.

Rexroth, Kenneth. "Chinese Poetry and the American Imagination." In *The New Directions Anthology of Classical Chinese Poetry*, ed. Eliot Weinberger, 209-12. New York: New Directions, 2003.

—. "The Influence of French Poetry on American." In *World Outside the Window: The Selected Essays of Kenneth Rexroth*, ed. Bradford Morrow, 143-70. New York: New Directions, 1987.

Ribeyre, Félix. *Cham: Sa vie et son oeuvre*. Paris: Librairie Plon, 1884.

Ribeyrol, Charlotte. "John Singer Sargent and the *fin de siècle* Culture of Mauve." *Visual Culture in Britain* 19, no. 1 (2018): 6-26.

Ricci, Seymour de. "La Chine à Paris: Une conférence de Mme Judith Gautier." *Gil Blas*, November 19, 1912.

Richardson, Joanna. *Judith Gautier: A Biography*. London: Quartet Books, 1986.

———. *Théophile Gautier: His Life and Times*. London: Max Reinhardt, 1958.
Ringmar, Erik. *Liberal Barbarism: The European Destruction of the Palace of the Emperor of China*. New York: Palgrave Macmillan, 2013.
Rionnet, Florence. "Judith Gautier, 'Vous êtes un marbre, habité par une étoile,' la muse inspiratrice et la femme sculpteur," 305-23. In Daniel and Lavaud, eds., *Judith Gautier*.
Rodays, Fernand de. "Gazette des tribunaux, Cours d'assises: L'affaire du Chinois Tin-Tun-Ling." *Le Figaro*, June 12, 1875.
Rosny, Léon de. *La Franc-Maçonnerie chez les Chinois*. Paris: Alexandre Lebon, 1864.
Ross, Alex. *Wagnerism: Art and Politics in the Shadow of Music*. New York: Farrar, Straus and Giroux, 2020.
Rowbotham, Arnold H. "A Brief Account of the Early Development of Sinology." *The Chinese Social and Political Science Review* 7 (1923): 113-28.
Rubins, Maria. "Dialogues across Cultures: Adaptations of Chinese Verse by Judith Gautier and Nikolai Gumilev." *Comparative Literature* 54, no. 2 (Spring 2002): 145-64.
Saint-Raymond, Léa. "Tracing Dispersal: Auction Sales from the Yuanmingyuan Loot in Paris in the 1860s." *Journal for Art Market Studies*, Forum Kunstmark Cologne (2018). https://hal.archives-ouvertes.fr/hal-02986360.
Samoyault-Verlet, Colombe, Jean-Paul Desroches, Gilles Béguin, and Albert Le Bonheur, eds. *Le Musée chinois de l'impératrice Eugénie*. Paris: Réunion des musées nationaux, 1994.
SarDesai, D. R. *Vietnam: Past and Present*. Boulder, CO: Westview Press, 1998.
Savant, Jean. *La Vie sentimentale de Victor Hugo*, Livret 6. Paris: Jean Savant, 1985.
Schafer, Edward. "What and How Is Sinology?" *T'ang Studies* 8-9 (1990-1991): 23-44.
Schuh, Willi. *Die Briefe Richard Wagners an Judith Gautier*. Mit einer Einleitung, "Die Freundschaft Richard Wagners mit Judith Gautier." Erlenbach-Zürich: Rotapfel Verlag, [1936].
Schwab, Raymond. *The Oriental Renaissance: Europe's Rediscovery of India and the East, 1680-1880*. Trans. Gene Patterson-Black and Victor Reinking. New York: Columbia University Press, 1984.
Schwartz, Betty. "Le Marquis d'Hervey de Saint-Denys: Rêves et réalités," 3-51. In Luppé et al., eds., *D'Hervey de Saint-Denys, 1822-1892*.
Schwartz, William Leonard. *The Imaginative Interpretation of the Far East in Modern French Literature, 1800-1925*. Paris: Honoré Champion, 1927.
Serrano, Richard. *Neither a Borrower: Forging Traditions in French, Chinese and Arabic Poetry*. Legenda: Studies in Comparative Literature 7. Oxford: European Humanities Research Centre, 2002.
Shi, Yichao. "La Formation de Judith Gautier au chinois et à la culture chinoise (1863-1905)." *Revue d'histoire littéraire de la France* 3 (July-September 2020): 639-50.
———. "Voyager dans un monde de rêve: La reconstruction du temps et de l'espace dans *Le Dragon Impérial*." *Loxias-Colloques* 15, *Traversez l'espace*. https://revel.unice.fr/symposia/actel/index.html?id=1427.
Sifflet. "L'Aventure de Tin-Tun-Ling." *Le Gaulois*, April 21, 1881.
Silvestre, Armand. "Tin Tun Ling," 184-93. In *Portraits et souvenirs, 1866-1891*. Paris: Charpentier, 1891.
Simpson, Marc. "Sargent in Paris, 1874-85: The Omnivore's Delight," 23-31. In Ormond with Kilmurray, eds., *Sargent: Portraits of Artists and Friends*.
Souday, Paul. "Autour des prix littéraires." *Paris-midi*, December 24, 2010.
———. "Les Livres." *Feuilleton du Temps*, January 1918. *Recueil factice d'articles critiques sur Judith Gautier*, BnF 8-RF-59975.
Soulié de Morant, George. *Essai sur la littérature chinoise*. Paris: Mercure de France, 1912.
———. *Florilège des poèmes Song*. Paris: Plon, 1923.

St. André, James. "Retranslation as Argument: Canon Formation, Professionalization, and International Rivalry in 19th Century Sinological Translation." *Cadernos de Tradução* 11 (2003): 59-93.

Stabler, Jordan Herbert. *Songs of Li-Tai-Pè from the "Cancionerio [sic] Chines" of Antonio Castro Feijo: An Interpretation from the Portuguese.* New York: Edgar H. Wells and Co., 1922.

Starkie, Enid. *Arthur Rimbaud.* New York: New Directions, 1961.

Steegmuller, Francis. *Flaubert and Madame Bovary: A Double Portrait.* Rpt. New York: New York Review of Books, 2005.

Steiner, George. *After Babel: Aspects of Language and Translation.* New York: Oxford University Press, 1975.

Stevenson, R. A. M. "J. S. Sargent." *The Art Journal* 50 (March 1888): 64-69.

Stocès, Ferdinand. "*Le Livre de Jade* de Judith Gautier (Caractéristiques générales des éditions de 1867 et de 1902)." *Neige d'Août* 14 (Spring 2006): 35-54.

—. "Le mystère du *Livre de Jade* de Judith Gautier." *Histoires littéraires* 26 (April-June 2006): 49-76.

—. "*O Livro de Jade* de Judith Gautier: Caracteristicas gerais das edições de 1967 e de 1902." *Revue Oriente* 7 (2003): 3-20.

—. "Sur les sources du *Livre de Jade* de Judith Gautier (1845-1917) (Remarques sur l'authenticité des poèmes)." *Revue de littérature comparée* 319 (2006): 335-50.

Tailhade, Laurent. "Judith Gautier." In *Quelques fantômes de jadis,* 165-73. Paris: L'Édition française illustrée, 1919.

—. "Les Morts: Judith Gautier." In *La Médaille qui s'efface: Mémoires d'écrivains et d'artistes,* 225-35. Paris: Les Éditions G. Crès et Cie, 1924.

Takashina, Erika. "East-West Cultural Exchange in Art—France and the Orient in the 1880s (Part 5)." *Japan Spotlight* (January-February 2004): 54-56.

Tcheng Ki-Tong [Chen Jitong]. "Avant-propos." In *Les Chinois peints par eux-mêmes.* Paris: Calmann Lévy, 1884.

—. "Préface," ix-xiv. In Antonio Feijó, *Cancioneiro Chinez.*

Tcheng Ki-Tong, Général. *Les Plaisirs en Chine.* Paris: Charpentier and Co., 1890.

Teele, Roy Earl. *Through a Glass Darkly: A Study of English Translations of Chinese Poetry.* Ann Arbor: N.p., 1949.

Thomas, Andrea S. "Judith Gautier, Vers Libre, and the Faux East." *Symposium: A Quarterly Journal in Modern Literatures* 72, no. 2 (2018): 77-88.

Thomas, Greg M. "The Looting of Yuanming and the Translation of Chinese Art in Europe." *Nineteenth-Century Art Worldwide* 7, no. 2 (Autumn 2008). www.19thc-artworldwide.org/index.php/autumn09/93-the-looting-of-yuanming-and-the-translation-of-chinese-art-in-europe.

Thomas, Vance. "The Last of the Parnassians: Catulle Mendès." In *French Portraits,* 73-90. Boston: Richard G. Badger and Co., 1900.

Tin-Tun-Ling (Ding Dunling). "La Justice du fils du ciel." *Le Monde illustré,* June 13, 1868, June 20, 1868, June 27, 1868, and July 4, 1868.

—. "Le Jour de l'an en Chine." *La Petite Presse,* December 29, 1866, January 8, 1876, and January 1, 1882; *La Science pittoresque,* June 10, 1867; and *Le Monde illustré,* January 6, 1872.

—. *La Petite Pantoufle (Thou-Sio-Sié): Roman chinois.* Trans. M. Charles Aubert. Paris: Librairie de l'eau-forte, 1875.

Toussaint, Franz. *La Flûte de jade: Poésies chinoises.* Paris: L'Édition d'Art H. Piazza, 1922.

Tribunal de commerce de la Seine. *Note pour M. le marquis d'Hervey contre MM. Penon Frères.* Paris: Imprimerie centrale des chemins de fer. A. Chaix et Cie, 1868.

Tythacott, Louise. "Exhibiting and Auctioning Yuanmingyuan ('Summer Palace') Loot in 1860s and 1870s London: The Elgin and Negroni Collections." *Journal for Art Market Studies* 2, no. 3 (2018): 1-15. http://eprints.soas.ac.uk/26149.

—. "The Yuanmingyuan and Its Objects," 3-24. In Louise Tythacott, ed., *Collecting and Displaying: China's "Summer Palace" in the West*.
Tythacott, Louise, ed. *Collecting and Displaying: China's "Summer Palace in the West": The Yuanmingyuan in Britain and France*. New York: Routledge, 2018.
Un sportsman [alias]. "Le grand prix de Paris et la question des courses." *La Question* 17 (June 23, 1878): 114.
Valette, Lucien. "Un Chinois de Paris: Tin-Tun-Ling et Th. Gautier." *Le Voltaire*, November 18, 1886.
Vassy, Gaston. "La Représentation chinoise à Passy." *Le Figaro*, July 7, 1874.
Vedel, Émile. "Une académicienne." *Recueil factice des articles biographiques sur Judith Gautier*. BnF 8-RF-59973.
Venuti, Lawrence. *The Translator's Invisibility: A History of Translation*. New York: Routledge, 1995.
Verlaine, Paul. "Deux poètes français," 948-54. In *Oeuvres en prose complètes*.
—. "*Le Livre de Jade* par Judith Walter," 622-23. In *Oeuvres en prose complètes*. Originally published in *L'Étendard*, May 11, 1867.
—. *Oeuvres en prose complètes*. Paris: Gallimard, 1972.
Vermersch, Eugène. "Les Hommes du jour." Première série, no. 12 (1867), pub. in *Le Hanneton*, August 12, 1866. In Michael Pakenham, ed., "Introduction," x, *Portraits littéraires*.
Verne, Maurice. "La fille de Théophile Gautier vient de mourir." *Le Dimanche littéraire*, January 7, 1918. *Recueil factice d'articles biographiques sur Judith Gautier*, BnF 8-RF-59973.
Von Minden, Stephan. "Une experience d'exotisme vécu: 'Le Chinois de Théophile Gautier.'" *L'Orient de Théophile Gautier. Bulletin de la Société Théophile Gautier* 12 (1990): 35-54.
Wagner, Richard and Cosima. *Lettres à Judith Gautier*, ed. Léon Guichard. [Paris]: Gallimard, 1964.
Waleffe, Maurice de. *Quand Paris était un paradis: Mémoires 1900–1939*. Paris: Société des éditions Denoël, 1947.
Waley, Arthur. "Chinese Lyrics." Review of *Chinese Lyrics from The Book of Jade*, by James Whitall. *Times Literary Supplement* 917 (August 14, 1919): 436.
—. "The Limitations of Chinese Literature." In *One Hundred and Seventy Chinese Poems*, 17-21. New York: Knopf, 1919.
Waley, Arthur, trans. *The Book of Songs*. London: Allen and Unwin, 1937.
—. *The Book of Songs: The Ancient Chinese Classic of Poetry*, ed. Joseph R. Allen, foreword by Stephen Owen. New York: Grove, 1997.
Wallon, Henri. "Notice sur la vie et les travaux de M. Aignan-Stanislas Julien, membre ordinaire de l'Académie." *Comptes rendus des séances de l'Académie des Inscriptions et Belles-Lettres*, 19e année 4 (1875): 386-430. http://www.persée.fr/web/revues/home/prescript/article/crai_0065-0536_1875_num_10_4_60293.
Walter, Judith (Judith Gautier). "Chine-Japon-Siam." *Le Moniteur universel*, November 12, 1867, 6.
—. "Collection chinoise de M. Négroni." *L'Artiste: journal de la littérature et des beaux-arts* (April 15, 1864): 188-89.
—. "La Légende de Tie-Ouang, l'empéreur des Taepings." *Le Moniteur du soir*, October 17, 1864.
—. *Le Livre de jade*. Paris: Alphonse Lemerre, 1867.
—. "Livres d'Étrennes, II: *L'Oraison dominicale*, de Lorenz Frolich. *La Terre et les mers*, de Louis Figuier." *L'Artiste: Revue de l'art contemporain* (December 15, 1863): 262-63.
—. "Soirs de lune: Petits poèmes chinois." *Revue du XIXe siècle* 6 (April 1866): 338-40.
—. "Variations sur des thèmes chinois d'après les poésies de Li-taï-pé, Thou-fou, Than-jo-su, Houan-tchan-lin, Haon-ti." *L'Artiste: Journal de la littérature et des beaux-arts* (January 15, 1864): 37-38.
—. "Variations sur des thèmes chinois d'après des poésies de Su-tchou, Sou-ton-po, Thou-fou, Li-taï-pé et Kouan-tchau-lin." *L'Artiste: Journal de la littérature et des beaux-arts* (June 1, 1865): 261.
Wang, Yu. *La Réception des anthologies de poésie chinoise classique par les poètes français (1735–2008)*. Paris: Classiques Garnier, 2016.

Wang Qi 王琦. *Li Taibo quanji* 李太白全集. Rpt. Taipei: Heluo tushu, 1976.
Wang Yaoqu 王堯衢, ed. *Gu Tang shi he jie* 古唐詩合解. Rpt. Taipei: Wenhua tushu gongsi, 1968.
Wang Zhongwen 王仲聞, ed. *Li Qingzhao ji jiao zhu* 李清照集校註. Beijing: Renmin wenxue chubanshe, 1979.
Weber, Eugen. *France, Fin de Siècle*. Cambridge, MA: Harvard University Press, 1986.
Whitall, James, trans. *Chinese Lyrics from the Book of Jade*. London: Erskine Macdonald, [1919].
White, Diana. "Préface." *Album de poèmes tirés du Livre de jade*, 3-6. London: The Eragny Press, 1911.
Will, Pierre-Étienne. "Abel-Rémusat l'orientaliste," 1-13. In Will and Zink, eds., *Jean-Pierre Abel-Rémusat*.
Will, Pierre-Étienne, and Michael Zink, eds. *Jean-Pierre Abel-Rémusat et ses successeurs: Deux cent ans de sinologie française en France et en Chine*. Paris: Académie des Inscriptions et Belles-Lettres, 2020.
Wolfgang, Otto. *Die Porzellanpagode*. Vienna: Glorietteverlag, 1921.
Wolseley, Lt. Col. G.-J. *Narrative of the War with China in 1860*. London: Longman Green, Longman and Roberts, 1862.
Yan Yu 嚴羽. *Canglang shihua jiaoshi* 滄浪詩話校釋, ed. Guo Shaoyu 郭紹虞. Beijing: Renmin wenxue chubanshe, 1961.
Yeh, Catherine. "The Life-Style of Four *Wenren* in Late Qing Shanghai." *Harvard Journal of Asiatic Studies* 57, no. 2 (December 1997): 419-70.
Yoshikawa, Junko. "*Le Livre de Jade* de Judith Gautier, traduction de poèmes chinois: Le rapport avec sa création du poème en prose." *Études de langue et littérature française* 96 (March 2010): 15-29. https://www.jstage.jst.go.jp/article/ellf/96/0/96_KJ00007641735/_pdf.
Yriarte, Charles. "Louis Bouilhet." *Le Monde illustré*, 24 July 1869, 53.
Yu, Pauline. "'Your Alabaster in This Porcelain': Judith Gautier's *Le Livre de jade*." *PMLA* 122.2 (March 2007): 464-82.
—. "Judith Gautier and the Invention of Chinese Poetry." In *Reading Medieval Chinese Poetry: Studies in Text, Context, and Culture*, ed. Paul Kroll, 251-88. Leiden: E. J. Brill, 2014.
Zhao Diancheng 趙殿成. *Wang Youcheng ji jian zhu* 王右承集箋諸. Rpt. Taipei: Heluo tushu, 1975.

Index

Note: Figures are indicated by an italic *f* following the page number.

Abel-Rémusat, Jean-Pierre, 19-20, 50, 77
Académie Française, 18, 26, 235-36
Academy of Ladies (Académie des Dames), 235
acrostic poems, 184
Against Nature (À Rebours) (Huysmans), 171-73, 175
Album of Poems Drawn from the Book of Jade (Album de poèmes tirés du Livre de jade) (Pissarro), 238-39, 240*f*, 241*f*
Alexéiev, Basile, 249
Allouard-Jouan, Emma-Marie, 167
ancient-style poetry, 73, 80, 105, 133
Anglo-French expedition, 26, 32, 34, 100-101, 179
anthologies: in China, 104-6; in France, 106
Arène, Paul, 94, 228
armchair sinology, 26
art for art's sake, 5, 228
Aubry, Raoul, 40
"Autumn evening" ("Le soir d'automne") (Gautier), 126-27, 234
"Autumn Evocations" ("Qiu xing") (Du Fu), 202-6
Autumn (L'Automne) section, 123-29
"Autumn's rise: a poem in eight songs" ("Montée d'automne: poème en huit chants") (Gautier), 202-6

avant-garde style, 1, 14, 98, 159, 183
Ayscough, Florence, 196-97

Ban Jieyu (Lady Ban), 112-13, 118, 119, 139
"Banqueting at the Tao family pavilion" ("Yan Tao jia tingzi") (Li Bo), 134-35, 234
Barnes, Julian, 172
The Bats (Les Chauves-souris) (Montesquiou-Fézensac), 171
Baudelaire, Charles, 2-3, 5-6, 34, 106, 121-23
Benedictus, Louis, 161, 244
Bergerat, Émile, 54, 168, 236
Berlioz, Hector, 157
Bertrand, Aloysius (Louis Jacques Napoléon), 121-22, 173, 219, 220, 225
Bethge, Hans, 231-33
"The big rat" ("Le gros rat") (Gautier), 130-31
Birds' Meadow (Le Pré des Oiseaux) house, 162-64, 163*f*, 244
"Birdsong in the evening" ("Chant des oiseaux, le soir") (Gautier), 108-9, 110, 137
Blémont, Émile, 228
"Blessings of the moon" ("Les bienfaits de la lune") (Baudelaire), 122-23
Böhm, Gottfried, 135-37, 136*f*, 173, 230, 234
Boissier, Gaston, 236
Bo Juyi, 200
Bonnières, Robert de, 10-11

Bonnier-Ortolan, Pierre-Elzéar, 63
The Book of Jade: Echoes of the Far East brought into Italian verse following the readings of Madame J. Walter (Massarani), 174
The Book of Jade (Le Livre de jade) (Gautier) (1902): collection overview, 183–91; Court (La Cour) section, 180, 200–206; Du Fu tribute in, 186–87, 197; expansions and corrections, 191–200; Ham Nghi (Xuan Tu) and, 183–85; impact on contemporary poetry, 219–24; Juven, Félix and, 180–83, 191; Li Bo tribute in, 186, 194–95, 197–98; Lovers section (Les Amoureux), 180, 191–92; prose poems and, 219–26, 229, 247–48; retranslations and, 226–32; Song dynasty section, 193, 206–8; Yu Geng in, 178, 187–91, 188f, 189f
The Book of Jade (Le Livre de jade) (Gautier) (1908), 247
The Book of Jade (Le Livre de jade) (Gautier) (1928), 247
The Book of Jade (Le Livre de jade) (Gautier) (1933), 247
The Book of Jade (Le Livre de jade) (Walter/Gautier) (1867): artistic connections through, 150–54; Autumn (L'Automne) section, 123–29; Bonnières, Robert de on, 10–11; "Chinese madrigals" in, 104–7; commentary on, 5–12; Coppée, François on, 9–10; cover of, 3, 4f; France, Anatole on, 11; Gourmont, Rémy de on, 11–12; Hugo, Victor on, 8–9, 17, 30, 156; International Exposition (1867), 100–104, 102f; invention *vs.* translation, 1–16; Lovers section (Les Amoureux), 107–16; The Moon (La Lune) section, 116–23; Poets (Les Poëtes) section, 141–49; research for, 82–85; Summer Palace pillage spoils, 30–32; Travelers (Les Voyageurs) section, 129–31; Verlaine, Paul on, 6–8, 11, 90, 220; War (La Guerre) section, 137–40; Wine (Le Vin) section, 132–37
The Book of Songs, 71–73, 77–78, 80, 104–5, 108, 130, 184, 191–93

Bouilhet, Louis, 51, 82
Boxer Rebellion (1899-1901), 179
Bruce, James, 27–28
Bülow, Cosima von, 161
Burlingame, Anson, 59
Burty, Philippe, 170
"By the western window" ("De la fenêtre occidentale") (Gautier), 140

Callery, Joseph-Gaëtan-Pierre-Marie, 47–49
calligraphy, 1, 3, 49, 180–83
Callot, Jacques, 121
Campion, Charles Philippe, 19
Cazalis, Henri, 151
Céard, Henry, 123
Champollion, Jean-François, 19–20
Chapon, Alfred, 101, 102f
Chen Jitong, 103, 175–77, 252
Chevalier of the Legion of Honor, 26, 237–38
China Mail, 64
Chinese culture, 1, 6, 34, 77, 94, 175–77, 191
"Chinese evening" ("Soir de Chine") (Gautier), 242–43
The Chinese Flute (Die chinesische Flöte) (Bethge), 231–33
Chinese Lyrics (Chinesische Lyrik) (Heilmann), 229–30
Chinese Lyrics from the Book of Jade (Whitall), 226
"Chinese madrigals," 104–7
The Chinese Painted by Themselves (Les Chinois peints par eux-mêmes) (Chen Jitong), 175–76
Chinese poetry: ancient-style, 73, 80, 105, 133; Ding Dunling (Tin-Tun-Ling) and, 50–55, 53f, 68–71; Du Fu and, 73–76; Hervey-Saint-Denys's anthology, 78–82, 79f; "Moonlit Evenings: Little Chinese Poems" (Walter/Gautier), 86; recent-style, 73, 75; translation challenges, 71–78, "Variations on Chinese Themes" (Walter/Gautier), 85–86
Chinese Songbook (Feijó), 174
Chinese Songs from the Book of Jade by Judith Mendès (Böhm), 173, 230

Chinese Tales (Contes chinois)
(Abel-Rémusat), 34
Classic of Poetry (Book of Songs). See *The Book of Songs*
Claudel, Paul, 229, 235
Clermont-Ganneau, Charles Simon, 39–41, 69
"Climbing Cloud Dragon Mountain" (Su Shi), 142–43
Collection of a Broken Heart (Zhu Shuzhen), 215
Collection of Jades for Rinsing (Shu yu ji) (Li Qingzhao), 215
Collège de France, 18, 23, 26, 49–50, 77, 84
colonialism, 14
Coloured Stars: Versions of Fifty Asiatic Love Poems (Mathers), 226
"Complaint from the women's quarter" ("Gui yuan") (Wang Changling), 139
"Complaint on the jade steps" ("Yu jie yuan") (Li Bo), 119
Comte, Charles-Edouard, 62
Confucianism, 57, 71, 73, 208
Contemporary Parnassicle (Arène), 106, 228
The Contemporary Parnassus (Mendès), 92, 94–95, 106
Coppée, François, 9–10
Cordier, Henri, 23
couplets, 121–22, 129
Court (La Cour) section, 180, 200–206
"Crows calling at night" ("Wu ye ti") (Li Bo), 109–10, 117
Cui Guofu, 124

d'Annunzio, Gabriele, 248
Daoism, 145–46, 200, 250
Dardenne de la Grangerie, Marguerite, 84, 90–91
Davis, John Francis, 78, 80
Debussy, Claude, 123, 164
"Dedicated to Li Taibo the twentieth day of the twelfth month" ("Envoi à Li-Tai-Pé: Le vingtième jour du douzième mois") (Gautier), 147
Dehmel, Richard, 230

Della Rocca de Vergalo, Nicanor, 220
Demiéville, Paul, 249–50
De Noé, Charles Amédée (Cham), 25f, 26
"Departure of a friend" ("Le départ d'un ami") (Gautier), 195, 224
"Departure of a great leader" ("Le départ du grand chef") (Gautier), 138–39
"Despair" ("Désespoir") (Gautier), 212–15
Détrie, Muriel, 15
Devéria, Gabriel, 61–62
Ding Dunling (Tin-Tun-Ling): arrest and imprisonment, 59–63; brief history, 46–50; credit in *The Book of Jade*, 3, 180, 183; death of, 67–68; Gautier, Théophile and, 40–45, 41f, 42f, 43f; importance of, 46; literary career of, 55–58, 82–85, 152–53; *The Little Slipper (La Petite Pantoufle)*, 64–66; research with Gautier, 82–85, 90, 100, 104–5, 113–14, 152; Tang-dynasty poetry and, 107, 113; as tutor to Gautiers, 50–55, 53f, 68–71, 236
"Discussion of the Lyric" ("Ci lun") (Li Qingzhao), 212
Dou Tao, 111
Dreyfous, Maurice, 60
Drouet, Juliette, 156
Du Fu: "Autumn Evocations" ("Qiu xing"), 202–6; "Gazing over the wilds" ("Ye wang"), 161; impact of, 73–76; Li Bo and, 147–49; "Song of the eight immortals of drinking" ("Yin zhong ba xian ge"), 133; "Spending a spring night in the chancellery" ("Chun su zuo sheng"), 202; "Spring gaze" ("Chun wang"), 74–76; "Thinking of Li Bo on a spring day" ("Chun ri huai Li Bo"), 146–47; tribute in *The Book of Jade*, 106, 114–17, 133, 186–87, 197; "Twenty couplets sent to Li Bo the twelfth" ("Ji Li shi er Bo er shi yun"), 147
Dumas, Alexandre, 55–56
Dupin, Charles, 101

Eliot, T. S., 222
Eragny Press, 238–39

Essay on Chinese Literature (Soulié de Morant), 216-17
"The eternal characters" ("Les caractères eternels") (Gautier), 148-49
Eureka: A Prose Poem (Poe), 2
"Evening walk on the plain" ("Promenade le soir dans la prairie") (Gautier), 116-17

Fabre, Gabriel, 234
Fan Alin, 47
"Farewell" ("Les adieux") (Gautier), 137-38
"Farewell to a friend" ("Song youren") (Li Bo), 195-96, 224
Farforovyi pavil'on (The porcelain pavilion) (Gumilev), 227-28
Feijó, António, 174-75, 227
feminism, 237, 252
Fenollosa, Ernest, 222
Ferrère, Raoul, 101, 103
Le Figaro, 58, 67, 101
First Opium War (1839-1842), 26
Flaubert, Gustave, 21, 34, 51, 82, 98, 152, 238
Fleischer, Max, 230
Fletcher, John Gould, 221-22
Flowers of Evil (Les Fleurs du mal) (Baudelaire), 34, 106
folk songs, 71, 73, 108-11, 114, 139, 191, 194
"Forbidden flower" ("Fleur défendue") (Gautier), 194
Foreign Peoples (Les Peuples étranges) (Gautier), 153-54
De Fouquières, André, 249
France, Anatole, 11, 12, 176, 248, 251, 252
Franckenstein, Clemens von, 231
Franco-Prussian War, 63, 161
French sinological influence and research: birth of, 17-26; Ding Dunling (Tin-Tun-Ling) and, 40-45, 41f, 42f, 43f, 50; introduction to, 17
"From the Palace" (Herbert Giles), 223

Gaspard of the Night (Gaspard de la Nuit) (Bertrand), 121
"gathering of flowers" metaphor, 185
Gautier, Estelle (sister), 37, 50, 54, 60, 67-68, 70-71, 70f, 157

Gautier, Judith: brief history, 1-12, 13f; celebrity status, 235-46, 237f; on Clermont-Ganneau, Charles Simon, 39-41; death of, 244, 245f; France, Anatole on, 12; marriage, 91-92, 93f, 95-99; obituaries of, 248-49; publication accomplishments, 12-16, 108-9; Schwartz, William Leonard on, 15
Gautier, Judith, artistic connections: Chinese admirers, 175-78; Hugo, Victor, 8-9, 17, 154-57, 155f; Sargent, John Singer, 166-68, 183; statesmen and diplomats, 173-75; through *Book of Jade*, 150-54; Wagner, Richard, 154, 157-62, 158f, 159f; Yamamoto Hōsui, 168, 169f, 171
Gautier, Théophile (father), 1-5, 12, 32-45, 35f, 104, 152, 181, 236, 247-48
Gautreau, Amélie Avegno, 166-67
"Gazing over the wilds" ("Ye wang") (Du Fu), 116
Gillot, Charles, 171
Giquel, Prosper Marie, 177
De Goncourt, Edmond, 25, 34, 50-51, 101, 152
De Goncourt, Jules, 25, 34, 50-51, 101
Goncourt Prize, 235-36
De Gourmont, Rémy, 11-12, 151-52, 177, 249, 252
Grant, James Hope, 27
Grisi, Carlotta (aunt), 1, 12
Grisi, Ernesta (mother), 1
Grisi, Giulia/Julia (cousin), 1, 12
Grison, Georges, 41
De Guignes, Chrétien-Louis Joseph, 19-20
De Guignes, Joseph, 19
Gumilev, Nikolai, 227-28
Guo Songtao, 177
A Gust of Wind (Sargent), 167

Ham Nghi (Xuan Tu), 183-85, 216, 244
Han dynasty, 193, 205
Han Wo, 124
Happy Life (Vie heureuse), 235
Haussermann, John, 234
Heilmann, Hans, 229-30, 234
Heine, Heinrich, 122

Henschke, Alfred, 230-31
heptasyllabic quatrain, 87, 105-6, 133, 139, 143, 183, 194, 201-2
De Heredia, José-Maria, 5
d'Hérisson, Maurice, 28-29
Hervey-Saint-Denys: on challenges of translation, 78, 200; Chinese poetry, 78-82, 79f; impact of, 22-26, 24f, 25f, 50; International Exposition and, 100-104, 102f; literary references to, 176; *Poetry of the Tang Dynasty* (Hervey-Saint-Denys), 78-82, 79f, 106, 153, 186, 223; translations by, 111, 113, 118, 123-26, 131, 192, 205, 251
He Zhizhang, 147
Hirth, Friedrich, 233
Hodson, L. W., 239
Holmès, Augusta, 96, 160
Holz, Arno, 230
"The house in the heart" ("La maison dans le coeur") (Gautier), 114-16, 226, 229, 231
Houssaye, Arsène, 85, 122
Howells, William Dean, 225
Hugo, Victor, 8-9, 17, 30, 154-57, 155f
Hung, William, 250
Huysmans, Joris-Karl, 171-73, 175

Il Libro di giada (Massarani), 227
The Imperial Dragon (Le Dragon impérial) (Mendès/Gautier), 150-51, 156
"In imitation of the old song 'Autumn nights are long'" ("Xiao gu qiu ye chang") (Qian Qi), 127-29
"In praise of Li Taibo" ("Louange à Li-Tai-Pé") (Gautier), 146-47
"Insomnia" ("Insomnie") (Gautier), 202
"In the palace" ("Dans le palais") (Gautier), 200-201

The Jade Flute: Chinese Poems (La Flûte de jade: Poésies chinoises) (Toussaint), 228-29
"The jade staircase" ("L'escalier de jade") (Gautier), 119-21, 123, 175, 197-98
Jessome-Nance, Barbara, 16
Jesuits, 17-20, 28, 34, 77, 80-81
"The Jewel Stairs' Grievance" (Pound), 223
Le Jockey, 7-8

Judith Gautier (Sargent), 167
Julien, Stanislas, 20-22, 48-49, 77, 85
Juven, Félix, 180-83, 191, 219

Kenner, Hugh, 252
Khayyam, Omar, 186, 220
Kleczkowski, Michel Alexandre, 23, 48
Komyoji Saburo (Mitsouda Komiosi), 170
Krysinska, Marie, 220

Lacroix, Albert, 162
Lafargue, Gustave, 62
Lagrené, Marie Melchior Joseph Théodose de, 26-27
Lang, Andrew, 64
Lan-Yin, 66
L'Artiste, 31, 85, 86, 107, 197
Lattimore, David, 250
Laughlin, James, 227
Lauth, Laura, 16
L' École des langues orientales vivantes (School of Vernacular Oriental Languages), 19, 22, 48, 49, 50, 153
Leconte de Lisle, Charles-Marie, 5-6, 98
Legge, James, 222
Lemerre, Alphonse, 1, 5, 92, 151, 180
De Lesseps, Jules, 100
Leyrer, Viktor, 230
La Liberté, 150-51
Li Bo: "Banqueting at the Tao family pavilion" ("Yan Tao jia tingzi"), 134-35; "Complaint on the jade steps" ("Yu jie yuan"), 119; "Crows calling at night" ("Wu ye ti"), 109-10, 117; Du Fu and, 147-49; "Farewell to a friend" ("Song youren"), 195-96; Henschke, Alfred and, 230-31; impact of, 36, 84, 88-89, 106, 108-9, 111, 112, 115-16; "Listening to a flute on a spring night in Luoyang," 87-88; "Quiet night thoughts" ("Jing ye si"), 130-31; "River song" ("Jiang shang yin"), 143-45, 148; *The Song of the Earth* (Mahler) and, 232-35; tribute in *The Book of Jade*, 186, 194-95, 197-98
Librairie Plon, 247
Liégeois, Caroline-Julie, 60

Li Hongzhang, 193, 229
Linked Pearls of Tang Poetry, 106
Li Po and Other Ideographic Poems (Li-Po y otras poemas ideograficos) (Tablada), 228
Li Qingzhao (Li Yi'an), 187, 206-18, 250
"Listening to a flute on a spring night in Luoyang" (Li Bo), 87-88
Li Tai Pe, the Emperor's Poet (Li Tai Pe der Kaisers Dichter) (Franckenstein), 231
The Literary Life (La vie littéraire) (France), 176
The Little Slipper (La Petite Pantoufle) (Ding Dunling), 64-66, 65f
Liu, James J. Y., 108
Liu Shixun, 242-43
Louÿs, Pierre, 184
Lovers section (Les Amoureux), 107-16, 180, 191-92
Lowell, Amy, 197

Madame X (Sargent), 166-67
Mahler, Gustav, 232-35
Mallarmé, Stéphane, 82, 92, 94-95, 151, 172
"La Marguerite" (Théophile Gautier), 36, 84, 92
Massarani, Tullo, 174, 227
Mathers, Edward Powys, 226
mauve print color, 181, 183
Mendès, Catulle (husband), 6, 54, 91-92, 93f, 95-99, 157, 160, 181, 208, 220-21, 236
Meng Hua, 15
Méritens, Eugene de, 101
Merrill, Stuart, 225-26
Meyer-Zundel, Suzanne, 91, 99, 161, 184, 193, 242-44, 246
Min Ling, 15
Mohsin-Khan, 90-91, 220, 243
Le Moniteur universel, 2, 38, 98, 103-4
Montauban, Charles Guillaume, 27
De Montesquieu, Charles-Louis, 6, 68, 91
De Montesquiou-Fézensac, Robert, 171
The Moon (La Lune) section, 116-23
"Moonlit Evenings: Little Chinese Poems" (Gautier), 86, 107, 118, 119
Moreau, Gustave, 172

"The mysterious flute" (Gautier), 87-89

Napoléon, Louis Jacques (Aloysius Bertrand). *See* Bertrand, Aloysius
The Necklace of Days (Le Collier des jours) (Gautier), 181
De Négroni, Jean-Louis, 27, 29, 31
Neumann, Friedrich, 21
Neumann, Robert, 231
New Songs from the Jade Terrace (Yutai xinyong), 105
De Noailles, Anna, 235
De Noblet, Agnes, 177-78, 251-52

"Oath of love" ("Voeu d'amour") (Gautier), 200
"On the edge of the small lake" ("Au bord du petit lac") (Gautier), 119
Opium Wars, 179
orientalism, 14, 49-50, 82, 252
Ou Jian, 59-60

"Palace song" ("Gong zhong ci") (Zhu Qingyu), 200-202
palindromes, 111, 137
"The paradise of poets" ("Le Paradis des poètes") (Gautier), 242
Paris apartment home, 164-66, 165f
Paris-Artiste, 159
Paris International Exposition (1867), 100-104, 102f, 179
Paris International Exposition (1900), 179
Parnassus (Le Parnasse or Parnassian), 5, 6, 34, 92, 94, 141, 152
Pasdeloup, Jules, 92, 159
Pastels in Prose (Merrill), 225-26
Pauthier, Guillaume, 21-22, 36, 48
Pavie, Théodore, 36
"The pavilion of the young king" ("Le pavillon du jeune roi") (Gautier), 123
"The peaceful river" ("Le fleuve paisible") (Gautier), 118
Perny, Paul, 22, 23
Persian Letters (Montesquieu), 6
La Petite Presse, 58

Pissarro, Esther, 238–39
Pissarro, Lucien, 238–39
Poe, Edgar Allen, 2
Poems of China (Poèmes de Chine) (Blémont), 228
Poems of the Dragonfly (Poèmes de la libellule) (Gautier), 168, 170–71
"A poet looks at the moon" ("Un poète regarde la lune") (Gautier), 118
Poetry of the Tang Dynasty (Poésies de l'époque des Thang) (Hervey-Saint-Denys), 78–82, 79f, 106, 153, 186, 223
poetry styles: acrostic, 184; ancient-style, 73, 80, 105, 133; avant-garde, 1, 14, 98, 159, 183; couplets, 121–22; prose poems, 2, 7, 10–11, 121–23, 173, 219–26, 229, 247–48; quatrains, 54, 73, 87–89, 116–19, 124, 130, 132, 139–40, 173–75, 187, 194, 198–201, 229, 239; recent-style, 73, 75; *vers libre* (free verse), 220–21. *See also* Chinese poetry
Poets (Les Poëtes) section, 141–49
"The poet walks up a mountain enveloped by fog" ("Le poëte se promène sur la montagne enveloppée de brouillard") (Gautier), 141–42
Poiteau, Émile, 247–48, 253
Pollak, Theobald, 232
Pont-Jest, René de, 176–77
The Porcelain Pagoda (Die Porzellanpagode) (Leyrer), 230
The Porcelain Pavilion (Fleischer), 230
"The porcelain pavilion" ("Le pavillon de porcelaine") (Gautier), 133–37, 136f, 234
Les Portes rouges (The red gates) (Gautier), 184
Potteau, Jacques-Philippe, 52
Pound, Ezra, 222–24, 252
Pourvourville, Eugène-Albert de, 250
Pozzi, Samuel Jean, 167–68
"Prince Teng's tower" ("Teng wang ge") (Wang Bo), 123–24
prose poems, 2, 7, 10–11, 121–23, 173, 219–26, 229, 247–48
Proust, Marcel, 25, 26, 171, 172
pseudo-Chinese label/translations, 5–6, 10, 57, 250

Qianlong, 28
Qian Qi, 127–29, 199, 233–34
Qian Zhongshu, 60
Qing dynasty, 106, 147, 193, 231
quatrains, 54, 73, 87–89, 116–19, 124, 130, 132, 139–40, 173–75, 187, 194, 198–201, 229, 239
"Quiet night thoughts" ("Jing ye si") (Li Bo), 130–31
Qu Yuan (Qu Ping), 146

racism, 5, 14, 54–55
recent-style poetry, 73, 75
"The red flower" ("La fleur rouge") (Gautier), 137–38
Régamey, Félix, 157, 159
"The return of the swallows" ("Le retour des hirondelles") (Gautier), 122
Rexroth, Kenneth, 222, 223, 225, 227
Rijn, Rembrandt van, 121
Rimbaud, Arthur, 220
ritual hymns, 71
"River song" ("Chanson sur le fleuve") (Gautier), 144–45
"River song" ("Jiang shang yin") (Li Bo), 143–45, 148
The Romance of the Mummy (Gautier, Théophile), 2
romanticism, 5, 51
Rosny, Léon de, 22–23
Rothschild, Alphonse de, 25

"The sages dance" ("Les sages dansent") (Gautier), 143, 145–46
Saionji Kinmochi, 170
Sandburg, Carl, 225
Sargent, John Singer, 166–68, 183
School of Vernacular Oriental Languages. *See* L' École des langues orientales vivantes
Schwab, Raymond, 251
Schwartz, William Leonard, 15
Second Opium War (1856), 27
The Second Strand of the Necklace (Le Second Rang du collier) (Gautier), 181
Selections of Refined Literature (Wen xuan), 105

Sentimental Education (Flaubert), 21
Serrano, Richard, 15–16
sexism, 14
"The shadow of the orange leaves" ("L'ombre des feuilles d'oranger") (Gautier), 113–14
Shang dynasty, 184
Shi Chong, 135
Shi jing. See The Book of Songs
Si-Tien-Li, 95
"Some good luck on the path" ("Une bonne fortune sur le chemin") (Gautier), 194
Song dynasty, 85, 141–42, 177, 193, 206–8
"song lyrics" (ci), 206–7
"Song of complaint" ("Yuan ge xing") (Ban Jieyu), 112
"Song of enduring regret" ("Chang hen ge") (Bo Juyi), 200
"Song of farewell to spring" ("Song chun ci") (Wang Wei), 132
The Song of the Earth (Mahler), 232–35
"Song of the eight immortals of drinking" ("Yin zhong ba xian ge") (Du Fu), 133
"Song of the faithful wife" ("Jie fu yin") (Zhang Ji), 113
Souday, Paul, 253
Soulié de Morant, George, 216–17, 250
"Sound after sound, a long song" ("Sheng-sheng man") (Li Qingzhao), 212–15
"Spending a spring night in the chancellery" ("Chun su zuo sheng") (Du Fu), 202
"Spring, river, flower, moon, night" ("Chun jiang hua yue ye") (Zhang Ruoxu), 118, 229
"Spring gaze" ("Chun wang") (Du Fu), 74–77
"Springtime chill" ("Froideur printanière") (Gautier), 209–12
Stabler, Jordan Herbert, 174–75
Steiner, George, 224
Stocès, Ferdinand, 15
Study of Judith Gautier by Lamplight (Sargent), 168
Su Hui, 111, 137–38
Summer Palace. See Yuanmingyuan Palace (Garden of Perfect Brightness)

Sun Baoqi, 178, 239, 242
Sun Jiagu, 59, 153
Su Shi, 85, 141–43

Tablada, Jose Juan, 228
Taiping conflict, 100
"Taking Leave of a Friend" (Pound), 224
Tallandier, Jules, 247
Tang dynasty (618–907), 23, 36, 66, 72, 75–76, 78, 80–83, 105–8, 112–13, 153, 176, 186, 192–93, 206, 223, 228–29, 233, 242
Tan-Jo-Su (Than-jo-su), 86, 112, 229
tanka form, 170
Taschereau, Jules, 84
Teele, Roy Edward, 251
"The fan" ("L'Éventail") (Gautier), 112
Theocritus, 7
"Thinking of Li Bo on a spring day" ("Chun ri huai Li Bo") (Du Fu), 146–47
Ting-Tun-Ling. See Ding Dunling (Tin-Tun-Ling)
"To eight great poets who drank together" ("À huit grands poètes qui buvaient ensemble") (Gautier), 133, 197
"To forget one's thoughts" ("Pour oublier ses pensées") (Gautier), 132–33
"To His Excellency the Late Yu Geng" (Gautier), 243–44
Tones, 75
Toussaint, Franz, 228–29, 249
Travelers (Les Voyageurs) section, 129–31
Treaty of Nanking (1842), 26
Treaty of Tianjin (1858), 27
Treaty of Whampoa (1844), 27
Turgan, Julien, 98
"Twenty couplets sent to Li Bo the twelfth" ("Ji Li shi er Bo er shi yun") (Du Fu), 147

"Variations on Chinese Themes" (Walter/Gautier), 85–91
"Vengeance" ("Vengeance") (Gautier), 192–94
Verlaine, Paul, 6–8, 11, 90, 123, 220
Verne, Jules, 56

vers libre (free verse), 220-21
Villiers de l'Isle-Adam, Auguste, 98, 151, 160, 173
"The virtuous wife" ("L'épouse vertueuse") (Gautier), 113, 138, 199
Vogelweide, Walther von der, 162
Voltaire, 18

Wagner, Richard, 154, 157-62, 158*f*, 159*f*, 246
Wagner, Siegfried (godson), 161, 244, 246
Waley, Arthur, 72, 107-8, 250-51
Walter, Judith (pseudonym), 1-2, 6-8. *See also* Gautier, Judith
Wang Bo, 123-24
Wang Changling, 139-40
Wang Wei, 132
De Ward, Louise, 23
War (La Guerre) section, 137-40
Weiss, Emil Rudolf, 231
Whitall, James, 226, 234
White, Diana, 239
"The white page" ("La feuille blanche") (Gautier), 141
Wine (Le Vin) section, 132-37
Wolfgang, Otto, 230
Wolseley, Garnet, 29
"A woman facing her mirror" ("Une femme devant son miroir") (Gautier), 119, 229
"A woman loyal to her duties" ("Une femme fidèle à ses devoirs") (Gautier), 113

"Written in imitation of Cui Guofu's style" ("Xiao Cui Guofu ti") (Han Wo), 124-25

Xiao Gang, 105
Xiao Tong, 105
Xuanzong, 194
Xu Ling, 105

Yamamoto Hōsui, 168, 169*f*, 171
Yang Guifei (Yang Yuhuan, Yang Taizhen), 194, 200
"A young girl's cares" ("Le souci d'une jeune fille") (Gautier), 124
"Youth" ("Jeunesse") (Gautier), 194
Yriarte, Charles, 51, 55
Yuanmingyuan Palace (Garden of Perfect Brightness), 26-32, 28*f*, 101
Yu Geng, 178, 187-91, 188*f*, 189*f*, 191, 193, 219, 243, 252
Yu Wang, 15

Zeng Jize, 177
Zhang Deyi, 22, 23, 59-60
Zhang Ji, 113, 138, 199
Zhang Ruoxu, 86, 118, 229
Zhang Wei, 199
Zhao Mingcheng, 206, 207-8
Zhi Gang, 59, 153
Zhu Qingyu, 200-202, 239
Zhu Shuzhen, 215

GPSR Authorized Representative: Easy Access System Europe, Mustamäe tee
50, 10621 Tallinn, Estonia, gpsr.requests@easproject.com

www.ingramcontent.com/pod-product-compliance
Lightning Source LLC
Chambersburg PA
CBHW022032290426
44109CB00014B/830